Fear of Judging

Fear of Judging

Sentencing Guidelines in the Federal Courts

Kate Stith
and
José A. Cabranes

The University of Chicago Press
Chicago & London

The University of Chicago Press, Chicago 60637
The University of Chicago Press, Ltd., London

07 06 05 04 03 02 01 00 2 3 4 5

ISBN: 0-226-77486-4 (paper)

Library of Congress Cataloging-in-Publication Data

Stith, Kate.
Fear of judging : sentencing guidelines in the federal courts/Kate Stith and José A. Cabranes.
p. cm.
Includes bibliographical references and index.
ISBN: 0-226-77485-6 (cloth : alk. paper).—ISBN: 0-226-77486-4 (pbk. : alk. paper)
1. Sentences (Criminal procedure)—United States. I. Cabranes, José A. II. Title.
KF9685.S75 1998
345.73'0772—dc21 98-13344
CIP

♾ The paper used in this publication meets the minimum requirements of the American National Standard for Information Sciences—Permanence of Paper for Printed Library Materials, ANSI Z39.48–1992.

For

Ann Carter Stith

Richard Taylor Stith, Jr.

Carmen López Cabranes

the late Manuel Cabranes

[L]egal history shows . . . periodic waves of reform during which the sense of justice, natural law, or equity introduces life and flexibility into the law and makes it adjustable to its work. In the course of time, however, under the social demand for certainty, equity gets hardened and reduced to rigid rules, so that, after a while, a new reform wave is necessary.

Morris Raphael Cohen (1933)

CONTENTS

PREFACE

Our subject is the revolutionary new system for the punishment of federal crimes, in place since 1987—the federal Sentencing Guidelines. These Guidelines are the creature of congressional enactments and of a newly created federal rule-making agency, the United States Sentencing Commission.

Our reservations about and proposals for reforming this system are tempered by a recognition that the Guidelines are likely to remain substantially intact for some time to come. This is true for several interrelated reasons: because major reforms in the law are always slow in coming; because reshaping, redirecting, or eliminating any bureaucracy in our country, as elsewhere, is a Herculean endeavor (witness the long, and ultimately successful, efforts to abolish the Interstate Commerce Commission and the Civil Aeronautics Board); because this system of rules and procedures lends an appearance of having been constructed on the basis of science and technocratic expertise, giving it a threshold plausibility to a general public not familiar with its actual contours and operation; because its principal critics, federal judges, for all their vaunted independence and high status, are poorly positioned and generally unable to influence national legislative policy; because criminal sentencing is a highly charged political issue; and because the very complexity and intricacy of this large body of rules is likely to discourage any observer—policymaker, legislator, or lay citizen—tempted to take an interest in how federal crimes are punished.

That said, we believe the continuing and unavoidable discussion of this important and controversial system, and its eventual reformation, may be served by a description and analysis of why and how this elaborate machinery of government came into existence and how it actually works (or does not work). To do this we have been required, by the very nature of the beast, to provide a considerable amount of detail. A political or philosophical overview—the stuff of a lecture or a series of lectures—could not by itself adequately convey how these labyrinthine rules function today.

In our research, discussion, and teaching of this subject over several years we have been aided by the efforts of several research assistants, most notably Sharon M. Bunzel, Jonathan Cedarbaum, Jonathan Mirsky, Carlos G. Muñiz, and Steve Y. Koh, all now graduates of Yale Law School, and Eric Cavallero, a graduate student in philosophy at Yale. (Steve Y. Koh was co-author of a law review article on which part of chapter 2 is based.) We have also benefited from the perspectives of several former law clerks, including Marc R. Bruner, Marinn F. Carlson, Jamie G. Heller, Robert K. Kelner, William G. Malley, Michael A. Scodro, Patricia M. Small, and Brian S. Weinstein. Other Yale Law School (and, in a few cases, Yale College) students contributed through their research assistance either to specific citations in this book or to our knowledge of particular corners of the criminal law. These students include Rachel Beattie, Ramamoorthi Bhaskar, Jacob Buchdahl, Elizabeth Cavanagh, Robert Edwards, Christopher Ford, Jason Freier, Noel Hartman, Xiao-Hong Jing, Stephen Juris, Erez Kalir, Abigail Kaufman, Brooke Libby, Paul Morf, Jennifer Newstead, Anne Oh, Lori Lynn Phillips, Jeannie Sclafani-Rhee, Allyson Serxner, and Michele St. Mary. Gene P. Coakley of the Yale Law School library was of great assistance in tracking down legislative and other materials.

We appreciate the comments on a draft of this book that we received from three persons who were involved, at one stage or another, in bringing the federal Sentencing Guidelines into existence: Leonard Orland, an authority on the law of crimes and sentencing and a professor at the University of Connecticut Law School; Denis G. Hauptly, a long-time student of the federal courts who is now Senior Director at West Product Development in St. Paul, Minnesota; and David A. Lombardero, formerly Chief Counsel at the Sentencing Commission and now counsel to the Los Angeles office of the national law firm of Hughes Hubbard & Reed. Over the years we have also received helpful comments and advice from three persons with long and distinguished careers in public service and, in particular, criminal justice as practiced in the federal courts of Connecticut and the region: Maria Rodrigues McBride, the Chief United States Probation Officer for the District of Connecticut; Richard A. Reeve of the New Haven Bar, a longtime Assistant Federal Public Defender in Connecticut; and John H. Durham, a career state and federal prosecutor who has served for many years as Chief Assistant United States Attorney for the District of Connecticut and who serves at this writing (by interim appointment of the Attorney General) as the United States Attorney for Connecticut.

We acknowledge with thanks the patience of John Tryneski, our editor at the University of Chicago Press, with whom we first tentatively broached the possibility of this project some five years ago. Akiba Covitz, a Senior Research Associate at Yale Law School, provided invaluable assistance in preparation of the index, while Robert E. Caceres and Leslie Keros expertly oversaw final preparation of the manuscript. Professor Stith appreciates the support of Yale Law School for her research on the Sentencing Guidelines and her work on this book, with particular gratitude to Dean Anthony T. Kronman and Professors Abraham S. Goldstein and Daniel J. Freed for their friendship and insights through the years.

Of course, these persons bear no responsibility for any limitations of this study, nor do they necessarily share the views we have expressed.

We are also grateful to several publishers for permission to reprint previously published material. A portion of chapter 2 originally appeared in Kate Stith and Steve Y. Koh, "The Politics of Sentencing Reform: The Legislative History of the Federal Sentencing Guidelines," *Wake Forest Law Review* 28 (1993): 223; reprinted with permission of *Wake Forest Law Review.* Portions of chapters 3 and 7 originally appeared in Kate Stith and José A. Cabranes, "Judging under the Federal Sentencing Guidelines," *Northwestern University Law Review* 91 (1997): 1247; reprinted with permission of *Northwestern University Law Review.* The flowchart in appendix D originally appeared in *The Washington Post,* 6 October 1996, A20–21. © 1996, The Washington Post. Reprinted with permission.

Finally, our children—Jennifer, Amy, Alejo, and Ben—have heard much about the book their parents were writing. We hope each will conclude in the years ahead that this volume was worth the effort and the attendant interruptions of family life.

Kate Stith
José A. Cabranes

March 16, 1998
New Haven, Connecticut

INTRODUCTION

On November 1, 1987, two centuries of sentencing practice in the federal courts came to an abrupt end. A regime of "Sentencing Guidelines" prescribed by a federal administrative agency went into effect. The purpose of the new regime was to divest the independent federal judiciary of the power to determine criminal sentences. Federal judges would still be the formal authority through which criminal sentences would be pronounced. But the new regime sought to strip them of authority to determine the purposes of criminal sentencing, the factors relevant to sentencing, and the proper type and range of punishment in most cases. Henceforth, these powers would rest with a newly formed bureaucracy, the United States Sentencing Commission, located in Washington, D.C. Our subject is the remarkable reform movement that culminated in the establishment of the federal Sentencing Guidelines, the sentencing system created under this new administrative regime, the operation of that system in practice, and the consequences for federal criminal justice.

Our own perspectives are based on more than abstract research. Of necessity, they are informed by our professional experiences working in the federal criminal justice system. The principal author served as an Assistant United States Attorney in the Southern District of New York and as a Special Assistant to the head of the Criminal Division of the Department of Justice in Washington in the era of the old sentencing regime, before embarking on a career as a teacher of criminal law at Yale Law School. The coauthor (and husband of the principal author) was a United States District Judge in Connecticut for fifteen years, imposing sentences under both the old and the new regimes, and now serves as a United States Circuit Judge for the Second Circuit, where he regularly reviews appeals of sentences imposed by district judges. We have been publicly skeptical of the Sentencing Guidelines regime and its effects on the criminal justice system.[1]

In this book we set out in some detail what we know about this new sentencing regime, identify some of its notable defects (as well as some of its conceded merits), and offer some suggestions on how legislators and policy-makers might begin to remedy those defects. While we are not particularly sanguine about the prospects for a significant counter-reform in the near term—history teaches that it is always easier to create a bureaucracy than it is to reform or dismantle one—we begin with the simple premise that our subject is central to our country's vision of justice and how it ought to be administered. We share the conviction that it is not too soon to begin the serious discussion of a new cycle of reform—one which, in the words of the philosopher Morris Raphael Cohen, "introduces life and flexibility into the law and makes it adjustable to its work."[2]

THE SENTENCING COMMISSION was established by the Sentencing Reform Act of 1984, legislation originally introduced by Senator Edward M. Kennedy, passed by nearly unanimous votes in both the Senate and the House, and enthusiastically signed into law by President Ronald Reagan. The 1984 Act sought to achieve "certainty and fairness" in the federal sentencing process by eliminating "unwarranted disparity" among sentences for similar defendants committing similar offenses.[3] Two hallmarks of this legislation were the elimination of parole and, for the first time, the provision for appellate review of sentences. These achievements have been overshadowed, however, by the most far-reaching and dramatic provision of the Sentencing Reform Act: the charge to the newly established Sentencing Commission to develop and implement a system of mandatory sentencing guidelines.

The transfer of formal sentencing authority from federal judges to the Sentencing Commission is probably the most significant development in judging in the federal judicial system since the adoption in 1938 of the Federal Rules of Civil Procedure. The new regime replaces the long-standing tradition that afforded judges broad discretion to determine criminal sentences within statutory limits. Despite the use of the term *guidelines,* the sentencing rules issued by the Sentencing Commission are binding on the federal judiciary.

In addition to transforming the judge's role in criminal sentencing, the new regime transforms the federal criminal law itself. In the American constitutional tradition, there has heretofore been a formal distinction between the process of crime definition (the responsibility of the legislative branch) and the process of criminal sentencing within the maximum penalties provided by statute (the responsibility of the judiciary and, for several generations, of parole officials as well). The major exception to this division of authority has been those few occasions in which Congress has mandated a minimum, as well as a maximum, term of imprisonment for particular crimes. The Sentencing Guidelines represent a radical departure from this tradition. Although a formal distinction between crime definition and criminal sentencing persists, the federal Sentencing Guidelines effectively function as an adjunct to the substantive criminal statutes enacted by Congress. Statutory law continues to prescribe the formal elements of particular crimes. But now, for purposes of determining punishment, these elements are supplemented by the factors that the Sentencing Commission has prescribed in its Sentencing Guidelines. In essence, the Sentencing Commission has identified a multitude of new "Guidelines crimes," each a variant of one or more statutory crimes and each with its own mandated range of punishment.

The sentencing hearing has thus been transformed into an adjudicatory process, in which the sentencing court determines which "Guidelines crimes" the defendant has committed. The defendant may be formally convicted of one crime at trial (or by plea of guilty), only to be sentenced for additional criminal conduct defined in the Sentencing Guidelines.[4]

The Sentencing Guidelines are the rules promulgated by the Sentencing Commission for the regulation of the criminal sentences imposed by federal district judges. As of 1997, the Commission's much-amended Guidelines Manual consists (including appendices) of more than nine hundred pages of technical regulations and amendments, weighing close to five pounds—which may be usefully compared to, for example, the Internal Revenue Code, which weighs in at just under four pounds.[5] The Sentencing Guidelines are almost a parody of the overly detailed, inflexible legal structures that lawyer and author Philip K. Howard criticized in his 1994 best-selling book, *The Death of Common Sense.*

The centerpiece of the Guidelines is a 258-box grid that the Commission calls the Sentencing Table, which we have reproduced in appendix A. The horizontal axis of this grid, entitled "Criminal History Category," adjusts severity on the basis of the offender's past conviction record. The vertical axis, entitled "Offense Level," reflects a base severity score for the crime committed, adjusted for those characteristics of the defendant's criminal behavior that the Sentencing Commission has deemed relevant to sentencing. The Guidelines, through a complex set of rules requiring significant expertise to apply, instruct the sentencing judge on how to calculate each of these factors. The box at which the defendant's Criminal History Category and Offense Level intersect then determines the range within which the judge may sentence the defendant. As an examination of appendix A reveals, the sentencing range in each box is small, the highest point being 25 percent more than the lowest point.

There are two circumstances permitting a judge to "depart" from the calculated Guidelines range. The first is where the defendant has provided substantial assistance to law enforcement authorities, with the important caveat that the prosecutor must first file a motion for a below-Guidelines sentence. The judge cannot sentence a cooperating defendant to a lesser term on his own accord or on the defendant's motion. The perceived transfer of discretion from the judge to the prosecutor (both in these circumstances and more generally under the Guidelines) is a central reason for judicial discomfort with the new regime.[6]

The second situation in which a judge may depart, up or down, from the Guidelines is where a judge is able to demonstrate on the record that there are factors or circumstances in the case at hand that have not been adequately factored into the Guidelines' sentencing rules. While the Supreme Court has held that a judge's decision to depart cannot be reversed on appeal unless it constitutes an "abuse of discretion,"[7] again there is a caveat. The Court has made it clear that the federal appeals courts should not permit departures by sentencing judges on grounds that have been either (a) proscribed by the Sentencing Commission, or (b) already considered by the Commission.[8] The Commission, in turn, has sharply constrained departures from the Guidelines by declaring that a defendant's personal history—including a history of misfortune or disadvantage, service to his country or his community, family responsibilities, and employment history—generally may *not* be a basis for departure. Moreover, the Guidelines themselves prescribe precise, quantitative sentencing weights for most other circumstances that have historically been taken into account by judges to mitigate or enhance punishment: the individual defendant's role in the offense, the actual amount of harm caused, and the defendant's acceptance of (or failure to accept) responsibility for his criminal conduct. These factors, too, are generally off-limits to sentencing judges as grounds for departure from the Guidelines. The result is that the judge's authority to depart from the Guidelines is notable not because it offers opportunities to individualize a criminal sentence, but because those opportunities are so limited.

Once the sentencing judge pronounces sentence, either within or beyond the Guidelines range, the defendant and the government may each obtain appellate review of the judge's calculations, including each subsidiary determination made by the judge in the calculation of the Criminal History Category or Offense Level (the two axes designed to yield the sentencing range). They may also obtain appellate review of the lawfulness of the judge's departure, if any, from the prescribed Guidelines range.

While the Guidelines have thus introduced radical changes in sentencing law and procedure, the resulting sentences themselves also represent a distinctive break from prior practice in the federal courts. Most notably, the Guidelines prescribe a sentence of confinement for all but the most minor federal offenses (indeed, only 23 of the 258 boxes in the Sentencing Table contemplate even the possibility of a nonincarcerative sentence). Before the Guidelines, about 50 percent of all federal defendants received nonimprisonment sentences; in the last decade, that percentage has dropped to less than 15 percent. Moreover, under the Sentencing Reform Act, offenders sentenced to prison may not obtain early release on parole, which has been abolished.[9]

The new system has distressed many who are most intimately involved in the criminal justice process. Judges, prosecutors, defense attorneys, and probation officers find themselves operating in a labyrinthine system of rules devised by a distant and alien administrative agency. The rules themselves, which generally ignore individual characteristics of defendants, often seem to sacrifice comprehensibility and common sense on the altar of pseudo-scientific uniformity. If the new regime really did—if it *could*—eliminate unwarranted disparity in criminal sentencing, perhaps the considerable effort of the various participants to decipher and apply the Guidelines could be regarded as well spent. Ironically, however, disparity—different sentences for defendants whose crimes and criminal histories seem similar—may be as great under the Guidelines as it was under the discretionary system it replaced.[10] Moreover, the sentencing hearing today can be nearly unintelligible to victims, defendants, and observers, and even to the very lawyers and judges involved in the proceeding. Too often, when it is all over, neither the judge nor the lawyers are able to explain coherently, much less justify or defend, the sentence imposed. The Sentencing Commission itself has become, in the words of a recent Chief Counsel to Senator Kennedy, "the Rodney Dangerfield of federal agencies: . . . [d]espised by judges, sneered at by scholars, ignored by the Justice Department, its guidelines circumvented by practitioners and routinely lambasted in the press."[11]

Many federal judges have been openly and strongly critical of the Guidelines.[12] A recent survey of federal judges by the Federal Judicial Center reported that nearly three-fourths of federal trial judges and more than two-thirds of appellate judges believe that mandatory guidelines are "unnecessary"[13]; a poll conducted in 1993 by the American Bar Association reported that nearly half of all federal judges want simply to "scrap" the Guidelines.[14] Significant dissatisfaction with the Guidelines continues within the defense bar, even (perhaps particularly) within that small segment that has become thoroughly steeped in them.

Yet as the Sentencing Guidelines have become ever more entrenched, many of the critics appear (understandably) to have become resigned to them. Probation officers, in particular, have made an irredeemable investment in the new regime, and their status has arguably been enhanced. Most federal prosecutors, too, have come to appreciate the power they now exercise free from countervailing judicial authority. In addition, with each passing year, there are fewer probation officers or prosecutors who have had experience with a non-Guidelines system. Even among judges, the criticism of the Guidelines has begun to dissipate[15]—especially as new judges are appointed, some of whom may welcome reduced responsibility over criminal sentencing. In any event, judges as a group aspire to be vigilant law-abiders, and the Guidelines—whatever their faults, whatever they may have done to the quality of criminal justice in federal courts—are, of course, the law.

We harbor the hope, however, that this new regime is temporary. We hope that the time will come when we can look back on the years of these Sentencing Guidelines as a period of transition between the old, fully discretionary sentencing system and a new, lasting regime of guided judicial discretion in criminal sentencing. After a decade of experience under the federal Sentencing Guidelines, it is time to reassess the foundations of the crusade that led to their enactment, appraise their performance, and chart a course for the future of sentencing in the federal courts.

The federal Sentencing Guidelines were born of an uneasiness with the very concept of authoritative discretion, a naive commitment to the ideal of rationality, and an enduring faith in bureaucratic administration. One of our objectives is to explain and document how and why the present regime of Sentencing Guidelines came into being. In chapter 1, we explore the history of federal criminal sentencing, including previous reform movements. In chapter 2, we chronicle the legislative history of the Sentencing Reform Act of 1984, the appointment of the Sentencing Commission, and how the Sentencing Commission in turn constructed the Sentencing Guidelines. We also note related developments such as the evolution of statutory minimum sentencing and the creation of less complex sentencing guideline systems in a number of states. In explaining and critically evaluating the federal Sentencing Guidelines, we hope to place them within a larger historical and political perspective. The Guidelines *juridify* criminal sentencing (to use Max Weber's term)—that is, they encumber sentencing law with minute formal distinctions and administrative detail—much as has occurred in certain other areas of law, such as the law of torts and contract. The endless specification of formal rules in the Sentencing Guidelines, their neoclassical preoccupation with artificial order, and their attempt to mechanize justice may seem anachronistic in what many intellectuals insist is our "post-modern" or "post-Enlightenment" age. In a time of discontent and fierce competition among value systems, the Guidelines represent the continuing triumph of the administrative state.

A second objective of this volume is to explain how the Guidelines have changed the quality of sentencing in the federal courts. Chapter 3 explores the changes both in the sentencing process and in the jurisprudence of criminal sentencing. In its quest for sentencing free of "unwarranted disparity," the Commission found it necessary to pigeon-hole crimes and offenders along complex gradients of severity and to greatly confine judicial discretion in all but "atypical" or "extraordinary" cases. But every case that comes before a judge for sentencing is different and special, and no set of rules—simple or complex—can be appropriate for every case. The attempt by the Sentencing Commission to develop a system of rules that would both ensure uniformity *and* recognize the variability of crimes and offenders has generated inordinate complexity and confusion in Guidelines definition and application, imposed burdens on both trial and appellate courts, generated case law jurisprudence that is at once trivial and voluminous, dehumanized the sentencing process, and undermined the moral dimension of sentencing and punishment. At the same time, as we document in chapter 4, the ability of the Sentencing Guidelines to eliminate sentencing "disparity" is dubious at best. There is considerable variation in Guidelines application among different federal districts, different judges, and different prosecutors. Inevitably, some prosecutors, probation officers, and judges have been disposed to implement the new sentencing rules without compromise or concession, while others have strained to achieve greater flexibility. The exercise of what we term "hidden" discretion by both judges and prosecutors mocks the precision and obduracy of the Guidelines' sentencing calculus, while at the same time contributing to disparity in sentencing outcomes and cynicism about the criminal justice system.

We readily concede that not every reader will share our disappointment with the consequences of the prevailing system of sentencing in the federal courts. Those who adhere fully to a neoclassical aspiration for rationality in human affairs, and who would seek to minimize opportunities for discretionary judgment, may be pleased with some of the very consequences we find lamentable. Our portrait of sentencing under the Guidelines may be welcome to these readers, if only to confirm that their vision of "progress" has found a place in our public order. We hope, however, that a fuller understanding of the processes and possibilities of justice under the Guidelines will stimulate some reconsideration of views.

Others may share our concerns and share also our determination to provide a workable alternative to the Guidelines as they now exist. The third and final objective of this volume is to suggest avenues for redirection of criminal sentencing policy in the federal courts. We recognize that it is unlikely that the present system of Guidelines will simply be abolished in the near future. Accordingly, in chapter 5 we propose modifications that would address some of their most troubling consequences, in particular those that may threaten or cast a shadow over constitutional norms. Any system of mandatory sentences alters the constitutional balance of powers among the judiciary, the executive, and the legislative branches; we believe that it is possible, without radical alteration of the Sentencing Commission or its Guidelines, to restore some measure of authority to sentencing judges to consider the totality of the circumstances presented by a case and to serve as a check on possible prosecutorial or legislative overreaching. Moreover, the fact that the Sentencing Guidelines effectively operate as a criminal code, supplementing statutory criminal prohibitions, has due process implications that have not yet been adequately addressed; we propose that the organized federal judiciary consider simple but meaningful changes in sentencing procedures that would attend to these due process concerns.

Also in the final chapter of the book, we set forth a vision of more comprehensive reform, one that would involve elimination of the Sentencing Guidelines as we know them. We do not reject out of hand all the reforms of the Sentencing Reform Act—indeed, we embrace some of these. In particular, we do *not* seek a return to the previous system of unconstrained and unreviewable sentencing discretion. We are convinced that appellate review of sentences is critical to a just sentencing regime; abuse of discretion by trial judges is reviewable in every other context, and we see no reason why sentencing decisions should be an exception. On the basis of the study in the previous four chapters, however, we propose a system of sentencing guidelines that truly provides "guidance" for the exercise of discretion by federal trial judges, rather than one which imposes mandates and fosters elaborate judicial factfinding. Unlike the present Sentencing Guidelines, the outline we propose is neither visionary nor comprehensive. We hope, however, that it is at once politically viable and responsive to the human yearning for justice.

CHAPTER ONE

Sentencing Reform in Historical Perspective

[T]hat if the person . . . shall swear or affirm falsely, such person shall . . . be punished by fine or imprisonment, or both, in the discretion of the court before whom the conviction shall be had, so as the fine shall not exceed one thousand dollars, and the term of imprisonment shall not exceed twelve months.

An Act to Regulate the Collection of Duties (1789)

[T]he almost wholly unchecked and sweeping powers we give to judges in the fashioning of sentences are terrifying and intolerable for a society that professes devotion to the rule of law.

Judge Marvin E. Frankel (1973)

The History of Federal Criminal Sentencing

Judicial Discretion and Its Discontents

From the beginning of the Republic, federal judges were entrusted with wide sentencing discretion.[1] The great majority of federal criminal statutes have stated only a maximum term of years and a maximum monetary fine, permitting the sentencing judge to impose any term of imprisonment and any fine up to the statutory maximum. Although juries in state courts often had sentencing authority in the early years of our nation, in the federal system sentencing has always been a duty of the judge.[2] For over two hundred years, there was virtually no appellate review of the federal trial judge's exercise of sentencing discretion.[3]

The earliest federal criminal statutes set the pattern. The first Congress enacted a criminal proscription even before it established the federal courts in 1789. The law provided that upon conviction for bribery of a customs official, the defendant

> shall . . . be punished by fine or imprisonment, or both, in the discretion of the court . . . , so as the fine shall not exceed one thousand dollars, and the term of imprisonment shall not exceed twelve months.[4]

The following year, the Crimes Act of 1790 catalogued a variety of federal crimes. It provided severe punishment for treason, murder, and piracy; relatively short maximum terms of imprisonment for most other crimes; and, very occasionally, some form of corporal punishment, usually at the discretion of the court.[5] Thus, for example, the crime of larceny on the high seas was punishable by a fine "not exceeding the four-fold value of the property so stolen" and a lashing "not exceeding thirty-nine stripes," while the crime of manslaughter was punishable by a fine of up to a thousand dollars and imprisonment "not exceeding three years."[6]

Congress also occasionally enacted mandatory minimum sentences of imprisonment, though the minimum terms were seldom severe. The first federal statute specifying a minimum term of incarceration appears to have been enacted in 1798. It provided a minimum term of three years, and a maximum term of ten years, upon conviction for fraud on the Bank of the United States.[7] The judge had discretion to sentence the defendant within the statutory terms provided by Congress. Because no federal prisons were built until the end of the nineteenth century, all federal prisoners served their sentences in state prison facilities.[8]

Throughout most of the nineteenth century, the only sentence that was ever mandated in federal law was the death penalty, for the most serious offenses.[9] Even here, significant discretion was exercised, though not by judges in formal sentencing. Rather, discretionary authority not to enforce capital punishment was exercised by: (1) prosecuting authorities, who might choose not to prosecute rather than subject a wrongdoer technically guilty of a capital crime to hanging; (2) juries, who through their power of "nullification" could decline to convict, however strong the evidence;[10] (3) judges, in their interpretation of the law;[11] and (4) the President, through the pardon power granted expressly in the Constitution.[12] The de facto discretionary nature of de jure "mandatory" capital sentences has been a hallmark of criminal sentencing throughout the history of the common law in England and the Colonies as well as in the American Republic.[13] A similar fate has befallen other harsh mandatory statutory penalties for drug and gun crimes in modern times.[14]

After the Crimes Act of 1790, Congress apparently never again provided for corporal punishment. It did, however, provide for minimum terms of imprisonment in a variety of laws throughout the nineteenth century, especially, it appears, for offenses related to the mails.[15] Even here, however, the range of judicial discretion was quite large,[16] and on occasion Congress made explicit reference to it. For instance, a provision of the Post Office Act of 1825 directed that a person harming a mailbag shall "pay a sum, not less than one hundred dollars, nor exceeding five hundred dollars, or be imprisoned not less than one year, nor exceeding three years, at the discretion of the court before whom such conviction is had."[17] Indeed, it appears that even when Congress specified a minimum term of imprisonment, federal courts could exercise authority not to incarcerate the defendant by either delaying imposition of sentence or by "suspending" its execution.[18]

Much more common than statutory minimum sentences were statutes that provided only for a maximum penalty. A typical provision is found in the Post Office Act of 1872: for unlawfully detaining letters, a postal employee shall "forfeit and pay a penalty of [*sic*] not exceeding five hundred dollars, or be imprisoned not more than one year, or both, at the discretion of the court."[19] In the intervening century, the only material alteration in this particular statute has been to increase the maximum penalty to five years' imprisonment.[20]

ALTHOUGH THE STRUCTURE of the federal criminal law and the nature of judicial sentencing discretion remained remarkably constant for some two hundred years, this apparent consistency masked considerable intellectual and political ferment regarding the proper scope of judicial authority in sentencing. The ideas of the sentencing reformers of the 1970s did not spring out of thin air. Rather, the intellectual origins of the federal Sentencing Guidelines are to be found in the Enlightenment's critique of natural law in favor of positivism and rationalism in the regulation of social relations.

One ambition of Enlightenment thinkers was to rationalize and systematize the processes of governance. For instance, Montesquieu argued for the "separation of powers" into legislative, executive, and judicial functions; the legislature, most responsive to the people, should have sole authority to enact laws, while the judges would exercise neither legislative nor executive power.[21] Our Constitution, drafted by men highly attuned to Enlightenment ideals, reflects this aspiration. Yet as our history has unfolded, the "separation of powers" in the federal government has never been complete. The demands of governance have required the creation of new agencies of government. One of the most important developments of our constitutional history has been the growth of a powerful and operationally autonomous *administrative* sector of the federal government—a sector that performs executive, legislative, *and* judicial functions. The Sentencing Commission, like other agencies in the administrative sector of government, does not fit the formalistic "separation of powers" model proposed by Montesquieu.

At the same time that they considered broad questions of political organization, Montesquieu and others also addressed more specific issues of policy, including the systematization of criminal punishment. The most celebrated Enlightenment thinker on crime and punishment was Cesare Beccaria, who obtained his law degree at the University of Pavia in 1758.[22] For Beccaria and his followers (most prominently Thomas Jefferson[23] and Jeremy Bentham[24]), the deterrence of crime was the only proper purpose of criminal punishment.[25] While Montesquieu and other Enlightenment philosophers had proposed reduced reliance on the death penalty on grounds of disproportionality to harm caused and blameworthiness,[26] Beccaria advanced an argument grounded in the need for both general and specific deterrence.

In Beccaria's view, deterrence was not achieved through severe penalties, which "make[ ] the criminal all the bolder . . . so that he commits several crimes in order to escape punishment for [the first]."[27] Rather, the best way to achieve deterrence and to control crime was through precise specification of offenses in advance by the legislature. For each such offense, the corresponding penalty should offset any benefit derived from the crime. Beccaria thus proposed fixed, mandatory penalties that would be precisely scaled according to the offender's injury to society.[28]

Although Beccaria did not propose that the specification of offenses and penalties be delegated to an "independent" administrative agency or anything like it (such institutions were unknown at that time), he did clearly insist that the judiciary's role be reduced to the minimum necessary for adjudication. Like Montesquieu, Beccaria vigorously criticized the tradition of common law crimes—that is, criminal prohibitions recognized over the centuries in judicial precedent, but not legislatively codified. The tradition of common law crimes had survived in the American states even after ratification of the Constitution. (Indeed, most of the serious felonies that legislatures proscribe by statute today were derived from the common law, including manslaughter, arson, robbery, and rape.)

The classic criminology of Beccaria, with its emphasis on certainty and uniformity of punishment through a gradient of sanctions prescribed according to the seriousness of the crime, was adopted in the French Penal Code of 1791, but never took hold in common law countries.[29] Although federal criminal statutes reflected Enlightenment thinking to the extent that they provided for relatively few capital crimes and for relatively short maximum terms of imprisonment for most other crimes, neither the federal government nor the states ever embraced Beccaria's condemnation of the exercise of judicial discretion in criminal cases. Common law crimes—both those previously defined by the courts and those that might be created by analogy in the future—were expressly recognized by state constitutional or statutory provisions in most of the original thirteen states as well as in many that subsequently joined the Union.[30] The elimination of common law crimes fared better in the federal courts. Justice Story, a distinguished student of the common law and a preeminent supporter of federal rights over states' rights, insisted that the federal judiciary had authority under the Constitution to recognize nonstatutory crimes against the federal government.[31] Yet the Supreme Court decided in the early nineteenth century that the concept was inconsistent with the principles of separation of powers and limited delegation of powers to the federal government.[32]

Still, Congress continued to accord great discretion to federal judges to interpret broadly worded criminal statutes,[33] as well as to fashion appropriate penalties within statutory maximums. Congress did occasionally provide some guidance to sentencing judges: an 1825 statute, for instance, contained the vague maxim of sentencing proportionality "according to the aggravation of the offense."[34] More commonly, federal criminal laws employed an explicit and open-ended delegation of sentencing to "the discretion of the court."[35] Federal law never sought or purported to achieve the certitude and the exactitude (in either the definition of offenses or the prescription of sentences) demanded by Beccaria—that is, until the enactment of the Sentencing Reform Act of 1984.

Like Beccaria in the eighteenth century, the federal Sentencing Guidelines today seek to replace the discretionary power of judges with an elaborate, less intuitive, and more "scientific" system for the administration of penal sanctions. In doing so, they reveal an intellectual affinity not only to Beccaria, but to a continuous tradition of Enlightenment and post-Enlightenment thinkers who have carried into the twentieth century Beccaria's dream of establishing a self-contained calculus of penology. It is interesting to note, however, that Bentham—with whom this project is perhaps most commonly associated—actually came to reject the ideal of a mechanized system of justice, adopting instead the premise that "inflexible rules in fact considerably increase the scope for arbitrariness of decision."[36] But while Beccaria's greatest student thus came to recognize the limitations of the master's vision, others continued to seek a fully rationalized and mechanized system of sentencing rules.

Indeed, the Sentencing Guidelines bear a remarkable resemblance to the effort of one of Beccaria's philosophical heirs from early in this century, Professor Enrico Ferri. Ferri's Italian penal code commission, appointed in 1919, propounded "a new and autonomous systematization of legislative norms in accord with the advance of scientific doctrines." The Ferri system insisted on a comprehensive specification of factors relevant to a sentence, along with instructions on penal arithmetic for adding these factors together.[37] One commentator's description of the judicial role under Ferri's system might as well have been written about the federal Sentencing Guidelines of today:

> The Ferri system is so mechanical and complicated in conception and design that one has a picture of a judge checking up on whether, say, "circumstances of greater dangerousness" numbered 1, 3, 7, 10, 12, and 17 and "circumstances of less dangerousness" numbered 2, 4, 6, and 8 are applicable to a defendant before him; ascertaining which of the numerous sanctions or combinations thereof are pertinent; then, using a computing machine to figure out just how much incarceration is called for in the application of the individual's sentence and where.[38]

It is worth noting that Italy never sought to implement Professor Ferri's elaborate system.

The Purposes of Punishment and the Rise of the Rehabilitative Ideal

The traditional flexibility of American sentencing practices reflects two powerful currents in our nation's history: first, an uncertainty about the purposes of the criminal sanction, and second, the ideal (for more than a century) of the rehabilitation of offenders.

The idea of proportionality in sentencing has been part of our tradition since biblical times.[39] In exercising the wide sentencing discretion assigned by Congress, a federal judge's task has been to allocate punishment fairly for each crime and each criminal who comes before the court. The difficult issue has always been, "proportionate to what?" Should punishment be proportionate to the *injury or harm* caused by the crime, or should it be proportionate to the *blameworthiness* of the defendant? What consequences of punishment should courts consider in determining proportionality? A criminal sanction has two effects on the general citizenry: it discourages others from committing the crime (*general deterrence*) and it protects others by the *incapacitation* of the defendant. The criminal sanction in any given case has additional effects on particular individuals: it may discourage the defendant from committing more crimes (*specific deterrence*), it may *rehabilitate* the defendant, and it may have either beneficial or deleterious effects on the victims and on the family and associates of the defendant. It is safe to say that in more than two hundred years of criminal sentencing in the federal courts, judges have taken into account all of these considerations.

Federal judges exercising sentencing discretion have always considered a wide variety of aggravating and mitigating factors relating to the circumstances of both the offense and the offender. In *Lyon's Case*

(1798), for instance, Judge Patterson in the federal circuit court of Vermont sentenced the defendant, convicted of seditious libel, to only four months in prison with a fine of one thousand dollars, which was well below the statutory maxima. The judge stated that Lyon's

> position, so far from making the case one which might slip with a nominal fine through the hands of the court, would make impunity conspicuous should such a fine alone be imposed. What, however, has tended to mitigate the sentence which would otherwise have been imposed, is . . . the reduced condition of your estate.[40]

In another case in which a bank president was convicted of making a false report to the Comptroller of the Currency, the federal appeals court affirmed the conviction but noted that it would "have been better pleased . . . if the sentence imposed had been less severe." The appeals court went on to note, however, that it was not authorized to review the sentence and that in any event "the more full and accurate knowledge of all the facts and circumstances . . . which was possessed by the trial judge enabled him, probably, to better determine what was adequate punishment."[41]

For the purposes of determining an appropriate sentence, sentencing judges frequently received evidence that was irrelevant or otherwise inadmissible on the issue of guilt or innocence, including testimony about the defendant's reputation and the circumstances that led to the commission of the offense.[42] In sentencing a postal employee to practically the minimum term provided for theft from the mails, for instance, a judge in 1869 referred to the defendant's "former good reputation," the fact that this was his first criminal offense, the "temptation which in an evil hour, for yourself and friends caused you to stumble and fall," and the "comparatively small" amount stolen.[43]

From the nation's beginnings, the federal government, like most states, appears to have practiced a hybrid philosophy of punishment. On the one hand, the civic ideal of reformation through punishment had attracted significant adherents in America by the end of the eighteenth century, paralleling the religious (and literary) idea of salvation through suffering. Associated most prominently with the Pennsylvania Quaker physician Benjamin Rush and his friend Benjamin Franklin, the ideal of personal reformation was at the heart of the movement to transform existing penal institutions into more humane institutions of treatment and reform.[44] Rush and his Philadelphia Society for Alleviating the Miseries of Public Prisons were also concerned with general deterrence, but they disputed Beccaria's postulate that fixed, certain sentencing was most effectual in this regard. Rush argued in 1793 that "the kinds of punishments that might be employed should be specified by law but their duration should not be fixed, save as a possible maximum. The limitations of punishment in specific cases within the prison should not be known to the prisoners."[45] As one historian has noted, it appears "that in the physician's mind was a clear foreshadowing of an indeterminate sentence."[46]

On the other hand, this period was also marked by substantial retributory sentiment in criminal law and practice. For example, despite the objectives of proportionality and reform stated in its constitution, New Hampshire in 1791 provided the death penalty for eight crimes: treason, murder, rape, sodomy, breaking and entering, arson at night, robbery, and counterfeiting.[47]

The pure ideal of retribution as the basis of a theory or system of penology is most often associated with Immanuel Kant. For Kant, neither deterrence nor reform of the criminal were proper purposes of punishment, because each required purposeful infliction of pain as "a means to promote some other good for the criminal himself or for civil society."[48] Though Kant, like other contemporaries, considered proportionality to be critical,[49] he rejected the utilitarian approach of Beccaria and others. "The law concerning punishment," he famously asserted, "is a categorical imperative, and woe to him who rummages around in the winding paths of a theory of happiness looking for some advantage to be gained by releasing the criminal from punishment or by reducing the amount of it."[50] Kant's retributive imperative—to do justice in the particular case—is echoed throughout nineteenth- and twentieth-century commentary on the criminal law.[51]

In the courts of nearly every state, as well as in the federal courts, the various purposes of punishment were to be achieved primarily through imprisonment and fines. The earliest European penitentiaries reflected the religious concept of crime as sin and punishment as penance.[52] Whatever motivation inspired the establishment of penitentiaries in the New World, there is little doubt that, by the early nineteenth century, reform through atonement, either in solitary repentance or in the expiation of hard labor, had become the guiding philosophy of imprisonment in America as well.[53]

Critics of judicial sentencing discretion have ventured that, in continuing to sentence defendants to fixed terms "largely on the basis of judgments concerning particular offenses," rather than the offenders' prospects for rehabilitation, nineteenth-century judges were apparently oblivious to the reformatory goals of incarceration.[54] This assessment may rest on a modern understanding of individual reform, which measures "rehabilitation" by the absence of recidivism after release from prison. There was in fact no inconsistency between the concept of reform pursued by prison authorities in the first half of the nineteenth century and the then-prevalent judicial sentencing philosophy, which suggested the longest sentences for the most hardened criminals.[55] It was reasonable to suppose that those who had committed the most heinous offenses would also require more time and more punishment for atonement and moral cleansing. Newly enacted federal statutes specifying imprisonment "at hard labor" (sometimes at the discretion of the judge) were consonant with the understanding of reformation pursued in the nation's penitentiaries.

By the middle of the nineteenth century, these early theories of reform through isolation or hard labor—through court-ordered suffering—gave way under the weight of failure[56] to a new understanding of rehabilitation. The twin foundations of the new dispensation were, first, that inmates should be provided an incentive for betterment, and, second, that experts—not judges—should determine when sufficient improvement had taken place. Reformers criticized the prevailing system of criminal sentencing because it could not be readily adapted to this new rehabilitative model.[57] In particular, they attacked judicial authority over criminal sentencing. As one early proponent of rehabilitation argued, "One of the greatest improvements in the administration of our penal code would be to withhold from the judges all discretion as to the time for which convicts shall be confined."[58]

This late-nineteenth-century complaint about judicial discretion, however, was *not* the same as that of the reformers of the late twentieth century. The reformers of our day fear that discretion leads to unduly disparate sentences for similar crimes by similar offenders.[59] The concern in the previous century was that judges were ill-positioned to determine the appropriate length of a term of incarceration. In the view of proponents of rehabilitation, the duration of imprisonment, whatever the crime, "should be not for weeks, months, or years, but until that end for which alone [an offender] should be put [in prison] is accomplished; that is, until reformation has evidently been affected."[60] Additionally, they argued, without the incentive of early release for good behavior, prisoners seemed increasingly to engage in unruly and violent conduct.[61] In thus proposing that the length of imprisonment should be determined by executive (prison or parole) authorities *after* the judicial imposition of an indeterminate sentence, the reformers who advocated rehabilitation as a penological goal departed from the basic tenet of Beccaria—that all punishment by the state must be precisely specified in advance by the positive law enacted by legislatures.

The efforts of criminal justice reformers in the late nineteenth and early twentieth centuries were an integral part of the Progressive Movement, which sought to address (if not to eliminate) the many forms of social deviancy. The emergence of the social work profession, the development of courts specializing in offenses by juveniles, and the founding of settlement houses are other prominent examples of this movement.[62] By the early twentieth century, the rehabilitative model of punishment had assumed primacy.[63] The problem of disorderly prison behavior was addressed by the enactment of statutes, first by the states and eventually by Congress, providing for what was (and still is) termed "good time" credit. Federal law, for instance, originally provided for a deduction of five days from an offender's sentence for each month of good behavior in prison.[64] Prison officials and reformers also promoted the adoption of a formal system of indeterminate sentencing. Under indeterminate sentencing, penal experts—rather than legislatures in enacting penal statutes or judges in pronouncing sentence—decide when incarcerated prisoners should be released.

In 1881, New York enacted one of the first general indeterminate sentencing and parole laws. The statute provided that courts in "imposing sentence shall not fix or limit the duration thereof." Rather, the "managers of the reformatory" would decide the duration of every term within the maximum statutory term provided for the crime at issue.[65] Other states adopted systems that provided for indeterminate terms of imprisonment for each crime, either set by statute or set by the sentencing judge, and established parole authorities.[66] Consistent with this trend toward sentence indeterminacy, many states that had relied on jury sentencing also abolished or sharply curtailed this practice.[67]

It was not until 1910 that Congress established a system of federal parole,[68] thereby providing both the incentive for rehabilitation and the possibility of expert determination that a prisoner had been rehabilitated and should be released from confinement. The adoption of the rehabilitative ideal in the federal system differed from the experience of the states in one significant respect, however: it did not involve any change either in the structure of statutory sentencing provisions or in the wide discretion accorded to federal trial judges. Thus, a 1909 federal criminal code revision, designed to eliminate gross inconsistencies that had accumulated in federal criminal law over the previous 120 years, continued to provide specific maximum penalties and maximum fines for each crime and required judges to sentence defendants to particular terms at or below the maximum.[69] In fact, the major difference between the penalty provisions of the 1909 code and the statutes it replaced was the elimination of most minimum terms of imprisonment, thereby ostensibly *increasing* judicial sentencing discretion.[70]

As a formal matter, the introduction of parole the following year significantly reduced federal judicial authority over the duration of prison sentences because parole authorities, not judges, would determine each federal prisoner's actual release date. From the judge's perspective, however, this limitation on judicial sentencing power was comprehensible and consistent with the traditional judicial role in sentencing. Since the late nineteenth century, federal prisoners had been able to earn "good time" credits that reduced their actual time in prison to a shorter term than the nominal sentence imposed by the judge.[71] Moreover, while the 1910 parole legislation provided parole authorities with the discretion to release offenders even earlier than the good time calculus alone would allow, judges had significant control over an offender's parole release. No offender could be released until he had served at least one-third of his nominal sentence, unless the judge at the time of sentencing specified immediate eligibility for parole.[72] As a result, judges could formulate their sentences so as to assure that the defendant would serve at least a particular minimum amount of time in prison (one-third of the nominal sentence) and usually no more than twice this minimum.

Of equal significance, federal trial judges retained the important authority to sentence the defendant to *no* time in prison. This procedure was first developed in Massachusetts during the nineteenth century on the theory that imprisonment was not necessary or proper for the rehabilitation of certain individuals.[73] Even under those few statutes that provided for minimum prison terms, federal courts continued on occasion to order a "suspension" of sentence—a power state courts had also assumed and exercised.[74] While the Supreme Court held in 1916 that federal courts had no authority to permanently "suspend" a statutorily specified minimum term of imprisonment,[75] this power was restored in 1925 when Congress enacted the National Probation Act. The Act authorized judges to suspend the execution of a sentence—"upon such terms and conditions as they may deem best"[76]—in all cases except those where the offense of conviction was punishable by death or life imprisonment (treason, murder, rape, mutiny, and piracy). In common parlance, the judge could place the defendant "on probation." Moreover, if and when the defender violated the terms of his probation, the judge could order him confined for up to the maximum term of the previously "suspended" sentence. The only directions to the court in the statute were that probation be imposed if "the ends of justice and the best interests of the public as well as the defendant will be served thereby."[77] By 1925, all 48 states also had probation systems.[78]

During the next sixty years, federal sentencing law underwent numerous modifications, including alterations in the administrative structure of parole[79] and special sentencing provisions for certain classes of offenders.[80] In its essential aspects, however, the system remained unchanged.[81] Congress continued to enact criminal statutes that stated only maximum terms of imprisonment and maximum fines, and within these maxima judges were authorized to impose any sentence—including probation alone, with imprisonment "suspended."[82] For the clear majority of cases, the term of imprisonment imposed by the judge set the possible minimum (usually one-third)[83] and the probable maximum (usually two-thirds, assuming the offender earned all of the good time credit available to him). A study of federal parole undertaken in the early 1970s found that where defendants were sentenced to prison, judges authorized immediate eligibility for parole in only about one-quarter of cases.[84] Moreover, as Congress was well aware, some statutes that appeared to specify minimum terms of imprisonment did not create *mandatory* minimum terms because they did not preclude suspension of the sentence and placement on probation; nor did they preclude placement on parole before expiration of the minimum term.[85]

In most cases, probation and fines remained statutory alternatives to imprisonment, though it was not until recent decades that federal judges began to take advantage of the many different *forms* of probation—which could range from virtually no post-conviction restrictions to significantly restricted liberty, depending on the conditions of release and the closeness of the prescribed supervision.[86] From the 1950s until the introduction of the Sentencing Guidelines in the late 1980s, nearly half of all persons convicted in the federal courts received nonprison sentences.[87] (This apparent uniformity, interestingly, masks significant growth in the scope of federal criminal law and changes in federal prosecutorial priorities over these decades.) The next most common form of sentence was a "split sentence," whereby an offender's prescribed term of imprisonment was suspended, and he was required to serve up to six months in prison, followed by a term of probation of up to five years.[88]

Advocates of the rehabilitative ideal would have preferred less judicial authority over sentences and even greater authority conferred on parole officials. The latter were regarded as "experts" in understanding character and criminal disposition. Their decisions could be based on the "facts" rather than on the politics of legislatures or the emotions of courtrooms. Ideally, in the view of proponents of rehabilitation, neither the legislature nor the court would set any term of imprisonment. Rather, all correctional decisions would be made by psychiatrists and other experts, who would "utilize every scientific instrumentality" to achieve protection for society with minimum constraints on the citizenry.[89] Professor Sheldon Glueck of the Harvard Law School, an eminent advocate of the rehabilitative model, enumerated the objectives of sentencing:

> (1) The treatment (sentence-imposing) feature of the proceedings must be sharply differentiated from the guilt-finding phase. (2) The decision as to treatment must be made by a board or tribunal specially qualified in the interpretation and evaluation of psychiatric, psychological, and sociologic data. (3) The treatment must be modifiable in the light of scientific reports of progress. (4) The rights of the individual must be safeguarded against possible arbitrariness or other unlawful action on the part of the treatment tribunal.[90]

Although they served by executive appointment in the federal system,[91] parole commissioners were nonetheless insulated from immediate political pressures. They served fixed terms, and their decisions to release or not release particular prisoners from confinement were largely hidden from public, legislative, or judicial scrutiny. Typically, the occurrence of a crime receives greater publicity than a subsequent guilty plea and sentence, and public interest in a case has usually faded by the time the parole authority makes a decision. Significantly, those who cared or aspired to serve as parole administrators usually came from a common tradition steeped in the rehabilitative ideal.

The federal system never adopted indeterminacy in sentencing to the extent it was adopted by some states. Although no state entirely removed the influence of legislators and judges on criminal sentences, in many states both statutory terms and the forms of sentence that judges were permitted to impose became highly indeterminate. By the early 1970s, California (the state perhaps most committed to the rehabilitative model) sentenced nearly all serious offenders to an indeterminate term of between one year and life in prison. The duration of almost all prison sentences in California was determined by parole authorities.[92] In the federal system, on the other hand, parole authorities continued to be limited in nearly every case by the sentencing judge's pronouncement of sentence. Unless the judge specified immediate parole eligibility, parole could not be granted before one-third of that sentence was served, nor in most cases would the defendant serve more than two-thirds of his nominal, publicly announced sentence.

Criminal Sentencing and the Substantive Criminal Law

Throughout much of our nation's history, the adjudication of guilt has been deliberately separated from sentencing and punishment. The "criminal law" has been understood by scholars, legislatures, and courts alike to consist simply of the definition and proof of the elements of crimes and defenses to crimes. Everything else that might relate to just punishment—the character, history, and motivation of the offender, the particular circumstances of the crime, relevant social and cultural needs—has been relegated to sentencing, the back-end of the criminal justice process. In this sense, the criminal law and criminal sentencing have been understood to be complementary systems, the former concerned with the requirements for just conviction and the latter concerned with the wholly separate question of just punishment.

The divorce of criminal law from criminal sentencing was essential and pervasive during the ascendancy of the ideal of rehabilitation. Some theorists of the criminal law even insisted that the rationale for a law of crimes was unrelated to the rationales for criminal punishment. Thus H. L. A. Hart, one of the leading legal thinkers in the period following the Second World War, posited a distinction between the "general justifying aim" of the criminal law and the justifications for punishment in each particular case.[93] One widely shared understanding is that even if deterrence of crime is the general aim of a system of criminal prohibitions, "just desert" (or retribution) should be a limit on the distribution of punishment. Within this limitation, each individual sentencing decision may be justified by appealing to other objectives that the sentencing authority determines are relevant in the case at hand. These objectives may be either retributive or utilitarian, the latter including rehabilitation or specific deterrence of the particular offender.

Legislatures and courts likewise have sought to distinguish issues relating to the substantive creation, definition, and proof of crimes from issues relating to criminal sentencing. Following the approach of the common law, modern legislatures in this country have continued to define crimes by reference to an *actus reus* (prohibited conduct) and a *mens rea* (the requisite state of mind with which the prohibited conduct is undertaken). Both elements of a crime have been defined in statutes at a broad level of generality.[94]

The preference for a substantial degree of generality in the criminal law has been remarkably constant and pervasive in the United States, shared by legislatures and law reformers alike. The broad scope of criminal statutes has had several significant consequences. First, it has left to the courts the critical task of interpreting and applying the elements of each criminal prohibition, initially at the trial level and then on appeal. Courts have played a particularly important role in insisting that the element of criminal mens rea requires something akin to conscious knowledge or awareness of one's behavior, without which conduct may not be justly classified as "criminal."[95]

Second, criminal statutes have generally left to the courts the task of linking the circumstances of the commission of a crime to the seriousness of that crime. Typically, a statute will make at most a single distinction concerning the relative seriousness of different circumstances (for instance, distinguishing "robbery" from "armed robbery," or "burglary during the day" from "burglary at night"). Rarely in the last two centuries have legislatures attempted to define with precision different severity levels for a single type of crime by further specification of the circumstances in which the crime is committed. For instance, in theory one might further subcategorize "armed robbery" into several different crimes: a robber might use a knife or might use a gun, he might threaten witnesses or he might ignore them, he might be working alone or he might be part of a larger conspiracy. Yet ordinarily a statute will broadly encompass all the different ways of committing the crime of armed (or "aggravated") robbery.[96]

Necessarily, the use of broad categories in crime definition has left to sentencing authorities, whoever they may be, the task of distinguishing between more and less serious crimes within the same category. Moreover, because criminal sentences in both state and federal courts have not been appealable for most of this nation's history, the task of determining the relative seriousness of offenses was left to the individual trial judge. Without appellate review of sentencing, there has been almost no "common law" of sentencing in this country.

The broad (and often vague) scope of statutory criminal prohibitions has also inevitably left important issues of interpretation and application to prosecutorial authorities. For example, federal law prohibits any "use of the mails" for the purpose of executing any "scheme or artifice to defraud, or for obtaining money or property by means of false or fraudulent pretenses, representations, or promises."[97] Many commercial transactions might arguably fall within the terms of this broadly crafted statute. The practical reach of the mail fraud statute has largely been determined, in the first instance, by federal prosecutors,[98] with periodic limitations or admonitions by the federal courts.[99]

The Model Penal Code Reform

During the ascendancy of the ideal of rehabilitation, the criminal law developed in a way that accentuated the gulf between the substantive criminal law and criminal sentencing. This gulf is best exemplified by the reforms stimulated at mid-century by the Model Penal Code promulgated by the American Law Institute (ALI). The object of the Model Penal Code, developed during the 1950s and first promulgated in 1962, was to rationalize the substantive criminal law. The Code is written in simple, clear language and covers the whole spectrum of criminal behavior in remarkably few provisions. It was not, however, accompanied by any comparable rationalization of the sentencing process. The drafters of the Model Penal Code quite deliberately fostered a discretionary sentencing system by providing for only a few categories of offenses, each with a wide and indeterminate sentencing range. Sentencing authorities were expected to take account of the complexities and ambiguities of human conduct that the Code deliberately ignores or glosses over.

In the years immediately before and following the Second World War, law reformers had undertaken significant "restatement" and codification efforts in other areas of the law, including a nationwide overhaul of both civil procedure and administrative law. In the wake of these efforts, the prestigious ALI—a selective national organization of elite lawyers, judges, and law professors—undertook to systematize and reform the nation's substantive criminal law. The criminal codes of most jurisdictions, including the federal system, were a hodgepodge of provisions enacted at different times, with many overlapping provisions, archaic prohibitions, and abstruse and anachronistic language. New criminal prohibitions had been piled on top of old, without regard for the consistency or comprehensibility of the whole. Work on the ALI's Model Penal Code began in 1952, and culminated in the publication of an Official Draft nearly a decade later. Though never adopted on the federal level (for reasons we shall subsequently note), the Model Penal Code was enacted, in whole or in part, by a majority of states in the ensuing quarter of a century.

The greatest contribution of the Model Penal Code, and the reason for its special attractiveness to state code reformers, is its unification and simplification of criminal offenses into a limited number of broad categories. The Code retains traditional distinctions between more and less serious crimes, but reclassifies them in a more consistent and systematic manner: first, by distinguishing between misdemeanors (punishable by no more than one year in prison) and felonies; and, second, by distinguishing among three broad classes of felony (first, second, and third degree).

In addition, the Code clarifies the concept of mens rea. Under the Code, mere negligence, even gross negligence, is usually insufficient to establish criminal culpability. Rather, all serious crimes require a mens rea of "purpose," "knowledge," or "recklessness." These levels of mens rea replace the enormous number of ambiguous and confusing terms of the common law (such as "wilfully," "maliciously," "deliberately," "corruptly," "improperly," "fraudulently," and "with malignant heart") that had found their way over the centuries into penal statutes around the country.[100]

In its attention to consistency, generalization, and systematization, the Code is clearly a "reform." But the Code also thoroughly embraces the rehabilitative ideal dominant at the time of its development, declining even to recognize retribution as a proper justification for punishment of crimes. Indeed, the Code deliberately avoids even use of the word "punishment"—it instead uses the terms "sentence" or "disposition," sometimes coupled with the term "treatment."[101] The Code's only reference to the idea of retribution as a justification for criminal punishment is its statement, in commentary, "wholly reject[ing] the idea that . . . the state is . . . justified in imposing the misery of prison on someone solely because the person has done something very bad and therefore 'deserves' a severe penalty."[102] For the drafters of the Code, the seriousness of a crime turns almost entirely on the offender's mens rea. Indeed, the Code uses the term "culpability level" as a *substitute* for the older term mens rea.[103]

All sentencing under the Code is indeterminate. For instance, a person convicted of a second-degree felony "may be sentenced to imprisonment . . . for a term the minimum of which shall be fixed by the Court at not less than one year nor more than three years, and the maximum of which shall be ten years."[104] The Code makes all persons convicted of felonies immediately eligible for probation instead of imprisonment, and provides that imprisonment should be imposed only if it "is necessary for protection of the public."[105]

Following the usual Anglo-American approach, the Code defines crimes broadly, providing a general actus reus element and an accompanying mens rea. For instance, the prohibition on trespass provides (in part) that "a person commits an offense if, knowing that he is not licensed or privileged to do so, he enters or surreptitiously remains in any building or occupied structure."[106] Each crime encompasses many varieties of criminal behavior. Indeed, in pursuit of its goals of systematization, unification, and consistency, the Code is written at an even more general level than most of the criminal provisions it was designed to replace. Theft offenses, in particular, were in most jurisdictions an array of overlapping and inconsistent prescriptions that had accumulated over the decades. The Code attempts to consolidate all theft into a single offense, and even as it recognizes many different forms of theft, it avoids ambiguous terms that had developed to distinguish among forms of theft (such as larceny, embezzlement, theft by trick, and so on) throughout the centuries of common law development.[107] Within the broad category of theft, the Code does not seek to specify subsidiary elements distinguishing more from less serious crimes. That is left to the process of sentencing.

In essence, the Code reformers were able to construct a nearly seamless, closed system only by arbitrarily limiting the contours of the law of crimes. The Code is perfectly logical and complete in and of itself, but that is because it does not attempt to address difficult questions concerning the varieties of criminal conduct and criminal motivation. It does not include in its definitions of crimes those distinctions that are difficult to specify through formal, *ex ante* prescription. Thus, in the Code, criminal mens rea breaks down into four simple concepts—purpose, knowledge, recklessness, and negligence. We all know, however, that the mind of an offender—indeed, the mind of any person—is infinitely more complex than this. The older, common law terms such as "wilful," "corrupt," "with malignant heart" and so forth were not subject to easy systematization on a single scale of culpability, but they did reflect an attempt to capture in the criminal law some of the complexity, ambiguity, and irrationality of life itself.

The Code's solution was not so much to *deny* these deeper and more profound issues of criminal justice as to *ignore* them by shunting them off to the far more open-ended, indeterminate sentencing process—reflecting, in part, the fact that law faculties had long regarded sentencing as a "soft" sub-speciality of criminal law, populated primarily by aficionados of psychiatry, sociology, social work, and other such branches of the "social" sciences.

The Code did attempt to systematize the sentencing process to some extent. For example, it lists the types of factors that *may* be relevant to a decision on a sentence. The most significant sentencing guidance provided in the Code is a list of eleven subjective factors that, if present in a given case, militate against a sentence of imprisonment. These factors concern the defendant's motivation, provocation, contemplated harm, amenability to treatment, and the like, and also the conduct of the victim and the impact of a prison sentence upon dependents of the defendant. For example, the Code instructs the sentencing judge to consider whether "the defendant acted under a strong provocation," whether "there were substantial grounds tending to excuse or justify the defendant's criminal conduct, though failing to establish a defense," whether "the defendant . . . has led a law-abiding life," and whether the "character and attitudes of the defendant indicate that he is unlikely to commit another crime."[108] The Code expressly states, however, that these considerations are "not controlling [on] the discretion" of the sentencing judge.[109]

In thus distinguishing between crime definition and criminal sentencing, and in opting for simple and broad categories of crime and a sentencing framework that is both subjective and only loosely systematized, the Code reformers proclaimed that a just criminal law cannot be achieved solely by the application of comprehensive categories and universal prescriptions. As Professor Gerard E. Lynch of Columbia Law School has recently pointed out, the Code opted for discretion over prescription, and it did so not only directly in its sentencing provisions, but also indirectly in its substantive crime definitions as well. In Professor Lynch's words: "[T]he drafters' preference for broad sentencing discretion affected the very structure of the Code's highly-influential substantive definitions of particular crimes."[110]

Yet, as we shall see below, the same intellectual forces that motivated the Code reformers in their effort to impose a closed, internally consistent systematization of the substantive criminal law would also exert pressure on the indeterminate sentencing system that the Code embraced. The Code's formula—systematized criminal law and indeterminate sentencing—was inherently unstable.

The Criminal Procedure Revolution

The Model Penal Code reform was concerned only with the *substantive* criminal law. Almost simultaneously, criminal *procedure* underwent an extraordinary reform. Originating in the lower federal courts and certain state courts, the rationalization and systematization of criminal procedure soon became primarily the province of the Supreme Court of the United States.

During the 1960s, in particular, the Court as a matter of constitutional interpretation imposed a host of new procedural constraints on the criminal justice system of every jurisdiction in the land.[111] For the most part, however, these new rules of criminal procedure pertain only to the areas of *investigation* (e.g., requiring that police obtain judicial warrants in most cases before engaging in a search for evidence of a crime) and *adjudication* (e.g., requiring appointment of counsel in every case, requiring that the defendant's plea of guilty be knowing and voluntary, and procedural requirements related to jury selection and trial).

The criminal procedure revolution has not, as yet, been fully applied to the stage of criminal *sentencing*. To the contrary, the Court's seminal case of *Williams v. New York,* decided in 1949, explicitly embraced the traditional separation of adjudicatory procedures from sentencing procedures, and declined to place significant due process restraints on the latter. Noting that "the due process clause does provide [many] salutary and time-tested protections where the question for consideration is the guilt of a defendant," Justice Black went on to explain that "[a] sentencing judge, however, is not confined to the narrow issue of guilt."[112] The implication was that the "salutary and time-tested protections" of due process are simply inapplicable to sentencing. Indeed, *Williams* and its progeny held that most of the procedural requirements of adjudication—such as juries, proof beyond a reasonable doubt, confrontation of witnesses, the prohibition of double jeopardy, aspects of the privilege against compelled self-incrimination, and the rules of evidence, including those relating to hearsay and prejudice—do not apply to sentencing.[113]

Clearly, this judicial tolerance of, even insistence upon, relatively informal and nonadversarial sentencing proceedings is historically grounded on the demands of a discretionary and rehabilitative model of sentencing. *Williams* explained that, in order to achieve case-by-case assessment of the defendant's character and rehabilitative potential, the sentencing authority must be permitted to take into account any information that might be useful. Without regard to the rules of evidence, without regard to the standard of proof beyond a reasonable doubt, and without regard to other due process limitations, the sentencing authority could consider any information that might shed light on the crime the defendant had committed, other crimes he had committed, or other aspects of his life choices and character. As Justice Black stated in *Williams:*

> Retribution is no longer the dominant objective of the criminal law. Reformation and rehabilitation of offenders have become important goals of criminal jurisprudence. Modern changes in the treatment of offenders make it more necessary now than a century ago for observance of the

distinctions in the evidential procedure in the trial and sentencing processes.[114]

Thirty years later, in *United States v. Grayson,* the Supreme Court upheld a sentencing judge's discretionary decision to increase the sentence the judge otherwise would have imposed because the defendant had perjured himself at trial.[115] More recently, the Court upheld a statutory provision in Pennsylvania that requires an enhanced sentence based on unconvicted conduct,[116] and Wisconsin's statutory enhancement for racially motivated crimes.[117] In the latter case, the Court noted that "[t]raditionally, sentencing judges have considered a wide variety of factors in addition to evidence bearing on guilt in determining what sentence to impose," and that "motive for committing the offense is one important factor."[118] For similar reasons, the Supreme Court refused to impose limitations as to the type and source of information available to parole officials in deciding whether to release a sentenced convict to the community.[119]

Beginning in the 1970s, however, some nonconstitutional constraints were imposed upon the sentencing proceeding. Amid calls by reformers for greater procedural protections at sentencing, the Federal Rules of Criminal Procedure were amended to require that the defendant have access to most parts of the presentence report prepared by the probation officer for the use of the sentencing court.[120] Some federal courts required findings of fact and a standard of proof of at least a "preponderance of the evidence" with respect to all disputed matters that the sentencing judge chose to consider in setting sentence.[121]

Still, the criminal procedure revolution extended only marginally into the area of criminal sentencing. It could not be further extended without upsetting a premise upon which the system of indeterminate sentencing was built: the broad discretion accorded to the sentencing judge.

The Revolt against Discretionary Sentencing

The Collapse of the Rehabilitative Ideal

The post-war reforms of substantive criminal law and criminal procedure might not have been realized had there not been open-ended and discretionary sentencing at the end of the process. When the drafters of the Model Penal Code rewrote the substantive criminal law and the Supreme Court rewrote the law governing investigation and adjudication, they postulated a sentencing process that was flexible and dependent upon human judgment. Discretionary sentencing provided some opportunity, at the end of the criminal justice process, to correct or adjust any untoward consequences of the closed, formal rules governing the previous stages of the process.

Yet, once the rationalizing reforms in the area of crime definition, investigation, and adjudication had been completed, the sentencing process appeared curiously unorganized and unsystematic. Indeterminate sentencing was at odds with movements toward systematization, orderliness, and *ex ante* specification of law that characterized other branches of the criminal law and the modern age more generally. Max Weber had predicted that Western societies in the twentieth century would experience a process of increasing growth of law, a process he called *juridification.* Legal subject matter would be systematized so that it would constitute a deductive, logical, and seamless system of rules. In Weber's wonderful metaphor, law would become "a slot machine into which one just drops the facts (plus the fee) in order to have it spew out the decision (plus opinion)."[122] The extended project of the American Law Institute to formalize and rationalize the substantive prohibitions of the criminal law and the nearly contemporaneous efforts, led by the Supreme Court, to formalize the rules governing criminal investigation and adjudication, are examples of the juridification predicted by Weber.[123]

The federal Sentencing Guidelines would soon provide another example. As Code reform and the revolution in criminal procedure were underway, criticisms of indeterminate and discretionary sentencing surfaced in various quarters with increasingly regularity. One important group of critics were advocates of prisoners' rights. If in theory the purpose of indeterminate sentencing was to permit rehabilitation in prison, they argued, in practice this often meant the use of prison to *incapacitate* those who could not be rehabilitated.[124] In this view, the rehabilitative premise was too often a sham, and indeterminacy had the effect of increasing the average length of nominal prison terms meted out in court and the amount of actual time served.[125] Moreover, uncertainty concerning release dates and the disparate treatment of offenders who had committed similar crimes were said to contribute to growing prison unrest during the 1960s and 1970s.[126]

Criticism also arose from within the psychiatric community. In the early decades of this century, the psychiatric profession had appeared to accept without equivocation the responsibility for predicting dangerousness and for deciding the extent of rehabilitation.[127] By the early 1970s, however, the voice of the profession seemed less certain, with many asserting the unreliability of psychiatric prediction and noting inherent conflicts between medical and legal objectives.[128] Other reformers objected that preventive detention after conviction, as well as such detention before conviction through the setting of high bail, was unjust because it resulted in incarceration of "many persons who would not have committed a crime if released, along with the few who would have."[129]

At the same time, more conservative political forces from outside the academic sentencing reform movement criticized judicial and parole discretion in sentencing on the ground that a focus on rehabilitation too often resulted in excessively lenient treatment of offenders who had significant criminal records or who had committed serious crimes.[130] The vehemence of this criticism grew as crime rates increased throughout the 1960s and 1970s and, with them, the number of media accounts of parolees (or even of persons who had actually completed their parole terms) who committed new, violent crimes.[131]

While these criticisms were directed at both parole and indeterminate judicial sentencing, the most sustained criticism was aimed at the asserted "disparity" in the sentences meted out by judges. As early as the 1920s and 1930s, some social scientists had observed that the differing temperaments, backgrounds, and personalities of judges accounted for some of the variation in criminal sentences.[132] Others claimed that sentencing severity was correlated with individual characteristics of defendants, including criminal record, sex, employment history, education, income, and race.[133] Despite their disagreements as to the causes of disparity, both groups of critics shared the view that illegitimate considerations were influencing the exercise of judicial discretion.

During the 1960s and 1970s, numerous studies were published purporting to show rampant, irrational variation in judicial sentencing and parole practices in federal as well as state courts. Especially significant for future debates was a study based on a questionnaire sent in 1972 to federal district judges in the Second Circuit (comprising New York, Connecticut, and Vermont). The committee that organized the study was chaired by Judge Marvin E. Frankel of the United States District Court for the Southern District of New York. Frankel was a highly respected judge and a former teacher of criminal law at Columbia Law School. The questionnaire asked the judges to impose sentences in a series of hypothetical cases, and the results of the study, published in 1974, were said to show "glaring disparity" in sentencing.[134] The methodological shortcomings and limitations of this and other studies of disparity in the federal courts, which we discuss in chapter 4, did not receive nearly as much attention as the study's startling conclusions.

In addition to empirical investigations of the phenomenon of sentencing disparity, the 1960s and 1970s witnessed a series of proposals to lessen the scope of judicial discretion in sentencing. The earliest proposals were relatively mild. Both the Model Penal Code[135] and the Model Sentencing Act (the latter developed by the National Council on Crime and Delinquency)[136] adopted the dominant penal philosophy of rehabilitation and the indeterminate sentence. They proceeded, however, on the premise that rehabilitation could not be expected to occur in the dehumanizing and often crowded and harsh settings of modern American prisons, and they sought to constrain judicial authority to impose sentences of imprisonment. The Model Penal Code, for instance, included a provision requiring that the sentencing judge impose a nonimprisonment sentence *unless* "imprisonment is necessary for protection of the public."[137] Moreover, both model codes sought to bring some order to sentencing processes. The Model Sentencing Act urged that before every sentence an arm of the court (such as the probation office) conduct a presentence investigation, as was already required in the federal courts, and that judges be required to provide factual findings and reasons for a sentence.

Few states adopted the sentencing provisions of the Model Penal Code or the Model Sentencing Act *en toto*. Nonetheless, it appears that the underlying objective of these proposals—to reduce reliance on incarcerative sentences—came to be realized in the sentencing and parole policies of many states.[138] We may never know whether the model laws were a cause of greater leniency or simply reflected a variety of factors in the larger culture that contributed to reduced reliance on imprisonment. Whatever its cause, hindsight reveals that the apparent leniency with which some *state* criminal justice systems treated criminals, including the growing perception of "revolving door" justice in crowded urban courts, was an important factor in achieving a political consensus in Congress for the strict *federal* Sentencing Guidelines promulgated some twenty-five years after the model statutes were developed. As one commentator explained: "When the headlines announce 'Convicted Killer with Life Sentence Released on Parole After Six Years in Prison,' a sense of frustration prevails."[139]

Also in the 1960s, President Lyndon B. Johnson appointed the National Commission on Reform of the Federal Criminal Laws, known as the "Brown Commission" after its chairman, Edward G. Brown, Sr., then Governor of California. The final report of the Commission urged an overhaul of federal criminal provisions to eliminate inconsistent and overlapping offense definitions and sentencing provisions.[140] The Commission also generally recommended appellate review of sentences—but did not directly address whether, or how, to guide either judicial discretion in sentencing or the standards governing appellate review of sentences. The Commission also declined to address the issue of parole.

For reformers who saw disparity as the fundamental flaw in criminal sentencing—an issue we address in detail in chapter 4—the limited reforms proposed in the model sentencing laws and considered by the Brown Commission were insufficient and ineffectual. These reforms would do little to address the numerous disparities in the American criminal justice system, disparities powerfully portrayed in the report issued by the President's Commission on Law Enforcement and Administration of Justice in 1967. This thoughtful and influential document, *The Challenge of Crime in a Free Society,* noted, among other matters, the existence of disparities in criminal sentencing. While commending the sentencing provisions of the Model Penal Code as a starting point for reform, the report urged all states to adopt statutory codes that would "include criteria designed to help judges exercise their discretion in accordance with clearly stated standards." Finally, the report urged greater use of sentencing councils and appellate review of sentences in order to "correct[ ] unjust and ill-considered sentences, particularly those in which the punishment imposed is grossly inappropriate."[141]

The criminal justice system's reliance on discretionary decision-making was further criticized in a pivotal book published in 1969. *Discretionary Justice: A Preliminary View,*[142] by Professor Kenneth Culp Davis of the University of Chicago Law School, one of the nation's preeminent scholars of administrative law, explored, among other things, the broad authority of police, prosecutors, judges, and parole officials in criminal cases. In Davis's view, the model sentencing laws, though considerable achievements, did not go far enough in reducing sentencing disparity.

Davis's analysis and proposals may have seemed radical at the time. In retrospect, however, Davis was far more nuanced and less rigid than those who followed in his wake. He did not propose to do away with all discretion in the criminal justice system. Although Davis respected legal complexity in other contexts (he admired, for example, the Internal Revenue Code and its accompanying four thousand pages of administrative regulations),[143] Davis did not urge that a comparable system of exhaustive *ex ante* rules be developed to govern criminal sentencing. Rather, Davis underscored that in "many circumstances, the mechanical application of a rule means injustice." Indeed, he warned against "confus[ing] the existence of discretionary power with the abuse of discretionary power," and he noted that "creativity is impossible without discretion."[144]

With regard to sentencing, Davis contemplated structures to guide discretion, not binding and complex sentencing rules. Specifically, he urged the development of case studies involving recurring patterns of crime and criminality, from which sentencing narratives would be prepared. Judges "would be free to use [these narratives] as guides" in their own sentencing decisions. Davis suggested that "*if supported by a strong vote of a large number of judges*," these guides could be an effective way to "structure" the exercise of judicial discretion. He also urged that sentencing judges be required to explain their decisions on the record, and that these decisions be subjected to appellate review like nearly every other trial court decision.[145]

Over the next five years, Davis's analysis was followed by increasingly urgent calls, especially but not entirely from the political left, for restrictions on judicial sentencing discretion and replacement of indeterminate with determinate sentencing.[146] Notable examples of these proposals included those that appeared in *Struggle for Justice* (1971), published by the American Friends Service Committee,[147] *Kind and Usual Punishment* (1973), written by the activist Jessica Mitford,[148] and a report issued by The Twentieth Century Fund Task Force on Criminal Sentencing (1976).[149]

The rapporteur for the last of these was Professor Alan M. Dershowitz of the Harvard Law School, a long-time and especially articulate critic of indeterminacy in sentencing and of rehabilitation as a purpose of criminal sentencing.[150] Serving on The Twentieth Century Fund Task Force were, among others, Edmund G. Brown, Sr., who had chaired the Brown Commission, and Andrew Von Hirsch, then a professor of criminology at Rutgers University and now at Cambridge University in England. Von Hirsch also served as executive director of the Committee for the Study of Incarceration, which was headed by former Senator Charles E. Goodell and included Professor Dershowitz among its members. As the principal author of that Committee's report, *Doing Justice* (1976), Von Hirsch called for presumptive criminal sentences fixed in advance. Invoking Immanuel Kant, Von Hirsch rejected the rehabilitative philosophy that supported indeterminate sentencing, urging that the appropriate rationale and measure of punishment should be "just deserts."[151] Meanwhile, the conservative thinker Ernest van den Haag weighed in, also counseling that retribution is the proper basis for criminal punishment.[152] Other influential scholars on the political right argued that society could and should seek utilitarian ends in the criminal justice system, especially general deterrence[153] and incapacitation.[154]

At about this time a study of rehabilitation programs was published by Robert Martinson, a prominent sociologist. He asserted that "with few and isolated exceptions, the rehabilitative efforts that have been reported so far have had no appreciable effect on recidivism."[155] Martinson's widely circulated views seemed to be the death knell for an indeterminate sentencing system based on rehabilitative goals, and it gave further impetus to calls for a new system of fixed sentences determined in advanced either by the legislature or by an administrative commission on sentencing. In a subsequent study, Professor Francis A. Allen of the University of Michigan Law School documented that by the mid-1970s, the rehabilitative ideal was in steep decline.[156] The movement toward determinate, rather than discretionary, sentences was in full gear.[157]

The Contribution of Judge Marvin E. Frankel

The most influential of all the criticisms of judicial sentencing discretion was that of Judge Marvin E. Frankel, who had organized the Second Circuit sentencing study in 1972. His book, *Criminal Sentences: Law without Order,*[158] published the following year, would thereafter confer upon him the title of "father of sentencing reform"—a title bestowed by no less a figure than Senator Edward M. Kennedy, who would become the chief sponsor of the Sentencing Reform Act of 1984.[159] Judge Frankel served with distinction for fifteen years as a federal trial judge in New York City. It was during his tenure as a United States District Judge in one of the outstanding trial courts in the land, and with the full authority of his office, that Frankel published his rhetorically powerful indictment of the sentencing authority he himself then exercised—powers he described as "almost wholly unchecked and sweeping" and that he found "terrifying and intolerable for a society that professes devotion to the rule of law."[160]

Frankel's book contained an equally powerful call to action: the creation of an administrative agency, a "Commission on Sentencing," with "the function of actually enacting rules . . . making law" in the form of "binding guides" on sentencing courts.[161] On the day his call was answered—November 1, 1987—Frankel had been engaged in the private practice of law for nearly a decade. His book, however, had remained the cornerstone of the movement to replace judicial discretion in criminal sentencing with certainty and administrative expertise.

Frankel was deeply skeptical of judicial discretion and, indeed, of judges. He explained that even federal judges, who traditionally enjoy a high reputation in the legal profession, were "a mixed bag."[162] The occupant on the bench at any given sentencing may be "punitive, patriotic, self-righteous, guilt-ridden, and more than customarily dyspeptic," even though "judges in general, if only because of occupational conditioning, may be somewhat calmer, more dispassionate, and more humane than the average of people across the board."[163] The result was, in Frankel's view, "arbitrary cruelties perpetrated daily."[164] At the same time, Frankel expressed great faith that an administrative sentencing commission "of prestige and credibility" could be established, composed of "people of stature, competence, devotion, and eloquence" that would have available "computers as an aid toward orderly thought in sentencing."[165] Frankel explained that he had "in mind the creation eventually of a detailed chart or calculus to be used . . . in weighing the many elements that go into the sentence . . . that would include, wherever possible, some form of numerical or other objective grading."[166] Frankel's views were echoed in many of the subsequent pleas for sentencing reform, while little attention was paid to the few voices that questioned either the need for his proposed transformation of federal sentencing law or its wisdom.[167]

In 1974, Yale Law School, with funding from the Daniel and Florence Guggenheim Foundation, conducted an in-depth workshop on sentencing disparity. The workshop ultimately resulted in draft legislation for the creation of federal sentencing guidelines.[168] In addition to Judge Frankel, the workshop's members included Jon O. Newman, a United States District Judge in Connecticut (who would subsequently be elevated to the Court of Appeals for the Second Circuit) and an important supporter of the move to sentencing guidelines;[169] Ronald Gainer, a career official of the U.S. Department of Justice, who years later would become the Department's *ex officio* representative to the Sentencing Commission during the crucial initial years when it wrote its first set of Guidelines;[170] and Professor Daniel J. Freed of Yale Law School, a nationally respected authority on sentencing. Freed had long been concerned with unwarranted disparity in criminal sentencing and would later support the enactment of the Sentencing Reform Act. He would thereafter become increasingly disenchanted with the Sentencing Commission and the sentencing system it created.[171]

While Freed's workshop examined the phenomenon of judicial sentencing disparity, the *Yale Law Journal* was examining the operation of parole and, in particular, the failure of the federal parole board to use its powers to reduce sentencing disparity. In the midst of the *Yale Law Journal* project, federal parole authorities announced that they would thereafter promulgate and be governed by a detailed Guideline Table.[172] According to the parole study subsequently published in the *Yale Law Journal* (with a foreword by Judge Newman), the new Guideline Table promised to provide "a scientific and objective means of structuring and institutionalizing discretion in parole release decision making. In so doing, the Guidelines also attempt to minimize the effects of sentencing disparity."[173]

Like the Sentencing Guidelines grid that would follow over a decade later (see appendix A), the parole system's Guideline Table consisted of a two-dimensional matrix, with one axis representing severity of the offense and the other a score based primarily on the defendant's prior criminal record.[174] The matrix was itself a graphical representation of an important change in policy perspective that had taken place: equality of treatment replaced rehabilitation as the overriding determinant of release decisions. The following year, Congress enacted a new parole statute that adopted this new approach, thereby codifying the transformation of parole from an indeterminate, rehabilitative model to a uniform, nondiscretionary model.[175] The statute required that within three months of entering a correctional facility, every prisoner must be informed of his presumptive release date as calculated under the Parole Commission's written guidelines.[176]

For many sentencing reform advocates, the transformation of parole from an indeterminate system grounded in the ideal of rehabilitation to a more uniform and nondiscretionary system was insufficient. Their goal was the complete elimination of parole. Moreover, in the view of reformers, parole was not the only, or even the most pernicious, source of undue disparity. In their view, parole guidelines could not be counted on to eliminate disparity in prison sentences.[177] It was necessary to attack the source of the problem: the discretion exercised by sentencing judges. Judge Frankel and other reformers would not be satisfied until Congress established a system of sentencing rules that would be binding on federal trial judges.

CHAPTER TWO
The Invention of the Sentencing Guidelines

The proponents of the bill . . . argue in essence that judges cannot be trusted. . . . Judges cannot write guidelines.

Senator Charles McC. Mathias (1984)

The commission would require prestige and credibility. It would be necessary to find for it people of stature, competence, devotion, and eloquence. The kinds of people—a matter broached here for discussion—could include lawyers, judges, penologists, and criminologists. They should also include sociologists, psychologists, business people, artists, and, lastly for emphasis, former or present prison inmates.

Judge Marvin E. Frankel (1973)

[W]e had hoped that a sentencing commission could serve a positive function in . . . even acting as a buffer, shielding the legislature from the political pressures to respond to ever increasing demands for punitive sanctions and helping to control burgeoning prison populations.

Professor Leonard Orland (1993)

Congress Invents the Sentencing Commission

In 1975, Senator Kennedy hosted a dinner for Judge Frankel and other leading scholars of the criminal justice system. It was this gathering that the *New York Times* later reported to be important in convincing the Senator to sponsor sentencing-reform legislation, which he first introduced later that year.[1] Senator Kennedy was moved not only by Judge Frankel's book, but by the Second Circuit study on disparity and the Yale Law School reform proposal calling for the creation of a sentencing commission to establish binding sentencing guidelines.[2] Kennedy came to view sentencing in the federal courts as "a disgrace," "a national scandal," a "glaring flaw," in "utter disarray," "hopelessly inconsistent," "arbitrary," and "desperately" in need of reform.[3] He introduced versions of his sentencing reform bill in each of the next four Congresses,[4] until at last it was enacted as the Sentencing Reform Act of 1984.

One of us has recounted in detail[5] the subtle legislative transformation of Senator Kennedy's reform from an essentially anti-imprisonment, antidiscrimination measure into a conservative, law-and-order measure hailed by President Ronald Reagan as a way to "crack down" on criminals.[6] As the sentencing bill became "tougher" on crime, it also became "tougher" on federal sentencing judges. Its initial inspiration was a mistrust of judicial discretion, and this theme became ever stronger over the course of four Congresses. Liberals and conservatives alike evinced a deep suspicion of discretionary judgment by federal judges; Congress was determined to limit it by delegating sentencing authority to an administrative agency that promised to be more responsive to Congress itself.

The Politics of the 1970s

The legislative origins of the Sentencing Reform Act of 1984 may be found in the failed efforts of the 1970s to achieve a recodification of the federal criminal law. Following the promulgation of the Brown Commission's report in 1971, bipartisan reformers sought to replace the diverse and disconnected federal criminal laws with a streamlined and simplified criminal code. The recodification drive foundered in the mid-1970s, however, in the face of intense liberal opposition to several relatively tangential provisions of the recodification bills.[7]

Senator Kennedy seized the opportunity presented by the probable defeat of criminal code reform. Working with his top aide on criminal matters, an energetic and gifted young lawyer named Kenneth G. Feinberg, the liberal Massachusetts Democrat drafted code reform legislation and sentencing reform provisions that would have broad, bipartisan appeal. In a move that was typical of his highly successful legislative career,[8] Senator Kennedy forged an alliance with two conservative Senate leaders—Senator John L. McClellan of Arkansas, the Arkansas Democrat who was then chairman of the Judiciary Subcommittee on Criminal Laws and Procedure, and Senator Strom Thurmond of South Carolina, the ranking Republican member of the Judiciary Committee.[9] Senator McClellan was nearing the end of his long political career and wished to leave criminal code reform as his lasting legacy. In alliance with Senator Kennedy, Senator McClellan agreed in 1977 to accept a version of the recodification bill stripped of its most controversial provisions, with Senator Kennedy's sentencing reform bill thrown in as a "sweetener" for liberals.[10]

This initial alliance reflected Senator Kennedy's early realization that the promise of reducing judicial sentencing discretion might be appealing to conservatives as well as liberals. Senator Thurmond in particular took a strong, independent interest in sentencing reform, spurred by his disdain for the view "that each offense and offender should necessarily be approached from the lenient perspective" and by his preference for "guidelines and policy statements that have teeth in them."[11]

Over the next four Congresses, between 1977 and 1984, the Senate's Judiciary Committee five times adopted and reported to the full Senate legislation containing versions of Senator Kennedy's sentencing reform bill.[12] Each of these bills had the stated objectives of avoiding "unwarranted sentencing disparity" among defendants "with similar records who have been found guilty of similar conduct" (by providing for sentencing guidelines and appellate review), and promoting "honesty in sentencing" (by providing for the elimination of parole).[13] Each of the bills also contained the basic features of the sentencing regime that would finally be enacted as the Sentencing Reform Act of 1984:

(1) the elimination of rehabilitation as a purpose of incarceration, along with the virtual elimination of parole as a mechanism of early release from prison. The post-prison supervisory function of parole would be continued instead in the form of a "term of supervised release" set at the time of the original sentencing;[14]
(2) the establishment of a "sentencing commission"—a multi-member "independent commission in the judicial branch";[15]
(3) a direction to the sentencing commission to develop and promulgate "sentencing guidelines" that would specify a 25 percent sentencing range for each case;[16]
(4) an expectation, recorded in the accompanying Senate Judiciary Committee report, that the commission's "guidelines" would be "sufficiently detailed and refined to reflect every important factor relevant to sentencing for each category of offense and each category of offender, give appropriate weight to each factor, and deal with various combinations of factors";[17]
(5) a direction to the Sentencing Commission to "consider" the "relevance" of both offense characteristics and personal offender characteristics, including age, education, vocational skills, employment record, and family ties and responsibilities;[18]
(6) a provision for appellate review of sentences;[19] and
(7) *no* provision for citizens or other affected persons to obtain judicial review of the final rules issued by the sentencing commission (as the federal Administrative Procedure Act provides with respect to executive branch agencies where the rules are alleged to be "arbitrary, capricious, an abuse of discretion, or otherwise not in accordance with law").[20]

Senator Kennedy's earliest proposals differed from the bill finally enacted in several respects. Most significantly, the initial bills anticipated that the complex sentencing rules issued by the putative sentencing commission would be essentially *advisory* rather than *prescriptive.* As Senator Kennedy explained at the time, his legislation "would require only that the sentencing judge 'consider' the sentencing range" set forth in the guidelines.[21] Indeed, Senator Kennedy made clear that the sentencing range set by the guidelines should be only one of several factors the sentencing judge would consider. The 1977 bill also instructed the judge to consider the four overarching purposes of sentencing (retribution, deterrence, incapacitation, and rehabilitation), as well as "the nature and circumstances of the offense being sentenced, and the history and characteristics of the defendant."[22] The judge could impose a sentence outside the guidelines range as long as he stated on the record "the specific reason" for doing so.[23]

Senator Kennedy's proposed system of advisory sentencing guidelines was transformed into a system of presumptive sentencing rules in 1978, as a result of the adoption on the Senate floor of an amendment proposed by Senator Gary Hart, the Democrat from Colorado. Senator Hart, who had been the sponsor of a competing sentencing reform bill providing for entirely determinate sentences,[24] sought the addition of language that would require the sentencing judge to impose a sentence in the guideline range *"unless the court finds that an aggravating or mitigating circumstance exists that was not adequately taken into consideration by the Sentencing Commission in formulating the guidelines and that should result in a different sentence."*[25] Senator Kennedy accepted the amendment, and this provision remains (with certain subsequent modifications) the key prescription limiting the power of sentencing judges to "depart" from the guideline sentencing range.[26] Senator Kennedy's original bill also contemplated only limited appellate review: the party wishing to appeal had to petition the appellate court for permission to do so, and the appellate court could reverse only if the sentence handed down was "clearly unreasonable." By contrast, the bill eventually adopted gave an absolute right to appellate review and empowered appellate courts to vacate sentences outside the Guidelines that are "unreasonable."[27]

Another Senate floor amendment curtailed more generally the role that federal judges would henceforth play in criminal sentencing. As originally introduced by Senator Kennedy and Senator McClellan in May 1977, the sentencing reform bill provided that the sentencing guidelines would be drafted by "an independent commission in the judicial branch," with all nine members *appointed by the Judicial Conference* (the federal judiciary's policy-making and governing body).[28] After the bill was reported out of committee, Senators Kennedy and McClellan agreed to an amendment sponsored by Senator Hart that provided that all the commissioners would be appointed by the President. The total number of commissioners was reduced from nine to seven, and only three had to be federal judges. The President would be required, however, to select these three judicial commissioners from a list of seven judges submitted by the Judicial Conference; only the four nonjudges would be subject to Senate confirmation.[29] As it turned out, later Congresses would further diminish the judiciary's role in sentencing reform, thereby guaranteeing that electoral politics and the politics of crime would be decisive factors in the sentencing regime of the future.

By 1980, when Ronald Reagan was elected President, the more substantive provisions of Senator Kennedy's sentencing bill had lost much of their original liberal, reformist aura. The bill that was reported to the Senate floor in 1980 completely eliminated parole, categorically prohibited judges from imposing sentences of imprisonment for rehabilitative purposes, and expressly discouraged consideration in sentencing of the background and personal characteristics of the defendant.[30]

WHILE THE SENATE strongly supported Senator Kennedy's efforts (and had in 1978 passed a bill that contained both comprehensive code reform and sentencing reform),[31] the House Judiciary Committee remained a continuing obstacle to the enactment of sentencing reform.[32] Chaired by Peter W. Rodino, Jr., of New Jersey, the Committee did not report a sentencing reform bill until 1980,[33] and that bill proposed far less radical reforms. Drafted by liberal Massachusetts Democrat Robert Drinan (who chaired the relevant subcommittee), the House bill would have retained a system of parole administered by a parole board and would have created a special committee within the federal judiciary itself to develop advisory sentencing guidelines. The accompanying House committee report explained: "Because judicial discretion in sentencing is a cornerstone of the criminal justice system, assigning the task of developing guidelines to the Judicial Conference is only logical."[34] Representative Rodino subsequently explained: "[A] presidentially appointed panel can too easily be dominated by political interests. The temptation to seek public approval by appearing tough on crime and therefore to propose standards biased in favor of prosecution and incarceration might prove too great."[35] Not convinced of the need to alter either federal criminal law or criminal sentencing, however, the House Judiciary

Committee did not press its position, and its bill never came to the floor for a vote.

The Politics of the 1980s

By the early 1980s, the political configuration of Washington had changed considerably. Ronald Reagan was in the White House, and, with the Republicans assuming control of the Senate, Senator Thurmond became chairman of the Judiciary Committee. Moreover, because Senator Kennedy opted to become the ranking Democrat on the Labor and Human Resources Committee, Senator Joseph R. Biden of Delaware became the ranking Democrat on the Judiciary Committee. Working with Senators Biden and Thurmond, Senator Kennedy did not let federal sentencing reform die. Many states were already moving toward more determinate sentencing systems by reducing the statutory range of sentences, shrinking the discretion of parole officials, and, in a few states, adopting sentencing guidelines systems.[36]

With growing public concern about crime and a new President keenly interested in expanding federal law enforcement efforts, Senator Kennedy repackaged his sentencing reform bill as one title of an anticrime bill. In 1982, both the House and Senate Judiciary Committees reported bills substantially increasing penalties for narcotics and gun crimes,[37] and in 1984 Congress enacted an assortment of crime bills providing for mandatory minimum terms of imprisonment.[38] The Senate Judiciary Committee twice adopted and reported general anticrime legislation cosponsored by Senators Thurmond and Biden; both bills included Senator Kennedy's sentencing reform legislation as a separate title.[39] When presented as part of the "Violent Crime and Drug Enforcement Improvements Act of 1982" and the "Comprehensive Crime Control Act of 1984," sentencing reform passed the Senate by an even larger margin than it had in 1978.[40] In both 1982 and 1984, Senator Charles McC. Mathias, the liberal Maryland Republican and senior member of the Judiciary Committee, was the only member of the Senate to vote against the crime bills.

Consistent with the "get tough" approach of the Comprehensive Crime Control Act of which it was a part,[41] the 1984 version of the Senate's sentencing proposal reflected the desire to address crime forcefully and contained several new provisions requiring sentences of substantial imprisonment for repeat offenders and drug offenders.[42] Without discussion or citation to empirical evidence, the Senate adopted a floor amendment instructing the projected Sentencing Commission that "in many cases, current sentences do not accurately reflect the seriousness of the offense."[43]

By 1984, the Senate bill also prescribed an even smaller role for federal judges in writing the sentencing guidelines. The bill passed almost unanimously by the Senate in early 1984 provided that of the seven commissioners, only *two,* rather than three, would be judges.[44] Moreover, the Attorney General or his designee would sit *ex officio* on the Commission as nonvoting members. Finally, unlike all previous versions of the bill, the 1984 version did not require the President to designate judicial members of the Commission from the list submitted by the Judicial Conference. The President only had to "consider" these names, and all seven commissioners—including the judges—had to be confirmed by the Senate,[45] thereby assuring that the judges named to the commission would, in effect, be selected by relevant senior members of the Judiciary Committee.

Both Senate supporters of the sentencing reform bill and President Reagan were candid in expressing their mistrust of federal judges. At one point Senator Mathias sought an amendment, drafted by the Judicial Conference, that would have placed responsibility for sentencing guidelines in the Conference itself. He explained that judges had more experience in sentencing than would a new bureaucracy in Washington, and noted that the Judicial Conference had long had responsibility for drafting the federal rules of practice and procedure. Most fundamentally, he complained that presidential appointment of sentencing commissioners would permit too much executive control over the Commission and "is no more appropriate than granting such power to a consortium of defense attorneys."[46]

The response from advocates of sentencing reform was clear: judges were the *problem* and as such could hardly be part of the *solution.* In the words of the conservative Nevada Republican, Senator Paul Laxalt:

> The proposed amendment would place the primary responsibility for the sentencing guidelines on the judges themselves. The present problem with disparity in sentencing, however, stems precisely from the failure of Federal judges—individually and collectively—to sentence similarly situated defendants in a consistent, reasonable manner. There is little reason to believe that judges will now begin to do what they have failed to do in the past.[47]

The Reagan administration explained that "[t]he judge, while trained in the law, has no special competence in imposing a sentence that will reflect society's values."[48] Senator Kennedy noted on the Senate floor,

"With all due respect, . . . judges themselves have not been willing to face this issue and . . . remedy this situation."[49] A frustrated Senator Mathias ventured that the Senate bill betrayed "a profound mistrust of the Federal bench. . . . The proponents of the bill . . . argue in essence that judges cannot be trusted. You cannot trust a judge . . . you must not trust a judge. Judges cannot write guidelines."[50]

Despite this overt distrust of judicial discretion and the extraordinarily limited role that the 1984 bill left for the judiciary in appointing commissioners and developing the sentencing guidelines, the measure still proclaimed that the Commission would be an "independent commission in the judicial branch." This provision had been in Senator Kennedy's original bill (calling for Judicial Conference designation of all commissioners),[51] and it remained in the bill as finally enacted (providing for presidential appointment and Senate confirmation of all commissioners).[52] The primary reason for this obfuscation was apparent: supporters were fearful that the Supreme Court might hold the Sentencing Commission unconstitutional unless it were considered part of the judicial, rather than the executive, branch of government.[53] Moreover, the insistence that the Sentencing Commission was part of the "judicial branch" made the proposed reforms appear less radical than they were.

While skeptical of the ability of judges to exercise judgment, write guidelines, or even designate sentencing commissioners, the Senate did enlist the federal courts of appeals in *enforcing* the guidelines. Under the sentencing reform legislation enacted in 1984, both the defendant and the prosecution may appeal on the ground that a sentence outside the guidelines range is "unreasonable" *or* on the ground that the Sentencing Guidelines have been "incorrectly applied."[54] In chapter 3 we discuss the role of appellate courts in the "new jurisprudence" of sentencing under the Guidelines.

LIKE THE SENATE, the House of Representatives also felt the public's growing concern about crime. Yet the House Judiciary Committee, widely considered to be more liberal than the House as a whole,[55] refused to accede to a system of mandatory sentencing guidelines as a response to this concern. Beginning in 1981, the Subcommittee on Criminal Justice of the House Judiciary Committee was chaired by John Conyers, Jr. of Michigan, who had long opposed mandatory sentencing guidelines because he believed that justice required "leaving judges free to tailor sentences to the unique circumstances involved in each case."[56] Like Chairman Rodino of the full Judiciary Committee, Representative Conyers was also concerned that administrative sentencing guidelines would lead to "an escalation" of sentences due to "political pressure."[57] With Conyers declining to agree to the Senate's sentencing reform proposal, that title was deleted from the Thurmond-Biden anticrime bill when it passed the House in 1982 during the final days of the 97th Congress.[58] Similarly, in 1984, despite President Reagan's public criticism of the House for holding up passage of legislation that would "crack down on criminals,"[59] the subcommittee never acted on the Comprehensive Crime Control legislation that had passed the Senate so overwhelmingly.

Under Representative Conyers, as under Representative Drinan (who had retired from the House and returned to law teaching, at Georgetown University), the House subcommittee questioned the very premise of the Senate bill: that there was rampant, unjustifiable sentencing disparity in the federal courts due to the exercise of discretion by sentencing judges.[60] The House Democrats were more dubious about the extent of disparity and more disposed to attribute that which did exist to prosecutorial charging practices. It is thus not surprising that the House was more disposed toward advisory guidelines, rather than the binding guidelines of the Senate bill. Nor is it surprising that the House was prepared to give federal judges themselves a leading role in developing any sentencing guidelines.[61]

Accordingly, the only sentencing reform proposal reported to the House floor by the House Judiciary Committee in 1984 was a stand-alone compromise measure that was neither as flexible and nonprescriptive as desired by Conyers, nor as rigid and mandatory as the Senate's bill.[62] Instead, the House bill provided for determinate parole terms and the establishment of a part-time commission within the Judicial Conference to draft advisory guidelines. The House bill also would have required the sentencing judge to impose the "least severe" sentence that would meet the four general purposes of sentencing. Finally, in addition to providing for guidelines to channel judicial discretion, the House bill required the Department of Justice to limit prosecutorial discretion by issuing guidelines for charging decisions and plea negotiations.[63]

Representative Conyers, ever dubious about codification of sentencing factors in the form of specific regulations, actually cast the lone Democratic vote in the House Judiciary Committee against the compromise bill.[64] On the other end of the Committee's ideological spectrum, Republicans were also dissatisfied with the compromise proposal. All but one Republican joined a brief minority report that urged passage of the Senate sentencing bill instead. The minority report sought elimination of parole and urged that sentencing guidelines be mandatory in order to prevent "unwarranted deviation on the part of trial judges." The report concluded that the compromise "seems to have been drafted more with the offender in mind than society."[65]

With the House Judiciary Committee refusing even to consider the Comprehensive Crime Control Act that had passed the Senate, the only sentencing reform bill before the full House in 1984 was the compromise measure providing for advisory guidelines developed by the judiciary itself. It appeared that a regime of mandatory sentencing regulations had again been forestalled.[66] This state of affairs may have pleased Representative Conyers, Senator Mathias, and most federal trial judges, but it was not acceptable to almost everyone else that mattered—a large and unusual alliance that included House and Senate Republicans, President Reagan, Senator Kennedy, Senator Biden, and liberal sentencing reform advocates.

IN THE END, THIS broad political coalition supporting mandatory sentencing guidelines prevailed by employing the parliamentary device of "attaching" the Senate's version of the Comprehensive Crime Control Act (including Senator Kennedy's Sentencing Reform Act) to a continuing appropriations resolution.[67] Under House rules, such urgent funding bills could not be amended once reported to the House floor. But Representative Dan Lungren, a California Republican who had joined the minority report of the House Judiciary Committee, invoked a little-used parliamentary device that was then permitted under House rules, and that could have the same effect as a motion to amend.[68] In late September, with the end of the fiscal year looming, Lungren moved to have the critical funding measure formally "recommitted" to the Appropriations Committee with instructions to "return" the measure to the House floor with the Senate's Comprehensive Crime Control Act attached.[69] With President Reagan having castigated the House for failing to enact the crime bill, Lungren's fellow Republicans could be counted on to vote for his motion. Democrats, too, were supportive; House Speaker Thomas P. O'Neill, Jr. of Massachusetts—an ally of Senator Kennedy and on the verge of retirement after decades of service—subsequently explained that he had reluctantly advised House Democrats that they could "go ahead" and vote for the recommittal motion.[70]

Lungren's strategy succeeded; his motion to recommit, with accompanying instructions, was approved 243 to 166.[71] With this masterful parliamentary maneuver, the intransigence of the House Judiciary Committee had finally been overcome. Once the Senate's crime bill was attached to the funding measure in the House, it was sure to be enacted because of the urgency of the continuing appropriations resolution. That omnibus bill already had appended to it numerous provisions of special interest to a Congress that was not only facing the end of the fiscal year, but an election as well. These circumstances led Republican Representative Trent Lott of Mississippi to refer to the measure as a "pickup train for all those loose cars that might otherwise be left in the railyards in this 98th Congress."[72] The omnibus resolution (including the crime control measure and other recently attached titles) passed the full House later the same day that Representative Lungren had successfully moved for its recommittal.[73]

When the resolution went to the Senate for final passage, Senator Mathias was able to alter the sentencing title in a few particulars. With the agreement of Senators Thurmond, Kennedy, Biden, and Orrin G. Hatch of Utah, the Sentencing Reform Act was amended to change the number of judges to serve on the Sentencing Commission from two back to three.[74] The sponsors also finally agreed to amend the Act to include the language that Senator Mathias had proposed earlier in the year,[75] requiring the sentencing judge to "impose a sentence sufficient, but not greater than necessary, to comply" with the four general purposes of sentencing listed in the statute.[76]

President Reagan—whose support of the Comprehensive Crime Control bill had been so enthusiastic that it was referred to as "Mr. Reagan's Bill"[77]—signed the omnibus funding bill, including the Sentencing Reform Act of 1984, on October 12, 1984. With broad, bipartisan support, sentencing reform was at last enacted into law.

The Commission Invents the Guidelines

The expectation of Marvin E. Frankel and other advocates of federal sentencing guidelines was that an administrative agency would be insulated from direct political pressures of the sort that, in their view, lead to law-and-order sloganeering and needless harshness in criminal sentencing. Thus insulated, the projected commission would proceed with care and expertise—and with a degree of political anonymity that would reduce the risk of public controversy—to create a just regime of sentencing. Under this new system, like defendants committing like offenses would be treated alike, and arbitrariness, in the form of undue leniency or undue harshness, would be eliminated.[78]

In reality, the United States Sentencing Commission from its inception has been highly visible to bar and bench, acutely sensitive to the political environment in which it operates, and controversial. Although sentencing commissions were created in some states both before and after the federal Sentencing Commission, no state commission has approached the federal Commission in prominence and ambition—or in funding.[79]

The Sentencing Commissioners

The political sensitivity of the Commission's assignment largely explains why a full year passed between enactment of the Sentencing Reform Act and the Senate's confirmation (by voice vote) of President Reagan's seven nominees for commissionerships on October 18, 1985. The year was marked by much jockeying in Washington over who would be appointed to serve on the Commission. The seven people ultimately nominated by President Reagan to become the first United States Sentencing Commissioners reflected the diverse political forces that had led to enactment of the Sentencing Reform Act, as well as the enduring senatorial role in the making of Presidential appointments that require the "advice and consent" of the Senate. While several of the nominees had extensive experience in politics or in social science research, the group as a whole had remarkably little experience in either the practice of criminal law or the sentencing of convicted criminals.

Indeed, the only member of the Commission with *any* sentencing experience was its Chairman, Judge William W. Wilkins, Jr. of South Carolina. Wilkins had been the first district judge appointed by President Reagan in 1981—though immediately after appointing him to chair the Sentencing Commission in 1985, the President elevated him to the United States Court of Appeals for the Fourth Circuit. Previously, Wilkins had served as a legislative aide to Senator Strom Thurmond and had managed Thurmond's 1972 reelection campaign. A colonel in the South Carolina National Guard, Wilkins was the editor-in-chief of the University of South Carolina Law School's law review, briefly engaged in private practice, and served as a state district attorney prior to his appointment to the federal bench.[80] Effectively designated for his appointment by Senator Thurmond, Wilkins was a strong proponent of tough and binding sentencing guidelines.

If Judge Wilkins was the personal designee of Senator Thurmond, then-Judge Stephen G. Breyer of the Court of Appeals for the First Circuit in Boston was the personal designee of Senator Kennedy. During his ten years on the faculty of the Harvard Law School, Breyer had specialized in administrative law—the law governing regulatory and other government agencies.[81] On leave from his professorial position in the late 1970s, Breyer had served as chief counsel of the Senate Judiciary Committee under the chairmanship of Senator Kennedy. In that role he had helped to shepherd the Senator's sentencing reform proposals through the Senate and had gained the trust and admiration of Senators Thurmond and Hatch and other Republicans, as well as Senator Kennedy's Democratic colleagues on the committee.[82] Breyer's political sophistication and his ability to forge compromises and build a consensus proved to be invaluable during his service on the Commission, while his temperament and intellect were well-suited to the task that lay ahead. Breyer was an advocate of the deregulation of economic markets,[83] but of scientific and rational administrative regulation of the noneconomic "market" of criminal sentencing. In terms reminiscent of Judge Marvin E. Frankel's call for the establishment of a federal sentencing commission, Breyer has written an elegant volume celebrating the "several virtues inherent in many administrative systems: rationalization, expertise, insulation, and authority."[84]

The last of the three judges initially appointed to the Commission was George E. MacKinnon, a semi-retired (or "senior") appellate judge in Washington, D.C. and a good friend of Chief Justice Warren E. Burger. Like the Chief Justice, MacKinnon was from Minnesota and had been a ranking Justice Department official during the Eisenhower Administration. In 1969, when President Nixon appointed Burger to become Chief Justice, he chose MacKinnon to take Burger's place on the United States Court of Appeals for the District of Columbia. It was well-known in the federal judiciary and beyond that MacKinnon was a favorite of the Chief Justice; Burger had previously appointed MacKinnon to other special, and highly sensitive, judicial panels (e.g., as presiding judge of the judicial division charged with appointing special prosecutors under post-Watergate legislation, and as presiding judge of the special court charged with reviewing applications for search warrants related to foreign intelligence). Over the years, MacKinnon had earned a reputation as the most conservative judge on the District of Columbia Circuit. He was 79 years old when he was appointed to the Commission, and his service as a Commissioner would stretch over eight years.[85]

Three other Commissioners were, until their appointments, full-time professors. Ilene H. Nagel, a sociologist by training who had written vigorously and critically of judicial sentencing discretion, taught at the law school of the University of Indiana at Bloomington.[86] A pivotal figure on the Commission, Nagel quickly became the target of complaints of many of the Commission's initial staff members. She was the Commission's most outspoken public defender, its most vigorous critic of judicial discretion, and a tenacious advocate of increasing the severity of federal sentences.

Paul H. Robinson was a professor of law at Rutgers University in Camden, New Jersey (he moved to Northwestern University Law School in Chicago in 1992). His scholarly work included articles on criminal law urging precise legislative specification of all elements and degrees of culpability in the definition of crimes.[87] Robinson had served as the chief counsel of Senator John L. McClellan's Subcommittee on Criminal Laws and Procedure in 1977, when the Senator originally cosponsored the Sentencing Reform Act with Senator Kennedy. As recounted below, Robinson would be the only dissenting Commissioner when the Guidelines were finally promulgated in 1987—dissenting on the ground that the Guidelines failed to articulate guiding principles and were *insufficiently* detailed and rigid.

The third full-time academic appointed to the Commission was Michael K. Block, a professor of management and economics in the University of Arizona's business school who specialized in econometrics research on the criminal justice system. Block believed that the Commission's mandate was to seek "social efficiency" in criminal sentencing, and he would unsuccessfully seek to have the Commission give greater consideration to social science research and cost-benefit analysis in developing its Guidelines.[88]

The final Commissioner was Helen G. Corrothers, then serving as a member of the United States Parole Commission (which was to be phased out pursuant to the Sentencing Reform Act). Though she brought a diversity of background and experience to the Commission (having been a prison warden and long-time civil servant), she appears not to have played a significant role in the elaboration of the initial set of Guidelines.[89]

One of the most important members of the Commission was not even a voting member, but, rather, the *ex officio* representative from the Department of Justice. Ronald Gainer, who was Associate Deputy Attorney General in the Reagan Administration, perhaps knew each of his fellow commissioners better than any of them knew each other, for he had helped to coordinate the search for the nonjudicial members of the Commission. Gainer was a strong proponent of determinate sentencing and a critic of judicial discretion.

The Search for Governing Principles

The newly established Commission was confronted with a mandate at once ambitious and ambiguous. The overriding statutory directive to the Sentencing Commission was to eliminate "unwarranted disparity."[90] The concept of disparity that is *unwarranted,* however is intelligible only in the context of some accepted criteria for determining what disparity is *warranted*—that is, what factors should be taken into account in sentencing. Yet Congress in the Sentencing Reform Act had failed to adopt any particular philosophy of punishment. The Act simply identified the four generally recognized justifications for criminal penalties—retribution, deterrence, incapacitation, and rehabilitation—as goals for the sentencing court to "consider" and for the Sentencing Commission to "assure" in its Guidelines.[91] The statute cross-referenced this list of purposes no fewer than eighteen times, in instructions both to the Commission and to sentencing judges. Nowhere, however, did the statute acknowledge the tensions among these four rationales. Nor did the statute acknowledge the vast uncertainty and disagreement over what particular types of penalties are most efficacious in achieving any of these purposes.

To the contrary, the Sentencing Reform Act simply instructed the Commission to develop Guidelines that "reflect, to the extent practicable, advancement in knowledge of human behavior as it relates to the criminal justice process."[92] To the extent that the task of the Commission was to determine the efficacy of alternative sanctions in achieving the purposes of criminal punishment, "science" and "expertise" were indeed required. This seems to be a reasonable and appropriate mandate to an administrative agency. Justice Harry Blackmun's opinion for the majority in *Mistretta v. United States,* the 1989 case upholding the constitutionality of the Sentencing Reform Act,[93] adopts this understanding of the Commission, depicting it as an "expert body" engaged in a process of "rationaliz[ation,] an essentially neutral endeavor."[94] But the Commission's more fundamental assignment—to *identify* the proper purposes, or combination of purposes, of criminal sentencing[95]—is inescapably political and ideological. Justice Antonin Scalia's admonition, in dissent in *Mistretta,* that the Commission is a "junior-varsity Congress," is a recognition of the fundamentally political nature of the Commission and its various statutory mandates.[96]

In addition to statutory charges to eliminate disparity and to achieve the purposes of sentencing, the Sentencing Commission was saddled with a variety of other, more specific statutory directions, many of which discouraged individualized sentences and encouraged greater severity in criminal sentencing.[97] Thus the Sentencing Reform Act, though it seemed to leave to the Sentencing Commission the key decisions on how to reduce disparity and how to achieve "the purposes of sentencing" for all categories of federal criminal cases, did not give the Commission a clean slate upon which to draft its Guidelines. Each of the specific statutory directions to the Commission was implicitly based on some sense of the *purposes* of sentencing or of the *efficacy* of particular penal sanctions. Moreover, the various directions to the Commission were not easily reconcilable. How, for instance, could the Commission increase sentence severity for certain broad classes of criminals[98] without running the risk of causing federal prison capacity to be exceeded at least temporarily?[99] How could the Commission ensure "sufficient flexibility to permit individualized sentences"[100] under a regime that reflected the "general inappropriateness" of considering most personal characteristics[101] and that imposed sentencing ranges varying by only 25 percent?[102]

These ambitious and discordant statutory mandates affected the Commission's ability to pursue an intelligible and consistent philosophy of punishment. As we explain here, the Commission ultimately decided against the articulation of any such philosophy. Unlike state authorities that had replaced discretionary regimes with determinate sentencing,[103] neither the Congress nor the Sentencing Commission sought to resolve the obvious tensions among the competing purposes of sentencing or to choose a single purpose to predominate over all others. Without an agreement on objectives, however, the Commission was left without a basis for deciding what sentences would be most appropriate for particular crimes. It should therefore come as no surprise that the Commission has never presented empirical evidence or substantial argument to support the proposition that its rules achieve, even imperfectly, any of the four well-established possible objectives of criminal sentencing—retribution, deterrence, incapacitation, or rehabilitation.[104]

Only two of the original Commissioners, Robinson and Block, urged the Commission to formulate guidelines that would reflect a comprehensive sentencing philosophy. For Robinson, the proper role of sentencing was to achieve retribution—to give an offender his "just deserts." In particular, Robinson believed that no defendant should be allowed to get away with "free harm"—that is, every incremental amount of harm caused by the defendant must result in an incremental increase in his sentence. The best way to implement this idea, Robinson believed, was through a sentencing calculus that assigns weight to each incremental unit of harm or threatened harm resulting from a crime.[105] He thus proposed a detailed and complex sentencing system that assigned a particular quantitative weight to every aggravating factor and every mitigating factor (especially those directly related to circumstances of the offense). Every species of criminal behavior proscribed by federal law would then be ranked in accordance with its seriousness.

The preliminary (draft) Guidelines issued by the Commission in September 1986,[106] which was largely produced by Robinson, incorporated these ideas. The draft provoked a uniformly negative reaction from federal judges, sentencing reform advocates, attorneys, and even some federal prosecutors.[107] Kenneth Feinberg, who as a young Senate aide had helped draft the early versions of the Sentencing Reform Act and who had become a prominent Washington lawyer, complained that the preliminary draft tried to do "too much, too fast"; he urged that the Commission seek rules that are "much simpler" and "leave more discretion with the sentencing judge."[108] Commissioner Breyer later remarked that the preliminary draft was "the perfect version of guidelines for God, but God was the only one who could administer it."[109] Indeed, the Commission itself would refer to the draft as an "academic fantasy" requiring "elaborate new factfinding" and "complex mathematical formulae." The difficulty of clearly defining and implementing Robinson's system, complained the Commission, raised "the likelihood that different judges would apply the system differently to similar cases."[110] It is a sad irony that the same criticisms apply to the Guidelines that the Commission ultimately promulgated, as we discuss in chapter 4.

Block, who was trained in law and economics, had a different vision of the future of sentencing in the federal system. His vision was also "scientific," but it differed greatly in substance from Robinson's. Block was a proponent of one version of the general deterrence, "crime-control" theory of punishment, which was the major theoretical competitor of Robinson's just-deserts approach. Block's particular approach, associated with the law and economics movement in the academy, is usually referred to as "optimal penalty" theory. Block argued that the Sentencing Reform Act had rejected what he called a "moral desert" basis for sentencing and had mandated an objective of efficiency in punishment—that is, punishment that minimizes the total cost of crime to society. In Block's view, the Sentencing Reform Act was "as clear as any legislative product could be in [its] mandate to 'do efficiency,'" and he noted that the Supreme Court, in upholding the constitutionality of the statute, had emphasized the "neutral" and "apolitical" nature of the Commission's statutory assignments.[111] In order to implement Block's vision, the Commission would have been required to consult or conduct social science research concerning the efficacy of various criminal sanctions in deterring different crimes, and then impose punishments that minimized the total social cost of crime.[112] One reason the Commission ultimately rejected Block's approach was that neither existing social science research nor the Commission's own research efforts, largely overseen by Professor Nagel, provided an empirical basis for the elaboration of provably "efficient" sentencing rules.

In the end, the Commission formally adopted neither of the approaches just described. In the Introduction to the Guidelines Manual, after alluding to the just-deserts and the general deterrence approaches to punishment, the Commission explained that it had found it difficult to choose between the two and thus simply had decided not to decide which approach should prevail, either generally or with respect to specific crimes. The brief treatment of the subject in the Guidelines Manual ended with the improbable assertion that "[a]s a practical matter, in most sentencing decisions both philosophies may prove consistent with the same result."[113] An article subsequently published by Breyer suggests that the Guidelines achieved an "important compromise" between the two approaches by relying on "past sentencing practice" instead of either philosophical vision.[114]

While it is true that the Commission did not settle on a particular principle of punishment, some parts of the Guidelines seem clearly to be based upon one principle to the exclusion of others. In every instance, the principle as applied calls for relatively severe penalties. For instance, the long sentences required for both repeat offenders and drug offenders may be seen as a response to the need for incapacitation of these offenders; the increase in severity for white-collar offenses reflects the need for deterrence; and the increase in severity for varieties of violent crime and sex offenses reflects the need for retribution.

Moreover, while as a whole the Guidelines do not reflect a single philosophy of punishment, the Commission appears to have been significantly influenced by Robinson's proposed strict, quantitative sentencing calculus. To a greater extent than required by the Sentencing Reform Act,[115] the Guidelines are structured to ensure that every unit of additional harm is met with an additional unit of punishment,[116] and thus reflect the influence of Robinson's vision of precise criminal sentencing rules driven by quantification of harm. The sentencing instructions issued by the Commission in 1987, and the many amendments issued in the ensuing decade of rule-making, contain detailed descriptions of a large number of proscribed acts and of the many circumstances in which these crimes may be committed. In a manner similar to the Robinson draft, the Guidelines assign a precise quantitative value to each aspect of criminal conduct, along with a series of instructions for calculating each defendant's final Offense Level (along the vertical axis of a Sentencing Table) and his Criminal History Category (along the horizontal axis of the Table). In cases where there is no lawful ground for departure from the Guidelines, the sentencing judge has discretionary authority only in choosing a point within the final Guidelines sentencing range.[117]

The maximum point of each range is no more than 25 percent greater than the minimum point of the range; this is a far cry from the pre-Guidelines era, when judges had authority to sentence at any point within the statutory sentencing range. We have reprinted the Sentencing Table as appendix A.

Given the structure of the Guidelines ultimately issued by the Commission, it is remarkable that Robinson was the only Commissioner to dissent—passionately and publicly—from the final Guidelines issued in April 1987. He complained that the Guidelines were not sufficiently detailed in their ranking of offense components, permitted too many "free harms," permitted too much judicial discretion, and were not based on any principled philosophy of punishment.[118]

The Commission has made no further mention of the issue of sentencing philosophy since its general and superficial discussion of the purposes of criminal sentencing in 1987.[119] Nowhere in the forest of directives that the Commission has promulgated over the last decade can one find a discussion of the rationale for the particular approaches or definitions adopted by the Commission; nor can one find any efforts to justify the particular weights it has elected to assign to various sentencing factors. Finally, the Commission has never explained why it chose to exclude a variety of factors (especially those relating to the personal history of the defendant) from the sentencing calculus. As a result, in applying the Guidelines, the courts are often without information regarding the underlying policies or objectives that the Commission is seeking to achieve through its sentencing rules.

The Commission has been able to avoid having to justify its decisions in part because of its unique legal status. Like many other administrative agencies, the Commission's proposed rules become law unless disapproved by legislation. That is, Congress must pass a bill disapproving a proposed Guideline, and if the President vetoes the bill, it can become law only by a two-thirds vote of both houses of Congress. If Congress fails to adopt such disapproval legislation within 180 days, any Guideline or other rule proposed by the Commission becomes legally binding on all affected.[120]

The Commission, however, is unlike other rule-making agencies in the federal government in that it need not provide explanations for its rules, nor respond to criticisms of its proposed Guidelines.[121] Although the Sentencing Reform Act required that the Commission publish proposed rules prior to final promulgation,[122] it did not impose any of the other procedural requirements that govern most other federal agencies.[123] It was not until the summer of 1997 that the Commission issued regulations dealing with its own internal practices and procedures.[124] The result, as one noted administrative law scholar has explained, is that

> [t]he commission does not have a regularized process for accepting or responding to petitions for the issuance of new guidelines. Its advisory committees do not hold open meetings. . . . [T]he most glaring shortcoming in the federal [sentencing] commission's process [may be] its "statement of basis and purpose" for final guideline amendments. While most rule-making agencies provide thorough explanations of their final rules, including the factual evidence supporting the rule, and respond to important comments from opponents, the commission's explanations for its final guidelines are strikingly terse and conclusory.[125]

The Commission need not explain or justify its Guidelines because, unlike the rules of other federal agencies, the Sentencing Guidelines may not be challenged in court on the ground that they are "arbitrary" or "capricious."[126] This means that, unlike most other regulatory bodies, the Commission never has to defend itself or its work product in court.[127] It writes the Guidelines, but others—judges, prosecutors, probation officers, and defense attorneys—must implement them and, when called upon in the performance of their duties, defend them.

The Commission issued its final proposed Guidelines in April 1987. By law, they would become effective six months later, except to the extent amended or delayed by Congress. The Senate Judiciary Committee, preoccupied with the nomination of Judge Robert H. Bork to the Supreme Court, conducted only a brief, one-day hearing on the Guidelines in late October.[128] In the House of Representatives, on the other hand, John Conyers' Subcommittee on Criminal Justice held hearings on a total of six days in May, June, and July. Individual judges, academic researchers, and representatives from criminal defense organizations testified in outright opposition to the Guidelines, while others—including the representative of the American Bar Association and some of the judges representing the Judicial Conference—sought a significant delay in their implementation so that the Commission could revisit various policy decisions it had made.[129]

For the most part, however, the immediate reaction to the proposed Guidelines when they were issued in April 1987 was muted. Federal trial judges and others who doubted the wisdom of mandatory guidelines were seemingly mollified by a revised draft that the Commission had issued only a few months earlier, in late January.[130] That draft had been praised by many judges and others for its simplicity and flexibility, at least as compared with the initial (Robinson) draft;[131] in public hearings, only the Department of Justice had expressed a preference for the earlier approach.[132] When the final Guidelines were issued in April, some press accounts initially reported that they were more flexible than either of these earlier drafts,[133] though Chairman Wilkins was quoted as noting that "the final draft strikes somewhere between the two [earlier] drafts."[134] Kenneth G. Feinberg, the former Kennedy aide who had been critical of the Commission's preliminary draft, believed that the final Guidelines "strike a careful balance"; rather than being "mandatory," they are "designed to provide a road map to assist judges."[135] Meanwhile, Judge Breyer advised readers of the *New York Times* that the Guidelines are "fairly neutral," rather than being either "hard" or "soft" on crime, and would "automatically cure" disparity because they would require that all defendants within a given category be given the same sentence.[136] By one inside account, Breyer was the guiding force behind the final version issued in April, having realized the January draft lacked sufficient support on the Commission; the final Guidelines were even referred to as "Breyer's draft."[137]

When the final Guidelines were first unveiled, Chairman Wilkins raised the possibility of some delay in their implementation for field-testing.[138] But Representative Lungren charged that any delay would result in continued undue leniency in criminal sentencing, and, as a congressional staffer was reported to have remarked, "Once it's framed that way, the ball game's over."[139] None of the Commissioners who testified before Congress on the final Guidelines pressed for delay, and the Department of Justice urged that no reconsideration was necessary.[140] Accordingly, the Sentencing Guidelines became effective without delay or legislative amendment on November 1, 1987.

The Guidelines promulgated in 1987 consisted of over 300 pages of directives, and since that time the Guidelines Manual published each year by the Commission has grown to over 900 pages, divided into two volumes. (The second volume consists entirely of a chronological listing of the over 570 amendments to the Guidelines that the Commission has promulgated since 1987.) These directives are presented under a variety of headings or labels within the Guidelines Manual. Some of the rules are formally denoted "Guidelines," but other directives are called "Policy Statements" or "Commentary." Although the Sentencing Reform Act only requires the Commission to submit formal Guidelines to Congress,[141] the Commission has also submitted important Policy Statements as well as rules embedded within the Commission's Commentary interpreting formal Guidelines. The Supreme Court has made it clear that Policy Statements and Commentary that directly relate to particular

Guidelines are as authoritative and as binding on judges as the Guidelines themselves.[142] Accordingly, we refer to all of the Commission's rules, whatever their formal label, as "Guidelines" unless the formal label is legally significant in context.

The Severity of the Sentencing Guidelines

Having decided not to adopt (or not to articulate) any particular purpose of punishment to guide the development of its guidelines, the Commission had to choose some other basis for determining the Guidelines' content. One critical issue was how to determine the appropriate measure of sentence *severity*. The resolution of this issue called upon the Commission to determine a calculus for linking the amount of harm (which, under Robinson's influence, the Commission had determined was of critical significance) to an appropriate prison sentence. The Commission also had to decide which factors in addition to the amount of harm caused should be relevant to a criminal's punishment.

As the Commission has told the story, it generally sought to answer these questions by replicating "past sentencing practice"—drawing on a detailed analysis of 10,500 cases sentenced in the federal courts during the year 1985 and on consideration of a less-detailed compilation of nearly one hundred thousand additional cases. The Commission explained that the data were used in two ways: to determine "relevant . . . distinguishing factors" and to determine the overall severity level of Guidelines sentences.[143] In a law review article published in 1988, Breyer noted that, because the Guidelines are based upon "actual past practice," the Guidelines "would come fairly close to replicating the average pre-Guidelines sentence handed down to particular categories of criminals."[144]

Basing the Guidelines on past sentencing practice—as the Commission apparently voted to do and as several Commissioners,[145] as well as outside observers,[146] apparently believe was done—was both politically adroit and defensible in principle. Had the Commission attempted to formulate a coherent theory concerning the proper purposes of punishment, it would risk adoption of a moral stance that would be objectionable to a significant proportion of reasonable people with views on the matter. A utilitarian/deterrence/efficiency approach (such as Block sought) would have shocked those (such as Robinson) who take a deontological, just-deserts approach. In a pluralistic society, sentencing rules derived from actual practice may be as close as a commission can come to achieving or representing a consensus on the purposes of punishment. Rules based on past practice avoid apparently unsolvable disagreements over sentencing philosophy and sentencing severity, while offering the promise of a reduction of "disparity." Although the average sentence for each crime would assertedly remain the same, variations around the average would be significantly reduced because each judge would be directed to impose the same average sentence. Some state sentencing commissions had explicitly sought to replicate past practice, usually pursuant to specific legislative direction.[147] Though not required to do so by statute, the United States Sentencing Commission had a statutory basis for relying largely on past practice, at least in its initial set of Guidelines: Congress had, after all, directed the Commission to look to current actual time served in prison "as a starting point" for the construction of the federal Guidelines.[148]

Both Robinson and Block criticized the decision to construct the Guidelines largely on the basis of average past practice. After leaving the Commission in 1989, Block wrote that the decision to replicate past practice had permitted the Commission to avoid, perhaps for all time, the need to develop a "consistent sentencing philosophy."[149] Robinson was even more disparaging, referring to Guidelines sentences as "bastardized."[150] In his dissent from the Guidelines, Robinson stressed a second sentence in the statutory directive concerning past practice—that, although the Commission could use past averages as a "starting point," it was not "bound" to these averages "and shall independently develop a sentencing range that is consistent with the purposes of sentencing."[151]

In fact, the Commission diminished the advantages of relying on past sentencing practices by *failing to do so in any systematic way.* The Commission interpreted the Sentencing Reform Act's requirement of *severe* sentences for career offenders and for many convicted of violent and drug offenses[152] to require *more severe* sentences than had been imposed in the past.[153] Moreover, wherever Congress had enacted a mandatory minimum sentence, as it already had done for drug dealing and as it would do with increasing frequency throughout the 1980s,[154] the Commission developed Guidelines that require sentences substantially above the statutory minimum in most cases.[155] The Commission further acknowledged that it had sought to increase sentence severity for "white collar" crimes,[156] apparently on the assumption that Congress was referring to this type of crime when it inserted the oracular statement that "in many cases, current sentences do not accurately reflect the seriousness of the offense."[157] More generally, the Commission asserted portentously and without further explanation that it had elected to raise sentences for violent crimes "where *the Commission was convinced that they were inadequate.*"[158] In fact, these categories of offenses, for which the Commission conceded it purposely deviated from past practice—drug cases, fraud and other white collar cases, and cases involving threatened or actual violence—actually far outnumber the remaining categories of cases.[159]

Even for those categories of cases in which the Commission did indeed seek to replicate past sentencing averages, the Commission's data analysis was limited, and possibly compromised, in several fundamental respects. The Commission conceded that for several categories of offenses it simply did not have sufficient data to ascertain average past practice.[160] Moreover, the Commission's past practice data were obtained only from the presentence reports for its sample of 10,500 cases—not from court records of actual judgments entered by judges. The Commission simply correlated the mention of particular facts in the presentence report[161] (such as whether the defendant used a weapon, the nature of his role in the offense, the amount of harm caused, etc.) with the sentence ultimately imposed. The Commission thus had no way of knowing whether sentencing judges actually relied on particular facts alleged in the presentence reports. Moreover, the "relevant sentencing factors" that the Commission kept track of in its sample of presentence reports related almost entirely to the offense committed, with very little consideration of the particulars of the offender being sentenced—factors such as age, education, family and community ties, military service, rehabilitative potential, and so on. Except for the defendant's prior criminal record and drug use, each of the factors examined by the Commission related only to particulars of the crime itself (such as the "quantity" of harm caused) and the defendant's role in the crime (such as whether he supervised others or played a minor role).[162]

It is therefore not surprising that the Guidelines themselves also rely primarily on factors relating to the offense[163] and that they specifically provide that most background or personal information on defendants (including age, education, military service, family and community ties, and the like) are "not ordinarily relevant" to determining the defendant's Guidelines sentencing range.[164] Congress had directed the Commission to determine the relevance of these background factors, in terms that suggested Congress's own skepticism about their relevance but that did not foreclose their consideration.[165] The Commission might have responded to this congressional directive by undertaking an empirical analysis of the past sentencing data—the data on which it purportedly based its Guidelines—to determine the importance, if any, of these factors. Instead, the Commission's declaration that such factors are generally irrelevant was a policy decision made by the Commission itself, without the benefit of empirical research, public explanation, or public comment. The Commission also apparently made a conscious decision to ensure that a criminal record would "dramatically affect" the severity of a sentence.[166] Unfortunately, the Commission never explained publicly—or even noted—the extent to which this policy choice could or would yield a deviation from past practice.

AN INEVITABLE RESULT of the Commission's determination to ensure that the Guidelines were at least as severe as past practice (and in many cases more severe) was a marked increase in the percentage of defendants sentenced to prison rather than to probation. Pursuant to the decisions of the Commission, the average term of imprisonment within a given crime category was at least equal to past practice. The range around this average, however, was greatly reduced—thereby reducing (for virtually every federal crime) the percentage of defendants who receive a sentence that includes no time in prison. The growth in the use of imprisonment in the Guidelines era is striking. While before the Guidelines nearly 50 percent of federal defendants were sentenced to probation alone,[167] that figure is now less than 15 percent.[168] For female offenders, the increased reliance on imprisonment is especially marked. There are, remarkably, no data available on the percentage of women who received probation (rather than imprisonment) in the pre-Guidelines era.[169] We do know, however, that the number of women in federal prisons has grown even faster than the number of men, while the percentage of women defendants sentenced in federal court has actually decreased slightly in the Guidelines era.[170]

If the Guidelines reflected past practice, one would expect that the reduced reliance on probation would be offset by a reduction in the median prison sentence, so that the overall severity level of federal sentences would be unchanged. On average, however, time served in prison has *increased* in the Guidelines era. The severity of sentences under the Guidelines thus derives from two, independent sources: the reduced frequency of nonincarcerative sentences and an increase in the length of incarcerative sentences. Table 1 below demonstrates the combined effect of these factors by comparing the average sentence for major categories of crime, pre- and post-Guidelines. In constructing this table, we have followed the Commission's practice of treating defendants sentenced to probation as having received a sentence of "zero months'" imprisonment. Hence, the table's averages reflect the sentence severity for *all* offenders.[171]

Importantly, table 1 provides a comparison both of *nominal* sentence length imposed by the judge and *actual* sentence length. The latter is

TABLE 1. **Average Sentence for All Offenders**

	Pre-Guidelines 1977–1986 (in months)[a]		Guidelines 1989–1996 (in months)[b]		Increase (in months)	
	Sentence Length	*Estimated Time Served*	Sentence Length	*Estimated Time Served*	Sentence Length	*Estimated Time Served*
All crimes	28	*13*	50	*43*	22	*30*
Robbery	146	*52*	107	*91*	−39	*39*
Fraud	15	*8*	11	*9*	−4	*1*
Drugs	47	*22*	77	*65*	30	*43*
Immigration	11	*7*	17	*14*	6	*7*

Note: Offenders sentenced to nonprison sentences are treated as having received "zero months'" imprisonment; see also *supra* note 171.

a. Bureau of Justice Statistics, Sourcebook 1979, tbl. 6.39; Sourcebook 1980, tbl. 6.26; Sourcebook 1981, tbl. 5.20 & tbl. 6.41; Sourcebook 1982, tbl. 5.19; Sourcebook 1983, tbl. 5.23; Sourcebook 1983, tbl. 6.43; Sourcebook 1984, tbl. 5.16; Sourcebook 1984, tbl. 6.47; Sourcebook 1985, tbl. 5.21; Sourcebook 1985, tbl. 6.46; Sourcebook 1986, tbl. 5.16; Sourcebook 1986, tbl. 6.42; Sourcebook 1987, tbl. 5.23; Sourcebook 1987, tbl. 6.56.

b. Id., Sourcebook 1990, tbl. 5.29; Sourcebook 1991, tbl. 5.41; Sourcebook 1992, tbl. 5.44; Sourcebook 1992, tbl. 5.45; Sourcebook 1993, tbl. 5.49; Sourcebook 1993, tbl. 5.50; Sourcebook 1994, tbl. 5.32; Sourcebook 1993, tbl. 5.50; Sourcebook 1994, tbl. 5.33; Sourcebook 1995, tbl. 1995; U.S.S.C. Annual Report 1995, tbl. 18 & tbl. 19; U.S.S.C. 1997b, tbl. 13 & tbl. 14. These statistics reflect only defendants sentenced under the Guidelines.

the more relevant number, because it reflects the time actually served, on average, by defendants convicted in federal court. Parole having been abolished under the Guidelines,[172] offenders now serve a greater proportion of their nominal sentences than they did in the pre-Guidelines period. The maximum "good time" allowance in the Guidelines regime is 15 percent, meaning that every offender serves at least 85 percent of his or her nominal sentence.[173] In the pre-Guidelines era, on the other hand, offenders served only 47 percent of their nominal sentences on average.[174] The percentage varied for different crime categories. Defendants convicted of robbery, who tended to receive long sentences, actually served just over one-third of these sentences on average; defendants convicted of fraud, who received shorter sentences, served over half their nominal sentences on average. Accordingly, table 1 deflates pre-Guidelines nominal sentences by the appropriate percentage for each sub-category of crime, reflecting the impact of parole policies on actual time served. Table 1 also deflates all Guidelines sentences by the maximum reduction permissible in the Guidelines era, the 15 percent "good time" allowance. (This may have the effect of somewhat *understating* the actual time served under Guidelines sentences, since it is unlikely that all federal offenders receive this maximum permissible "good time.")

As table 1 reveals, the increase in average time served is due in large part to the very long terms of drug offenders, who are subject to statutory mandatory sentences and especially severe Guidelines sentences that build upon those statutory minimums.[175] (In 1994, Congress enacted what has come to be known as the "safety valve" provision, which permits judges to sentence certain nonviolent drug offenders without regard to statutory minimums. However, this statutory change did not greatly alter *the Guidelines'* formulae for drug offense severity.[176]) The increase in the average sentence for robbery is largely attributable to the Commission's unexplained decision in 1989—two years after the Guidelines were first issued—to ratchet up the severity of sentences for robbery and firearms offenses, apparently without regard to past practice.[177] As both Congress and the Commission subsequently provided for increased sentence severity for a variety of crimes, the Commission's modest estimate in 1987 of the impact of the Guidelines on total federal prison population quickly became out-dated.[178]

There is little doubt that each of the political choices that the Commission made regarding sentence severity fell within its delegated authority. Indeed, the statutory finding that "in many cases, current sentences do not reflect the severity of the offense"[179] was an open invitation to increase federal sentences generally. It is hardly surprising that the Commission accepted this invitation. The Commissioners were appointed by a President whose party had long been critical of the failure of the criminal justice system to stem the rising rates of serious crime across the nation, and their work product was both highly visible and formally subject to review by a Congress disposed to enact its own severe, mandatory sentencing statutes. One straightforward way of reducing sentencing disparity is to reduce the possibility of relatively lenient sentences.

Rather than forthrightly acknowledging the enhanced severity of the penalties it was prescribing, however, the Commission confused the issue, thereby undermining its credibility. The Commission never explained for which categories of crime existing practice was, in its view, "inadequate," nor how it arrived at this determination, or how it quantified the magnitude of the inadequacies. Its 1987 prison impact analysis was complicated and seemed unduly conservative in forecasting only a small (7 percent) increase in federal prison population attributable to the Guidelines.[180] In fact, the Commission arrived at this percentage only *after* projecting as a "base" the increased prison population resulting from statutory mandates, including the direction in the Sentencing Reform Act itself that certain offenders be sentenced "at or near the statutory maximum."[181] Moreover, when the Commission decided to increase sentencing severity for robbery and other crimes soon after the Guidelines were promulgated, this decision was not accompanied by any further prison impact analysis or reference to past practice.

ALTHOUGH THE COMMISSION'S lapses in explaining the bases and severity of its Guidelines may have been caused by time pressure, inadequate data, and dispersal of authority within the Commission, some of the Commission's critics—including top staff members of the Commission—suggest otherwise. The Commission's first staff director and its first chief counsel quit even before the Guidelines were promulgated, and one Commission official was quoted as saying that "everything I did was changed by some mysterious person, who turned out to be [the Chairman's] law clerk."[182] A lawyer who later served as chief counsel to the Commission complained that after the initial Guidelines were issued, "any semblance of deference to past practice or any other form of rationalization [was] abandoned" and that the Commission "actively suppresse[d] research and analysis of data."[183] Similarly, a professor who served as chief economist at the Commission flatly asserted that in subsequent Guidelines the Commission "has altered data and presented other data in deliberately misleading ways."[184] Another staff economist who left the Commission in 1989 was quoted in the *Washington Post* as complaining that there "was always a feeling that certain commissioners wanted us to get high numbers."[185] When Commissioner Block resigned later that year, he complained that the Commission "at this point lacks any real commitment to research as a basis for sentencing law. I have no problem suggesting high sentences as long as they can be supported by data."[186]

A subsequent review of the Sentencing Commission's management difficulties by the United States General Accounting Office was more circumspect but still harshly critical. The GAO report referred to "organizational disarray," "troublesome . . . direct control by individual commissioners over major research projects," and a "concern" that "research [could] reflect the perspectives and interests of the commissioner conducting the project." The GAO report and others asserted that the Commission was unable to retain respected professionals to serve in key staff positions, and that its research and data collection efforts were highly politicized.[187]

Whatever the causes, the result was significant and increasing skepticism among interested observers and among members of the judiciary who followed the Commission's work closely.[188] Almost from the moment it issued its Guidelines in April 1987, the Commission operated in an environment poisoned by mistrust—mistrust engendered not only by the radical changes in sentencing law that it was implementing, but also by its incomplete and questionable data and its dubious public assurances that the Guidelines followed past sentencing practices.

Real-Offense Sentencing

In addition to issues of sentencing philosophy and severity, Congress passed to the Commission the responsibility to determine whether defendants should be sentenced on the basis of their "real-offense" behavior or simply on their "offense of conviction." The two approaches are vastly different. An offense-of-conviction approach to criminal sentencing would determine the severity of a sentence by reference to the statutory elements of the crime for which the defendant is convicted (after trial or a plea of guilty); the purest expression of this approach would sentence every defendant convicted of a particular crime in precisely the same way. A real-offense approach considers additional facts about the criminal behavior of the defendant, beyond the formal elements of the crime of conviction. These might include the magnitude of harm caused, the manner in which the crime was committed (by stealth, threats, fraud, etc.), the duration of the crime, and the motivation for the crime.

As a theoretical matter, the consideration of factors that relate not to the offense, but to the defendant himself—such as criminal record, family and employment circumstances, military record, and other personal characteristics—might be thought irrelevant under *both* offense-of-conviction and real-offense sentencing systems. Generally, however, such offender-based considerations have been regarded as more consistent with a real-offense approach.[189] Accordingly, for the sake of clarity, we use the term "real offense" to include all nonstatutory factors related to the defendant's criminal and other behavior.

Despite the significance of the issue, neither the Sentencing Reform Act of 1984 nor the accompanying Senate Report had given the Sentencing Commission a clear or definitive direction on which of these approaches to adopt. Several of the specific statutory directives to the Commission, however, strongly point toward a broad, real-offense approach to sentencing.[190] In particular, the Sentencing Reform Act requires that the Commission consider "the circumstances under which the offense was committed," "the nature and degree of the harm caused," "the public concern generated by the offense," and the defendant's criminal record.[191] An offense-of-conviction approach would not permit any consideration of the different ways in which a single statutory crime may be committed, or of the defendant's role in the offense, his past record, or a variety of other factors historically relevant to the sentencing decision.[192] Moreover, the sponsors of the Act shared the concern of sentencing reformers that an offense-of-conviction approach would result in undue concentration of power in the hands of prosecutors.[193] Basing a defendant's sentence only on the statutory charges to which he pleads guilty would seem to give prosecutors significant authority over the ultimate sentence; the government could ensure a lenient sentence by permitting a plea to a relatively minor charge, or seek a more severe sentence by refusing to accept such a plea.

The Commission decided in the end to construct Guidelines that "contain a significant number of real-offense elements."[194] Indeed, the Guidelines take into account real-offense behavior (that is, facts in addition to or beyond the statutory elements of the crime) in five major ways.

Offense Categories and Base Offense Levels

The Guidelines generally devalue the relevance of the statutory offense by classifying all federal crimes into nineteen generic groupings. Then, these nineteen offense categories are further subdivided on the basis of "specific offense characteristics"—that is, additional aggravating factors, usually not referred to in the relevant statutes, that the Sentencing Commission has determined should affect the severity of criminal punishment.

An appendix to the Guidelines Manual cross-references each federal crime to one or more of the Commission's generic categories. These nineteen categories are an adaptation of the proposed recodification of federal criminal law that Congress considered in the early 1970s,[195] and match that massive effort in both structure and ambition. The Guidelines categories simplify and rationalize over five hundred different federal statutory prohibitions into neat (though inevitably overlapping) groupings:

"offenses against the person"
"offenses involving property"
"offenses involving public officials"
"offenses involving drugs"
"offenses involving criminal enterprises and racketeering"
"offenses involving fraud or deceit"

"offenses involving prostitution, sexual exploitation of minors, and obscenity"
"offenses involving individual rights"
"offenses involving the administration of justice"
"offenses involving public safety"
"offenses involving immigration, naturalization, and passports"
"offenses involving national defense"
"offenses involving food, drugs, agricultural products, and odometer laws"
"offenses involving prisons and correctional facilities"
"offenses involving the environment"
"antitrust offenses"
"money laundering and monetary transaction reporting offenses"
"offenses involving taxation"

Finally, a subchapter on broad doctrinal categories includes conspiracy and accomplice liability.

For each category of crime, the Commission specifies a numerical Base Offense Level; for instance, the Base Offense Level for "larceny, embezzlement, and other forms of theft" is four;[196] that for "criminal sexual abuse" is twenty-seven.[197] If a listed "specific offense characteristic" is present in a particular case, the assigned Base Offense Level must be increased (or, occasionally, decreased) by the number of points specified for that characteristic.[198] The numerical point value assigned to a particular characteristic (for instance, use of a weapon) varies from one crime category to another.[199]

The identification of precise point values for each specific offense characteristic reflects the Commission's determination to minimize the need for sentencing judges to exercise their judgment in the application of the Guidelines. For instance, the Base Offense Level for crimes within the generic category "aggravated assaults" must be increased by six points if there was permanent or life-threatening bodily injury, by four points if there was serious bodily injury, or by two points if there was any other type of bodily injury.[200] The point values assigned to some specific offense characteristics were apparently initially derived empirically by the Commission's staff and were subsequently modified and elaborated upon pursuant to the Commission's own policy choices.[201]

The most common specific offense characteristic found in the Sentencing Guidelines is *quantity*—with the result that the severity of a sentence is heavily dependent on quantifiable factors such as the amount of drugs in a drug conspiracy, the amount of money stolen in a bank robbery, or the number of unlawful aliens harbored in an illegal immigration scheme. Implicit in the quantity-driven approach, of course, is Commissioner Robinson's idea that no incremental harm should occur without an incremental increase in punishment.[202] While penal codes have historically made a few, bright-line distinctions in the degree of a crime on the basis of the amount of harm (money stolen or drugs sold, for instance),[203] the Sentencing Guidelines take the concept of quantification much further—making minute distinctions in quantity, far beyond the gradations any criminal code has attempted. The Guidelines provide, for instance, that an embezzlement in which less than a hundred dollars is taken is assigned a Base Offense Level of four, while embezzlement of between a hundred and a thousand dollars has a Base Offense Level of five. The Base Offense Level continues to increase the more money the defendant obtained—to a Base Offense Level of twenty-four when the amount involved is more than $80 million.[204] A similar approach governs the Base Offense Level tables for other crimes where some type of harm may be measured in continuous quantitative increments (e.g., narcotics crimes, fraud, and other forms of theft).

Quantification of harm was an attractive approach for the Commission, at least initially, because it permitted the agency to distinguish among defendants on the basis of apparently objective and precisely measured criteria. Tying sentence severity to quantity of harm would thus reduce the scope of judicial discretion and achieve a reduction in measurable sentencing disparity among defendants, while suggesting the use of a scientific method.

Unfortunately, the Sentencing Commission has nowhere stated, much less explained, why these quantifiable differences in harm caused are *appropriate* measurements of the extent of individual culpability, or why they are more significant than other sentencing factors that receive less weight in Guidelines sentencing calculations. Why, for instance, should the bank robber who is handed a bag containing $5,000 be punished differently from the bank robber who happens to be handed a bag containing $15,000? Why is one gram of hashish oil equivalent to fifty grams of marijuana? Indeed, the Commission has never explained the rationale underlying *any* of its identified specific offense characteristics, why it has elected to identify certain characteristics and not others, or the weights it has chosen to assign to each identified characteristic.

One effect of quantification, of course, is to increase the severity of a sentence significantly when there is a high measurable loss. Of perhaps greater significance is that the weight placed on quantifiable loss results in some Offense Level calculations that may be considered to be *insuffi-*

ciently severe. The Commission's Guidelines for alien-smuggling, for instance, provided for a Base Offense Level of nine; two points were added if the offense involved between six and twenty-four aliens, four points if there were between twenty-five and ninety-nine aliens, and six points if the offense involved more than a hundred smuggled aliens.[205] But, remarkably, the Commission declined to provide a special offense characteristic relating to the often deleterious health and safety conditions under which aliens may be transported into the United States.[206] Because of their reliance on quantifiable offense characteristics, the Guidelines give relatively short shrift to more subjective, less-easily-measured aggravating factors relating to both harm and culpability.

Relevant Conduct

A second way in which the Guidelines reflect a commitment to real-offense sentencing is the adoption of the principle of "relevant conduct." This principle requires an upward adjustment from the defendant's Base Offense Level not only for identifiable specific offense characteristics, but also for *any additional criminal behavior related to the present offense*—other crimes he committed and other crimes committed by his accomplices. Under the Guidelines, courts are required to take such uncharged (or even acquitted) conduct into account if the conduct is proved by a "preponderance of the evidence" at the sentencing hearing.[207] Judge Wilkins, the first Chairman of the Commission, asserted in a law review article published in 1990 that the relevant conduct principle is the "cornerstone" of the federal Guidelines.[208] Wilkins explained that this real-offense feature "significantly reduces the impact of prosecutorial charge selection and plea bargaining by ensuring that the court will be able to consider the defendant's real-offense behavior in imposing a guideline sentence."[209]

This "cornerstone" of the sentencing system—whose contours require over nine single-spaced pages of explanation in the Guidelines Manual (see appendix B)—is one that lawyers and judges have found remarkably abstract and difficult to apply. Moreover, as we observe in chapter 3, the attribution of other crimes through the relevant conduct principle is entirely the invention of the United States Sentencing Commission; the "principle" of "relevant conduct" is unknown outside of the federal Sentencing Guidelines.[210] We discuss procedural aspects of proof of "relevant conduct" in chapter 5.

Offense Adjustments

The third way in which the Guidelines employ real-offense sentencing is by identifying certain offense circumstances that require further adjustment of the Base Offense Level. Unlike "specific offense characteristics," these general adjustments apply to all offense categories. Some of these adjustments involve aspects of the criminal conduct itself—such as the upward adjustment when the victim is especially vulnerable[211] and the upward adjustment when the defendant played a major role in the offense.[212] Others involve arguably separate crimes committed before, during, or after the crime of conviction—such as the upward adjustment when the defendant attempted to obstruct or impede the administration of justice during investigation, prosecution, or sentencing.[213] The most common adjustment is a two- or three-point reduction in Offense Level when the defendant demonstrates his "acceptance of responsibility" for the crime.[214]

Criminal History Score

The fourth way in which the Guidelines take account of circumstances beyond the offense-of-conviction is their treatment of the defendant's prior criminal record. Criminal history functions as a factor requiring a substantial upward adjustment of the defendant's sentencing range. The very format of the Guidelines' Sentencing Table—the two-dimensional grid containing 258 different sentencing ranges—underscores the significance of past criminal record. Whereas the vertical axis of the Sentencing Table represents Offense Level (as shaped by the various definitions, offense factors, and adjustments discussed above), the horizontal axis of the Sentencing Table is devoted entirely to the defendant's Criminal History Category. In this respect, the structure of the Sentencing Guidelines' treatment of criminal history is nearly identical to the treatment of criminal history in federal parole policies before the Sentencing Reform Act of 1984. Whereas the Sentencing Table contains 258 cells, however, the Parole Commission's Guidelines Table contained only 32 cells.[215]

There are six Criminal History Categories in the Guidelines. Category I, the lowest, covers defendants with a total "criminal history score" of zero or one; Category VI, the highest, covers defendants with a score of thirteen or more. A defendant in a high Criminal History Category will receive a more severe punishment than a defendant in a low category, even if he has committed the same crime and has the same calculated Offense Level.[216] This is, of course, in keeping with the fundamental mandate of the Sentencing Reform Act to avoid sentencing disparity "among defendants with similar records who have been found guilty of similar criminal conduct."[217] (See appendix C for one example of the complexity of the criminal history rules.)

The Parole Commission considered criminal history solely as a good measure of the likelihood of recidivism, but the Sentencing Commission proceeded on the further premise that criminal history is also relevant to the degree of retribution, or "just deserts," warranted in the present case; [218] it is apparently for this reason that the Commission decided that an offender's criminal history should have a dramatic impact on the severity of the sentence imposed.[219] The Sentencing Commission also adopted complicated rules governing how to count ("group") prior convictions,[220] adopted a rule giving extra weight to past violent offenses, and chose not to weigh a prior offense by either the offender's age or how long ago the offense was committed. Most importantly, and unlike the Parole Commission, the Sentencing Commission did not construct its Criminal History formulae on the basis of empirical data.[221]

The apparent precision of the Guidelines' criminal history rules masks numerous asymmetries and sources of disparity that the Commission has never sought to explain or justify. Because criminal history points are based only on nominal sentence length, defendants with recent prior records are treated the same as those whose convictions took place long ago.[222] Moreover, all prior sentences of the same nominal length are treated the same, whether or not the underlying criminal conduct has any relation to the current offense. Thus, a defendant convicted of white collar fraud who recently served a short prison sentence for a previous fraudulent scheme receives the same criminal history enhancement as does the white collar defendant who ten years ago served a sentence for drug possession.

Departure from the Guidelines Range

The rules on "departure" from the prescribed Guidelines range are a fifth way in which the Guidelines implement a real-offense sentencing system. The Sentencing Reform Act itself authorizes sentencing judges to "depart" from the calculated sentencing range if "there exists an aggravating or mitigating circumstance of a kind, or to a degree, not adequately taken into consideration by the Sentencing Commission in formulating the guidelines that should result in a sentence different from that described."[223] But both the statute and the Commission discourage departure, especially *downward* departure, in a number of ways.

Most importantly, departures are generally discouraged in the new regime through the operation of rules on appealability—that is, the rules that govern whether and when a decision by a sentencing judge may be appealed. The Sentencing Reform Act treats the decision whether to depart—on whatever basis—differently from all other decisions of the sentencing court. Every other factual and legal determination that affects the defendant's final sentencing range is appealable by either side. That is, the defendant may argue that the sentencing court erred on the high side in calculating either his Offense Level or his Criminal History Category, while the government may argue that the court erred on the low side. If the court decides *to depart,* this decision is appealable by the aggrieved party, on the grounds that departure is unlawful or unreasonable under the circumstances.[224] If, on the other hand, the sentencing court decides *not to depart* from the prescribed Guidelines range, this decision cannot be appealed by either side.[225] Under this asymmetric rule of appealability, a decision to depart risks an appeal and reversal, while a decision to adhere to the prescribed sentencing range insulates the judge from second-guessing (at least as to his departure decision) by an appellate court. The slightest comprehension of human nature will suggest that this asymmetry accomplishes the result it is intended to accomplish—namely, to discourage judges from departing.[226]

The Commission has also directly circumscribed judicial power to depart. Although the language of the Sentencing Reform Act can be read to empower the sentencing court to decide the circumstances that are not "adequately" factored into the Guidelines,[227] the Sentencing Commission has taken the position that *it* has plenary authority to decide which grounds for departure are warranted and which grounds are not warranted.[228] In a few instances, the Commission has identified a ground for departure and assigned a precise numerical value to it—so that the "departure" operates as an optional adjustment to the defendant's Offense Level.[229] Significantly, however, the Commission decided *not* to exercise its asserted authority to provide an exhaustive list of all possible bases for departure, and *not* to quantify most departures it does identify. Instead, the Commission has listed a variety of grounds that may warrant departure, without assigning point values to most of these; moreover, the Guidelines explicitly note that sentencing courts may identify other factors that warrant departure in particular cases.[230]

The twelve circumstances identified by the Commission as warranting upward departure in Offense Level relate mostly to circumstances of the offense—such as the presence of physical injury, extreme psychological injury to victims, abduction of victims, and use of dangerous weapons.[231] Often, these grounds are already factored in as "special offense characteristics" for particular offense categories; in these cases, only an extraordinary circumstance would warrant further enhancement by means of a departure.[232]

The most important basis for upward departure relates not to the defendant's crime, but to his criminal record. The Guidelines encourage upward departure along the Criminal History axis if the defendant's calculated Criminal History Category "does not adequately reflect the seriousness of the defendant's past criminal conduct or the likelihood that the defendant will commit other crimes."[233] Accordingly, while the threshold Criminal History calculation is based only on past *convictions*, the defendant's final Criminal History score may be based on evidence of prior arrests, dismissed charges, and even charges on which the defendant has been acquitted.[234] In the most recent year for which data are available, nearly half of all upward departures from the Guidelines sentencing range were made on the ground that the calculated Criminal History Category was too low.[235]

Downward departures are generally discouraged. The Guidelines list only five grounds relating to the offense itself, each of which is analogous to situations in which the substantive criminal law recognizes a partial or full defense to a crime (provocation by the victim, legal justification, legal coercion or duress, diminished mental capacity, and voluntary abandonment and disclosure).[236] In an interesting development, several appellate courts have discovered a sixth approved ground for downward departure within the covers of the Guidelines Manual.[237] This ground is not mentioned in the portion of the Guidelines explicitly governing departures, but in a single sentence of the Introduction to the Manual referring to the possibility of a sentence of probation where the defendant has committed a "single act of aberrant behavior."[238] Although it is doubtful, at best, that the Commission intended thus to create a sixth approved ground for downward departure,[239] it has not sought to amend the Guidelines so as to override this judicial effort to permit more flexibility in sentencing of first offenders.

With respect to most other sentencing factors that relate to the *offender*, rather than to the *offense*, the Commission has gone out of its way to limit downward departures. The Commission did not merely fail to mention many arguably relevant offender characteristics on its list of approved grounds for departure. The Sentencing Reform Act directed that the Guidelines be "entirely neutral" as to race, sex, religion, national origin, and socioeconomic status.[240] The Commission responded by adopting a Policy Statement prohibiting sentencing judges from ever taking these factors into account.[241] The Commission also chose to prohibit ever taking into account drug or alcohol dependence as a basis for *downward* departure,[242] and to direct that most other personal circumstances of the defendant are "ordinarily inappropriate" bases for departure. (The latter decision by the Commission goes beyond the provision in the Sentencing Reform Act itself that the listed factors are "generally inappropriate" considerations in imposing sentences of *imprisonment.*[243]) The personal circumstances the Commission considers ordinarily irrelevant include age, employment history, and family ties and responsibilities.[244] The last of these may partially explain why the percentage of female offenders receiving incarcerative sentences has increased even more than the percentage of male offenders.[245] Judges in the previous era had significantly more discretion to take into account the effect that imprisonment of a single parent would have on minor children.

After promulgating its initial Guidelines in 1987, and in response to a series of decisions by the federal courts of appeals upholding several offender characteristics as bases for downward departures,[246] the Commission issued a set of preemptive Policy Statements that prohibit departures on the basis of the individual life circumstances of the defendant in most cases. Thus, the Commission proclaimed in 1991 that additional factors not "ordinarily" relevant to departure are "[p]hysical condition or appearance, including physique,"[247] and "prior good works."[248] The Commission broadly defined the latter to include charitable work, public service, and even service in the nation's armed forces. The Commission was even more emphatic about the defendant's "[l]ack of guidance as a youth and similar circumstances indicating a disadvantaged upbringing." These life disadvantages, the Commission decreed, are simply "*not relevant grounds* for imposing a sentence outside the applicable guideline range."[249]

In response to discontent, especially in the federal trial bench, regarding these tightening strictures on departure authority, the Commission in 1994 amended its general Policy Statement on departures to emphasize that a circumstance described by the Commission as not "ordinarily" relevant may nonetheless be a basis for departure, if the circumstance is "present to an unusual degree" and "distinguishes the case [at hand] from the 'heartland' cases covered by the guidelines."[250]

The notion that the Guidelines are aimed only at cases in the *heartland* of each crime category is curious. In fact, the Guidelines are, as Congress directed, quite comprehensive. They fully meet the high expectations stated in the Senate Report accompanying the Sentencing Reform Act of 1984; they are

> sufficiently detailed and refined to reflect every important factor relevant to sentencing for each category of offense and each category of offender, giving appropriate weight to each factor, and deal[ing] with various combinations of factors.[251]

Prior to the 1994 amendment, the "heartland" concept appeared in a single sentence in the Introduction to the Guidelines Manual.[252] The tentative and open-minded tone of that Introduction was praised even by Guidelines critics.[253] But the Introduction's earnest suggestion of the modesty and simplicity of the rules that are to follow—as reflected, for instance, in the proposition that the Guidelines are intended only for crimes in the "heartland"—was belied by the ensuing effort systematically and comprehensively to cover almost all situations that a sentencing judge might encounter in a criminal case.

In fact, until the 1994 amendment explicitly incorporated the heartland concept in the Policy Statement on departures, this idea had been noticed only on a few occasions—most conspicuously, in a law review article by Judge Breyer[254] and a later judicial opinion by Breyer when he was Chief Judge of the United States Court of Appeals for the First Circuit in Boston.[255] The Supreme Court appeared to follow suit in 1996 in *Koon v. United States*.[256] As we explain in chapter 3, the *Koon* decision unanimously adopted the reasoning of then-Judge Breyer, but it left ambiguous (at best) whether the "heartland" concept promises greater opportunity for the exercise of discretion by sentencing judges.[257]

By far the most significant basis for departure relates directly to neither the offense being punished nor the character of the offender being punished, but to the defendant's service in the prosecution of others. Implementing a 1986 amendment to the Sentencing Reform Act,[258] the Guidelines invite the sentencing judge to depart downward where the defendant has provided "substantial assistance" to law enforcement authorities.[259] Substantial assistance is by far the most common basis of all departures. Of all departures granted in 1996, more than 60 percent were downward departures for substantial assistance to authorities.[260] Approximately two-thirds of all downward departures were made on this basis.[261]

Of both practical and symbolic significance, however, is the Commission's decision to limit this departure authority to cases in which *the prosecutor requests the court* to depart downward.[262] Cooperation with authorities is the *only* commonly occurring sentencing factor that the Commission chose to make a basis for the exercise of judicial discretion, rather than a binding sentencing instruction from the Commission; yet the judge may not exercise this discretion unless he receives the prosecutor's approval. Congress has provided that defendants who obtain such a prosecutorial motion may be sentenced even below statutory minimum requirements.[263]

The significance of substantial assistance departures in the punishment of federal crimes is increasing. Whereas in 1989 substantial assistance departures occurred in less than 4 percent of all federal sentencings, by 1994 this proportion had grown to nearly *20 percent*.[264] That is, one-fifth of all offenders in federal court received sentences below the levels which the Guidelines would otherwise have mandated because the prosecutor and the judge agreed that they deserved a lower sentence for providing substantial assistance to authorities in the prosecution of others.

Conclusion

For many years commentators and national commissions have criticized Congress's failure to codify the large and dispersed body of federal criminal laws.[265] When it enacted the Sentencing Reform Act of 1984, Congress had long since cast aside the earlier effort of bipartisan reformers to recodify federal crimes. Yet those who still imagine that a federal criminal code is a thing of the future should consider that fact that the federal criminal law has already been extensively rationalized, revised, and recodified—not by the United States Congress but by the United States Sentencing Commission. Indeed, one long-time student of criminal code reform has referred to the Sentencing Commission as "the empowered successor of the Brown Commission."[266] Unlike the Brown Commission, which merely advised Congress on code reform, the Sentencing Commission has full lawmaking power unless both houses of Congress (and the President) reject its Guidelines.[267]

The Commission's Guidelines supplement congressionally enacted laws as the effective federal criminal code. Within the statutory maximum or minimum set for the offense of conviction, the conduct for which a defendant will be punished is determined by the confluence of factors that the Sentencing Commission has decided are relevant to punishment. Today, in every criminal prosecution in every federal courtroom in the land, the acts for which defendants must be held responsible include, in addition to those proscribed by statute, those "real-offense" factors that the Sentencing Commission has identified under the headings of "offense conduct," quantity and other "specific offense characteristics," "relevant conduct," aggravating and mitigating "adjustments," "criminal history score," and permitted bases for "departure."

In sum, by establishing a Sentencing Commission with authority to issue detailed and binding sentencing rules, the Sentencing Reform Act set in motion a process that has transformed the substantive criminal law itself. In the next two chapters, we consider how this new regime has affected the quality of judging in the federal courts and the exercise of discretion over sentencing outcomes. In the final chapter, we consider certain due process implications of mandatory "real offense" sentencing.

CHAPTER THREE

Judging under the Federal Sentencing Guidelines

To a judge striking the balance among these claims, with all the discretion and perplexities involved, his task seems as plain an example of the exercise of moral judgment as could be; and it seems to be the polar opposite of some mechanical application of a tariff of penalties fixing a sentence careless of the moral claims which in our system have to be weighed.

H. L. A. Hart (1958)

The whole point of the guidelines was to hem in district courts with a set of rules created by the Commission and enforced by the courts of appeals.

Frank O. Bowman (1996)

Sentencing in the Guidelines Era

The Traditional Ritual

We take it as an established truth of our constitutional order that the criminal justice system exists not only to protect society in a reasonably efficient and humane way, but also to defend, affirm, and, when necessary, to clarify the moral principles embodied in our laws. In the traditional ritual of sentencing, the judge pronounced not only a sentence, but society's condemnation as well. The judge affirmed not only society's need to punish, but also its right to do so. Central to that venerable ritual was the presiding judge's exercise of informed discretion. The judge's power—duty—to weigh *all* of the circumstances of the particular case, and *all* of the purposes of criminal punishment, represented an important acknowledgment of the moral personhood of the defendant and the moral dimension of crime and punishment.

Justice has sometimes been represented by the blindfolded icon, *Justicia.*[1] This ancient metaphor is appropriate for adjudication. In deciding guilt or innocence, it ought not to matter whether the defendant is rich or poor, whether the defendant has erred in the past, or suffered unusual disadvantages, or even whether he or she is likely to break the law again. The decision on guilt or innocence is properly blind to these circumstances, blind to everything but the question of whether the defendant's actions and accompanying mental state instantiate the abstract features specified in a criminal statute. The character of this determination is represented by the icon's scales. Essentially a matter of weighing evidence and determining facts, the process of adjudication has more in common with scientific than with moral reasoning.

But *Justicia* usually is depicted also holding a sword, representing not the power to determine guilt or innocence, but the power to punish. Before that power is exercised, before the sword is raised, *Justicia* must lift the blindfold.[2] When it comes to the imposition of punishment, the question is always one of degree. The need is not for blindness, but for insight, for equity, for what Aristotle called "the correction of the law where it is defective owing to its universality."[3] This can occur only in a judgment that takes account of the complexity of the individual case.

FOR ALMOST TWO CENTURIES, trial judges in the American federal system bore much of the burden—and at times all of the burden—of achieving a just sentence within the maxima set by statute. While other actors participated in the sentencing process, the trial judge retained ultimate discretionary authority to fashion the sentence. In this century, the judge shared sentencing responsibility with parole officials in cases of imprisonment, but in the federal system the influence of these officials was limited. As we have noted in chapter 1, federal parole policies from their inception required that most federal prisoners serve between one-third and two-thirds of their nominal (that is, judicially imposed) prison sentences. Mindful of the relevant parole parameters (including, in the last decade of discretionary sentencing, published parole guidelines), the federal trial judge was able to exercise considerable control over the actual amount of prison time that would be served.[4]

Probation officers also played a substantial role at sentencing, but they facilitated, rather than diminished, the sentencing authority of the court. The probation officer in the federal system is an employee of the judicial branch, and traditionally has acted as a confidential adviser to the court. In the discretionary sentencing era, the officer's most important function was to prepare a presentence report for the judge, a copy of which (with the exception of a confidential sentencing recommendation to the judge) was provided to the prosecution and to the defense prior to the sentencing hearing.[5] In recent decades, a typical report included summaries of both the prosecutor's and the defendant's versions of the offense, information on the disposition of the cases of codefendants, and information on the application of the parole guidelines to the case at hand. But the largest section of the presentence report dealt with the personal history and circumstances of the defendant: family background, education, military service, work history, criminal record, dependents, and activities (good and bad) in the community.

Prior to the implementation of the Sentencing Guidelines, the official instructions to probation officers explained that the presentence report's "primary purpose is to aid the court in determining the appropriate sentence," and required that the report include "[a]n assessment of the problems of the defendant and a consideration for the safety of the community."[6] The final section of the report, not released to either the government or the defendant, contained the probation officer's recommendation to the judge of an appropriate sentence. The probation officer's major threshold recommendation, in many cases, dealt with the issue of whether the defendant should receive a prison sentence or probation. In the event that a period of imprisonment was recommended, the probation officer would suggest a particular term, based in part on the national sentencing statistics available for the offense in question, as well as on the officer's informed judgment. But the role of the probation officer in sentencing was purely advisory, in both theory and practice.

The pre-Guidelines roles of the prosecutor and the defense attorney at a federal sentence hearing varied widely, but they never approached the significance of the judge's role. We explore in chapter 4 the exercise of prosecutorial discretion, both before and during the Guidelines era. For now it is enough to note that in many districts, including those with which we are most familiar, prosecutors generally refrained from rendering specific sentencing recommendations to the judge, and the judge would neither elicit nor condone such recommendations. In other districts, prosecutors could and would forcefully argue for a significant term of imprisonment, or they might urge a lenient disposition (perhaps joining in a defendant's request for a term of probation).[7] In a case where the defendant had provided useful information to law enforcement officials concerning the criminal activities of others, the defense and the prosecutor might each describe to the judge the nature and significance of this cooperation. While on rare occasions a judge accepted a plea of guilty and sentenced on the basis of a sentence agreement between the parties, the judge always retained authority to reject the agreement of the parties.[8] Moreover, unlike nearly every other significant decision a judge makes in criminal or civil cases, the exercise of sentencing authority was virtually unreviewable: criminal sentences were not appealable by either side.[9] As we note at greater length in chapter 5, the lack of appellate review was, in our view, the major failing of the traditional sentencing system.

The significance of the judge's role at sentencing was unmatched by the role he played in other stages of the criminal case. In the adjudicatory stages of a criminal case, the primary actors are the prosecutor and the defense attorney. The prosecutor, in fashioning an indictment and a trial strategy, decides what facts can be proved beyond a reasonable doubt, the manner in which evidence will be presented, and the inferences the jury may reasonably be called on to make. In turn, the defendant and defense counsel decide which charges to contest and how best to contest them. The judge's role at this early, pretrial stage is, in many respects, secondary. If a plea of guilty is entered to one or more counts of the indictment, the judge's primary concerns are to ascertain the voluntariness of the plea[10] and to ensure that there is a factual basis for a guilty plea.[11]

In a criminal trial, the judge's role is in some ways even more passive than at a guilty plea hearing. At the trial stage, the judge is significantly constrained by requirements of procedural regularity. The roles among the participants are clearly demarcated—judge, parties, counsel, witnesses, and jurors. Throughout most of a trial, the judge's role is largely reactive. His most significant judgments are usually those concerning the admissibility of evidence. These evidentiary decisions are made on the basis of applicable rules and principles, the particular factual circumstances presented, and the judge's own legal experience. At the end of the trial, the judge instructs the jury on the law, but these instructions are almost invariably drawn directly from relevant appellate opinions and from standard ("pattern") jury instructions. At least in the absence of television cameras, the judge at a criminal trial takes a back seat to the attorneys and witnesses, and, at the moment of consequential decision, to the jury.

At a traditional sentencing hearing, however, the complex interplay of various actors, characteristic of the adjudicatory stage, resolved itself into a single axis of tension between the defendant (now convicted) and the judge (robed and seated behind the high bench). No longer serving primarily as an arbiter between the parties, the judge was now called upon to exercise the ultimate authority of the state.

Those present at a sentencing proceeding in a federal court (at least in those courtrooms with which we are familiar) witnessed a ritual of manifest moral significance. It was critical that this proceeding took the form of a face-to-face encounter between individuals. The sentencing judge might have a wide audience. The audience included victims, their families and friends, the family and friends of the defendant, the general public, and even the appellate courts that might be called upon to review the judge's presentencing decisions (although generally not, under the old regime, the decision on the sentence itself). But the judge *addressed* only one person when imposing a sentence and ordering the entry of the judgment of conviction. This solemn confrontation was predicated on the fundamental understanding that only a person can pass moral judgment, and only a person can be morally judged.

In emphasizing the human face of justice,[12] we are not blind to the limitations of the traditional sentencing hearing. Human judgment is fallible. Unfortunately, this is a fact of our existence for which there can be no easy technological solution. By replacing the case-by-case exercise of human judgment with a mechanical calculus, we do not judge better or more objectively, nor do we judge worse. Instead, we cease to judge at all. We process individuals according to a variety of purportedly objective criteria. But genuine judgment, in the sense of moral reckoning, cannot be inscribed in a table of offense levels and criminal history categories.

This does not mean that judgment, as we understand it, is a matter of subjective "feeling." Judgment proceeds from principles. These principles can and should be stated, rationally discussed, attacked, and defended. The greatest deficiencies of the pre-Guidelines regime were its failure to provide for review of the decisions of sentencing judges and its failure to ensure that the sentencing judge's exercise of discretion was informed by authoritative criteria and principles. But it is in the nature of moral and juridical principles that they must be informed by a particular set of facts before they can be applied.[13] Only a person can perform this task. Anthony Kronman has called this irreducibly human capacity for judgment "practical wisdom" or "prudence."[14] It is a trait of character acquired by life experience. It can never be reduced to a body of universal rules.

The New Ritual

The federal Sentencing Guidelines retained the traditional venue of sentencing while effectively abandoning the substance of the traditional sentencing rite. The Guidelines have replaced the traditional judicial role of deliberation and moral judgment (inherently imperfect) with complex quantitative calculations that convey the impression of scientific precision and objectivity. The judge on the elevated bench remains a visible symbol of society's moral authority, but the substance and meaning of this ancient staging is gone in most cases. The federal Sentencing Guidelines as they are now constructed seek not to *augment* but to *replace* the knowledge and experience of judges.

With a far more limited role, the federal trial judge in today's sentencing ritual has little or no opportunity to consider the overall culpability of the defendant before him. The Guidelines themselves determine not only which factors are relevant (and irrelevant) to criminal punishment, but also, in most circumstances, the precise quantitative relevance of each factor. In 1996, the last year for which information is available, more than forty thousand individuals were convicted and sentenced in the federal district courts of this country.[15] In each of these forty thousand sentencings, the sentencing judge was required to follow complex and abstract rules and to make minute arithmetic calculations in order to arrive at a sentence. Each step of a sentence calculation under the Guidelines represents what mathematicians call a "minimal pair": The judge must decide whether a given factor deemed relevant by the Sentencing Commission is present or absent in the case at hand. Each decision step requires the judge to add or subtract points ("levels")—generally no more than two at a time—that will ultimately determine the sentence of the defendant.

This sequence of minimal-pair decisions offers little opportunity for judicial reasoning. The judge's prescribed role is largely limited to factual determinations and rudimentary arithmetic operations. Moreover, the Sentencing Commission has taken pains to limit sharply the judge's authority to depart from the sentencing range that these arithmetic calculations yield. As we discuss later in this chapter, the Guidelines are comprehensive—encompassing many different contexts and circumstances in which federal crimes may be committed—and, absent approval from the prosecutor, the sentencing judge may depart from the Guidelines only in the atypical case.[16] One judge has recently likened his role in sentencing to that of a "notary public";[17] another has compared the sentencing judge's role under the new dispensation to that of "an accountant."[18]

The hallmark of judging in the common law tradition is the judge's application of general principles to specific facts, a process by which the general principles are themselves refined, explained, and, indeed, reconsidered.[19] In sentencing, the Guidelines have sought to minimize the opportunity and authority for judges to reason and to apply general principles of law to particular circumstances. Instead, the Guidelines require judges to address many quantitative and definitional issues in excruciating detail, while staying away from larger questions relating to culpability and the purposes of criminal punishment. Every hour a judge spends analyzing the Guidelines is an hour that might instead be directed toward application, and thus further refinement and development, of common principles and standards of criminal sentencing.[20] Nor are the Sentencing Guidelines themselves the product of such judgments. As we have discussed in chapter 2, the Commission was politically and institutionally incapable of articulating general principles and then applying these principles to exemplary situations.[21] While it would perhaps be possible, as a logical exercise, to derive from the Guidelines some common standards and principles that animate them, the Guidelines themselves—which are simply directives for computing severity levels and criminal history scores—do not reveal any such reasoning. The sentencing judge is left to engage not in judgment or moral reasoning, but in minute parsing of administrative regulations.

The sentencing proceeding itself has been recast from a discretionary into a formal adjudicatory process, in which the court makes findings of fact that translate into sentencing requirements under the Guidelines. By largely eliminating from the sentencing proceedings the power of any individual to consider the circumstances of the crime and of the defendant in their entirety and to form a judgment on that basis, the Guidelines threaten to transform the venerable ritual of sentencing into a puppet theater in which defendants are not persons, but *kinds* of persons—abstract entities to be defined by a chart, their concrete existence systematically ignored and thus nullified. The judge who conducts the sentencing is now, by design, little more than the instrument of a distant bureaucracy. Like the law in Kafka's parable,[22] the real power of the court has receded into an impenetrable state agency, nearly inaccessible both to the convicted offender and to his victims. These persons may implore the court to consider the full circumstances of the crime and of their humanity, but the judge is not permitted to consider many of these circumstances in determining the general severity of the defendant's punishment. Indeed, the range of attitudes and gestures we commonly associate with sentencing—defiance or contrition on the part of the defendant; vengeance or forgiveness on the part of his victims; condemnation, admonition, or forbearance on the part of the judge—become strangely inappropriate, even cruelly farcical in this setting.

Without moral authority, neither mercy nor moral condemnation is possible. Under the Guidelines, mercy, by which the full application of the law is relaxed in furtherance of the law's ends, has been rendered largely obsolete. Without the possibility of mercy, rigid adherence to the law cannot express severity of judgment. No moral judgment can be expressed at all.

The result is that the sentencing hearing often takes on the spirit of the Guidelines themselves: the hearing has become dry, complicated, mechanistic, and frequently incomprehensible to courtroom observers, including the parties. The discussion centers on "base levels," "points," "scores," "categories," and other Guidelines terminology. A recent article in the *Washington Post* captured the terms of discourse at a sentencing hearing under the Guidelines:

> "The court finds that the base offense level is 20," the judge began. "Pursuant to Guidelines 2K2.1(b)(4), the offense level is increased by two levels [to 22]. . . . The Court notes that the criminal convictions . . . result in a total criminal history category score of 18. At the time of the instan[t] offense . . . the defendant was serving a parole sentenc[e] in two causes of action. And pursuant to Sentencing Guidelines 4A1.1(D), 2 points are therefore added. The total criminal history points is 20. And according to the Sentencing Guidelines Chapter 5, Part A, 20 criminal history points establish a criminal history category of 6 . . . [As a result] the guideline range for imprisonment is 84 to 105 months."[23]

The same series in the *Washington Post* included a flow chart of a typical federal sentencing proceeding, which we have included as appendix D.

Nothing so dramatically illustrates the transformation of the sentencing hearing under this new regime than those cases where, after thirty or forty minutes of discussion in this double-speak, the sentencing judge realizes that parties and spectators in the courtroom are staring ahead in dazed numbness, having lost all sense of what is happening. That is when the judge feels bound to pause, to try to reassure courtroom observers, in comprehensible language, that the principal interlocutors in the courtroom do indeed understand what they are talking about, and that what is going on, though perhaps unintelligible to them, is indeed honest and fair. This is sometimes an awkward and embarrassing moment for the judge, who must try to explain a proceeding that may appear as arbitrary to the judge as it does to observers in the courtroom.

The observer who comes to the contemporary federal courtroom to witness the dramatic passing of judgment on a member of the community—to observe the drama of catharsis, appeals for mercy, appeals for severity, and the reasoned judgment that takes all of this into account—is sorely disappointed. That observer finds in today's federal courtroom precious little discussion of the human qualities of the victim or the defendant, of the inherently unquantifiable moral aspects of the defendant's crime, or of the type of sanction that would best achieve any of the purposes of sentencing. The "purpose" of sentencing in the new regime, he will learn, is nothing more and nothing less than compliance with the Sentencing Guidelines.

The New Probation Officer

In parsing and applying the Guidelines, the judge is significantly informed and aided by the probation officer. Although the Guidelines do not grant the probation officer new formal powers, they have transformed the role the officer plays at sentencing. Rather than providing guidance to the court in its exercise of sentencing discretion, the probation officer now undertakes a kind of preliminary adjudication of all issues made relevant by the Sentencing Guidelines. No longer serving as a conduit for the parties to present their respective versions of the offense to the judge, the presentence report today gives a single version of the facts—one determined, in principle, by the probation officer himself. The officer then provides his Guidelines calculus, applying the Guidelines to the facts as he finds them and computing a recommended sentencing range. Together, these two functions—independent fact-finding and autonomous Guidelines calculation—make the probation officer the "'special master' of guidelines facts"[24] and the primary enforcer of the Guidelines.

"Independent" Fact-Finding

The enhanced investigatory function of the federal probation officer is reflected in the rules governing presentence reports. When the Guidelines went into effect, the Federal Rules of Criminal Procedure were amended to require preparation of a presentence report in nearly all cases; the defendant no longer has the right to waive its preparation. As recently further amended, the Federal Rules require that the presentence report advise the court as to "the classification of the offense and of the defendant under the categories established by the Sentencing Commission . . . that the probation officer believes to be applicable to the case."[25] Probation authorities at the Administrative Office of the United States Courts in Washington have provided even more specific directives to officers in the field: they may not "withhold from the court reliable information" even if the prosecutor and defense attorney attempt "by agreement" to "eliminate relevant information."[26] The most recent instructions from Washington likewise refer to the "probation officer's role as *the court's independent investigator.*"[27]

It bears noting that federal probation officers are generally not trained for criminal investigation; one officer has delicately explained that many of the skills required for investigation—including the evaluation of the reliability of information and the credibility of witnesses—"were previously not considered within their province."[28] In fact, most federal probation officers have been trained in social work.[29] It is therefore ironic, as Sharon Bunzel has observed, that in the new sentencing regime, probation officers need not devote significant attention to who the offender is (and how he came to be that way).[30] The Guidelines render largely irrelevant to the determination of the sentencing range much of the background information about a defendant as a person, unless the information is so extraordinary that it arguably makes the case "atypical" of the criminal offenses addressed by the Guidelines.[31] And even in the extraordinary case, personal background about the defendant is never *required* for the sentencing decision,[32] because departure from the Guidelines is itself never required.

That probation officers are in fact not equipped or able to engage in criminal investigations may have even more pernicious consequences. In practice, many probation officers simply report the facts of the case as directly recounted to them by the prosecutor on the case,[33] noting where the defendant takes issue with this assessment of the facts. If a probation officer is disposed to do more than this, or believes that the prosecutor and defense attorney have conspired to hide important facets of the defendant's conduct, he most commonly will seek out the law-enforcement agents (the police or the FBI, for instance) who investigated the criminal case, going behind the backs of the parties in order to ferret out alleged conduct of the defendant that is relevant under the Guidelines.[34] What "independent" investigation of a case means, then, is "independent" from the prosecutor and the defense attorney. The police or federal agents, in turn, will advise the probation officer of their own view of the case—what the defendant's role "really" was, how much drugs were "really" involved, and so on. As Professor Gerard E. Lynch has noted:

> In effect, the "independent" investigative role of the probation officer . . . provides an opportunity for the police or law-enforcement agents to assert their version of what happened, and their views on an appropriate sentence, directly to the court, by-passing the prosecutor's censorship.[35]

There is good reason to be cautious about the reliability of raw "facts" reported by law-enforcement agents operating independently of prosecutors. The prosecutor preparing allegations for an indictment (or for a sentencing hearing) may well have a better understanding of the litigation potential of these allegations and be more aware of the legal and factual ambiguities of evidence than the law-enforcement agent who has transcribed interview notes or prepared police reports without the opportunity to consider other perspectives on the "facts" he has obtained.

Guidelines Application

The second function of the probation officer is to apply the law as stated by the Sentencing Commission to the facts that the probation officer finds and reports. Probation officers are now the Guidelines "experts" in the courtroom—trained in Sentencing Commission workshops and remotely guided by its manuals, worksheets, and telephone "hotline."[36] The probation officer's familiarity with the evolving law of Guidelines application is critical because the Guidelines findings and calculations in the officer's presentence report are the inevitable focus of the sentencing hearing under the new sentencing regime.

Guidelines application, however, is a species of legal reasoning, no matter how mechanical it may be in form. Several years ago, the Federal Courts Study Committee, created by an Act of Congress to study the future of the federal courts, expressed skepticism as to whether probation officers were appropriate personnel for this task, noting that "[a]lthough district judges have great confidence in the federal probation service, there is a growing concern among judges, prosecutors and defense lawyers that the new sentencing regime imposes on these officers responsibilities . . . for which they may not be particularly well trained or well suited."[37]

The degree of legal knowledge required to perform this function is indicated by the fact that several years ago all federal probation officers were provided training in WestLaw and LEXIS, the on-line computer services for legal research, in order to be able to keep abreast of appellate jurisprudence on the Sentencing Guidelines.[38] But it is not clear that mere access to such information can take the place of legal training; one probation officer has noted that "[t]o be really good . . . at [the] task of presentence writing, the probation officer will need to employ a new kind of reasoning—syllogistic—heretofore foreign to probation work."[39]

Ironically, the new role of the probation officer in a system where the judge's discretionary authority has been so diminished may in many courtrooms have the effect of *reducing* the probation officer's real influence over the sentencing outcome. In the previous era, the officer could, through his insights and perspectives about the defendant, influence the judge's exercise of discretion. In the present era, the probation officer too often is reduced to seemingly rote application of rules, with little opportunity for creative insight or professional judgment.

Defense attorneys have explained that they are reluctant to speak openly with the probation officer about the defendant, for fear that any revelation might trigger an upward adjustment under the Guidelines.[40] Indeed, "some defense counsel have come to regard the probation officer as a second prosecutor, whose purpose is to review and then raise the guideline calculations of the government."[41] As a result, it is now the common (and perfectly understandable) practice of defense counsel to instruct their clients, as well as their clients' relatives and friends, to decline to cooperate with probation officers prior to sentencing, or to do so only if defense counsel is present.

The relationship between the probation officer and the prosecutor has also been strained.[42] Although many probation officers rely primarily on the prosecutor in drafting the presentence report's version of the offense, prosecutors have an incentive not to be forthcoming with the probation officer in cases where the defendant's agreement to plead guilty has been tendered with the expectation that certain allegations will *not* be considered in the calculation of the sentence.[43]

The probation officer may stand in a quasi-adversarial position even in relation to the judge. At the very least, the officer stands, as never before, at arm's length from the judge. As a formal matter of law, federal probation officers remain part of the judicial branch of the federal government, and they continue to be appointed by the judges of the district courts.[44] And because of the presumed expertise of the probation officer and the tedious and often mechanical work of computation under the Guidelines, many trial judges are disposed to defer to the officer's judgments over the objection of one of the parties.[45] One judge has explained: "We find ourselves giving probation reports cursory attention because we are usually just checking the probation officer's addition."[46]

Yet probation officers who vigorously play the role of "guardian of the Guidelines"[47] may appear to judges to be indistinguishable from a third party in the case. They may appear to be precisely what the Sentencing Commission expects them to be—*de facto,* though not yet *de jure,* agents of the Commission, charged with diligent implementation of a system that is designed to limit the authority of the judge.[48] That the Probation Office is formally a part of the judiciary is of little solace to the judges; after all, the Sentencing Commission and its bureaucracy are also located, by statutory prescription, "in the judicial branch" of the federal government.[49] When a party disputes a factual finding made in the presentence report, the judge may eliminate altogether the customary confidential meeting with the probation officer prior to a sentencing. Especially in cases where it is likely that the probation officer will be required to testify under oath at the projected hearing (requiring the judge, in turn, to resolve disputed issues of fact in part on the basis of the credibility of the probation officer), the judge may feel bound to "decline to meet and talk with the probation officer about the presentence report in an effort to avoid any claims of ex parte communications."[50] In addition, many judges at plea hearings will routinely give defendants a *Miranda*-style explanation of the role of the probation officer, including an admonition that anything they say to a probation officer can be used against them at sentencing.

Many judges are not at ease operating within such a system, and may be sorely tempted to manipulate their Guidelines calculations to avoid the results called for by the Guidelines. Where the Guidelines' mandated sentencing range seems inadequate or too harsh, the judge may be tempted to reconsider factual "findings" in order to alter the Guidelines calculation, or to devise a basis for departure that may be largely irrelevant to culpability in the case at hand but at least may pass muster in the court of appeals as a permissible basis for imposing a sentence different from the one prescribed by the Guidelines' sentencing calculus. One judge has recently described how his fact-finding and Guidelines application at sentencing hearings varies with the extent to which the prosecutor seems disposed to appeal the sentence, explaining that "the best departures" are "the ones that aren't appealed."[51] Another judge responded to a survey about the Guidelines by noting with disgust:

> [T]he Guidelines . . . have made charlatans and dissemblers of us all. We spend our time plotting and scheming, bending and twisting, distorting and ignoring *the law* in an effort to achieve a just result. All under the banner of "truth in sentencing"![52]

Many other judges are loathe to attempt maneuvers around the Guidelines, viewing such manipulation as lawless exercise of unsanctioned power. In any event, the prospect of appellate review constrains the ability even of willing judges to use the pretense of fact-finding to exercise sentencing discretion *sub silentio.*

It is not surprising, in these circumstances, that federal judges increasingly reject the probation officer's Guidelines calculations in favor of a sentence or sentencing range that the *parties jointly recommend* as part of a plea bargain.[53] To be sure, a judge who is disposed to follow a plea agreement that the parties have reached may be put in an awkward position when a probation officer formally reports that the agreement is grounded on what the officer views as inaccurate or incomplete statements of offense conduct. In response, some judges have directed probation officers to limit their investigations to the facts as stipulated by the parties,[54] while others have viewed a sentencing agreement between the parties as a legitimate alternative to the sentencing outcome that would likely be calculated under the Guidelines in the absence of the agreement.[55] Even though the judge is never legally bound to sentence in accordance with a plea agreement,[56] there may be good reasons for doing so in the Guidelines regime, as we explain further in the following chapter.

Jurisprudence in the Guidelines Era

The Nature of Guidelines Fact-Finding

The judicial fact-finding required by the Guidelines is both tedious and difficult. Little may hinge on the issue in dispute, because the existence of a particular aggravating or mitigating circumstance may ultimately have a small effect on the length of a sentence. Yet minor factual issues are often exceedingly difficult to resolve because they are complicated or ambiguous. Moreover, the detail and comprehensiveness of the Guidelines means that the sheer number of potential factual issues is immense. There are literally hundreds upon hundreds of definitional terms and factual specifications that sentencing courts may be called on to apply and about which appellate courts must generate innumerable, dense opinions. The primary significance of this elaborate jurisprudence spawned by the Sentencing Guidelines is that it aids in implementing this particular set of rules—in much the same way that rulings of administrative law judges in the Social Security Administration implement their particular legal regime, or that rulings of Internal Revenue Service officials implement the federal tax code.

In many other areas of the law that have become exceedingly technical or that require a particular expertise, Congress has created specialized tribunals. These include courts or administrative agency tribunals on the trial or appellate level dealing with social security entitlements, federal taxes, patents and copyrights, and bankruptcies. Criminal sentencing has not been removed (yet) from the federal courts of general jurisdiction.[57] Although a bureaucracy in Washington writes the rules, their application is left up to the federal courts. This is a time-consuming enterprise for district courts and appellate courts alike. About two-thirds of all criminal appeals in the federal system involve Guidelines issues.[58]

As an illustration of the nature of judging under the Guidelines, consider the distinction between "minor" and "minimal" participation in a crime. The Guidelines provide that the defendant's numerical Offense Level should be reduced by two points if he was only a "minor" participant in the offense, but by four points if he was a "minimal" participant.[59] Unless the prosecution and defense have agreed in advance to accept the characterization in the probation officer's presentence report, one party is likely to lodge an objection; even where the parties have agreed, the judge may (sometimes with the probation officer's encouragement) be doubtful about the proposed characterization.[60] In these cases, the judge must make a decision on this relatively arcane issue. Once the trial judge renders a decision, the distinction becomes the business of the federal courts of appeals. Literally hundreds of appellate opinions have been written on permutations of this distinction[61]—a distinction that is relevant only for applying the federal Sentencing Guidelines. One may find appellate opinions, for instance, on whether a sole participant in a crime may qualify for one or the other of these reductions;[62] whether either reduction applies when the other participants were undercover agents;[63] whether the adjustment is to be applied on the basis of the defendant's role in the offense of conviction only, or on the basis of all the activities that constitute relevant conduct;[64] when drug couriers qualify for one or the other adjustment;[65] whether drug "steerers" or middlemen qualify for one or the other adjustment;[66] and whether the defendant qualifies simply because he did less than the other participants, even if he did as much as most offenders usually do.[67]

The set of appellate opinions on the distinctions between "minor" and "minimal" participants is only one of many possible examples of the extraordinary effort that is required to implement the Sentencing Commission's mandates. Other issues that have become the subject of detailed discussion and analysis in the sentencing courtroom and in trial and appellate case law include:

- Which annual edition of the Guidelines Manual is to be applied at a sentencing—the manual in effect on the date of sentencing or the manual in effect when the crime was committed? Which of these editions should be used when crimes were committed over a span of several years? When the Sentencing Commission amends a portion of Guidelines "Commentary" after the crime was committed, may the new "Commentary" be used by the sentencing court?[68]
- What is the difference between "leadership" and "managerial" roles in a crime (which require different upward adjustments)?[69]
- How should a sentencing court calculate the weight of drugs when they are mixed with other ingredients or superimposed on other materials?[70]
- How should a court calculate the weight of marijuana when it is seized as dry leaf, as opposed to seizure as a living plant (roots and all)?[71]
- How should a court estimate drug quantity when *no* drugs are seized but the defendant has been convicted of conspiracy to deal in drugs?[72]

- For each of the nineteen crime categories listed in the Guidelines, how much planning constitutes "more than minimal planning"? When is such planning by others attributable also to the defendant?[73]
- Where the offense level is increased for "more than minimal planning," is it also appropriate to apply the upward adjustments for having had a "leadership," "supervisory," or "managerial" role in the offense? What about the upward adjustments for "use of a special skill" or for "concealment"?[74]
- How many acts constitute "repeated acts" (a question that arises in various factual settings)?[75]
- Does the required upward adjustment for tax evasion schemes employing "sophisticated means" apply when the taxpayer used cashier's checks and a separate bank account in his wife's name?[76]
- In order to apply the upward adjustment for an "unusually vulnerable victim," is the court required to find that the defendant intentionally selected his victim on this basis, or simply that the defendant *actually knew* of the vulnerability or *should have known* of the vulnerability?[77]
- Should the upward adjustment for "abuse of trust" apply only when the defendant had a relationship of trust with *victims* or also when he or she had such a relationship with others, such as nonvictim shareholders, constituents, or employers?[78]
- When and how should the court "group" multiple counts of conviction on firearms offenses (and how should the court account for timing, purpose, place, and types of weapons used)?[79]
- When should money laundering and fraud counts be "grouped" under the Guidelines' multiple-count rules?[80]
- Does a burglary constitute a "crime of violence" for purposes of applying the upward adjustments that are mandatory in the sentencing of "career offenders"?[81]
- How do the terms "crime of violence" and "controlled substance offense" in Guidelines §4B1.1 differ from "violent felony" and "serious drug offense" in the federal statute relating to enhancement of sentence for defendants previously convicted of such crimes?[82]

For the uninitiated, the most powerful evidence of the tediousness and complexity of sentencing in the Guidelines regime would be provided by a perusal of one of the many compendiums of appellate sentencing case law and other Guidelines "updates" published by both the Sentencing Commission and the Federal Judicial Center, as well as by academic and commercial enterprises.[83] These summaries—often listing in the briefest form the holdings of thousands of cases—are necessary, of course, because no federal judge, prosecutor, probation officer, or defense counsel could possibly have the time to read and make sense of the appellate sentencing opinions that may be relevant to a particular case. The compendiums are a monument to the effort that federal judges across the nation have devoted to applying the often unexplained, if not arbitrary, rules promulgated by the Sentencing Commission—an effort which, lamentably, is squandered on the obscure.

Indeed, the weighty volumes of Guidelines jurisprudence notwithstanding, a federal court rarely has the opportunity to address issues of just punishment in the context of the case at hand. Neither the trial courts nor the appellate courts have much occasion to address questions concerning the appropriate form of punishment (the choice between probation and imprisonment, for instance) or the appropriate length of punishment in a particular case. The explosion of case law on federal sentencing contains almost no discussion of the purposes of sentencing generally or in the specific case—almost no articulated concern as to whether a particular defendant should be sentenced in the interests of general deterrence, rehabilitation, retribution, and/or incapacitation. Usually, no reference is made to the nonquantifiable losses or pain suffered by victims of the offense; no mention of the experience, character, values, community and military service, or life accomplishments and failures of the defendant; no mention of the sentences received by codefendants.[84] There is almost no mention of these matters because, under the Guidelines, judges are simply not allowed to take them into account (barring "extraordinary" or "atypical" circumstances) except in selecting the defendant's precise sentence within the calculated Guidelines range—and *that* final decision by the sentencing judge can never be reviewed by an appellate court.

The Insignificance of Guidelines Jurisprudence

Even those issues that are potentially of lasting significance become, in the application of the Sentencing Guidelines, trivial and inconsequential. The insignificance of Guidelines jurisprudence is a consequence of policy choices made by the Sentencing Commission. First, the Commission almost never explains the reason behind a particular Guidelines rule. Second, in its rules, the Commission has chosen to invent new terms and has altered the meaning of well-established ones. Third, the Commission has been notably reluctant to permit the judges to participate in the elaboration of the rules it promulgates. It is emphatically true, of course, that the now-discarded system of fully discretionary sentencing, under which sentences could not be reviewed by appellate courts, did not permit the judicial development of sentencing principles and standards. *But neither does the Guidelines regime.*

The Guidelines as Diktats

Largely unencumbered by the requirements of the Administrative Procedure Act,[85] the Sentencing Commission has seldom explained its actions or its intentions—beyond the conclusory statements of its "Resolution of Major Issues" in the Introduction to its Guidelines Manual. The rules issued by the Commission, whether termed "Policy Statements," "Guidelines," or "Commentary," simply assert that some particular circumstances call for adjusting sentence length, while some other circumstances do not. Neither in proposing particular rules nor in ultimately promulgating them does the Commission explain *why* it is doing what it does.

As a result, the Guidelines are simply a compilation of administrative *diktats.* A set of unexplained directives may warrant unquestioning acceptance if they are thought to constitute divine revelation or its equivalent (the Ten Commandments come to mind), but this is not a common occurrence in human affairs—at least not in democratic societies. The Commission's primary argument in support of its Guidelines is implicitly an argument from authority—that is, the authority for these rules rests on the Commission's authority to issue them. The Commission's reluctance to explain itself to the public thus leaves us with a set of rules promulgated and enforced *ipse dixit* —because the Commission says so. In the absence of some reasoned explanation for a particular rule, it is difficult to understand, much less defend, the rule. This is surely one reason that the Administrative Procedure Act requires most federal agencies to explain and justify their rules and subjects these rules to judicial review for arbitrariness. The Commission, regrettably, is not subject to these requirements. Hence, unless there is reason to believe that the Commission has some hidden capacity to discover important truths, its argument from authority leaves the Guidelines with little or no independent validity or legitimacy.

New Concepts, New Confusion

A second reason that the federal Sentencing Guidelines are unlikely to have lasting significance is that the Sentencing Commission has so often chosen—without explanation—to define or apply terms differently from the way they are defined in the substantive criminal law, and even to invent entirely new concepts. Many of the terms employed by the

Guidelines appear, at first glance, to embody or restate principles that traditionally are relevant to a determination of criminal liability. But on closer examination, or on a review of their application over time, it becomes clear that the terms are used in idiosyncratic ways or in ways that are unknown both to the substantive criminal law and to the law of evidence.

For example, the Guidelines define "obstruction of justice" for the purpose of a sentence enhancement differently—indeed, much more broadly—than do the federal statutes defining the crime of obstruction of justice.[86] Our criminal law has long punished obstruction of justice, and over the centuries courts and legislatures have altered the precise contours of this crime. There is no reason to suppose that the current definition in federal law could not be improved upon, or that the current definition is necessarily the best definition for all purposes. It would undoubtedly be possible for a sentencing commission, or sentencing courts and appellate courts, to reinterpret the concept of obstruction of justice in a manner that would improve our understanding of the sort of obstructive conduct that deserves to be considered in sentencing decisions. Such thinking about this behavior and its punishment would begin with an explanation of why—and to what extent—a defendant's sentence for a particular crime ought to be enhanced because of the defendant's additional conduct of obstructing justice. Only then would rule-makers be ready to propose a definition of "obstruction of justice" for sentencing purposes. Yet it appears that the Sentencing Commission has never attempted any such inquiry. At the same time, because it has adopted a comprehensive codification of the meaning of obstruction of justice in its Guidelines and has decided the precise point value this behavior is "worth" in calculating the defendant's sentencing range, the Commission has effectively preempted the federal courts from undertaking this sort of inquiry.

Perhaps the most extraordinary conceptual invention of the Commission is the idea of "relevant conduct"—an idea whose significance looms large in the new sentencing regime, as we noted in chapter 2.[87] The concept, as it happens, is novel. Its scope is broader, for example, than the scope of the familiar evidentiary concept of "common scheme or plan,"[88] broader than the scope of "accomplice liability" in the criminal law,[89] and different from that of "conspiratorial liability."[90] Courts have had a difficult time deciphering and applying the Guidelines' principle of "relevant conduct," with the result that it has been applied in different ways by the various district courts and courts of appeals across the country.[91] The Commission itself found it necessary to amend its relevant conduct rules on no fewer than five different occasions in a six-year period.[92]

In light of the Sentencing Commission's notable reluctance to offer explanations for its various rules, and its decision to adopt new meanings for traditional common law terms, it is not surprising that conflicting interpretation and confusion have characterized the efforts of the courts to apply the Guidelines. In one two-week period in 1996, for instance, three different appellate panels gave three different answers to the question of how to calculate a sentence for a witness convicted of criminal contempt for refusing to testify at a trial.[93] The Guidelines provision on criminal contempt (§2J1.1) directs the sentencing court by a cross-reference to another section of the Guidelines Manual (§2X5.1) governing "other offenses" not specifically addressed in the Guidelines. The latter provision, in turn, directs the court to apply "the most analogous offense guideline." In the three appellate cases involving recalcitrant witnesses, one panel concluded that the most analogous guideline was that pertaining to "failure to appear by a material witness" (§2J1.5, with a Base Offense Level of six); [94] a second panel concluded that the "obstruction of justice" guideline (§2J1.2, with a Base Offense Level of twelve) was most appropriate;[95] the third panel concluded that the proper guideline was that pertaining to "misprision of a felony" (§2X4.1, with a Base Offense Level between four and nineteen depending on the underlying felony).[96]

The second and third panel opinions were issued only one day apart, *by two different panels of the same court of appeals.* And if that were not quite enough, these two panels were, coincidentally, reviewing two different sentencing decisions by the same district judge in the same prosecution. The result was that one appellate panel told the district judge he was wrong to use the "misprision of a felony" guideline to sentence a recalcitrant witness convicted of criminal contempt, while another panel of the same court told him one day later that he had been right to do so.[97] Confusion of this sort has contributed to erosion of confidence in the system of criminal sentences and spawned the small industry devoted to the compilation and explication of the case law under the Guidelines.

The Primacy of the Sentencing Commission

The massive effort of both trial and appellate courts to make sense of ambiguities, complexities, and gaps in the Guidelines is of little lasting value to the bar, the bench or the public. This is so because the Commission has gone out of its way to make it clear that it alone will determine the scope and application of concepts employed in the Sentencing Guidelines, regardless of any teachings of the substantive law of crimes or the experience of federal and state governments in elaborating the criminal law. The Commission's adamant refusal to share interpretive authority with the judiciary accounts, in part, for the complexity of the Guidelines. The Commission deliberately employed minute quantitative distinctions in the Guidelines precisely in order to minimize the opportunity for sentencing judges to make discretionary choices.[98]

The Commission has also sought to minimize opportunities for the appellate courts to contribute their perspectives on the meaning of key Guidelines principles and terms. When the courts of appeals have interpreted provisions of the Guidelines in ways that would enhance the authority of district judges to exercise their informed judgment, or differed among themselves in interpretation of particular language in the Guidelines, the Commission has almost invariably responded by promulgating a "clarifying" amendment to bring the appellate courts back into line—thereby cutting off any possibility of longer-term judicial development of sentencing law.[99] According to a staff report, the Commission by 1994 had issued twenty-nine such amendments.[100]

As one federal appeals judge (a former chief federal prosecutor in New Jersey) has explained, "[T]he Commission, through the amendment process, is now performing with respect to the guidelines essentially the same role that the Supreme Court plays with respect to the interpretation of other federal laws."[101] Unlike the Supreme Court, however, the Commission does not seek to explain or justify its resolution of conflicts.[102] The Supreme Court has welcomed the Commission's effort to reduce circuit conflicts,[103] a practice that regrettably also reduces the role of the courts of appeals and of the Supreme Court itself in giving meaning to the Guidelines.

It is perhaps ironic that the most coherent and sensible jurisprudence under the new sentencing regime concerns not application *of* the Guidelines, but a certain type of departure *from* the Guidelines. The Commission has insisted that certain factors may never be a basis for departure (including the defendant's socioeconomic status), has discouraged departure on other bases (including the defendant's disadvantaged background or military or community service), and has specifically encouraged departure for yet other reasons. It has not, however, sought to address exhaustively or comprehensively *all* the possible grounds for departure from its Guidelines.[104] This has afforded the courts a limited role in determining the factors that are relevant to a just sentence, both generally and in specific factual contexts. In the rules governing departures, the Guidelines list twelve grounds warranting an upward departure from the calculated Guidelines sentence,[105] and five grounds supporting a downward departure.[106] Additionally, the rules concerning criminal history[107] and obstruction of justice,[108] among others, specifically note that further adjustment (beyond the points specified in the Guidelines instruction) may be warranted if especially mitigating or aggravating circumstances are found.[109]

Some of these Commission-identified grounds for departure are closely analogous to concepts that have long played an important role in determining substantive criminal liability, including mens rea, self-defense, duress, justification, and diminished capacity.[110] Moreover, in a break with their usual approach, the Guidelines do not quantify the precise effect that the presence of one of these factors should have on the defendant's sentence. Rather, the Guidelines leave to the sentencing judge in the first instance, and to the appellate court on review, the task of fleshing out the significance for punishment of each of these circumstances. Appellate opinions explaining, limiting, justifying, and applying these Commission-identified grounds of departure are among the most thoughtful and significant of the genre.[111] These decisions discuss issues of culpability and just punishment in the particular case, often drawing upon the substantive criminal law as it has developed in statutes and at common law through the years.

Both sentencing judges and appellate courts have contributed a coherent sentencing jurisprudence primarily with respect to this limited set of "guided departures."[112] With respect to departures that are based on a circumstance not specifically countenanced by the Commission, appellate courts have often been bogged down by consideration of a threshold issue: whether the ground cited by the trial court as a basis for departure has already been factored into the Sentencing Guidelines.[113] As we discuss below, the case law here is speculative and trivial, addressing not whether a particular circumstance is relevant to just sentencing, but simply whether the Sentencing Commission can be said to have already considered the particular circumstance. That is, most jurisprudence concerning departure from the Guidelines, like most jurisprudence concerning application of the Guidelines, is useful for only one purpose: interpreting the federal Sentencing Guidelines.

The Hegemony of the Sentencing Commission

The federal courts of appeals have by and large faithfully enforced the Commission's decision to limit severely downward departures on the basis of personal characteristics of the defendant.[114] One survey of appellate case law reports that five circuit courts are overtly hostile to downward departures and two are deferential to sentencing courts, while the remainder are someplace in between.[115] Federal courts of appeals have reversed departures based on a defendant's especially minor role in a crime,[116] diminished mental capacity at the time of the offense,[117] age,[118] health,[119] family history,[120] mental condition,[121] familial responsibility,[122] employment record,[123] community service record,[124] post-arrest rehabilitative efforts[125] or religious activities,[126] duress stemming from drug addiction,[127] and exemplary military service.[128] Just as the Commission itself lists more grounds for upward departure than for downward departure, the appellate courts appear to be more receptive to departures enhancing a sentence.[129]

Whether upward or downward, however, departures are not authorized where, at bottom, the sentencing court simply disagrees with the Commission's assessment of the relative seriousness of the crime committed.[130] Not surprisingly, rigidities and disparities built into the Guidelines themselves and into federal criminal statutes are not grounds for departure. One much-discussed federal statute, for instance, provides for a hundred-to-one ratio in the quantities of powdered cocaine and crack cocaine that yield the same mandatory minimum sentence,[131] and the Guidelines' "Drug Equivalency" tables reflect this disparity. Every federal appeals court has held that this discrepancy is not a ground for downward departure for defendants convicted of trafficking in crack.[132]

A judge may not even depart on the ground of avoiding disparity itself, as when a codefendant with a greater role secures a lower prescribed sentencing range.[133] Nor may a judge depart upward on the ground of strong community sentiment regarding the defendant's antisocial behavior.[134] A sentencing judge may not justify a downward departure on the basis of a defendant's voluntary restitution of victims' losses, or the collateral consequences of his conviction (including deportation, loss of a job, civil forfeiture of the home, and effect on family and employees),[135] or on the ground that this particular defendant and related parties (such as his family) have already been punished more than adequately for the crime.[136]

Despite the hopes of some observers, this situation is not likely to change in light of the Supreme Court's 1996 decision in *Koon v. United States*.[137] In *Koon,* the Court unanimously adopted the notion that the Sentencing Guidelines govern "heartland" cases, and that judges may depart in cases outside the heartland. The heartland concept is at the center of some state sentencing guidelines systems (the Minnesota guidelines, for instance), but the federal Guidelines had seemingly rejected that approach in favor of a far more comprehensive and inclusive set of sentencing guidelines. As we noted in chapter 2, the word "heartland" had appeared only in a single sentence in the Introduction to the Guidelines when they were issued in 1987.[138] In 1994, a reconstituted Commission added a new paragraph expressly adopting the concept in the chapter of the Guidelines governing departures; the new provision recognizes that judges may depart in cases outside the "heartland" covered by the Guidelines, but admonishes that such departures should be "rare."[139]

Potentially more significant than its adoption of the heartland concept, *Koon* held that departures should be reviewed by appellate courts under an "abuse-of-discretion" standard.[140] Prior to *Koon,* appellate courts had simply followed the directions of the Sentencing Reform Act itself (1) to accept a sentencing judge's findings of fact unless they were "clearly erroneous," and (2) to give "due deference" to the judge's application of the Guidelines.[141] *Koon*'s articulation of an abuse-of-discretion standard could be interpreted as encouraging the courts of appeals to defer in most cases to a sentencing judge's decision to depart.[142] A cursory reading of the Court's decision in the *Koon* case may reinforce the media's initial misimpressions of the decision—that the Supreme Court has appeased district judges by giving them more discretion and mollified circuit judges by relieving them of much of the burden of Guidelines appeals.[143] The Court said, for instance: "We agree that Congress was concerned about sentencing disparities, but we are just as convinced that . . . district courts retain much of their traditional sentencing discretion."[144] To this remarkable statement, a leading proponent of the Guidelines regime has responded, "With the utmost respect to the Justices, this is pure banana oil."[145]

Few of the eleven federal circuit courts of appeals have understood *Koon* to herald a release from the strictures of the Guidelines.[146] This is because *Koon*'s expansive *dicta* regarding the scope of sentencing court discretion are difficult, if not impossible, to reconcile with the actual reasoning and holdings of the case. Of course, the life of the law *is* more than logic, and perhaps over time the case will be understood as a powerful signal from the Supreme Court that sentencing judges are due more deference. But two years after the decision was handed down, most courts of appeals have continued to subject departures—especially downward departures—to close scrutiny.[147]

In our view, *Koon* ultimately fails to afford relief from the rigidities of the Guidelines because it leaves undisturbed the major obstacle to meaningful judicial participation in criminal sentencing: the mischievous provision of the Sentencing Reform Act that prohibits judges from departing from the Guidelines on grounds already "adequately" considered by the Commission.[148] By the further terms of the Sentencing Reform Act, the judge in making the determination of "adequacy" cannot invoke any knowledge that he may have; "adequacy" is to be judged solely on the basis of "the guidelines, policy statements, and official commentary of the Sentencing Commission."[149]

The Supreme Court in *Koon* followed the lead of the federal courts of appeals in treating *any* consideration by the Commission as, *ipso facto,* "adequate" consideration.[150] Because no second-guessing of the Commission is permitted, sentencing judges and appellate courts are denied authority to consider the arbitrariness of any rule in the Guidelines themselves. In the words of one recent decision by a federal appellate court, *Koon* does nothing to alter the rule that "[a] sentencing court may not depart from an otherwise applicable guideline range simply because its own sense of justice would call for it."[151] The question of whether the applicable Guidelines calculation or sentencing range produces justice in a particular case is not open for consideration either by sentencing judges or appellate courts. *Koon* makes clear that the reviewing court must defer to a departure decision only if the circumstances identified by the district judge take the case out of the "heartland"—that is, if the circumstances have not already been factored into the Guidelines.[152]

As it happens, the Sentencing Commission *has* already considered, and the Sentencing Guidelines *have* already factored in, many if not all circumstances that are arguably relevant to criminal sentencing; this micro-management is one of the Guidelines' most notable features. The Guidelines have done this by prohibiting altogether the consideration of some factors[153] and by specifying the weight to be accorded other significant factors depending on the precise degree to which they are present.[154] The Guidelines are, as Congress intended them to be, comprehensive,[155] and *Koon* makes it clear that judges may not depart because they disagree with these comprehensive sentencing instructions. Judges may not depart because they disagree with the weight the Guidelines give to a circumstance in the *typical* case, or simply because they disagree with the Commission's prohibition on consideration of certain factors.

Moreover, with respect to commonly occurring circumstances that are not explicitly addressed by the Guidelines, *Koon* teaches that the benefit of the doubt must be given to the Commission; it must be assumed that the Commission has already taken the matter into account.[156] The real question is not whether the Commission actually took some factor into account, but whether the factor is rare enough to overcome a *presumption* that the Commission *has* taken it into account.

Koon thus leaves sentencing courts approximately where they were: with departure authority only in cases that are atypical in ways neither proscribed from consideration by the Sentencing Commission nor already "considered" by the Commission. *Koon* also leaves appellate courts approximately where they were: with supervisory responsibility to invalidate departures based on anything other than the "atypicality" of the case at hand. There is no room to question the reasonableness of the Commission's judgments about just punishment in the "typical" (or "heartland") case, nor to review any determination the Commission has made regarding the proper grounds for departure from the Guidelines ranges. Chief Judge Richard Posner puts it well: *Koon* reaffirms "the primacy of the Commission over the courts in determining the proper grounds for departures" from the Guidelines.[157]

THE HEGEMONY OF the Sentencing Commission thus remains intact. As one supporter of the present regime has succinctly explained, "The whole point of the guidelines was to hem in district courts with a set of rules created by the Commission and enforced by the courts of appeals."[158] Those who championed this "hemming in" of sentencing judges thought that the new system of administrative sentencing rules was necessary to bring consistency, coherence, and accountability to a federal sentencing process that was deficient in these respects.

Unfortunately, as we have suggested in this chapter, an unintended consequence of the Guidelines has been to rob the traditional sentencing rite of much of its moral force and significance. The new regime of bureaucratic sentencing inadvertently mocks the moral premises upon which the traditional ritual was based, while denying both sentencing judges and appellate judges the opportunity to develop a principled sentencing jurisprudence. In order for this regime of comprehensive, *ex ante* sentencing rules to function effectively, the defendant must be reduced to an "inanimate variable" in an equation,[159] the probation officer must operate as the "special master" of Guidelines facts,[160] the sentencing judge must weigh the crime according to the Sentencing Commission's calculus, and the role of the courts of appeals is simply to police the sentencing judges. Without principled foundation or application, the awesome power of the state to inflict suffering is wielded as an exercise in bureaucratic regularity, for which no one, ultimately, bears responsibility.

CHAPTER FOUR

The Battle Cry of Disparity

Only a few studies examined actual Federal sentencing decisions prior to the introduction of the guidelines. Together, they showed that sentencing was not greatly dependent on the judge that one drew. Rather, outcomes generally corresponded to differences in cases and offenders' characteristics that were commonly seen as legitimately considered. . . . Differences clearly thought to be unwarranted (e.g., by the offender's race or ethnicity) were found to be uniformly small or statistically insignificant.

Douglas McDonald and Kenneth E. Carlson (1993)

The Department's policy is only to stipulate to facts that accurately represent the defendant's conduct. If a prosecutor wishes to support a departure from the guidelines, he or she should candidly do so and not stipulate to facts that are untrue.

Richard Thornburgh, U.S. Attorney General (1989)

The widespread use of fact bargaining, and the lying to the court that is inevitable with the frequent use of such bargaining, is the dirty little secret in the prosecution of federal criminal cases.

Tony Garoppolo, Deputy Chief U.S. Probation Officer,
Eastern District of New York (1996)

Reduction of "unwarranted sentencing disparities" was a—probably *the*—goal of the Sentencing Reform Act of 1984.[1] As the Department of Justice explained in 1987, "Simply stated, unwarranted disparity caused by broad judicial discretion is the ill that the Sentencing Reform Act seeks to cure."[2] Congress's concern with reducing perceived or assumed disparities in federal sentencing is reflected in the debates leading up to the Act's passage,[3] in the Senate report accompanying it,[4] and in the text of the Act itself.[5] Indeed, the virtue of reducing sentencing disparity stemming from the exercise of judicial discretion was one thing that both conservatives and liberals in Congress could readily agree on, if for different reasons. Liberals believed that permitting the exercise of discretion compromised the ideal of equal treatment under the law, and conservatives were concerned as well that federal judges too often used their discretion to go easy on criminals.[6] The Sentencing Guidelines reflect this consensus by restricting the exercise of judicial discretion to a narrow sentencing range in each case and by limiting judicial departures from that range. The ranges of the Sentencing Table (see appendix A) are a small percentage of the statutory ranges that were available to judges in the pre-Guidelines era; it was presumably hoped that sentencing disparity would be reduced commensurately.

In our view, the fixation on reducing sentencing disparity that results from the exercise of judicial discretion has been a mistake of tragic proportions. It is not that the ideal of equal treatment is unworthy; rather, this ideal cannot be, and should not be, pursued through complex, mandatory guidelines. We reject the premise of sentencing reformers that *uniform* treatment means *equal* treatment, and thus that judicial discretion—insofar as it undermines uniformity—necessarily denies justice. We also reject the notion that reducing disparities "among defendants with similar records who have been found guilty of similar criminal conduct" (in the words of the Sentencing Reform Act[7]) ought to be the paramount objective in criminal sentencing. Uniform treatment ought to be *one* objective of sentencing, to be sure, but not the sole or overriding objective. A *just* sentence must also be a reasoned sentence and a proportional sentence, imposed through procedures that comport with basic understandings of fairness and due process of law in a constitutional scheme of checks and balances.

Ending "unwarranted disparity" has been the rallying cry of sentencing reformers and the Sentencing Commission. On the surface, this objective seems both obvious and uncontroversial. The trouble begins when we move beyond this slogan and ask what factors should be considered in deciding whether particular crimes and particular criminals are "similar" or "dissimilar" for purposes of sentencing. As the Senate Report on the Sentencing Reform Act itself conceded, "[t]he key word in discussing unwarranted sentence disparities is 'unwarranted.'"[8] Most might agree, for instance, that in deciding whether a particular crime is similar to another, one important criterion is the amount of direct harm caused. But how much should this matter? What about less tangible or easily measured harms, such as the effect of the crime on witnesses, employees, or the community at large? What should be the relative weight of factors other than harm, such as role in the offense, past criminal record, and likelihood (or unlikelihood) of rehabilitation?

The focus of the Sentencing Reform Act, moreover, was to reduce disparity resulting from the exercise of *judicial* discretion, But, of course, other participants in the criminal justice system *also* make key decisions and judgments that affect a criminal sentence. Prosecutors in the federal system, for example, have been afforded wide discretion in charging and plea decisions. In examining sources of sentencing disparity, it is important to look not only at decisions of judges, but also at the decisions of prosecutors and others that may precede the judge's sentencing decision. Denying sentencing discretion to judges may serve to reinforce or to leave uncorrected disparity and arbitrariness arising elsewhere in the criminal justice system.

Here we seek to move the debate beyond the shibboleth of "unwarranted disparity" to examine some of these complex issues. Our analysis suggests four major conclusions:

1. Inter-judge sentence variation was not as rampant or as "shameful" in the federal courts under the pre-Guidelines regime as Congress apparently believed when it enacted the Sentencing Reform Act in 1984.
2. No thorough empirical study has demonstrated a *reduction* in the total amount of disparity under the Guidelines.[9]
3. While reduction of inter-judge disparity is a worthwhile goal for sentencing reform, it is a complex goal, and a myopic focus on this objective can result in a system that too often ignores other, equally important goals of a just sentencing system. Uniformity can itself be "unwarranted": when unprincipled, blind uniformity itself promotes *inequality*.
4. Important sources of disparity remain in the Guidelines regime, some acknowledged and others hidden from view. In particular, the exercise of the prosecutorial function is, despite the efforts of both the Sentencing Commission and the Department of Justice, inevitably a wellspring of disparate treatment. This does not mean that prosecutorial discretion should be suppressed, but rather that prosecutors should exercise discretion in the open, where it can be observed and, if necessary, checked by judges.

Measuring Disparity before the Guidelines

Although the sponsors of the Sentencing Reform Act believed that unfettered judicial discretion had led to egregious sentencing disparities in the federal courts, very little of the empirical research that propelled the movement to enact sentencing guidelines actually concerned the federal courts. In the decade between Judge Marvin E. Frankel's influential call for an end to discretionary sentencing[10] and the enactment of the Sentencing Reform Act, over fifty empirical studies on sentencing practices were published, of which only seven examined the federal courts.[11] While proponents of a sentencing commission repeatedly held these studies up as powerful proof of the "shameful" disparities present in federal sentencing practices,[12] other assessments have reached far more modest conclusions.

A fair summary of these assessments is that *the more sophisticated the study, the less clear the evidence of unwarranted disparities.* After a recent review of the literature, David Weisburd concluded: "[T]he degree of capriciousness or prejudice evident in the sentencing behavior of Federal judges before the establishment of the guidelines has been often overstated."[13] The authors of another recent review, Douglas McDonald and Kenneth Carlson, reached a similar conclusion:

> Only a few studies examined actual Federal sentencing decisions prior to the introduction of the guidelines. Together, they showed that sentencing was not greatly dependent on the judge that one drew. Rather, outcomes generally corresponded to differences in cases and offenders' characteristics that were commonly seen as legitimately considered. Some differences existed that were controversial as to their desirability (e.g., differences in sentencing among Federal circuits) but could not be deemed necessarily invidious. Differences clearly thought to be unwarranted (e.g., by the offender's race or ethnicity) were found to be uniformly small or statistically insignificant.[14]

McDonald, a leading researcher on sentencing, had been one of the few voices in the years leading up to the Sentencing Reform Act to caution against the unsupported assumption that judicial discretion caused rampant disparities in sentencing.[15] In a detailed empirical study of New York state courts published in 1982, he had complained, "Despite wide acceptance of the notion that sentencing disparities are rife, the empirical evidence is far from persuasive. . . . The most common failing has been not to account adequately for the numerous factors which possibly affect sentencing decisions."[16] In the debates leading up to the Sentencing Reform Act,[17] however, little attention was paid to the voices of McDonald and the few others who questioned the wisdom of mandatory sentencing guidelines.[18]

Four studies proved especially influential in the congressional deliberations leading up to passage of the Act.[19] The Senate Report accompanying the Act devoted several pages to a summary of the studies' conclusions and even reproduced some of their statistical tables.[20] Two of the studies, both reporting on data from the early 1970s, were simply tabulations of sentencing *variation* across districts; they lacked any controls for either offender characteristics (even criminal history) or offense characteristics. One of these, undertaken by the United States Attorney for the Southern District of New York,[21] showed wide ranges in sentences among districts and circuits (for instance, "[t]he range in average sentences for forgery runs from 30 months in the Third Circuit to 82 months in the District of Columbia").[22] A larger study using sentencing data compiled by the Administrative Office of the United States Courts[23] employed the same simple methodology. The study showed that average sentence length for a series of federal crimes varied from district to district across the country, but again did not control for case mix.

Unsurprisingly, these same results are obtained under the Sentencing Guidelines. Judge Gerald Heaney has found substantial variation among sentences imposed under the Guidelines in four districts of the Eighth Circuit.[24] The Sentencing Commission's annual reports demonstrate similar nationwide variation in the means and ranges of sentences imposed for the same statutory crime. To take a typical example: In 1995 in the District of Columbia, only 30 percent of embezzlement offenders were sentenced to prison, and their average term was seven months. In the Eastern District of Pennsylvania, on the other hand, nearly 70 percent of these offenders received prison sentences, and the average term was twice as long (fourteen months). Meanwhile, in the Central District of California, just over half of those convicted of embezzlement were sentenced to prison, and they served a median sentence of only four and one-half months.[25]

After Judge Heaney published his study of the Eighth Circuit, the then-Chairman of the Sentencing Commission complained that the judge had merely examined variations in sentence without any offender or offense controls.[26] Judge Heaney in turn responded that Congress had relied, in part, on just such studies in proclaiming the existence of "rampant" sentencing disparities—suggesting that what is sauce for the goose is sauce for the gander.[27]

The other two studies relied on by the Senate sought to control for offender and offense characteristics. Both, however, concerned not actual sentencing behavior, but judges' responses to hypothetical or simulated cases. Of the two, the study that received greater attention was an experiment conducted in 1972, the results of which were published by the Federal Judicial Center in 1974.[28] The group that organized the experiment was chaired by Judge Marvin E. Frankel of the Southern District of New York, who the next year published his influential book denouncing judicial discretion in sentencing.[29] The study asked fifty district judges from the six districts in the Second Circuit (covering New York, Connecticut, and Vermont) to respond to a total of thirty hypothetical cases involving twenty different offenses. Two-thirds of the cases were based on actual presentence reports; nine were further modified to gauge the effect of varying particular characteristics of the offense or the offender; and the last case was entirely made up.

The results of the study were said to show "glaring disparity" among judges both in the decision whether to incarcerate and in the recommended length of imprisonment.[30] "The absence of consensus," the Federal Judicial Center report concluded, "is the norm."[31] The greatest disparity arose over a scenario involving extortionate credit transactions by a union official with no criminal record. The median sentence proposed was ten years' imprisonment, the most lenient sentence was three years, and the most severe was the statutory maximum of twenty years' imprisonment. The study was unable to identify any systematic basis for the sentencing variation, including even individual judges' general propensities to be tough or lenient.[32] Among the particular offense and offender characteristics isolated for analysis, only criminal history proved to have a significant influence on sentencing outcome.[33]

The Federal Judicial Center presented the results of its study in a tabular format that emphasized the degree of variation in recommended sentences. For each case, every possible sentencing combination of fine and imprisonment was listed separately, with the result that no more than two or three judges appeared to agree on the appropriate sentence. Small differences in recommended sentences (say, a $5,000 difference in the amount of the fine, with the same term of imprisonment) appeared to have as much significance as large differences in recommended sentences (say, a five-year gap in recommended prison terms).

The Second Circuit study had major difficulties, both in design and in analysis. First, there is no assurance that any judges, beyond those who helped to organize the study, approached it with the seriousness and deliberation that they would bring to a real case with a real defendant and real victims. The judges were simply mailed the case packets over the course of six weeks, responding with proposed "sentences" by return mail. One still-active district judge who participated in the experiment has asserted that he was not alone in treating the simulation as a "joke" because it was so utterly unlike the actual criminal sentencing process.[34] In addition to the skeletal nature of some of the presentence reports and the lack of face-to-face contact with the defendant, there was no advocacy by defense attorneys, prosecutors, victims, friends, or family.

Second, and quite significantly, the study failed to simulate the *presentencing* procedural history of the case, especially that relating to plea bargaining. Judges were not told the nature of the charges originally lodged against a defendant, what type of plea agreement the defendant had entered into, or any information regarding the prosecution's view of the case. Perhaps most importantly, the scenarios used in the Second Circuit survey reported no information on how the sentences imposed would be reduced through operation of parole and "good time." The study was conducted before federal parole officials adopted and published guidelines to govern their release decisions, and before estimates of the effect of parole policies were routinely provided to judges in presentence reports. Knowing how different judges accounted for this missing information would be essential to assessing the study. One scholar who led a re-analysis of the data of the Second Circuit study has reported that "much of the seeming difference in sentences . . . was simply a function of different understandings as to . . . how long the judge thought the defendant would actually serve."[35]

The other study using hypothetical data that figured prominently in the Senate Report on the Sentencing Reform Act was a sentencing simulation sponsored in 1981 by the U.S. Department of Justice.[36] Like the Second Circuit study conducted nearly a decade earlier, the Department of Justice study was based upon hypothetical presentence reports; sixteen hypothetical cases were presented covering only two offenses, bank robbery and fraud (as opposed to the thirty hypotheticals and twenty offenses used in the Second Circuit study). Rather than conduct the study by mail, the Department of Justice asked each participating judge, in the course of a 90-minute interview, to sentence all sixteen cases, as well as answer questions about sentencing philosophy and other matters.[37] Researchers controlled for the effect of parole by asking the judges to sentence defendants in "real" time.[38]

The results showed substantially more agreement among the judges concerning the decision whether to incarcerate than did the Second Circuit study, but still indicated considerable variation in recommended prison terms.[39] Through complex statistical inference, the authors of the Department of Justice study concluded that nearly half of this variation reflected the effect of the particular offense and offender characteristics built into the hypotheticals, while 21 percent of the variation could be ascribed wholly to "judge effect"—the tendencies of individual judges to be severe or lenient sentencers either generally or for specific crimes.[40] However, a more recent study of *actual sentences* in the pre-Guidelines period in three large, northeastern district courts, which apparently controlled for a greater number of case characteristics, found that "the disparity attributable to differences among judges before the sentencing reforms account[ed] for less than 5 percent of the total variation in sentences." [41]

DESPITE THE LIMITATIONS of simulation studies (and recognizing, as the authors of the Second Circuit study acknowledged, that these limitations probably cause the degree of sentencing variation to be exaggerated),[42] we believe that these studies were constructive. Although the claims of sentencing reformers were exaggerated, disparity in sentencing in the era of unreviewable judicial sentencing discretion did exist. Reform was needed that would permit judges to address this aspect of sentencing (but without neglecting other objectives of criminal justice). Most importantly, the lack of any appellate review of sentencing meant that the federal judiciary itself had no opportunity to examine the sentencing variability that did exist or to provide explanations (if there were explanations) for such variation. Federal appellate courts had no occasion to develop or expound general principles of sentencing justice. Without appellate review or appellate law on sentencing, sentencing judges themselves had little opportunity to refer to common principles or standards for sentencing, to contrast different cases, or to explain differing outcomes in cases that might appear, at least on the surface, similar to one another.

It bears emphasizing, however, that an examination of these early studies and other data from the pre-Guidelines period belies the notion that sentencing in the federal courts was "shameful," "lawless," or "arbitrary." In particular, every study of the *federal courts* in the pre-Guidelines era found that *race* was *not* a significant factor in explaining variation in sentences[43] (though it may be noted that the case mix in federal courts in previous decades did not include a large number of violent crimes, where the influence of race on sentences could arguably be more pronounced). A higher percentage of white offenders were sentenced to prison, but the average sentence imposed was slightly higher for blacks. Hispanic offenders were less often sentenced to prison and received lower sentences than whites or blacks on average, due apparently to their large representation in immigration prosecutions (which generally were treated leniently).[44]

On reflection, it is not surprising that lawyers, sentencing reformers, and members of Congress so readily accepted the more extreme claims of opponents of judicial discretion and the flawed studies that seemed to support these claims. The empirical studies appeared to confirm common knowledge. Virtually all of us have heard accounts featuring a "hanging" judge on the one hand, and a "bleeding heart" judge on the other. These salient anecdotes might be expected to create the perception of wide variability—even if most judges, most of the time, cluster in the middle rather than at either extreme.[45] In fact, review of the empirical studies shows that a significant part of the variation in sentencing outcomes was due to extreme (outlier) sentences by a small percentage of the participating judges, and with a few exceptions, the *same* judges were *not* outliers in all situations.[46]

At the same time that these simulation studies—whatever their limitations—purported to reveal significant disparity, they also provided an important glimpse into how judges reached different sentencing outcomes. Insight into this question had been sorely lacking because judges had never been required to explain their sentencing decisions on the record and sentencing decisions had never been subject to appellate review. The results of the Second Circuit study, for example, showed remarkable agreement among the judges in the ordinal ranking of crimes from least to most serious, but also showed that judges differed in translating these rankings into actual sentences.[47] As a later, in-depth examination of sentencing in white-collar cases concluded, "Judges who talk in similar general terms often come to different judgments, in particular cases, about whether or not to imprison or for how long."[48] Perhaps the most interesting conclusion of the 1981 Department of Justice study, at least in retrospect, is that inter-judge differences in sentencing outcomes "are not random events that occur without rhyme or reason."[49] Rather, such disparities

> are anchored in *patterned differences* regarding such matters as: (a) overall value orientations about the functions of criminal sanction; (b) judgments about the appropriate goal of case-specific sentences; (c) perceptions about the severity and the sentences themselves; (d) predispositions to sentence in a relatively harsh or lenient fashion; and (e) perceptions of the seriousness of particular attributes of a case.[50]

As one of the authors of the Department of Justice study cogently noted, elimination of sentencing disparity among judges cannot be achieved without eliminating disagreement over both the overall goals of criminal sentencing and the appropriate goal of sentencing in the particular case.[51] The federal Sentencing Guidelines cannot and have not eliminated these disagreements; they are designed, rather, to suppress them. Whether they have succeeded in doing so is addressed in the remainder of this chapter.

Have the Guidelines Reduced "Unwarranted Disparity"?

It has proven extremely difficult to design an empirical study that would answer the question whether the Sentencing Guidelines have reduced "unwarranted disparity" in the federal courts. In many studies, two distinct questions have been conflated:

1. Are defendants presently being sentenced in a manner that honestly and consistently applies the Guidelines?
2. Would honest and consistent application of the Guidelines yield a reduction in "unwarranted disparity"?

Current empirical studies are unable to answer even the first of these questions. Moreover, even if there were unequivocal support for the proposition that defendants are now being sentenced more uniformly—that the Guidelines are being applied honestly and consistently and thus are decreasing inter-judge disparity in sentencing—this would not necessarily signify that sentencing is now more consonant with the goal of equality than in the pre-Guidelines era.

The Commission's Analysis

In the Sentencing Reform Act, Congress directed the Sentencing Commission to carry out an evaluation of the Guidelines' effectiveness after their first four years of operation. One of the major concerns of this evaluation was disparity reduction.[52] The Commission conducted its self-evaluation in 1991, concluding that the Guidelines had achieved "significant reductions in disparity and the desired increases in uniformity,"[53] a viewpoint echoed in the assessments offered by some individual Commissioners.[54]

The Commission's major approach to measuring disparity was to compare similar cases from a pre-Guidelines year (1985) and a post-Guidelines period of nearly two years (1989–90). The Commission looked at sentences imposed for four offenses: bank robbery, bank embezzlement, heroin trafficking, and cocaine trafficking. "Bank robbery" was itself broken down into four subgroups based on the criminal history of the offender and on certain characteristics of the offense, while "bank embezzlement" was divided into two such subgroups—making for a total of eight offense/offender categories. The analysis conducted by the Commission compared the range of sentences and the mean sentence for each of these categories under the Guidelines to corresponding data from the pre-Guidelines period. The Commission acknowledged some problems with statistical significance, but claimed to find measurable reductions in disparity under the Guidelines for all eight categories.[55]

In fact, the Commission's confidence in its findings turns out to have been misplaced. The study's methodological shortcomings were summarized in the title of a General Accounting Office review of the Commission's effort: "Central Questions Remain Unanswered."[56] The Commission's sample sizes were extremely small—not more than ninety cases for any of the eight categories, and often many fewer than that. More troubling, the Commission chose not to compare *actual time served in prison,* but *nominal* sentences imposed. Because parole served to reduce the range of time actually served, nominal sentences in the pre-Guidelines era were more dispersed than actual sentences. By the same token, elimination of parole *by itself* reduces the range of nominal sentences imposed to achieve the same real time served. That reform, quite apart from any effect of the Guidelines, can be expected to reduce sentencing variation.[57] As the Commission's own former director of research complained in a review of the Commission's self-evaluation, comparing nominal sentences is "pointless" and "irrelevant" to a comparison of pre- and post-Guidelines disparity.[58] This researcher and others have noted that if the Commission had analyzed *actual* sentences and taken proper account of sample size, it would have found that five of its eight offense/offender groups do not show statistically significant reductions in sentencing variation.[59]

Nor did the Commission attempt to screen out the effect of mandatory minimum sentences that were established for many drug crimes in the Anti-Drug Abuse Acts of 1986 and 1988. Yet these mandatory minimums have the effect of making sentences for these drug offenses more uniform—quite apart from any contribution of the Guidelines themselves.[60] Most remarkably, the Commission eliminated from its calculations all Guidelines cases in which the defendant received a downward departure from the Guidelines range for substantial assistance to authorities.[61] These departures, which allow the sentencing judge to disregard the Guidelines range altogether, unavoidably introduce the possibility of considerable variation among sentences. Moreover, the frequency of such departures varies considerably from judge to judge and judicial district to judicial district.[62] We do well to recall that judges in the pre-Guidelines era took account of a defendant's "cooperation" with authorities;[63] surely this accounted for some part of the variation in pre-Guidelines sentences. It is inexplicable that the Commission would include such variation in its pre-Guidelines measurements of disparity, but exclude all such variation from its post-Guidelines analysis.

The most fundamental flaw in the Commission's 1991 evaluation of disparity, however, was that it categorized the cases only according to factors deemed relevant by the Guidelines. Indeed, the Commission did not even possess data for the latter half of 1990 regarding factors that the Guidelines do not consider relevant.[64] Hence, even if the data presented by the Commission in its evaluation could be said to support fully the Commission's celebratory conclusions, all that these data would really tell us is that the Guidelines were indeed being implemented. As Professor Albert W. Alschuler of the University of Chicago Law School has suggested, rather than showing that the Guidelines have reduced disparity according to some independently legitimate criterion, the Commission's 1991 study demonstrates simply that "the new regime has more consistently applied its own standards."[65]

In this respect, the 1991 report exemplifies a failing common to all disparity studies that rely exclusively on Guidelines-defined categories of criminal behavior: they share the premise that *no unwarranted disparity occurs when defendants are sentenced in accordance with the Guidelines.*[66] These studies assume that the factors taken into account in the Guidelines are warranted, that these are the only warranted factors, that the relative weights given to these factors by the Guidelines are warranted, and hence that "unwarranted disparity" exists if and only if there is deviation from the Guidelines.[67] To anyone who does not accept these assumptions, however, such studies will simultaneously overestimate the extent of arbitrary variation in the pre-Guidelines era, and fail even to recognize the arbitrariness that exists under the Guidelines regime.

Consider, for instance, a factor that the Guidelines treat as largely irrelevant to the sentencing decision: the age of the offender.[68] Under the Commission's approach to measuring unwarranted disparity, age would not be considered in selecting "comparable" pre- and post-Guidelines cases.[69] But let us imagine, not unreasonably, that the offender's age was important to many federal trial judges in their pre-Guidelines sentencing decisions, with a defendant's youth often militating in favor of a less severe sentence. If we examine, as the Commission did, a group of pre-Guidelines sentences defined only by the Guidelines criteria of criminal conduct and criminal history, we might find quite a wide range of variation. But once we include the offender's age as a factor, we might find that the sentences cluster into smaller subgroups in which the variation is less than in the larger, Guidelines-defined case groups. By leaving out factors that may have been applied with some consistency in pre-Guidelines sentencing decisions, measurements based on the Guidelines' own categories overstate the degree of *unprincipled* variation (or "unwarranted disparity") that was actually present in pre-Guidelines sentencing patterns. At the same time, these measurements ignore what many would consider to be sources of unprincipled uniformity under the Guidelines—for example, the fact that defendants who have committed the same crime, but who are of different ages, are subject to the same sentence. Any increased uniformity revealed by such studies is properly termed a reduction in "unwarranted disparity" only under the assumption that taking age into account is, indeed, "unwarranted."

Evidence of Inconsistent Guidelines Application

Even on its own terms—that is, defining as "unwarranted disparity" only that variation that comes from inconsistent application of the Guidelines themselves—the Commission's 1991 self-evaluation is challenged by other studies suggesting that the new regime has not even applied *its own standards* consistently. In an exhaustive study of sentencing practices in four judicial districts within the Eighth Circuit, Judge Gerald Heaney found wide variations among the districts in applying key Guidelines rules, including those relating to "acceptance of responsibility" and "substantial assistance" to authorities. Districts also varied greatly in within-range sentencing practices—some tending to sentence at the top of Guidelines ranges, and others sentencing at the bottom. Judge Heaney also found significant evidence of a new source of hidden disparity: variation among the four districts in the proportion of cases in which defendants receive unacknowledged below-Guidelines sentences. Much of this variation, he found, was due to the fact that plea bargaining and charging practices varied greatly among the four U.S. Attorneys' offices in the Eighth Circuit.[70]

A review of statistics in the Commission's annual reports indicates that the practices in the Eighth Circuit are not unique.[71] Gross patterns of inter-district variation in sentencing practices persist year after year.[72] Table 2 shows the variation among districts in the percentage of convicted defendants who received a downward departure for substantial assistance to the government. In 1991, for instance, departures on this ground were made in about 12 percent of cases nationwide. The use of such motions varied considerably, however, from less than 3 percent in some districts (Maine, the Western District of Kentucky, the Western District of Michigan, the Western District of Arkansas, and the Eastern District of Oklahoma) to one district in which a substantial assistance motion was granted in approximately 40 percent of all sentencings (the Eastern District of Pennsylvania).[73] By 1994, the nationwide use of substantial assistance departures had increased significantly, to nearly 20 percent of all cases.[74] Moreover, as shown by the standard deviations in table 2, the significant variation across districts in the use of substantial assistance departures has not subsided, and in fact has slightly increased, over time.[75] These sorts of regional disparities, which sentencing reformers documented in the pre-Guidelines regime and which were a major impetus to the massive restructuring of federal sentencing law,[76] thus

TABLE 2. **Percentage of Cases with Departure for Substantial Assistance**

	Mean (across all Districts)	Range	Standard Deviation
1990	7.5	n.a.	n.a.
1991	11.9	1.2–41	7.6
1992	15.1	4.0–48.8	8.5
1993	16.9	0.7–50.8	9.4
1994	19.5	3.9–49.3	9.3
1995	19.7	0–54.2	9.8
1996	19.2	4.4–47.5[a]	9.4[b]

Source: 1997b, 41–43. Data for each year before 1996 are drawn from the United States Sentencing Commission's Annual Reports for those years. 1990 Annual Report, tbl. U (by circuit only); 1991 Annual Report, tbl. 56; 1992 Annual Report, tbl. 50; 1993 Annual Report, tbl. 66; 1994 Annual Report, tbl. 33, at 831; 1995 Annual Report, tbl. 31. Data for 1996 are from U.S.S.C. 1997b, 41–43.

a. For the year 1996 we have excluded the District of the Northern Mariana Islands. That District had a departure rate of more than 85 percent. It had only 14 sentencings in 1996; in twelve of these, there was a downward departure for substantial assistance. The next highest departure rate for substantial assistance in 1996 was in the Eastern District of Pennsylvania (47.5 percent). The departure rate in previous years in District of the Northern Mariana Islands varied between 0 percent and 50 percent.

b. If the District of the Northern Mariana Islands is included in the 1996 data, the standard deviation for 1996 grows to 11.6 percent. (This particular District is included in the data for previous years, with little or no effect, however, on the standard deviation for those years.)

remain quite significant in a regime of supposedly uniform, nationwide sentencing standards.

Some of the variation in use of substantial assistance motions may be attributable to underlying differences in the types of cases in each district. Still, it bears noting that the magnitude of variation is large even in districts that one might expect to be quite similar. Consider a comparison between two districts consisting of a major northeastern city and its surrounding areas—the Southern District of New York (which includes Manhattan, The Bronx, Westchester County, and other northerly suburbs) and the Eastern District of Pennsylvania (which includes Philadelphia and its environs). In 1995, the substantial assistance departure rate for the Southern District of New York was 19.7 percent, right at the national average. Yet for the Eastern District of Pennsylvania, the rate was more than twice as high, at 42 percent.[77] This inter-district gap has persisted for years.[78] At the same time, another northeastern district containing several urban pockets, the District of Connecticut, has generally reported a rate of less than 10 percent for substantial assistance departures.[79]

While it would be tempting to conclude that inter-district inconsistencies in Guidelines application are entirely the result of the remaining sources of discretion in our sentencing system—most notably, the exercise of prosecutorial discretion—other evidence suggests that at least part of the problem lies with the Guidelines themselves. Portions of the Guidelines are inordinately difficult to apply uniformly because of their abstractness, complexity, and ambiguity.[80] We discuss both of these sources of sentencing disparity—prosecutorial discretion and variable application of the Guidelines—in the final two sections of this chapter.

Measuring Inter-Judge Disparity

In 1992, Professor Joel Waldfogel, a young economist at Yale, published a study using an elegant method of measuring disparity that, at least on its face, avoids the fundamental problem that we identified with the Commission's 1991 report. His study assumed nothing about which factors constitute "principled" bases for distinguishing among defendants at sentencing. The study thus sidestepped the thorny and contentious issues relating to the proper objectives of criminal punishment, the efficacy of various punishments, and the considerations that are proper or improper in criminal sentencing.[81]

Professor Waldfogel used a definition of sentencing disparity that measured neither gross, inter-district variation in criminal sentences nor variation according to the standards of the Guidelines themselves. Instead, he sought to isolate and measure the disparity that could be attributed to the identity of sentencing judges—that is, inter-judge sentencing variation. Rather than looking at different judges' sentences for "similar" offenses (which always raises the question, what is similar?), Waldfogel examined the average sentences of individual judges within a particular federal judicial district and asked whether there was more variability in these averages before or after implementation of the Guidelines.

As is so often true in economic analysis, the value of Waldfogel's measure of disparity depends on the accuracy of the assumptions that underlie it. *Assuming* that the judges within each district carry equivalent caseloads, and *assuming* that the sentencing inclinations of an individual judge are not offsetting, then comparing judges' average sentences is a good way to gauge the amount of inter-judge sentencing disparity. With respect to the first assumption, it appears now to be the norm in the federal system to assign cases randomly, though it is not clear to what extent this norm was routinely honored in past years.[82] Although we have not sought to test the accuracy of the second assumption, we note that the simulation studies conducted in the 1970s suggest that few judges were systematically lenient or harsh—that is, many judges tended to be relatively lenient in some cases, and relatively harsh in others.[83] This raises the possibility that comparing each judge's average sentence masks considerable variability within each set of sentences. Furthermore, the extent of this concealed disparity may well differ in the pre- and post-Guidelines regimes.

Still, Waldfogel's method is an especially appropriate way to measure the success of the federal Sentencing Guidelines on their own terms. The overriding objective of the Sentencing Reform Act was to reduce the discretion of individual judges in criminal sentencing. Reducing judicial discretion *means* reducing the role of the judge as an autonomous actor in the sentencing process. Waldfogel's approach to isolating inter-judge "disparity" permits at least a preliminary measurement of the extent to which the Guidelines have been successful in taking the judge out of the decisional process in criminal sentencing.

Waldfogel was able to derive judicial mean deviations for only three districts—the Southern District of New York, the Northern District of California, and the District of Connecticut. This limitation was due to his method of research: Waldfogel had to obtain his data by first-hand research in the Clerk's Office of each of the three districts, because the Sentencing Commission and the Administrative Office of the United States Courts have thus far refused to provide outside researchers with any data that contain judge-codes, which is necessary for more extensive research of inter-judge disparity.[84]

Despite these limitations, Waldfogel's results are intriguing. He discovered that in the years 1984 through 1987 (that is, prior to the Sentencing Guidelines), the mean deviation of judges' sentences around their district average was 4.2 months in Connecticut, 5.8 months in the Southern District of New York, and 4.2 months in the Northern District of California. In the years 1988 through 1990 (that is, *after* the Sentencing Guidelines went into effect), the mean deviation stayed approximately the same in the Northern District of California (at 4.4 months) but approximately doubled to 9.9 months in Connecticut and to 10.4 months in the Southern District of New York.[85] That is, Waldfogel's data suggest that inter-judge disparity (as he measured it) has actually increased under the Guidelines. A later, similar study by another researcher examined the Southern District of New York, the Eastern District of New York, and the Eastern District of Pennsylvania and concluded that inter-judge disparity (which was "very low" to begin with) had been "negligibly" reduced under the Guidelines.[86]

These results are surprising. One would expect that the Sentencing Guidelines (and concomitant statutory minimum sentences) would result in less inter-judge sentencing dispersion, inasmuch as they reduce the possibility of relatively lenient sentences. In recent years we have examined more extensive sentencing data than was available to Waldfogel. In 1993, the Sentencing Commission provided us some data that included a code for each judge (but not the name or other personal identifier for any judge) in *each* of the nation's nearly one hundred federal judicial districts. We ultimately included only forty-three of these districts in our analysis; like Waldfogel, we looked only at judges who sentenced at least ten cases in both the pre- and post-Guidelines eras, and we excluded districts with fewer than four such judges in order to avoid any possibility of identifying individual judges. Still, our data allowed for a broader application of Waldfogel's approach.[87] The results of this initial study were more in line with expectations than were Waldfogel's, but no more conclusive. We found that mean judicial deviation around the average district sentence had actually decreased in twenty-seven of the forty-three districts, had stayed the same in eight districts, and had increased in only eight districts. That is, our results suggested that, using the Waldfogel measure, there was *less* inter-judge disparity under the Guidelines in most districts.[88] Unfortunately, our sample was limited to cases involving certain white-collar crimes. Accordingly, it may not have been representative of all federal criminal sentencing and it was too small to ascribe statistical significance to our results. At this writing, we are part of a larger research study examining an even broader data set of sentencing outcomes since the Guidelines went into effect.[89] Until that study is completed, we are not in a position to judge whether Professor Waldfogel's intriguing and counterintuitive suggestion—that inter-judge disparity may have *increased* under the Guidelines—will be borne out.

Most importantly, however, even if we could definitively establish that the Guidelines have reduced inter-judge sentencing dispersion, this would not mean that the sentencing outcomes under the Guidelines are more "warranted" than the sentencing outcomes in the discretionary era. Any decrease in inter-judge sentencing variation caused by adherence to the Guidelines is only as principled as the set of choices reflected in the Guidelines themselves.

To take age as an example again, Waldfogel's measure of pre-Guidelines sentencing variation—the deviation of a particular judge's sentences from the district average—would reflect the variation caused by the fact that some judges, but not all judges, treated age as a significant mitigating factor in certain cases. In the post-Guidelines era, on the other hand, where all judges are prohibited from departing from the

Guidelines range on the basis of youth, there should be much less deviation resulting from age considerations. But whether this reduction in inter-judge disparity is *desirable* still depends on whether one accepts age as a relevant factor in sentencing. If one thinks that youth *is* an important mitigating factor in some cases, then one might prefer a set of outcomes in which at least some judges consider youth to a set of outcomes where no judge is permitted to consider youth. The prohibition on consideration of age may have replaced "unwarranted disparity" with "unwarranted uniformity."

A similar analysis could be applied to a factor that the Guidelines do strongly take into account, but that played a less significant role, on average, in sentencing in the pre-Guidelines era. The Guidelines, for instance, treat the quantity of drugs involved in an offense as a critical determinant.[90] Under this quantity-driven approach, the subset of offenders who are accountable at sentencing for trafficking in a given amount of drugs will be sentenced more uniformly under the Guidelines than they would have been in the discretionary era; using Waldfogel's measure, there will be less inter-judge disparity. Yet the primacy given to quantity under the Guidelines may group together cases in ways that mask morally and penologically significant differences between offenders—differences that may have been more fully captured in the variable pattern of pre-Guidelines sentencing. Measures of overall inter-judge disparity do not address or illuminate the extent to which greater uniformity is purchased at an unacceptable price. Inter-judge disparity could be reduced to zero, of course, if all judges gave exactly the same sentence in every case.

Because of their fixation on reducing sentencing disparity, reformers assumed that less inter-judge variation is *necessarily* better than more variation. We would agree, *ceteris paribus.* In our view, however, inter-judge uniformity is *worse* than inter-judge disparity if the uniformity comes at the price of prohibiting consideration of a morally relevant factor in sentencing or giving too much weight to a factor that is often not morally relevant. Sentencing *some people* justly is better than sentencing *no one* justly.

The Arbitrariness of Uniformity

We have argued that decreases in sentencing disparity, either within certain Guidelines-defined categories of criminal behavior or across judges for all cases, do not necessarily represent decreases in unprincipled or otherwise unwarranted disparity. We readily concede that readers who believe that the Sentencing Guidelines *do* sentence people justly—that is, that they invariably take into account morally relevant factors and assign the appropriate weight to each—will not be moved by this argument. We note, however, that many commentators have complained that the Guidelines' substantive content contributes to arbitrary uniformity in two ways.

First, the Guidelines' calculus focuses excessively on quantifiable measures of harm. Second, this calculus adopts a narrow conception of the offender characteristics that are relevant to sentencing. Professor Albert W. Alschuler, a thoughtful critic of the Guidelines, stresses the first of these problems in an article subtitled "A Plea for Less Aggregation."[91] Professor Stephen J. Schulhofer, an equally thoughtful supporter of mandatory sentencing guidelines and a consultant to the Sentencing Commission, stresses the second of these problems in his article subtitled "The Problem Is Uniformity, Not Disparity."[92] Alschuler and Schulhofer recognize both problems and note that they are interrelated.[93] By weighing some factors (most especially quantity of harm) so heavily, the Guidelines necessarily give less weight to other factors, especially at the higher ranges of the Sentencing Table. These relatively marginalized factors include personal characteristics of the offender, role in the offense, and prospects (or lack of prospects) for rehabilitation.

Remarkably, the Sentencing Commission itself has recognized that uniformity is not always a positive value in criminal sentencing. In 1991, the Commission issued a report that was harshly critical of *statutory* mandatory minimum penalties—sentencing minimums set by Congress for particular federal crimes. In the Commission's own words, such mandatory minimums cause "unwarranted disparity in sentencing" of similar offenders because they are not consistently applied.[94] At the same time, the Commission complained, "offenders seemingly not similar nonetheless receive similar sentences."[95] The Commission further argued that mandatory minimums "transfer sentencing power from the court to the prosecutor" and negate "honesty and truth in sentencing" because plea bargaining around the statutory minimums is "neither open to public review nor generally reviewable by the courts."[96] These complaints are equally true of the Guidelines themselves.[97]

The Commission's opposition to mandatory minimum penalties set by Congress has placed it on common ground with federal trial judges, thereby deflecting criticism toward Congress that might otherwise be focused on the Commission and its Guidelines. Yet the Commission, and indeed some sentencing reformers,[98] have not acknowledged the extent to which the Sentencing Guidelines suffer from the same inflexibility associated with the mandatory minimums set by Congress. The two phenomena (mandatory statutory minimums and mandatory Guidelines ranges) are different manifestations of the same "counter-reformation"[99] against discretionary sentences. Mandatory sentences and mandatory sentencing guidelines are both attempts to replace discretionary sentencing with determinate sentencing, both reflect a restrictive just-deserts sentencing philosophy, and both have ratcheted up the severity of criminal punishment. As we noted in chapter 1, the collapse of the rehabilitative ideal and a concern with inequality in sentencing in the 1970s led to increased demands for certainty and determinacy in punishment. In some jurisdictions, the result was sentencing guidelines; in others, determinate statutory sentences; in still others, abolition of parole; and often, as in the federal criminal justice system, all of these together.[100]

Thus understood, the federal Sentencing Guidelines are not an *alternative* to mandatory sentencing, as the Commission and many sentencing reformers insist, but a particularly complex *form* of mandatory sentencing. Instead of prescribing a mandatory minimum sentence for a particular statutorily defined crime, as Congress might do,[101] the Sentencing Commission prescribes a mandatory minimum sentence (i.e., the bottom of the sentencing range) for every Guidelines-defined "crime."[102] These Guidelines-defined offenses are, of course, more narrowly delineated than statutory crimes. One Guidelines-defined crime applies to bank robbers who stole $20,000, played a "minor" role in the offense, and are in Criminal History Category I; another to bank robbers who stole $20,000, played a "minimal" role, and are in Criminal History Category III, etc. In principle and structure, however, the two forms of mandatory sentence differ only in their specificity. Where no substantial assistance motion has been made and the case presented is in the "heartland," the judge in a Guidelines case has no authority to depart from the prescribed sentencing range.

Whichever of these forms a mandatory sentence takes, its application is to some extent inherently arbitrary. The arbitrariness of most statutorily mandated sentences is apparent on their face: all defendants, whatever their personal circumstances and whatever the circumstances of their crimes, are subject to the same minimum amount of punishment. If this punishment is warranted for one defendant (perhaps the stereotypical offender whom we may assume the legislature had in mind), it must be arbitrary and hence "unwarranted" for any defendant who differs from the stereotypical offender on morally cognizable grounds. The arbitrariness of a more complex mandatory scheme like the Sentencing Guidelines is perhaps not as great or as immediately apparent. The Guidelines do distinguish among defendants with respect to certain assertedly relevant factors. But the problem (again) is that if applying these distinguishing factors (and the relative weights assigned to them) yields the right sentence for one defendant, it will fail to yield the right sentence for any defendant who differs from the first in relevant ways not factored into the Guidelines.

Studies of sentencing disparity that accept the sentencing choices made by Congress and by the Sentencing Commission necessarily accept the arbitrariness implicit in these choices. For instance, the Guidelines provide that bank embezzlement of less than $10,000 shall have a Base Offense Level of eight, while bank robbery of less than $10,000 shall have a Base Offense Level of twenty. This difference in Offense Level leads to a sentencing range roughly *eight times* more severe for robbery than for embezzlement.[103] Is this degree of disparity warranted? Perhaps so—but the Sentencing Guidelines cannot and do not answer this question, and, as we have suggested in chapter 2, the Sentencing Commission has never attempted to answer any such question. The details of the Guidelines are a series of unexplained choices made by the Sentencing Commission—the consequences of which are borne by society at large and by the federal criminal justice system in particular.

An especially significant example of disparity resulting from arbitrary sentencing rules is examined in a December 1993 empirical analysis sponsored by the Department of Justice's Bureau of Justice Statistics. The study sought to determine whether variations in the sentencing of offenders in different racial and ethnic groups had been reduced or increased in the Guidelines era.[104] Examining both the pre-Guidelines simulation studies and pre-Guidelines empirical studies, the authors found that, prior to the Guidelines, blacks, whites, and Hispanics received similar sentences, on average, in the federal courts.[105] For Guidelines cases in 1989 and 1990, on the other hand, there were "substantial aggregate differences in sentences imposed on white, black, and Hispanic offenders." Whereas 72 percent of whites were sent to prison, the percentage of blacks was seventy-eight, and the percentage of Hispanics was eighty-five. Moreover, blacks received much longer prison sentences (41 percent longer) than did whites and Hispanics.[106]

Does this mean that there is now "racial disparity" in federal sentencing? The answer is "no" *if* we accept the choices that Congress and the Sentencing Commission have made regarding the factors relevant to criminal sentencing. In the words of the report:

> Nearly all of the aggregate differences among sentences for whites, blacks, and Hispanics during this period can be attributed to characteristics of offenses and offenders that current law and sentencing guidelines establish as legitimate considerations in sentencing decisions.[107]

The main reason that the sentences of blacks were longer than those of whites was the greater representation of blacks in crack cocaine prosecutions. In accordance with statutory mandatory minimum laws and Sentencing Guidelines that build upon those minimums, the average sentences imposed for crack cocaine offenses was twice as long as for offenses involving powdered cocaine.[108] Controlling for statutory mandatory sentences, and controlling for factors that are significant determinants of sentences under the Guidelines—such as criminal record and the quantity of drugs or other harm involved in the case—race was not a factor in sentencing.[109]

Yet the factors that Congress and the Sentencing Commission have insisted be significant determinants of sentences are themselves the product of *choices*—exercises of discretion, if you will—that may be as arbitrary as any choice made by a judge unconstrained by statutory or regulatory sentencing rules. With respect to sentencing for drug offenses, both Congress and the Sentencing Commission have chosen to require significant increases in the severity of punishment based on factors that tend to apply less often to white defendants than to black and Hispanic defendants. Most significantly, the statutory distinction between crack cocaine and powdered cocaine means that the same mandatory minimum penalty applicable to crack cocaine applies to 100 times that amount of powdered cocaine.[110] As the 1993 report for the Bureau of Justice Statistics explained, this statutory distinction can be viewed as a source of "racial disparity" in sentencing: if this difference in the treatment of crack cocaine did not exist, the differential between sentences for blacks and whites in the Guidelines era would be nearly halved, from 41 percent to 22 percent.[111]

The vast difference between crack cocaine and powdered cocaine for sentencing purposes is not solely due to statutory requirements. The Sentencing Commission has built upon *all* mandatory minimum penalties so that the Guidelines require far more than the statutory minimum in many cases. The 1993 report for the Bureau of Justice Statistics found that even if Congress took no action, the Sentencing Commission itself could significantly reduce the overall black/white sentencing disparity by revising its Guidelines to allow statutory mandatory minimums to trump the Guidelines rather than to act as a floor upon which higher Guidelines penalties are built.[112]

In sum, to be sentenced under the federal Sentencing Guidelines is not necessarily to be sentenced nonarbitrarily. Arbitrariness is built into the Guidelines themselves,[113] and indeed is inevitable in any system of mandatory sentencing rules. Applying the same objective, mechanical system uniformly to all cases is simply an objective, mechanical way of dispensing the arbitrariness that is inherent in the system. An *ex ante* set of sentencing instructions can spread only a relatively coarse grid over the infinitely complex field of human behavior. Ultimately, the arbitrarily uniform sentences it seeks to ensure—however successfully or unsuccessfully—stand at odds with the principle of equality that the sentencing reformers hoped to vindicate.

Discretion under the Sentencing Guidelines

The Guidelines regime contains many sources of sentencing disparity, both old and new, both visible and hidden. The complexity of the Guidelines, designed to repress the exercise of subjective judgment, has actually permitted significant and probably unavoidable variation in application. And although *judges* have less formal authority over criminal sentences than they did in the era of indeterminate sentencing, the Guidelines have enhanced the discretionary authority of *others* in the sentencing process. In this respect, practice under the Guidelines suggests the aptness of the "toothpaste tube" metaphor: by squeezing discretion out of the judicial domain, the Guidelines have required it to expand elsewhere, shifting the locus, but not necessarily the quantity, of disparity. Moreover, many of the present sources of disparate treatment, camouflaged and concealed, are less consonant with our constitutional values than the open and unabashed exercise of judicial discretion of the old order.

Judges, Defense Counsel, and Probation Officers

Judges

As the preceding discussion suggests, despite the effort of the Sentencing Commission to draft detailed and exhaustive sentencing rules, judges still retain some sentencing discretion. And differences among judges in the exercise of this discretion may result in disparity under the Guidelines, just as the exercise of discretion resulted in disparity in the pre-Guidelines era.

Two forms of judicial discretion—and hence, two sources of disparity resulting from exercise of the judicial function—are possible in the Guidelines era. We might call these two forms of discretion "open" and "hidden." Open discretion is authorized discretion: Judges openly exercise discretion whenever the Guidelines authorize the judge to make a value judgment (rather than simply a factual finding) in the course of sentencing. For instance, the Guidelines explicitly require judges to exercise discretion in setting the precise sentence within a particular Guidelines range. The Guidelines also contemplate that judges have discretion to decide not to depart even though there may be a basis for departure; it is for this reason that the federal courts of appeals have refused to review a judge's decision not to depart.[114] Finally, where there *is* a lawful basis for departure, judges face few if any limits on the magnitude of departure permitted. Although the Sentencing Reform Act itself requires that all departures be "reasonable," neither the Commission nor the federal courts of appeals have put much effort into placing constraints on the amount by which a judge may depart. By and large, the Guidelines only govern the *bases* for departure, not the *amount* of departure.[115]

A second type of judicial discretion is seldom acknowledged but inevitably occurs, to a greater or lesser extent, even in a system formally governed by a set of mechanical rules designed to achieve uniformity of outcomes. The exercise of "hidden" discretion under the Guidelines derives from the inevitable discretionary judgment that accompanies the application of rules by human beings. Put another way, there is always some "give" in the application of rules. For instance, even where the Guidelines carefully and explicitly make a distinction (between "minor" and "minimal" roles in the offense, for instance), different judges examining the same set of facts may in good faith arrive at different conclusions regarding the appropriate label to attach. Moreover, given that some indeterminacy is inevitable when rules are applied, judges (like other rule interpreters) may deliberately shape fact-finding and rule application so as to exercise what amounts to unauthorized discretion.

Judges will, of course, vary in the manner in which they exercise both open and hidden discretion. With respect to open discretion, some judges will tend to sentence at the high end of the sentencing range, others at the low end, and still others studiously in the middle. Some judges will search for grounds to depart, while others will be disposed to avoid departure (and thus avoid a ground for reversal). Some judges will take the occasion of an authorized basis for departure to exercise wide discretion, essentially jettisoning the Guidelines, while others will gauge the magnitude of departure according to the "structure and theory" of the Guidelines.[116] Finally, with respect to the exercise of hidden discretion, judges will certainly differ in the extent to which they exploit their fact-finding authority to shift the sentencing range in one direction or another. The anonymous judge quoted in the previous chapter, who characterized judicial practice under the Guidelines as "plotting and scheming, bending and twisting . . . to achieve a just result,"[117] no doubt speaks for some judges, even though other judges would never take such actions nor characterize their decisionmaking in this manner.

Defense Counsel

Another source of continuing sentencing disparity results from variation among defense counsel, particularly in their handling of Guidelines issues. It is true, of course, that in the pre-Guidelines regime the competence of defense counsel inevitably influenced whether defendants were convicted. But, because of the discretion afforded to judges at sentencing, the ability of counsel was less significant at this stage of the proceedings. In the complex Guidelines system, where sentencing outcomes rest largely on one's ability to understand the intricate calculus and to influence prosecutors and probation officers, "Guidelines competence" is vitally important.[118]

Studies have found significant variation in Guidelines competence among defense attorneys. One study showed that while federal public defenders generally know the Guidelines more thoroughly than their prosecutorial adversaries, this situation is reversed in some districts, with a visible impact on sentencing outcomes.[119] Private attorneys typically understand the Guidelines less thoroughly than do public defenders, sometimes hardly at all. Again, the extent of this gap varies from district to district, and from lawyer to lawyer.[120]

Probation Officers

In the Guidelines regime, probation officers also play a crucial role, as we have described in chapter 3. Their fact-finding function has been transformed and enhanced, and now they also have lawyer-like functions—interpreting and applying the law (i.e., relevant Guidelines provisions) to the facts as they find them. The varying capabilities, approaches, and sensibilities of probation officers unavoidably introduce a source of disparity into Guidelines sentencing.

While the probation officer performed a reportorial function before the enactment of the Guidelines,[121] the nature of this function has changed and its significance has increased in the new sentencing system. Instead of providing the judge with two versions of the offense (that of the prosecution and that of the defense), the presentence report now contains only one version—in theory, that of the probation officer.

Rather than simply advising the court of potentially relevant information, the presentence report is now the starting point of what amounts to an adjudicatory process, at the end of which the sentencing judge will render formal findings of fact that translate into sentencing requirements under the Guidelines.[122]

In undertaking this investigatory function, the probation officer necessarily exercises judgment. Of critical importance is the extent to which a probation officer goes beyond the prosecutor's initial offer of information, by independently investigating the factual descriptions that go into presentence reports. Anecdotal accounts[123] and a recent empirical study[124] suggest that the amount of independent fact-finding varies from district to district, officer to officer, and case to case. If probation officers are not disposed to engage in a thorough search for relevant information, their passivity will necessarily reinforce the control of prosecutors over sentencing. Yet, as we have suggested in the previous chapter, the reliability of an "independent" investigation, dependent as it is on law-enforcement reports, may itself be suspect.[125]

The second, and arguably the more significant, change in the probation officer's sentencing role is the addition of a legal, or legalistic, function—initial calculation of the Guidelines sentence.[126] Although judges are not required to accept the probation officer's calculation, it becomes a focus of the sentencing hearing and is accorded presumptive weight by many judges. But probation officers do not share a single, consistent interpretation of the Guidelines any more than do judges. Although Guidelines application is largely a mechanical function, the very generation of Guidelines calculations introduces another variable element into the sentencing process. A study by two researchers for the Federal Judicial Center indicates that probation officers can, and do, interpret the same Guidelines provisions in vastly different ways.[127] In 1991, Pamela B. Lawrence and Paul J. Hofer asked a nationwide, randomly selected sample of federal probation officers to interpret the "relevant conduct" rules (see appendix B) in a hypothetical but typical drug distribution case. For each of the three hypothetical defendants, the resulting Offense Level varied greatly. For one defendant, no single Offense Level was assigned by a majority of probation officers, with the Levels assigned ranging from 16 (by ten officers) to 32 (by three officers); the most frequent response was Offense Level 20 (by seventeen officers).[128]

One of the authors of the study asserts that a subsequent revision of the relevant conduct guideline (effective in November 1992) would "help prevent the most egregious error of application uncovered" in the study, but notes the "sobering fact" that "[a] significant number of defendants have been sentenced under an interpretation of the relevant conduct guideline that the Commission says is incorrect."[129]

Prosecutorial Discretion

While judges, defense attorneys, and probation officers are readily identifiable sources of continuing discretion in sentencing, critics of the Guidelines have focused primarily on the sentencing disparity said to result from the exercise of prosecutorial discretion. The consensus of these critics is that, while prosecutors have always had considerable discretion to affect sentencing in the federal system, they now have much more.[130] We would state the matter differently: prosecutorial discretion is now greater *relative* to judicial discretion in criminal sentencing. Both the Sentencing Commission and the Department of Justice have sought to constrain the scope of prosecutorial discretion in the Guidelines era, as we describe in detail below. Prosecutors nonetheless exercise significant influence over criminal sentences, as both Guidelines supporters[131] and more agnostic observers[132] have recognized.

The Nature of Prosecutorial Discretion

Prosecutors exercise sentencing discretion under the Guidelines at three critical points: in deciding upon a charge, in entering into plea agreements, and in filing motions for downward departures based on substantial assistance to law enforcement authorities.[133] Prosecutorial control over charge selection and substantial-assistance motions may, in turn, become a bargaining chip in the plea-bargaining process. Plea bargaining is absolutely crucial to sentencing outcomes in the federal courts. Roughly 90 percent of all convictions are the result of guilty pleas, and the great majority of these guilty pleas are the result of plea agreements between the defense and the prosecution. The proportion of convictions obtained by guilty plea in the federal courts has risen during the Guidelines era—from approximately 87 percent in 1986 and 1987, to 90 percent in 1994 and 92 percent in 1995.[134]

Each guilty plea is in some sense unique; charging decisions and plea-negotiations are, by their very nature, case-specific. One case may involve powerful evidence of guilt, a creative and energetic prosecutor, a busy or underpaid defense attorney, an unrepentant defendant, and a relatively empty docket. Another case may involve time-consuming but equivocal evidence, an overworked prosecutor, an imaginative and skillful defense attorney, a remorseful defendant, and a crowded docket.

The two cases may, in the words of the Sentencing Guidelines, involve the same "actual offense behavior,"[135] but the parties will be disposed to negotiate to very different outcomes.

Of course, prosecutors prior to the Guidelines also exercised discretion in charging, plea bargaining, and sentencing recommendations, but the exercise of prosecutorial discretion before the Guidelines seldom determined the sentence that would be imposed by the judge (except where the prosecutor agreed not to prosecute at all). The most prevalent form of plea bargaining in federal courts was charge bargaining,[136] in which the prosecutor agreed not to bring—or to drop—certain charges in return for a defendant's plea of guilty to others. That is, in most guilty-plea cases, the defendant would plead guilty to one or more counts of an indictment, and the prosecutor would move to dismiss the remaining counts. Or, where no indictment preceded the guilty plea, the prosecutor would agree not to bring other potential charges against the defendant. The reduction in charges was of value to the defendant both because it reduced the statutory maximum sentence that he faced and because it was a clear signal from the prosecutor to the judge that the defendant had saved judicial and prosecutorial resources and had, at least in part, accepted responsibility for his crimes. Where the defendant, in addition to pleading guilty, cooperated with the prosecution by providing assistance in the investigation or prosecution of others, one or both of the parties would bring this to the attention of the sentencing judge. Prosecutorial comment on the defendant's cooperation was another signal from the prosecutor to the judge that the government believed the defendant deserved a "reward" in the form of a reduced sentence.

Sometimes plea agreements resulted in more than implicit signals to the judge; at times prosecutors actually recommended that the defendant receive a long prison sentence, or no prison sentence, or a relatively short sentence. But, always, the judge retained full discretion to reject or ignore any such prosecutorial recommendations.[137] The Federal Rules of Criminal Procedure do provide a mechanism by which the parties may propose a binding sentence to the judge,[138] but the judge has always been free to reject the proposed sentence; in any event, such "binding" plea proposals were virtually unheard-of in many districts.[139] Put simply, federal judges were extremely reluctant to accept this form of plea precisely because to do so would suggest the transfer of sentencing authority from the judge to the prosecutor. It was, of course, the *judge's* great control over sentencing (within statutory limits) that led Judge

Marvin E. Frankel and other reformers to insist on binding sentencing guidelines, in order to replace individual judicial discretion with administratively promulgated sentencing rules.

From the outset, the United States Sentencing Commission was fully aware of the existence and nature of plea bargaining in the federal courts, and it understood that binding sentencing rules could have the effect of simply transferring discretionary power from judges to prosecutors. It was clear that sentencing rules tying the defendant's sentence to the charges to which he pled guilty would permit prosecutors to exercise increased control over the final sentence. Charge bargaining, a well-established practice in the federal courts, would become, for all intents and purposes, sentence bargaining—something the federal courts had rarely countenanced, and something not contemplated by the Sentencing Reform Act. That statute was intended to transfer control over federal sentencing to the Sentencing Commission it created, not to the Department of Justice. Indeed, this was a major reason why the Sentencing Commission adopted a strong "real offense" approach in its sentencing rules.[140] If the defendant's sentence is dependent not on the crime of conviction, but on the *actual offense* committed, then, the Commission apparently believed, prosecutors could not obtain control over sentencing through the process of charge bargaining.[141]

The Commission clearly understood that even limiting the significance of charge bargaining would not necessarily keep control over sentencing out of the hands of prosecutors. It is, after all, prosecutors—not the Sentencing Commission or the sentencing judges—who possess information about the defendant's "real offense." If mandatory real-offense sentencing reduces the significance of charge bargaining, what is to prevent prosecutors and defense attorneys from bargaining over the defendant's "real offense"? That is, what is to prevent plea bargaining over Guidelines characterizations and computations? This phenomenon of "fact bargaining," as it has come to be termed, was virtually unknown in the pre-Guidelines era.[142]

Recognizing the potential for "fact bargaining," the Commission attempted to avoid the problem by fiat—that is, by proscribing plea agreements that do not reflect the defendant's "real offense." The Commission's Policy Statements on plea bargaining, set forth in chapter 6 of the Guidelines Manual, seem to direct judges not to accept plea bargains that would alter the defendant's sentence as computed under the Guidelines. One rule expressly prohibits the sentencing judge from accepting a plea agreement that includes dismissal of any charges, unless "the court determines . . . that the remaining charges adequately reflect the seriousness of the *actual* offense behavior" and "will not undermine" the Sentencing Guidelines.[143] A second rule provides that, if a plea agreement includes a stipulation of facts relevant to sentencing, the stipulation must "set forth the relevant facts and circumstances of the *actual* offense conduct and offender characteristics" and "not contain misleading facts."[144] Moreover, a judge may not accept a plea agreement with recommendations, calculations, or stipulations that depart from the otherwise applicable Guidelines range unless the departure is "justifiable."[145]

Three other rules, emphasizing the "independent" role of the probation officer in the preparation of the presentence report, underscore the Commission's concern that the near-elimination of judicial discretion would contribute to increased prosecutorial control over sentencing.[146] First, the sentencing judge is told that he "shall defer" accepting any plea agreement until after he reviews the presentence report prepared by the probation officer.[147] A second rule states that "[a] thorough pre-sentence investigation" is "essential in determining *the facts* relevant to sentencing."[148] A third asserts that the sentencing judge is not bound by any stipulation of facts in a plea bargain between the parties and "may with the aid of the presentence report [i.e., with the aid of the probation officer] determine *the facts* relevant to sentencing."[149] The Commission recognized that federal judges have always had the authority to reject plea bargains, even those not recommending or specifying a specific sentence.[150] It was now expected that judges would exercise this authority "in a more active, vigilant manner"[151] (in the words of Judge William W. Wilkins, Jr., the Commission's first Chairman) to ensure that the Guidelines are not evaded.

Implicit in these rules are the following three premises: *first,* there are "actual" facts[152] (known or knowable) that describe the defendant's criminal conduct; *second,* the probation officer, regardless of his training or professional assets, is able to ascertain these "actual" facts; and *third,* the judge has a duty to impose a sentence based on these "actual" facts.

In our view, all of these premises are doubtful, or at least are so simplistic as to greatly distort and misrepresent the nature of litigation and proof. The "facts" of a case never exist apart from the evidence and the ability of the litigants to present this evidence convincingly in court. Testimony and other evidence is always (to one degree or another) ambiguous, incomplete, or conflicting. Hence the parties will contest its weight, the appropriate inferences to be drawn from it, and its relevance under the applicable law. As a result, there is always a range of uncertainty regarding what "facts" could or would be proved at trial.

This uncertainty regarding the provable facts is a central reason why the parties may be disposed to resolve a case through settlement rather than trial. When a prosecutor agrees to permit a defendant to plead guilty to a lesser offense, he has traded the possibility of acquittal on the greater offense in exchange for a sure conviction and sentence on the lesser offense; the defendant, in turn, avoids the possibility of more serious consequences. A second central reason for settlement is the opportunity cost of litigation for both sides. In particular, prosecutors seldom, if ever, have the resources to investigate every crime that comes to their attention. In many cases it would be unreasonable and contrary to the public interest to devote further investigatory and prosecutorial resources in order to prove every last plausible allegation against a particular defendant.

These two constraints inherent in litigation—uncertainty and cost—may dispose the parties toward settlement regarding sentencing "facts" in the Guidelines regime, just as they dispose parties toward settlement of criminal charges every day in every court in the nation. Suppose, for instance, that a defendant to be sentenced under the Guidelines is willing to plead guilty to drug dealing, but only if the quantity of narcotics attributed to him is limited to the quantity found in his possession when he was arrested. (As we have noted, the "real offense" approach of the Guidelines imposes greater mandatory penalties the larger the quantity of narcotics attributed to the defendant as part of his "relevant conduct."[153]) The prosecutor may have solid evidence that the quantity of drugs in the defendant's possession understates the defendant's liability under the Guidelines; perhaps he has phone records and statements made by other defendants that strongly point to the defendant's involvement in a larger drug operation. But this evidence may be impeachable, difficult to introduce in court, or otherwise uncertain. Significant additional investigatory and prosecutorial resources—perhaps including sentencing concessions to another trafficker who is a potential witness—may be required to convince the judge of the defendant's greater involvement in narcotics trafficking. In these circumstances, a prosecutor might reasonably prefer to stipulate to an amount of drugs which the defendant will not dispute, rather than devote further resources to litigating (and possibly losing) the additional allegations against him.

Suppose, continuing this real world hypothetical, that the prosecutor reports to the probation officer the lower amount of narcotics. Suppose further that the probation officer speaks with the investigating agent, and the agent advises the officer of the evidence strongly indicating the defendant's greater involvement. The Sentencing Commission would apparently view the prosecutor as hiding the "actual" facts and the probation officer as undertaking the prescribed "independent" investigation to report these "actual" facts. But who really has the "actual" facts? As we have suggested, in a courtroom *the only facts that count are those that can be proved, given the constraints of fragmentary evidence and litigation costs.* The prosecutor and defense attorney in most cases have more complete information for assessing *these facts* than does an investigating agent or probation officer. Gerard E. Lynch, formerly the chief of the Criminal Division in the U.S. Attorney's Office in the Southern District of New York and now a professor at Columbia Law School, has stated the matter with clarity:

> To a probation officer, influenced by reading police reports that purport to identify what "actually" happened, the [prosecutor's report] may look inaccurate. But the idea that the probation officer can or has "determined" the "actual" facts is more or less absurd.[154]

Perhaps recognizing the implausibility of the premises listed above, the Guidelines in the end equivocate on the issue of plea bargaining. First, in stating that judges may accept a plea agreement "that departs from the applicable Guidelines range" if there are "justifiable" reasons for doing so,[155] the Guidelines employ a conspicuously ambiguous term. Does "justifiable" refer simply to reasons that would constitute lawful grounds for judicial departure (with all the limitations imposed on that authority by statute, case law, and the Guidelines themselves[156])? Or are there "justifiable" reasons for accepting a plea bargain—such as the uncertainty of proof, limitations on judicial and prosecutorial resources, and prosecutorial priorities—that would not be lawful grounds for a sentencing departure in the absence of a plea bargain? In law review articles published after the Guidelines were promulgated, Chairman Wilkins suggested that the first interpretation was correct,[157] while Commissioner Breyer seemed to endorse the second.[158]

Even more confusingly, the Introduction to the Guidelines Manual states that "[t]he Commission decided not to make major changes in plea agreement practices."[159] At least one of the original Commissioners has acknowledged that this statement undercuts the effectiveness of the Manual's chapter 6 rules in controlling the extent to which plea bargaining may be used to evade the Guidelines.[160] Another of the original Commissioners (Chairman Wilkins) simply ignored this statement in listing Guidelines provisions that provide "significant protections" against prosecutorial "manipulat[ion]."[161]

In a retrospective law review article, then-Commissioner Breyer insisted that "the Commission has basically left the problem [of plea bargaining], for the present, where it found it."[162] Yet the Commission had "found" plea bargaining in a judge-controlled sentencing structure, and what it "left" in its wake is plea bargaining in a Guidelines-controlled sentencing structure. These are two different worlds. Before the Guidelines, prosecutors could only hope that judges would respond to the suggestions implicit in their charging strategy or explicit in their occasional sentencing recommendations. Now prosecutors know the rules the judges must follow; all that remains is to arrange, if not stack, the deck. As Schulhofer and Nagel have candidly recognized, "whoever controls the relevant facts and charges controls the sentence."[163] Plea bargaining that takes the form of "fact bargaining" under a regime of mandatory sentencing guidelines is, for all intents and purposes, *sentence* bargaining.

The Thornburgh Memorandum

While, at the end of the day, the Commission may have done little to limit prosecutorial discretion to shape or determine the sentence to be imposed, it was not alone in making efforts toward this end. In the wake of the Guidelines, and in response to the Commission's clear concern that the Guidelines would be undermined by rampant charge and fact bargaining, the Department of Justice abandoned its traditional, hands-off approach toward routine plea bargaining by federal prosecutors in the field.[164] In 1989, federal prosecutors received a new set of instructions on the subject from the Department of Justice in Washington. The "Thornburgh Memorandum,"[165] as it came to be known (after the Attorney General who issued it), announced strict limitations on the discretion exercised by individual federal prosecutors in charging and plea bargaining, and provided for monitoring and enforcement of these limitations. The key instruction on charge bargaining states:

> [A] federal prosecutor should initially charge the most serious, readily provable offense or offenses consistent with the defendant's conduct. Charges should not be filed simply to exert leverage to induce a plea, nor should charges be abandoned in an effort to arrive at a bargain that fails to reflect the seriousness of the defendant's conduct. [166]

The rule on fact bargaining is equally categorical:

> The Department's policy is only to stipulate to facts that accurately represent the defendant's conduct. If a prosecutor wishes to support a departure from the guidelines, he or she should candidly do so and not stipulate to facts that are untrue.[167]

The Thornburgh Memorandum thus imposed on prosecutors essentially the same standards that the Commission had sought to impose on judges and probation officers (in chapter 6 of its Guidelines Manual), with the exception that the Memorandum permits a United States Attorney to drop "readily provable" charges under certain circumstances not mentioned in the Sentencing Guidelines. For example, the Memorandum permits such charges to be dropped if the prosecutorial office "is particularly overburdened, the case would be time-consuming to try, and proceeding to trial would significantly reduce the total number of cases disposed of by the office."[168]

Given the intensely fact-specific nature of the judgments involved (what charges, after all, are "readily provable"?), the ability of higher-ups in the Department of Justice to restrict local discretion is severely limited. Indeed, every relevant study of prosecutorial practices in the field shows that the Thornburgh Memorandum has been, at best, loosely and unevenly implemented. The most detailed study of charging, sentence bargaining, and substantial assistance departure motions, undertaken by Commissioner Nagel and Professor Schulhofer in the early 1990s, found that prosecutors admit to efforts to shape or influence sentences beyond the strict confines of the Guidelines in approximately 25 percent of cases resolved by plea.[169]

That figure probably understates the extent of Guidelines manipulation for two reasons that the authors acknowledge only in passing. First, prosecutors are not likely to be fully candid with interviewers when asked whether and how often they deviate from the law and Department of Justice policies.[170] Second, Nagel and Schulhofer were able to observe only *post*-indictment bargaining.[171] When plea bargaining occurs after indictment, a paper trail usually documents the bargaining; one may infer that charge bargaining has probably occurred if the defendant does not plead guilty to all of the crimes for which he was indicted. For many federal offenses, however, charge bargaining occurs *prior* to indictment, leaving no paper trail.[172] In many white collar and organized crime cases, the subject of an investigation knows that he is under scrutiny because he is aware of subpoenas, search warrants, and other investigatory efforts by federal agents or prosecutors. In such cases, it is common for the prosecutor and the attorney for the subject or target of the investigation to reach a plea bargain even before arrest or indictment. A study of plea bargaining that does not include pre-indictment bargaining will miss all those cases in which the indictment *is* the bargain.

In apparent response to the concern that the limitations on plea bargaining in the Thornburgh Memorandum were not realistic or enforceable, in the fall of 1993 Attorney General Janet Reno issued a "clarifying" supplemental memorandum to all federal prosecutors.[173] That memorandum stated that "a faithful and honest application of the sentencing guidelines is not incompatible with selecting charges or entering into plea agreements on the basis of an individualized assessment of the [case]."

The significance of the "Reno Memorandum" is unclear. Although some observers suggested that Attorney General Reno had essentially "undone" the Thornburgh Memorandum,[174] the Attorney General herself later publicly insisted—in a letter to Senator Orrin G. Hatch, then the ranking Republican on the Senate Judiciary Committee (and soon to become the Committee's chairman)—that the policies enunciated by the previous Attorney General remained in effect.[175] In any event, prosecutors surely remain reluctant to acknowledge that they engage in plea bargaining in order to evade the strictures of the Sentencing Guidelines[176]—a practice that is, after all, prohibited by chapter 6 of the Guidelines. In the words of one experienced probation officer, "[t]he widespread use of fact bargaining, and the lying to the court that is inevitable with the frequent use of such bargaining, is the dirty little secret" of the Guidelines regime.[177]

A recent survey of chief federal probation officers indicates that Guidelines-evading bargaining is even more commonplace than Nagel and Schulhofer suggest (or, alternatively, that it has become more commonplace since their study in the early 1990s). The nationwide study, conducted by the chief federal probation officer in the District of Massachusetts,[178] confirms that plea bargains purporting to bind the court to impose a specific sentence are still the exception in the federal courts, though they apparently occur more frequently than in the pre-Guidelines era.[179] But in two-thirds of federal districts, pleas of guilty are often accompanied by an agreement that includes Guidelines stipulations or calculations.[180] Indeed, some districts and some individual district judges encourage such stipulations, and the court of appeals in one circuit has explicitly adopted the idea as part of the law of the circuit.[181]

Significantly, the survey of chief probation officers found that only 20 percent of these officers believed that the stipulations and calculations in plea agreements were accurate and complete in at least 80 percent of cases. Another 20 percent reported that such stipulations were inaccurate more than three-fourths of the time.[182]

The survey also suggested that prosecutors play a larger role in determining the scope and content of presentence reports than the Sentencing Commission had anticipated. The description of the offense in most presentence reports in most districts is prepared largely or exclusively on the basis of information provided by the prosecutor.[183] Fewer than half of the chief probation officers responding to the survey reported that prosecutors provide all available information.[184]

Just as important as the prevalence of surreptitious Guidelines manipulation through plea bargaining is the enormous variation in such practices from district to district and prosecutor to prosecutor. A probation officer in the Eastern District of New York reports that, while he knows of cases in his district in which a federal prosecutor has "falsely represent[ed] to the court that he or she has revealed all of the facts of the case that can be proven," his district is relatively "clean" in comparison to other districts from which he has received reports. He writes that his "colleagues in federal probation offices around the country have apprised [him] of the gross misrepresentations that are frequently made in plea agreements, and some defense attorneys have intimated to [him] the relative ease with which they have obtained favorable fact bargains in other districts."[185]

These anecdotal accounts from inside the federal criminal justice system are buttressed by the empirical studies to which we have previously referred.[186] As table 2 demonstrates, there is considerable inter-district variation in the use of downward departures for substantial assistance to authorities. Judge Heaney reported substantial inconsistency in the implementation of the Thornburgh Memorandum among the four judicial districts in the Eighth Circuit.[187] Nagel and Schulhofer also noted a variety of ways in which both that Memorandum and the Guidelines have been circumvented. The latter study reported that in some districts, for example, prosecutors relied heavily on substantial-assistance motions as their "preferred mode of guideline circumvention."[188] In others, prosecutors used charge dismissal when possible. In one district, prosecutors gave no role-in-offense reduction for small-time drug couriers; in other districts, they did.[189] Some districts had a fixed policy about the size of substantial-assistance reductions, while others made no recommendations about the size of the reduction.[190]

These studies of plea-bargaining techniques and evasions do not tell the whole story of the significance of prosecutorial discretion in the Guidelines regime. It is well understood that prosecutorial offices differ in their policies on what to allege as "relevant conduct" at the time of sentencing.[191] Even when a case goes to trial, prosecutors may exercise significant control over the sentence through their charging strategy. For some crimes, for example, the Guidelines' multiple-count calculus means that the more numerous the counts of conviction, the higher the sentencing range. In these circumstances, the prosecutor has an incentive to charge the defendant in numerous separate counts in the indictment, even though the separate counts may all define a single type of criminal behavior (for instance, a single defendant may be charged separately for each of the people he allegedly robbed on a single occasion).

For other crimes, the Guidelines provide an incentive for the government to go to trial on only one count—the one most easily proved—and then effectively to "convict" the defendant on further "counts" through application of the "relevant conduct" principle. As one judge has explained, "The Guidelines obviously invite the prosecutor to indict for less serious offenses which are easy to prove and then expand them in the probation office."[192] One brief recently filed by the government in the federal appeals court on which one of the authors serves noted, with candor, that the government had elected to prosecute the defendant only for robbery and to wait until the sentencing hearing to prove that the defendant should also be held responsible for an associated murder.[193]

Perhaps the most intriguing aspect of the Nagel and Schulhofer study of prosecutorial implementation of the Guidelines is not its statistical findings, but its catalogue of the reasons given by individual federal prosecutors for their efforts to evade the Guidelines. Among the factors mentioned are the intuitive or subjective concerns for overall fairness that the Guidelines were intended to squeeze out of the sentencing process. In deciding whether to find a way to lighten a sentence, for example, the prosecutors are reported to look to "human factors"; they judge whether the defendant is "salvageable"; they consider "the guy's background and . . . the circumstances."[194] Instead of fewer than 800 federal district judges[195] making these rough-and-ready determinations of overall sentencing fairness in an open process, they are now made by more than 3,000 Assistant United States Attorneys behind closed doors.

PROSECUTORIAL CHARGING, plea, and motion practices are thus a wellspring of sentencing disparity. We do not mean to suggest, however, that the existence of broad prosecutorial discretion is inappropriate or disturbing in and of itself. Indeed, nothing is surprising about the fact that prosecutorial practices vary from district to district, prosecutor to prosecutor, and even case to case. Such variation is inherent in the bargaining process, as we have suggested, and has always been a hallmark of the federal criminal justice system.[196] In the federal system, prosecutors have always enjoyed great discretion in deciding what cases to pursue and what charges to bring.[197] The federal courts have been reluctant to interfere absent evidence of invidious discrimination or improper selective prosecution.[198]

The major reason that such broad discretion has been accorded to prosecutors is the large number and complexity of factors that prosecutors must (legitimately) take into account in making charging and other decisions. These include many considerations that the Sentencing Guidelines, or any other sentencing authority, would recognize as relevant also to sentencing—including the nature and seriousness of the offense, the deterrent effect of prosecution, the defendant's culpability in the offense, the defendant's criminal history and a wide range of other personal circumstances, the charges against accomplices in the crime, and the defendant's willingness to cooperate in the prosecution of others.[199] In addition, prosecutors must pay attention to a variety of considerations that sentencing authorities ordinarily do not take into account after the defendant has been convicted—the strength or paucity of the admissible evidence, the priority accorded by the federal government as well as by the local community to prosecution of the particular offense, the capability and availability of prosecutorial resources and adjunct investigatory resources, the alternatives to prosecution, and the likelihood of prosecution in another jurisdiction.

We recognize that, subject to the general prohibition of invidious discrimination,[200] the exercise of discretion in all of these matters is critical to the prosecutorial function. Our concern is *not* that the exercise of prosecutorial discretion affects criminal sentences, nor are we troubled by the obvious fact that prosecutors sometimes exercise their discretion *in order* to affect the sentence. (And we are well aware that not every prosecutorial decision that happens to affect a sentence was made with that objective in mind; there are simply too many other considerations prosecutors take into account for that to be the case.) Our concern, rather, is that the exercise of broad prosecutorial authority over sentencing *within a system that severely limits the sentencing discretion of federal judges* means that the power of prosecutors is not subject to the traditional checks and balances that help prevent abuse of that power.

Our remedy would not be to attempt to limit or thwart the exercise of needed prosecutorial discretion, to insist that prosecutors ignore the impact of their decisions on sentences, or to pretend that prosecutors have no interest in criminal sentencing. These approaches, already tried by the Sentencing Commission in the rules of chapter 6 of the Guidelines and by the Department of Justice in the Thornburgh Memorandum, serve only to drive the exercise of prosecutorial discretion underground and permit discretion to flourish in even less visible and less accountable reaches of the criminal justice system.

Throughout the Guidelines era, for instance, there have been complaints that federal law-enforcement agents, especially those working in undercover operations, attempt to structure criminal transactions and the timing of arrests in ways that will enhance a target's sentence under the Guidelines.[201] Surely this is not the most appropriate locus of discretionary authority over sentencing. The federal courts and the Sentencing Commission have responded by permitting departure from the Guidelines where manipulation by investigating agents is so extreme as to effectively "entrap" a defendant into, for instance, purchasing a larger amount of drugs.[202] But neither the Commission nor the courts can possibly seek to prohibit law-enforcement personnel from taking into account the effect of their investigatory tactics on an offender's ultimate sentence under the Guidelines. The very essence of *ex ante* sentencing rules is to provide notice to all concerned—defendants, prosecutors, and investigators alike—of the consequences of different offense scenarios. *Of course* law-enforcement personnel will seek to employ their lawful authority to achieve the consequences they seek. Denying countervailing judicial discretion simply reinforces the control of both police and prosecutors over criminal sentences in the federal courts.

The problem, in sum, is not that prosecutors have discretion, or that the exercise of that discretion inevitably results in sentencing "disparities"—this is obviously true, and obviously unavoidable. The problem is that judges—the impartial arbiters under our constitutional order—have now been denied countervailing discretionary authority to restrain prosecutorial power.

CHAPTER FIVE
Prospects for the Future

It is our duty to see that the force of the state, when it is brought to bear through the sentences of our courts, is exerted with the maximum we can muster of rational thought, humanity, and compassion.

Judge Marvin E. Frankel (1973)

In the matter of punishing federal crimes, the greatest challenge facing policy-makers today is the restoration of the legitimacy of sentencing in the eyes of victims, litigants, the bar, the bench, and the general public. Although we are critical of the latest wave of sentencing reform, we are under no illusion that the Sentencing Guidelines will be easily discarded; hence we begin this chapter by proposing interstitial reforms that seek merely to ameliorate some of their most troubling aspects.

In our view, however, tinkering with the federal Sentencing Guidelines will not be sufficient to remedy their greatest defects. Thus, in the final section of this book we consider the possibility of a new wave of reform. We do not advocate a return to the pre-Guidelines system. Rather, we envision replacing the Sentencing Guidelines as we know them with a system of true guidance for judging. The structure we tentatively outline here would retain the most significant accomplishments of the Sentencing Reform Act of 1984—the establishment of written sentencing guidelines, the requirement that judges state the reason for their decisions, and the availability of appeal by either party.

Reforming the Guidelines

The Entrenchment of the Guidelines

We recognize that Congress is not likely in the near future to repeal those portions of the Sentencing Reform Act of 1984 that mandated the creation of the federal Sentencing Guidelines. The Guidelines have become deeply entrenched. Of the 751 active federal judges, 435 have been appointed since the Guidelines became effective in November 1987.[1] Many federal probation officers have also been appointed in the intervening decade, and few active federal prosecutors will have labored under any other regime of federal sentencing. Even those judges, probation officers, prosecutors, and defense attorneys who had experience in the federal criminal justice system before the advent of the Guidelines have now devoted a decade to learning and applying the new system. We do not expect that many will be disposed to devote energy to ousting a regime in which they have made such a substantial investment of time and effort.

Moreover, completely abolishing the Sentencing Guidelines would involve repealing not only most of the Sentencing Reform Act, but numerous other statutory provisions as well. In the last decade Congress has taken to referring explicitly to the Sentencing Guidelines in new federal criminal statutes, usually by instructing the Commission to provide a sentence "enhancement" for certain offenders.[2] For instance, in 1994 Congress instructed the Sentencing Commission to adjust the Base Offense Level for defendants convicted of possessing pornography depicting minors; the Guidelines must ensure a "base offense level of not less than 13, and . . . at least a two level increase for possessing 10 or more books."[3] These statutes are a "hybrid" form of mandate—somewhere between simple statutory mandatory sentences and the policy directives that encumbered the Sentencing Reform Act of 1984.[4] Most of these hybrid statutory mandates are functionally equivalent to the rules formulated by the Sentencing Commission itself. For the defendant, the prosecutor, and the judge, it matters little whether a "specific offense characteristic" or other mandatory adjustment has been established by the Sentencing Commission on its own initiative or pursuant to a statutory direction by Congress.

The Commission has publicly welcomed such congressional participation in Guidelines drafting,[5] preferring these legislative instructions that reinforce the Commission's rule-making functions to statutes that mandate minimum penalties for particular crimes. The latter form of legislation largely preempts the Guidelines. It should surprise no one that the Commission, recognizing that it is a creature of Congress, would prefer congressional directives that affirm and ratify the Guidelines' centrality in the punishment of federal crimes.

IN LIGHT OF THE entrenchment of the federal Sentencing Guidelines, we set forth here some modest proposals that we believe will ensure that the Guidelines are implemented with greater fairness and consistency. We hope these proposals will be of interest to a range of policy-makers and commentators who may continue to entertain widely divergent views of the Sentencing Guidelines as a whole.

Mandatory Sentencing: Implications for Checks and Balances in the Criminal Law

Any system in which punishment is prescribed in advance of the judge's formal imposition of sentence necessarily alters the distribution of authority among the three branches of our national government. Even as the exercise of prosecutorial discretion allows executive officials to fit the demands of the criminal law to the real cases that come to their attention, the exercise of judicial discretion allows judges to adjust criminal penalties to fit the real cases that come before the court. When judicial discretion is replaced by criminal penalties set *ex ante* by an administrative agency, the institutional balance of power is shifted. The most notable transfer of power, of course, is from the independent federal judiciary to the agency itself. While the Sentencing Commission is asserted to be "within the judicial branch" of the federal government, it is in fact dominated by nonjudges appointed by the President and confirmed by the Senate for a term of six years.[6] Moreover, this new agency has been accorded great powers. Once the Sentencing Commission decrees that particular statutory offenses shall be punished in a certain way, or that particular mitigating or aggravating factors shall affect the duration of a sentence, or that other factors are not relevant to punishment, these matters generally are placed beyond review by the courts—even though the agency's hard and fast rules may be arbitrary and their application may yield sentences that are unduly lenient, unduly severe, or otherwise unreasonable.[7]

As we observed in the previous chapter, mandatory sentencing schemes also inevitably shift power toward prosecutors: Because the sentencing rules are known in advance, prosecutors may greatly influence the ultimate sentence through their decisions on charges, plea agreements, and motions to depart for substantial assistance to law enforcement authorities. Although prosecutors have always had significant discretion in charging and plea bargaining, the prosecutor's decisions on these matters have far greater significance for sentencing in the Guidelines regime—they determine not only the maximum term of a sentence (as provided in the statute prohibiting the conduct), but, in many cases, the precise range of the sentence. The efforts of the Sentencing Commission and the Department of Justice to constrain prosecutorial discretion in the field during the Guidelines era have been equivocal and difficult to implement consistently across the nation.[8]

Most importantly, the judge has no effective check on the sentencing consequences of prosecutorial decisions. Because the Guidelines comprehensively and exhaustively specify the weights to be accorded to most factors relevant to sentencing, the judge's power to depart from the calculated sentence range is severely limited. In many cases, the judge has authority to depart only if there are residual factors present that the Sentencing Commission has not addressed because they are so insignificant or atypical.[9] The one recurring and important basis for departure recognized by the Guidelines is where the defendant has cooperated in the prosecution of others, but this basis is not available unless, in the words of the Supreme Court, the prosecutor agrees to "authorize the district court" to depart.[10]

It would not be difficult, however, to modify the structure of the Sentencing Guidelines to achieve a more appropriate balance of sentencing authority among judges, prosecutors, and the Commission. In a nutshell, the Guidelines can be amended to give judges fewer mandates and more choices. One may find in the present Guidelines a few instances in which the Commission has done just that, by enunciating sentencing policies not in the form of mandatory instructions but in the form of what we call "guided departures."[11] In these situations, the Commission has simply identified circumstances warranting departure, without attempting to specify the precise magnitude of a departure or conditioning a departure on approval of either party. Less often, the Commission has recommended particular weights to be accorded to identified grounds for departure.[12]

One might ask whether fewer mandates and more judicial authority are really needed; after all, judges already possess authority to sentence at any point within the 25-percent ranges of the Sentencing Table (reprinted in appendix A). Why is this not adequate to permit individualization of sentences and sharing of sentencing authority between the Sentencing Commission and the federal judiciary?

To ask the question in this way is to misunderstand both the essential structure of the Guidelines and the widespread dissatisfaction with the quality of justice under this regime. First, the 25-percent leeway built into the Sentencing Table is quantitatively insignificant in comparison to statutory sentencing ranges. Most federal felony statutes provide for a minimum sentence of no incarceration and a maximum sentence of at least five years imprisonment; for many crimes and for defendants convicted on more than one count, the maximum sentence is much higher. The ranges of the Sentencing Table are far smaller than these statutory ranges. In a case in which the defendant is statutorily exposed to between zero months and sixty months of incarceration—as is typical for a defendant convicted of a single, non-drug-trafficking felony—the Sentencing Table provides only a six-month sentencing range. (See, for instance, the range of 24 to 30 months provided for defendants with a calculated Offense Level of 17 and a Criminal History score of 0 or 1.) Six months represents no more than *10 percent* of the sentencing range that existed in the pre-Guidelines era. This quantitative relationship between statutory sentencing ranges and Guidelines sentencing ranges holds for nearly every federal crime. If one seeks a quantitative measure of judicial sentencing discretion under the Guidelines, the appropriate quantity would not be 25 percent, but 10 percent (and far less than that for defendants convicted on multiple counts).

More importantly, the exercise of sentencing judgment cannot be stated readily in percentage terms. As we have sought to explain in chapter 3, the most important capacity that judges bring to criminal sentencing is the ability to pronounce moral judgment that takes into account all aspects of the crime and the offender. Granting judges a small range within which to pronounce sentence ignores rather than responds to this need. Nor do sentencing ranges (of whatever magnitude) invite trial and appellate courts to participate in the development of sentencing principles and norms, or do anything to reduce the complexity and ambiguities of the Guidelines.

Much of the complexity of the present Guidelines stems from the attempt to specify the exact amount of each sentencing factor that yields an additional one-point adjustment in Offense Level or Criminal History score.[13] It would be far simpler to identify each factor warranting an adjustment and then to allow the sentencing judge a range within which to determine the appropriate value of the adjustment in the case at hand. Making greater use of guided departures (and thus reducing reliance on mandatory sentencing rules) is especially appropriate with respect to "real-offense"—that is, nonstatutory—factors that greatly affect the defendant's final sentencing range. The real-offense factors of greatest concern are "special offense characteristics" involving quantity of harm, "relevant conduct," and the weight accorded criminal history.[14] Of course, all departures ("guided" or otherwise) would be reviewed by the appellate courts under the statutory standard of "reasonable[ness]."[15]

In sum, relying less on precise and complex mandatory sentencing instructions and relying more on guided departures would enhance the sentencing authority of judges, permit a greater role for appellate courts, respond to due process concerns associated with "real-offense" sentencing,[16] and improve the comprehensibility of the Guidelines—all without abandoning the Sentencing Reform Act's stated objectives of rationalizing sentencing and reducing undue disparity. We therefore recommend:

The Commission should treat certain real-offense factors as bases for "guided departure" rather than as bases for mandatory adjustment of Offense Level and Criminal History Score.

Our recommendation potentially encompasses a wide range of reforms. For example, the Commission could make *all* "real-offense" elements of the Guidelines discretionary. The Guidelines sentence range would be set solely on the basis of the statutory elements of an offense and perhaps a single criminal history distinction between those with no significant criminal record and those with serious or numerous previous convictions;[17] all other factors, including particular aspects of criminal history, would simply be recognized grounds for departures of unspecified magnitude. On the other hand, the Commission could retain the mandatory nature of most of the Guidelines, transforming only a few selected factors into guided departures of specified magnitudes. Between these poles the Commission has available to it many possibilities. For instance, the Commission might treat "role in the offense" not only as a factor requiring small mandatory adjustments, up or down, in most cases (as the Guidelines now provide), but also as a basis for departure when the judge finds that the defendant's role in the particular case at hand dominates other considerations of individual culpability.

The Guidelines as a Criminal Code: Implications for Due Process

The combination of mandatory rules and "real-offense" sentencing raises important issues of due process. Although we do not argue that the present regime violates the Constitution, we believe that policymakers, including the organized federal judiciary, can ensure greater fairness in sentencing than the current system provides—fairness not only to the defendant, but to the government and the society the government serves.

The Sentencing Guidelines, as we have observed, function as an adjunct to the substantive criminal statutes enacted by Congress. While statutory law continues to determine the formal elements of particular crimes, for sentencing purposes these elements are now supplemented by factors that the Sentencing Commission prescribes in the Guidelines. In effect, the Commission has invented numerous new "Guidelines crimes," each a variant of one or another statutory crime and each with its own mandated range of punishment.[18] The sentence imposed on a defendant can never exceed the maximum provided by statute, but the statutory offense of conviction is otherwise rendered irrelevant at sentencing.

We do well to recall that no other jurisdiction with mandatory sentencing guidelines has adopted a "real-offense" approach of this kind, that this approach was implicitly encouraged but not mandated by Congress in the Sentencing Reform Act of 1984, and that the consequences of this approach are extraordinarily significant.[19] Many commentators have focused on the Guidelines' "relevant conduct" rules in criticizing the phenomenon of mandatory sentence enhancement without conviction (and without the procedural protections associated with convictions). But, as we have shown in chapter 2, "real-offense" sentencing is a pervasive feature of the Guidelines that goes well beyond relevant conduct. The conduct defined in the Sentencing Guidelines by the euphemistic terms "offense category," "specific offense characteristics," "adjustments," and "Criminal History" (as well as "relevant conduct") are often simply forms of additional or aggravating criminal behavior. To provide here an illustration and a brief reprise: Whatever the crime of conviction, a defendant's Offense Level *must be increased* by two additional points if the judge finds, by a mere preponderance of the evidence, that the defendant sought to "obstruct or impede the administration of justice," as that term is defined by the Commission.[20] In "Commentary" to the guideline on obstruction of justice, the Sentencing Commission further decrees that an attempted escape from custody constitutes one form of obstruction of justice.[21] Thus, for example, a defendant to be sentenced for bank robbery will have his sentence for the crime of bank robbery enhanced if the sentencing court finds that he attempted to escape from pre-trial or post-trial detention. As a formal matter, perhaps, the defendant is not being punished *for* a "Guidelines crime,"[22] but it cannot be denied that some of the defendant's punishment is *because* he committed a "Guidelines crime" (obstruction of justice).

The astonishment that observers from other countries (not to mention this country) express at the Guidelines' commitment to "real-offense" sentencing[23] likely stems in part from their knowledge of the powerful constitutional protections that we otherwise afford to persons charged with crimes. The Fifth Amendment to the United States Constitution assures that "[n]o person shall be held to answer" for a felony "unless on a presentment or indictment of a grand jury." That Amendment further provides that no one shall "be subject for the same offence to be twice put in jeopardy . . . nor be deprived of life, liberty or property without due process of law." And the Sixth Amendment to the Constitution requires that "in all criminal prosecutions, the accused shall enjoy the right to a speedy and public trial, by an impartial jury . . . and . . . be informed of the nature and cause of the accusation; [and] be confronted with the witnesses against him."

Yet under the Guidelines' "real-offense" approach, the defendant *must* be held responsible and sentenced for criminal conduct without recourse to a grand jury or to a petit jury, and without the basic procedural protections of a trial—most importantly, the requirement that the fact-finder be convinced beyond a reasonable doubt that the defendant has engaged in clearly specified criminal conduct. The standard of proof in sentencing proceedings under the Guidelines is "preponderance of the evidence,"[24] which typically is the standard of proof used in *civil* cases—indeed, this is the standard of proof customarily used in federal and state courts to resolve almost every factual dispute *except criminal liability.*

The Process Due

In the pre-Guidelines system, sentencing was not an adjudicatory process; it was not a matter of fact-finding, or of law-making. In exercising sentencing discretion, judges were asked to make *judgments* (concededly, highly subjective judgments) about the appropriate disposition of the defendant, in a legal framework that regarded rehabilitation as a principal rationale for criminal punishment.[25] In those circumstances, there was an understandably strong reluctance to place limitations on the types of information that judges could consider, or on the sorts of decision-making processes they could use. It seemed critical that a judge's sources of information and insight not be restricted through application of rules and standards that had been developed for the quite different function of adjudicatory fact-finding.

It was in this particular historical context that the Supreme Court in *Williams v. New York* (1949)[26] first upheld "real-offense" sentencing without limitations on the type of information that the judge might consider. *Williams* articulated the principle that the judge be permitted to inquire into "every aspect" of the defendant's life,[27] including criminal conduct of which the defendant did not stand convicted. This principle was codified in the United States Code in 1970, before determinate sentencing became an item on Congress's agenda.[28] In the era of discretionary sentencing, both this statute and *Williams* itself became the basis for rejecting a wide array of challenges to the lack of evidentiary rules and due process standards in sentencing proceedings.[29] Procedures and rules of evidence designed for adjudicatory proceedings seemed inherently ill-suited to a function that did not require any fact-finding at all. Indeed, it was not until the 1970s that any federal appellate court adopted *any* standard of proof (a "preponderance of the evidence" or otherwise) for sentencing hearings in the old regime.[30]

In the 1980s, as jurisdiction after jurisdiction began to move away from discretionary sentencing, the Supreme Court explicitly relied on *Williams* and its progeny to uphold various kinds of mandatory sentence enhancements. In *McMillan v. Pennsylvania* (1986), the Court explained that while the Constitution requires proof beyond a reasonable doubt for proof of the statutory elements of an offense, the lesser "preponderance" standard is acceptable for proof of an aggravating factor. In the statutory scheme examined in *McMillan,* proof of the aggravating factor triggered a mandatory minimum prison term but did not increase the maximum prison term to which the defendant might be sentenced.[31]

More recently, the Supreme Court affirmed the vitality of pre-Guidelines procedures in Guidelines sentencing proceedings. The Court held, first, that there is no constitutional double jeopardy bar to indicting, convicting, and punishing a defendant for conduct that has already served as the basis for a mandatory sentence enhancement in connection with a prior conviction.[32] In the illustration offered above, this would mean that even after the defendant has had his sentence for robbery mandatorily enhanced on the basis of an escape from custody, he may be separately prosecuted and sentenced for the statutory crime of escape. Secondly, following the lead of the federal courts of appeals and the Sentencing Commission itself,[33] the Court held in 1997 that the "preponderance" standard of proof is constitutionally permissible for mandatory sentence enhancement, even when the defendant has been acquitted of criminal charges relating to the conduct requiring the enhancement.[34]

The fact of the matter is that the "real-offense" sentencing of the Guidelines is materially different from the "real-offense" sentencing found in the federal courts in the era of discretionary sentencing. In the *Williams* era, fact-finding was virtually never a requirement at sentencing hearings. A federal judge could lawfully dispense *any* sentence within the maximum or minimum provided by statute, for any reason or for no (stated) reason. One federal judge aptly described the old sentencing system as one in which "Congress placed its faith in independent judicial officers to pronounce just sentences. . . . Upon proof of only the essential elements of the crime charged, this discretionary judicial sentencing power was fully released."[35]

The Guidelines have completely altered the character of the sentencing proceeding. It is now clearly an adjudicatory process—that is, Guidelines sentencing requires, first, the finding of facts, and, second, the application of prescribed rules to those facts. Sentence enhancement for uncharged criminal conduct is not a matter of discretion. Rather, the sentencing judge is *required* to consider the presence of any sentencing factor the Commission deems relevant. If a factor requiring adjustment under the Guidelines is found to be present, the judge is *required* to enhance the otherwise applicable sentencing range according to the Commission's carefully calibrated schedules. If the factor is found not to exist, the judge is *prohibited* from an adjustment on this basis. Unlike sentencing in the discretionary era (and unlike the sentencing scheme at issue in the 1986 case of *McMillan v. Pennsylvania*), the maximum term to which a defendant may lawfully be sentenced now depends on the judge's resolution of disputed facts.

"Real-offense" sentencing has thus been taken out of a discretionary system and transferred to a determinate system that is premised on the severe limitation of judicial discretion. In addition, the promise or possibility of rehabilitation is no longer available to justify sentence enhancements for related and unrelated criminal behavior, because Congress has determined that rehabilitation is not even a proper basis for incarceration.[36] As the respected Chief Judge of the United States Court of Appeals for the Eighth Circuit has noted with exasperation in a dissenting opinion: "*Williams*' whole underpinning is the . . . very system the Sentencing Reform Act of 1984 was passed to destroy!"[37]

The old and new regimes of "real-offense" sentencing thus differ both in theory (rehabilitative versus punitive) and in practice (discretionary versus mandatory). These differences are so fundamental that a few federal judges have argued that the foundational precedents from the discretionary era are simply inapposite and that aspects of the new sentencing system violate the basic due process requirements of the Constitution.[38] One federal appeals court has held that where the consequence of applying the "relevant conduct" rule is to increase a sentence dramatically, the burden of proof should be higher than the "preponderance of the evidence" standard prescribed by the Sentencing Commission.[39] Other courts have applied procedural protections normally associated with trial and pretrial practice to Guidelines sentencing.[40] Despite articulated discomfort with procedural aspects of Guidelines sentencing, however, the federal courts have been generally reluctant to require trial-like procedures at criminal sentencings, or, alternatively, to hold a fundamental feature of the regime—mandatory "real-offense" sentencing—unconstitutional.[41]

QUITE APART FROM any arguable requirements of the Constitution, there is the simple question of whether, as a matter of public policy, additional procedural protections in sentencing hearings are appropriate. This is a question probably best answered in uniform rules adopted by national policy-makers, based on the advice of interested parties and institutions, rather than in the episodic and fact-particular pronouncements of the twelve regional federal appellate courts.

Two national policy-making organizations might be well-positioned to undertake a comprehensive review of procedural fairness in a mandatory sentencing system: the United States Sentencing Commission itself and the Judicial Conference of the United States (the governing body of the judicial branch of the federal government). The Sentencing Commission has already addressed some procedural issues pursuant to its statutory authority to issue "general policy statements regarding application of the guidelines or any other aspect of sentencing or sentence implementation."[42] The Judicial Conference by statute plays the leading role in the adoption and amendment of the Federal Rules of Practice and Procedure.[43]

Due Process and the Sentencing Commission

To its credit, the Sentencing Commission has given some attention to the procedural aspects of sentencing under the Guidelines. The "Policy Statements" in chapter 6 of the Guidelines Manual recognize that fact-finding under a mandatory sentencing system is of critical importance,[44] provide for preparation of a presentence report in most instances,[45] instruct judges to permit the parties "an adequate opportunity" to dispute any factors relevant to sentencing under the Guidelines,[46] and encourage "reliable" fact-finding (albeit under a "preponderance" standard).[47]

In 1993, moreover, the Commission added to its "Commentary" on plea agreements a paragraph that "encourages" prosecutors to disclose to the defendant prior to any plea of guilty those "facts and circumstances . . . that are relevant to the application" of the Guidelines.[48] This 1993 amendment implicitly acknowledges the unfairness of having defendants plead guilty before they are advised of the "Guidelines crimes" for which they will be punished.

The Commission has not been prepared to go very far, however, in prescribing procedures at sentencing, despite its recognition of the essentially adjudicatory nature of the sentencing process. The Commission cautions that its "encourage[ment]" to prosecutors to provide notice to defendants about Guidelines sentencing factors "shall not be construed to confer upon the defendant any right."[49] In addition, the Commission has provided that "the court may consider relevant information without regard to its admissibility under the rules of evidence applicable at trial."[50]

In our view, the Sentencing Commission's efforts to achieve procedural regularity at sentencing are a good beginning. The Commission's rules, however, are not sufficiently attentive to the realities of the plea-bargaining process under the Guidelines[51] and to the greatly changed roles that prosecutors and probation officers now play in criminal sentencing.[52] Beyond making the important but obvious point that fact-finding at sentencing should be reliable, the Commission's Policy Statements prescribe few procedural safeguards to ensure that this objective is achieved.

It is understandable that the Commission's efforts are neither comprehensive nor responsive to the adversarial bargaining that inevitably occurs in the criminal justice system. As we have noted in the previous chapter, the major concern of the Sentencing Commission in chapter 6 of its Guidelines Manual has been to discourage evasion of the Guidelines by the parties and the judge. Accordingly, the Commission's policies are intended, first and foremost, to ensure that judges take into account the independent fact-finding of the probation officers and that judges do not accept plea bargains that avoid or evade the commands of the Guidelines.[53]

It is arguable that the Commission is not authorized by statute to address issues of procedural fairness under the Guidelines in any definitive manner. Although the Commission *is* authorized to promulgate "Policy Statements" on court procedures for implementation of the Sentencing Guidelines,[54] case law suggests that these policies (as opposed to the Commission's Policy Statements that relate to substantive Guidelines) may not be binding on federal judges.[55] In all events, it is clear that the Commission does *not* have the authority to amend the Federal Rules of Criminal Procedure, which govern practice and procedure in all criminal cases in the federal courts.[56]

The Federal Rules of Criminal Procedure

The Federal Rules of Criminal Procedure are, in our view, the most appropriate (indeed, the most obvious) place to consider changes in sentencing procedure that correspond to the revolutionary changes that have occurred in the substantive law of sentencing. The Rules Enabling Act, first passed by Congress in 1948, authorizes the organized federal judiciary to prescribe the rules of practice, procedure, and evidence for the federal courts, subject to the ultimate right of Congress to reject the judiciary's proposals.[57] The process by which amendments are made to the federal rules of procedure is far more open and comprehensive than the process prescribed for the issuance of Guidelines and Policy Statements by the Sentencing Commission. The Sentencing Commission issues potential amendments for public comment (sometimes including public hearings), then issues its final proposed amendments, at which point Congress has 180 days to review the amendments.[58] There have been few congressional hearings on any of the Commission's proposals, and only once has Congress rejected an amendment proposed by the Commission.[59] Moreover, under the terms of the Sentencing Reform Act, the Commission need not even abide by these procedural requirements in issuing Policy Statements, since the statutory requirements of public notice and of congressional review apply only to formal "guidelines."[60]

The process by which the Federal Rules of Criminal Procedure are adopted is far more thorough (indeed, *exhaustive*) and is more likely to be responsive to a variety of perspectives and concerns. Whereas proposed Guidelines and Policy Statements are promulgated by the Sentencing Commission without screening by any other body, proposals relating to the Federal Rules of Criminal Procedure are issued only after action by (1) an Advisory Committee (which is broadly representative),[61] (2) the Judicial Conference's Standing Committee on Rules of Practice and Procedure, (3) the Judicial Conference itself, and (4) the Supreme Court. In addition, Congress has an opportunity to reject or amend proposals relating to the Rules of Criminal Procedure, as it does with respect to rules issued by the Sentencing Commission.[62]

The present Federal Rules of Criminal Procedure were largely written in the pre-Guidelines era, and—with the notable exception of the Rule on the sentencing hearing itself—they barely acknowledge the existence of the federal Sentencing Guidelines. The Advisory Committee on Criminal Rules has apparently never conducted a thorough study of the operation of the Rules as a whole in a mandatory sentencing regime. More generally, the organized federal judiciary has declined to assess issues of substantive or procedural regularity under the Guidelines. The Judicial Conference even ignored a modest recommendation by the Federal Courts Study Committee in 1990 that the Conference establish a standing committee "to study proposed and actual guidelines and to provide advice on them to the Sentencing Commission, the federal judiciary, and the Congress."[63] The Judicial Conference has permitted the Sentencing Commission to play the leading role in reassessing procedural constraints in the age of Guidelines sentencing,[64] despite the fact that for the last fifty years Congress has delegated to the Conference prime responsibility for the rules of practice and procedure in the federal courts.

As a result of the Conference's deference to the Sentencing Commission, the Federal Rules of Criminal Procedure substantially reflect the reigning assumptions of the era before the Guidelines. There is a sharp differentiation between the formalities of the adjudicatory stages (indictment followed by trial or plea of guilty), and the less formal and more open-ended procedures of sentencing. At the adjudicatory stages, there are strict requirements of notice and proof. The defendant must receive notice of the indictment against him; the indictment itself must be "[a] plain, concise, and definite written statement of the essential facts constituting the offense" and include a reference to the statutory prohibition alleged to have been violated.[65] The defendant must be formally arraigned, with a copy of the indictment given to him and read to him (unless a reading is waived) before he is called upon to plead to the charges.[66] At the arraignment, the defendant may plead guilty, not guilty, or nolo contendere.[67] Within ten days of arraignment, the defendant may move the court to obtain from the government a bill of particulars containing further allegations of facts relating to crimes charged in the indictment.[68] If the defendant pleads not guilty and elects to go to trial, there are numerous rules governing the rights and duties of the parties with respect to motions before trial for the admission or suppression of evidence, depositions, subpoenas, trial venue, the selection of jurors, and the rendering of a verdict.[69]

Even where the defendant elects to plead guilty, the adjudicatory nature of the plea hearing is recognized in the Rules. Rule 11 (entitled "Pleas") provides that the judge must personally address the defendant in open court and ensure that he understands "the nature of the charge to which the plea is offered."[70] The defendant must be informed of the trial rights he is giving up by pleading guilty, including "the right to be tried by a jury, . . . the right to assistance of counsel, the right to confront and cross-examine witnesses, and the right against compelled self-incrimination."[71] The judge must, "by addressing the defendant personally in open court, determine that the plea is voluntary and not the result of force or threats or of promises apart from a plea agreement,"[72] and must further "mak[e] such inquiry as shall satisfy [the court] that there is a factual basis for the plea."[73]

The premise that sentencing is essentially *nonadjudicatory* is reflected in the further provision of Rule 11 that requires the judge to inform the defendant that, if his plea of guilty is accepted, "there will not be a further trial of any kind."[74] In the bygone era of indeterminate sentencing, this statement was accurate. After the defendant was found guilty by a jury or as a result of the entry of a guilty plea, there was no requirement for further adjudication of any kind; the sentencing hearing did not involve extensive fact-finding or rule application. Indeed, in many federal circuits there were no rules governing proof of facts thought by the judge to be relevant to a sentence. In this context, it was understandable that the defendant at a guilty plea hearing was given only limited information about his possible sentence. The Rule governing pleas simply required—as it still does—that the defendant pleading guilty be informed of "the mandatory minimum penalty provided by law, if any, and the maximum possible penalty provided by law."[75] In the era of discretionary sentencing, more notice was not possible or necessary because, within the statutory maximum and minimum, the type and length of sentence was entirely up to the court.

In 1989, after the Guidelines had gone into effect, Rule 11 was amended slightly to require that the judge advise the defendant pleading guilty not only of the statutory maximum and minimum for his offense, but also of "the fact that the court is required [at sentencing] to consider any applicable sentencing guidelines but may depart from those guidelines under some circumstances."[76] This modest amendment to Rule 11 only minimally acknowledges the revolutionary change in sentencing that occurred with the advent of the Guidelines. There is no requirement that the defendant be told that the "sentencing guidelines" to which the judge refers are mandatory, while the opportunities to "depart from those guidelines" are severely circumscribed. The Rule does not require that a defendant be given notice, prior to tendering his plea, of the facts that the government may allege which, if proven by a preponderance of the evidence, will affect the ultimate sentencing range prescribed by the Guidelines. Under the amended Rule 11, the defendant is still not advised that the conduct for which he will be held accountable at sentencing may bear little relation to the conduct to which he is pleading guilty. He is not advised that the sentencing range he will face depends upon how the Sentencing Commission has classified and characterized the statutory offense he committed and depends on other aspects of his conduct that the Sentencing Guidelines penalize or reward.[77]

Although the Rules of Criminal Procedure that govern indictments, trials, and pleas of guilty take no account of (and even deny) the adjudicatory nature of sentencing, the Rule that governs the sentencing hearing itself (Rule 32, "Sentence and Judgment") was amended significantly in 1993 to take account of the adjudicatory nature of Guidelines sentencing and, in particular, the increased significance of fact-finding at sentencing hearings. Thus, as Rule 32 is presently written, the defendant and the government must be given notice of the presentence report, an opportunity to object to proposed findings of the report regarding any Guidelines sentencing factor, and an opportunity (in the discretion of the judge) to present testimony and other evidence. The judge is required to resolve any factual dispute that will affect either the sentence mandated by the Guidelines or his decisions on whether to depart.[78]

The procedural protections afforded to a defendant at a sentencing hearing are not, however, as substantial as those available at a trial. As we have observed, the rules of evidence do not apply, the standard of proof is "preponderance of the evidence," there is no right to confrontation of adverse witnesses, and there is no recourse to a jury. Because the fact-finding requirements at a sentencing hearing are now so much more elaborate and significant than they were in the pre-Guidelines era, some commentators have urged the implementation of greater procedural safeguards at the sentencing hearing. One proposal is that the standard of proof at sentencing hearings under the Guidelines be raised from the low "preponderance" standard to a heightened standard such as "clear and convincing evidence," perhaps even to the standard at criminal trials of "proof beyond a reasonable doubt."[79] Another is that certain of the Federal Rules of Evidence, especially those relating to hearsay, be made applicable to sentencing hearings.[80] The concern of these commentators is that fact-finding at sentencing hearings is not sufficiently reliable, with the result that the defendant may be punished for conduct (such as "relevant conduct" or a "major" role in the offense) of which he is not "guilty beyond a reasonable doubt."

These proposals deserve careful consideration. A "preponderance of the evidence" standard seems inadequate to prove allegations that substantially affect the severity of a defendant's sentence. Under the present system, quantity of harm, relevant conduct, and other elements of the "real offense" often more than double the defendant's sentencing range. These rules provide a significant reward to prosecutors who, in the words of a former Chief Judge of the Court of Appeals for the Sixth

Circuit, determine to "indict for less serious offenses which are easy to prove and then expand them in the probation office."[81] Even prosecutors acting in complete good faith are implicitly encouraged to take advantage of a lawful means of bypassing the requirements of indictment and trial found in the Constitution and the Federal Rules of Criminal Procedure and to seek punishment of a defendant under the less stringent adjudicatory requirements of a sentencing hearing.[82]

It is doubtful, however, that the fact-finding process in sentencing hearings under the Guidelines is as unreliable as suggested by some critics. Our own experience supports the observation of one experienced federal trial judge that factual disputes in sentencing are relatively rare, and that when they occur, fact-finding by federal judges tends "to err on the side of the criminal defendant."[83]

The precise standards and requirements that ought to govern sentencing hearings in the federal courts may be debatable, but it seems clear that the organized federal judiciary ought seriously to consider these issues in a sustained, comprehensive review of procedural fairness under Guidelines sentencing. Even if the Supreme Court is not prepared to reconsider the applicability of *Williams* and its progeny to sentencing proceedings under the Guidelines, the federal judiciary has the institutional and administrative authority—and responsibility—to consider issues of fairness and justice beyond the constitutional minima enunciated by the Supreme Court in particular cases. We thus recommend:

> **The Judicial Conference of the United States should instruct its Advisory Committee on the Federal Rules of Criminal Procedure to reassess the present practices and procedures governing all aspects of sentencing, including a review of the relevant Policy Statements of the Sentencing Commission, with a view to proposing a comprehensive set of rules to govern the sentencing process.**

A "Notice of Sentencing Allegations"

The greatest procedural infirmity of the present system may not be the rules governing the sentencing hearing itself, but the rules for the adjudicatory stages that precede that hearing—in particular, the rules relating to entry of the defendant's plea. As we observed above, it is not until *after* he is adjudged guilty of the statutory offense (by plea of guilty or by trial) that a defendant must be advised of the allegations against him regarding relevant conduct and other "real-offense" factors that may dramatically increase the sentencing range prescribed by the Guidelines. The authoritative Notes of the Advisory Committee accompanying the 1989 amendment to Rule 11[84] insist that advising the defendant who pleads guilty of the existence of the Guidelines, and of the judge's power in some cases to depart from the Guidelines, is all that is needed to put the defendant and his counsel "on notice of the importance that guidelines may play in sentencing and of the possibility of a departure from those guidelines."[85] The Advisory Committee believed that further notice—for instance, of "which Guidelines will be important or which grounds for departure might prove to be significant"—is "impracticable, if not impossible." These matters, the Advisory Committee asserted, cannot be known "prior to the formulation of a presentence report and resolution of disputed facts" at the sentencing hearing.[86]

Yet the Advisory Committee's position that sentencing allegations simply cannot be made prior to a plea of guilty is not entirely consonant with the Sentencing Commission's more recent "encourage[ment]" to prosecutors, noted above, to inform the defendant prior to his guilty plea of Guidelines factors "then known" to the prosecutor.[87] In light of this recent concession by the Sentencing Commission, and more generally the due process concerns we discuss below, the Advisory Committee should consider amending the Criminal Rules to *require what the Sentencing Commission has already recommended.* Specifically, we recommend:

> **The Advisory Committee on Criminal Rules should consider adopting a provision requiring that by the time a final plea is entered, the government must inform the defendant of the mandatory sentencing factors the government intends to allege at sentencing.**

This recommendation[88] rests upon an acknowledgment of certain fundamental features of the new sentencing regime: the requirement that the judge impose a sentence on the basis of nonstatutory factors, and the concomitant requirement that probation officers independently ascertain the presence of such factors.[89] Requiring notice to the defendant would not eliminate these requirements of current law, but would provide safeguards in their implementation. It would eliminate the possibility that either the government or an inquisitorial third-party (the probation officer) will make new allegations *after* a defendant has entered his plea of guilty that, if proved, *require* additional punishment.

A Notice of Sentencing Allegations would serve a function similar to that performed by formal indictment or information,[90] except that the sentencing notice would concern Guidelines "crimes" rather than statutory crimes. The government should be permitted to serve and file a superseding Notice of Sentencing Allegations at any time prior to entry of a defendant's plea of guilty; this, like the possibility of a superseding indictment or information, would facilitate the plea process by allowing newly discovered or changed circumstances to be taken into account.

If such notice were required, then before a defendant decides to plead guilty on one count, he would know how many other offenses the government will seek to prove at sentencing. Or, for example, before he pleads guilty to a fraud involving $10,000, he would know whether the government intends to prove at his sentencing that the actual fraud involved $400,000.[91] Before a defendant enters a plea to any crime, he would know the factors the government will allege that would command an increase in Offense Level or Criminal History Category, such as having a "major" role in the offense, seeking to impede the administration of justice, and so on.[92]

The question that arises, of course, is how to proceed if the government (or the probation officer) subsequently learns of new allegations regarding the defendant or his offense—allegations which, if proven, would require a higher sentence under the Guidelines. Stating the question another way, how would the requirement of notice be enforced? There are two possible approaches, both of which would require some changes (though not especially radical changes) in plea and sentencing practices in the federal courts.

One possibility is to permit the defendant to withdraw his plea of guilty if, at the time of sentencing, the judge proposes to impose a sentencing enhancement of which the defendant had not received appropriate notice. This is the procedure already followed (both before and after the Guidelines) with respect to that small number of so-called "binding" plea agreements in federal court. If the judge after the sentencing hearing decides not to sentence in accordance with the "binding" agreement, the defendant is given the option of withdrawing the guilty plea he entered (which was premised on that agreement) and proceeding to trial.[93] This approach would effectively merge the guilty-plea hearing and the sentencing hearing in every case. Final acceptance of a plea of guilty would have to await preparation of the presentence report and resolution of disputed facts.[94] Yet such lack of finality in the tender of a plea would be troubling; a defendant bent on delay might seek to persist in tendering and then withdrawing guilty pleas. Moreover, this approach would not provide a means to enforce a notice requirement in cases where the defendant chooses to proceed to trial.

The most direct way to enforce a notice requirement for all defendants (both those who plead guilty and those who are convicted after trial) would be to provide that the defendant could not be sentenced on the basis of nonnoticed factors without his consent. This approach, too, would require some changes in plea and sentencing practices in the federal courts. In particular, the government would be afforded a strong incentive to complete its investigation of a case (and to learn the full extent of a defendant's criminal record) before, rather than after, it enters into a plea agreement—an incentive that seems unobjectionable on its face.

However, absolutely prohibiting consideration of sentencing factors that the government has failed to allege in its notice might well violate the statutory provision implementing the principle of *Williams v. New York,* which we noted previously.[95] This statute, 18 U.S.C. §3661, provides that there shall be "no limitation" on the information a judge may take into account at sentencing.[96] In 1997, in *United States v. Watts,* the Supreme Court explicitly invoked this statute in upholding the Sentencing Guidelines' mandate that "relevant conduct" and other mandatory enhancements under the Guidelines encompass criminal conduct (proven at the sentencing hearing) of which the defendant had previously been acquitted.[97] The Court concluded that, in light of section 3661, federal courts may not "invent a blanket prohibition against considering certain types of evidence at sentencing."[98]

Justice Scalia, in a concurring opinion in *Watts,* took the argument one step further, concluding that as long as section 3661 remains the law, even the Sentencing Commission may not adopt a rule excluding acquitted conduct from consideration at sentencing.[99] Justice Breyer (also in a concurring opinion) took issue with Justice Scalia, asserting the Commission's view that it does have such authority.[100] Indeed, at the time the Supreme Court issued its decision, the Sentencing Commission was considering whether to prohibit consideration of acquitted conduct.[101] (Two months after the Supreme Court's decision in *Watts,* the Commission announced that it would not amend the Guidelines to alter the treatment of acquitted conduct.[102])

As a narrow legal matter, there are good arguments on both sides of the disagreement between Justices Scalia and Breyer in *Watts.* But neither of those Justices, nor the Court itself in its unsigned, *per curiam* opinion, acknowledged the most obvious point: that section 3661—enacted during the era of indeterminate, discretionary sentencing—is exceedingly difficult to reconcile with the Sentencing Reform Act itself. Section 3661 places "no limitation" on the matters relevant to sentencing. Yet the very purpose of the 1984 reform was to limit the discretion of judges by giving the Sentencing Commission authority to determine henceforth what factors should be taken into account in sentencing in federal court.[103] The Sentencing Guidelines from start to finish violate at least the spirit of the earlier statute by mandating the particular weights that must be given to most information the judge receives and by excluding other factors from consideration altogether.

The Sentencing Commission has from its inception recognized the general incompatibility of the Sentencing Reform Act and section 3661. The Introduction to the Guidelines Manual expressly purports to limit application of section 3661 to those few occasions when judges retain discretion under the Guidelines—that is, in selecting a particular sentence within the Guidelines range and in determining whether there are lawful grounds for departure.[104]

Quite apart from the issues addressed by the Supreme Court in *United States v. Watts,* it does not seem advisable to adopt a rule categorically prohibiting sentencing judges from considering relevant matters that had not been in the Notice of Sentencing Allegations provided to the defendant. Such a rule would further enhance the prosecutor's effective authority over sentencing, at least for defendants who do not insist upon trial. If non-noticed factors are entirely off-limits to the sentencing judge, then a prosecutor who reaches an agreement with a defense attorney as to which factors shall be in the "notice" would effectively be deciding the defendant's sentence. Without countervailing authority to reject bargained-for exclusions from the Notice of Sentencing Allegations, the sentencing judge would be powerless to check the power of the prosecutor. In our view, plea agreements are most likely to conceal prosecutorial overreaching or abuse of discretion precisely when they are immune from review by independent judges who have authority to reject the agreement.

A better balance of authority would be to limit only the *mandatory* consideration of non-noticed sentencing factors. Judges would still be permitted to consider *all* matters, even those not in the Notice of Sentencing Allegations, in choosing a sentence within the Guidelines range or in deciding whether to depart. Thus, the Guidelines range could be mandatorily enhanced only on the basis of factors about which the defendant had received notice, but the judge would have discretion to depart from this range on the basis of any information from any source—even when that source is the prosecution itself. This approach would empower the judge to reject bargained-for limited notice, would ensure that the judge may take into account matters he learned at trial or other hearings in the case, and would ensure that no one, including the government and the probation officer, is precluded from bringing newly discovered evidence to the attention of the judge at sentencing.

The Guidelines as a Criminal Code: Implications for Plea Bargaining

The extent to which the Sentencing Guidelines now function as a criminal code prompts consideration of other reforms to make this code more coherent, workable, and realistic. It makes sense, for instance, to adopt the proposal of one thoughtful commentator, Professor Michael Tonry of the University of Minnesota Law School, to simplify the Guidelines by reducing the number of Offense Levels in the Sentencing Table (see appendix A).[105] There may also be merit in Tonry's proposals to permit judges to depart on the ground of substantial assistance even without prosecutorial approval,[106] and to permit greater use of probation for first-time, nonviolent offenders whose calculated Offense Levels are low.[107]

Our fundamental concern with the Guidelines as a criminal code, however, is not the severity of the punishment prescribed but, rather, the rigidity of the sentencing rules. The Guidelines fail to acknowledge the extent to which the formal demands of law are inevitably adjusted or tempered in implementation. By ignoring or attempting to suppress the adversarial bargaining that is inherent in litigation, the Guidelines drive the process of adjustment underground and hide from observers the decisions that actually shape a sentence.

Most criminal cases in the federal courts end in explicit or implicit plea bargains, just as most civil cases are resolved by settlement. Although over 90 percent of federal convictions are obtained by pleas of guilty, rather than by trial,[108] the Guidelines do not clearly permit the judge to impose a sentence based on a characterization of offense conduct agreed upon by the parties and proposed to the judge.[109] At least one court has read the Commission's Policy Statements as allowing "sentence bargaining" outside the Guidelines,[110] but, as we suggested in the previous chapter, these Policy Statements are, at best, ambiguous on the matter. They do not explicitly acknowledge any judicial authority to consider the parties' resolution of the case on a basis different from that prescribed by the Sentencing Guidelines. As we have observed, the result is that prosecutors and defense attorneys, though "officers of the court," may be sorely tempted to deny information to both the probation officer and the court that would fully reveal all arguably relevant aspects of their plea bargain.[111]

The current stance of the Guidelines may also place judges in an ethically uncertain position. When a plea agreement is proposed that appears fair and that purports to comply with the Guidelines, the judge might without further inquiry accept the agreement and state ("for the record") that he or she is applying the Sentencing Guidelines—even while the prosecutor, the defense attorney, and the probation officer know that the agreed-upon stipulations have the effect of avoiding or evading an otherwise-applicable Guidelines range. On the other hand, the judge may feel compelled to reject the agreement even though no one in the courtroom believes that the Guidelines sentence is appropriate in the case at hand. Neither option is particularly attractive to a judge who is committed to the rule of law.

Much, though not all, of the dissimulation, distrust, and discomfort generated by the Guidelines can be avoided if the Sentencing Guidelines (or, perhaps, the Federal Rules of Criminal Procedure) simply *authorized* judges to accept a plea agreement that resolves matters differently from the resolution contemplated by the Sentencing Guidelines in the absence of any agreement. By failing to acknowledge the plea bargaining that now occurs under the Guidelines, the Commission has driven that bargaining underground, often out of the view of both the probation officer and the judge.

We therefore recommend:

> **The Sentencing Guidelines should be amended to recognize the authority of the sentencing judge to impose a sentence in accordance with a plea agreement where the judge finds that such a sentence would achieve the purposes of criminal punishment at least as well as a sentence prescribed by the Guidelines.**

As our comments in the previous section suggest, we would under no circumstances *require* that judges accept a plea agreement proposed by the parties. There should be no limitation on the judge's power to review and reject the parties' proposed sentence, sentencing range, or stipulation of facts.

But we also believe that judges should have the authority to *consider* an agreement the parties have reached. In most criminal litigation the parties to the case will have a better sense than could the Sentencing Commission of the strength of the evidence, the cost of trial to all concerned, law-enforcement priorities, and the myriad circumstances relevant to just punishment of the defendant. Where adverse parties have arrived at an agreement (or partial agreement) that *both they and the judge* believe is appropriate and achieves the objectives of punishment specified by Congress (including, most importantly, the objectives of the Sentencing Reform Act of 1984),[112] we should defer to the judgment of these decision-makers who know the most about the case, rather than to the vagaries of sentencing rules constructed by persons who know nothing about the case. The Sentencing Reform Act itself is amenable to an interpretation that permits acknowledgment and acceptance of plea bargaining. The statute lists the Sentencing Guidelines as but one of several factors that sentencing judges should consider in imposing sentence (the most important other factors being "the nature and circumstances of the offense," "the history and characteristics of the defendant," the four general purposes of criminal punishment, and the "need to avoid unwarranted sentence disparities among defendants with similar records who have been found guilty of similar conduct").[113] Moreover, the statute broadly authorizes the Commission to issue Policy Statements regarding plea agreements.[114] The Commission's present approach is surely not the only one that is permissible under the statute.

Recognition of the inevitability (and often, indeed, the legitimacy) of bargaining outside the Guidelines would also clarify the role of the probation officer.[115] The Sentencing Commission's effort to direct the activities and responsibilities of probation officers has led to tension and confusion among all the participants in sentencing. Probation officers are, by statute, employees of the *court* and not the Sentencing Commission. Yet, as the Chief Probation Officer of the District of Connecticut has informed us, the Guidelines have caused "some confusion regarding the sentencing Judge's authority and responsibility to make the final decision on what goes into a [final presentence] report."[116] By law, the judge has final authority to decide the facts that determine sentence, and the Sentencing Commission should act to reaffirm that fundamental principle and restore the close working relationship between the court and probation officers.

The Responsibility of the Judiciary

Even if the Sentencing Guidelines are retained largely as we know them, judges themselves should accept greater responsibility for ensuring that federal sentencing law is rational and just. The Sentencing Commission and the Supreme Court each have recited the importance of the judicial role in ensuring just sentences. The Introduction to the Commission's Guidelines Manual states that "it is difficult to prescribe a single set of guidelines that encompasses the vast range of human conduct potentially relevant to a sentencing decision,"[117] and asserts that the Commission "views the guideline-writing process as evolutionary."[118] In recent years, the Commission has explicitly incorporated the "heartland" concept in its instructions to judges on departures[119] and has announced a desire to work with the judiciary to "simplify" the Guidelines.[120]

These initiatives, tentative though they are, may reflect subtle changes in the political environment, including significant personnel changes in the Commission as result of the passage of time and the turn of the political wheel. Perhaps we are witnessing the beginning of a new trend—one in which the Commission demands less unquestioned authority and introduces greater opportunities for the exercise of informed *judgment* in federal sentencing proceedings. But the signals from the Commission are decidedly mixed. Soon after announcing its interest in "simplification" in 1995, the agency announced that it would not reconsider fundamental political choices made by the Commission at the onset of its labors, such as the adoption of the relevant conduct principle.[121] More recently, it was announced that the plan to simplify the Guidelines "is on hold."[122] Most importantly, the present Commission has yet to suggest, much less achieve, any significant alteration of the structure of the Guidelines.

Even adoption of the "heartland" idea appears to offer little hope for meaningful relaxation of the strictures of the present regime. Although the Supreme Court's decision in *Koon v. United States* (1996) asserted, in the teeth of reality, that under the Sentencing Guidelines, "the district court retains much of its traditional discretion,"[123] *Koon* did not deliver on the promise of discretion. As we have noted in chapter 3, *Koon* denies sentencing and appellate courts any authority to question the reasonableness of the Commission's judgments about just punishment in the "typical" (or "heartland") case; nor may courts question the Commission's judgments about proper and improper grounds for departure from the Guidelines.

Both the Commission and the courts could do more to ensure that federal judges bear appropriate responsibility for achieving justice in the individual case and for developing the jurisprudence of sentencing. A useful step in this direction could be made if *Koon*'s abuse-of-discretion standard for reviewing departures from the Guidelines were combined with a willingness to let judges evaluate the adequacy of prescribed sentencing factors and the weights accorded them by the Guidelines. Under one approach, for instance, a task of the sentencing judge would be to determine whether the Commission's consideration of sentencing factors is adequate *in the case at hand*. If the sentencing court answers that question in the negative, it would have to identify the relevant factors not considered adequately by the Commission and explain why they warrant a sentence outside the Guidelines range in that particular case. One task of the appeals court would then be to decide, in the words of the Sentencing Reform Act, whether such a departure was "reasonable"[124]—

that is, whether the sentencing judge abused his discretion in determining that the Guidelines did not adequately identify or weigh the sentencing factors that should apply in the particular case at bar. There would be no irrebuttable presumption that consideration of a factor by the Commission is, *ipso facto,* adequate consideration (in the "typical" case or otherwise). Courts might well conclude that the Commission's consideration of certain sentencing factors is adequate and reasonable in most cases. If the consideration of other factors is repeatedly found to be inadequate, the courts would have a role in contributing to further development of sentencing standards and rules.

We recognize that to adopt a meaningful abuse-of-discretion standard for departures—one that permits both trial judges and appeals courts to assess the work of the Sentencing Commission—would require a significant deviation from the present jurisprudence of the federal Sentencing Guidelines.[125] The approach we suggest here would ensure that judges exercise the responsibility to determine just punishment in all cases, not just in the rare or atypical case, and not just in cases where the defendant has cooperated with authorities. It would also encourage the Commission to explain the reasoning behind its various prohibitions and prescriptions.

This reform would not require any statutory change. The language of the Sentencing Reform Act itself authorizes a departure if the sentencing judge finds "an aggravating or mitigating circumstance of a kind, or to a degree, not adequately taken into consideration by the Sentencing Commission in formulating the guidelines that should result in a sentence different from that [prescribed by the Guidelines]."[126] That standard permits, and arguably invites, the approach we outline here. Thus far, however, the federal judiciary has been unwilling to question the hegemony of the Sentencing Commission.

Starting Anew: Guidelines for Judging

We are confident that eventually the federal sentencing guidelines as we know them will be rejected or significantly modified. The realization that these Guidelines must be replaced will come slowly—perhaps by assertions of judicial authority or changing ideas on the part of the Sentencing Commission as it is reconstituted over time. Perhaps Congress itself will take the initiative to simplify and relax the Guidelines. Whatever the future holds, it is not too early to begin to consider what a new wave of sentencing reform might look like.

To do this, we should start with the simple recognition that the Sentencing Guidelines are based on a fundamental misconception about the administration of justice: the belief that just outcomes can be defined by a comprehensive code applicable in all circumstances, a code that yields a quantitative measure of justice more easily generated by a computer than by a human being.[127] We must recognize, in other words, that no system of formal rules can fully capture our intuitions about what justice requires. The federal Sentencing Guidelines of today are based on a fear of judging; they attempt to repress the exercise of informed discretion by judges. Instead, in the typical case, the judge is supposed to perform an automaton's function by mechanically applying stark formulae set by a distant administrator. The unhappy consequences of such a system are borne by all participants in the sentencing process, including the judges themselves. As one federal judge has put it, the Guidelines "tend to deaden the sense that a judge must treat each defendant as a unique human being. . . . [I]t is quite possible that we judges will cease to aspire to the highest traditions of humanity and personal responsibility that characterize our office."[128]

The desire to achieve objectively rational, technocratic solutions to human problems has deep roots in our intellectual traditions.[129] The Enlightenment thinkers who inspired our nation's Founders possessed an abiding faith in the power of reason and in their own power to explain the human and physical world in terms of a finite number of fixed laws. Similarly, the legal positivists of the nineteenth century hoped to reduce all laws to a single, comprehensive system of abstract rules. In our century, well-intentioned reformers have often proposed complex, centrally controlled regulatory regimes as a means of addressing many kinds of social ills. Some of these thinkers have contributed much to the progress of our nation, producing incalculable benefits in science, technology, medicine, and, to be sure, the law.

But our experience with technocratic and bureaucratic "solutions," in this country and across the globe, has also taught us that comprehensive systems often have ramifications that undermine the very purposes they were intended to further. Our faith in experts and planning can serve us well, despite its dangers, if we remain equally committed to another important element of our political and intellectual heritage: our distrust of centralized governmental institutions and our awareness of the ways in which institutions designed to serve us can become our masters. This skepticism acts as a powerful check upon creeping accretions of power and upon the erosion of liberty and justice. In the federal sentencing reforms of the 1980s, we let the first of these traditions capture and ultimately corrupt the second. Driven by our rationalist ambitions for an all-encompassing, technocratic "solution," we vented our fears of authority against the only sort of sentencing power that was recognizably human—that of the judge—and embraced its coldest and most impersonal alternative.

ONCE WE RECOGNIZE the irreducible need for individualized judgment and for humanity as well as rationality in sentencing, we can begin to see the shape that renewed sentencing reform must take. First, if judges are to exercise judgment rather than plug numbers into formulae, the process that should concern us most is that of choosing the men and women of whom we ask judgment: judges. This simple truth was so fundamental to the Founders that the Constitution itself protects the independence of the federal judiciary—through provisions for tenure during "good behavior" and salary protection—and ensures that no single official will fully control the appointment of federal judges. In this way, our forebears sought to assure the reasonably good judgment (if not necessarily the wisdom) of the federal bench, and to guarantee it the independence necessary for the exercise of that judgment.

Second, in determining how to constrain judges' discretion in sentencing we should look to the mechanism that has been used for centuries to impose such constraints in most other judicial matters: requiring trial judges to give reasons for their decisions, and then permitting litigants to seek review of those decisions in appellate courts. This basic model can also work well in sentencing and would rest on one of the genuine strengths of the system established by the Sentencing Reform Act of 1984: the appealability of sentences by both sides. Slowly but surely, a federal common law of sentencing would be created.

Under the system displaced by the Sentencing Reform Act, the individual federal judge exercised extraordinarily broad discretion over the nature and magnitude of the sentence: The judge might or might not follow the prosecutor's recommendation. The judge might or might not take into account the defendant's cooperation and adjust the sentence that would otherwise have been imposed. The judge might impose a short sentence of imprisonment combined with probation or might impose the maximum jail time permitted by the statute defining the offense of conviction. In theory and in practice, the moral and intellectual burden of determining the sentence fell largely on the trial judge. As long as the sentence was under the maximum (and above any minimum) set by statute, the decision as to the type and length of sentence was the judge's alone.

As it happens, this broad and virtually unreviewable authority was unusual for a federal trial judge. The discretionary power that a judge exercised in criminal sentencing went beyond the usual forms of judicial discretion and constituted what Callis called "*discretio specialis*," where the discretionary decision itself "is the absolute judge of the cause, and gives the rule."[130] While many issues that arise in criminal and civil cases are left to the discretion of the trial judge, most of these issues are ultimately reviewable by the appellate courts. Only in the preliminary stages of a civil case (in the management of the discovery process and other pretrial arrangements) does a federal trial judge exercise remotely comparable authority to that traditionally exercised in sentencing, and even there the judge is guided by articulated legal principles and standards. The judge's discretionary decisions during a trial may be appealed, and possibly reversed if the judge is found to have abused his discretion.[131]

The circumstances in civil and criminal cases in which a federal trial judge exercises his informed judgment subject to appellate review for "abuse of discretion" are many and varied, and deeply touch the lives and property of real people. To take simply one example of many highly discretionary judgments that we routinely expect judges to make, Rule 403 of the Federal Rules of Evidence advises that relevant evidence "may be excluded if its probative value is substantially outweighed by the danger of unfair prejudice, confusion of the issues, or misleading the jury." This is a broad and inevitably subjective standard of exclusion, which gives a judge great discretion to weigh the particular circumstances with which he is confronted at trial. But the judge's evidentiary rulings are appealable and may be reversed if the appellate court finds them to be arbitrary, inexplicable, or contrary to binding precedent. In addition to all evidentiary rulings, the judge must decide, among many other matters, whether to hold hearings of any kind, when to hold an evidentiary hearing, when to permit or end questioning, when to seal documents from public view, when to close courtroom proceedings to the public, when to allow the intervention or participation of new parties, when to permit sketching or television cameras in the courtroom, whether to excuse jurors or potential jurors, whether and when to hear legal arguments from *amici curiae* (interested persons who are not parties to the case), when to make on-site inspections, when to admit a criminal defendant to bail, when to grant a criminal defendant the opportunity to voluntarily surrender at a prison (rather than be remanded into custody immediately), whether to sever counts of an indictment, whether to accept the defendant's plea of guilty, whether to have an observer or defendant removed for courtroom misconduct, and whether to reveal the identity of a confidential informant.[132]

There can be no doubt that in the pre-Guidelines era, the sentencing decision was one of the most important discretionary decisions judges were obliged to make. What made sentencing authority truly extraordinary, however, was not the broad discretion the judge exercised, but rather, the fact that his decision was virtually unreviewable on appeal.[133] The lack of appellate review meant that the unreasonable or inexplicable—or even the bizarre—decision at this stage was beyond correction. In addition, no common standards or principles were articulated to guide the exercise of judgment in sentencing.

We believe that requiring district judges to explain their sentencing decisions on the record, with the availability of appellate review under an abuse-of-discretion standard, would ensure sentencing outcomes that are more reasonable and just than either the sentences under the old discretionary system or those under the Guidelines regime. If we have confidence in our federal judiciary, we can be assured that with this reform alone, unreasonable or inexplicable sentences will not stand and impermissible considerations (such as race, ethnicity, or religion) will not be tolerated. This should be our foremost goal—the avoidance of sentences that are arbitrary, unreasonable, or inexplicable *in context*, not the achievement of national uniformities devised by persons deliberately alien to the case at hand.

Why *not* start anew on the basis of these simple and historic strengths of American law? Other commentators have suggested that the Sentencing Reform Act itself might be retained, with only these ponderous Guidelines overhauled and restructured.[134] Yet the fundamental misconception of the Guidelines is that sentencing justice is synonymous, or nearly so, with the minimization of inter-judge sentencing variation. And this same misconception is at the heart of the statute that created the Sentencing Commission.

It took significant political courage to confront the issues of criminal recodification and sentencing reform in the mid-1970s. Liberals generally opposed the recodification effort, while conservatives were generally unlikely to support the liberal vision of sentencing reform.[135] As Senator John L. McClellan said of Senator Kennedy on the Senate floor in 1977:

> He did not have to get involved. With considerable commitment of time and a willing acceptance of the risks that inevitably accompany legislative involvement with controversial issues, he accepted the responsibility of identifying the major issues and worked with me in the spirit of give and take to attain a bill.[136]

Senator Kennedy and his cosponsors shepherded sentencing reform through the Senate not because it was the favorite cause of powerful interest groups on either side of the ideological spectrum, but because of a conviction that federal sentencing was in "utter disarray" and that judicial discretion worked to the disadvantage of those already disadvantaged by birth and social condition.[137]

Unfortunately, the Sentencing Reform Act was based on the notion that *judges* were the problem, and thus that the solution to the problem consisted of removing judges from the sentencing process as much as possible. Under the approach sought by sentencing reformers of the 1970s and early 1980s, what was needed was not a process to enhance or ensure sound judicial judgment, but one that would reduce or eliminate the very exercise of judicial judgment.[138] And the Sentencing Commission has zealously—*too* zealously, in our view—sought to achieve this objective in its implementation of the Sentencing Reform Act.

We believe that, despite their obvious good intentions, sentencing reformers were wrong to assume that federal judges were commonly arbitrary or discriminatory in meting out sentences and that the sentencing system over which they presided was incurably ridden with unfairness. Indeed, unwarranted sentencing outcomes (both unwarranted disparity and unwarranted uniformity) may be no less frequent now than they were before the Sentencing Guidelines greatly restricted the authority of the judge, though now the causes of unequal treatment may be less visible.[139] Moreover, there is every reason to believe that denying judges the opportunity to mitigate sentences on the basis of social disadvantage, when appropriate, works *against* poor and minority defendants. Beyond all of this, we now have a sentencing system of remarkable complexity and rigidity, one that is not easily understood by those who work with it every day, much less by the general public.

It can be argued that much of the blame (if "blame" is the right word) for the new regime of federal sentencing lies not with sentencing reformers, or with Congress, or with the Sentencing Commission, but rather, with the federal judiciary itself. The federal judiciary defaulted in two ways: first, by failing to address the issue of "sentencing disparity" when it emerged as a significant policy issue in the 1970s, and second, by failing to anticipate or explain to Congress why the proposed reforms were not in the public interest.[140] Throughout the years of energetic advocacy by sentencing reformers (including, most eloquently, Judge Marvin E. Frankel[141]), the organized federal judiciary failed seriously to consider the issue of variation in criminal sentences and the growing public perception of inexplicable or unfair sentences. If federal judges believed that the codification of sentencing factors in the form of complex, mandatory "guidelines" was an unnecessary and unwise response to the questions raised by reformers, they failed to make a timely effort to persuade those who disagreed with them.

It is possible that the judges anticipated that any such effort to discourage or forestall this reform movement would be futile. Compared to other political actors, judges are almost uniquely ill-suited to the task of influencing the shape of legislation. Judges lack the key ingredients for successful legislative lobbying and negotiation: their numbers are minuscule, and they can promise nothing in return.

In addition, judges have felt an understandable reluctance to engage in public disputes on matters of public policy—even when the debate involves the administration of justice, a subject about which judges surely *are* free to speak publicly. Although they may have been activists in politics or in the legal profession before assuming the bench, judges (and especially federal judges) are expected to stand apart from politics and political intrigue. The very independence of federal judges guaranteed by the Constitution is also responsible for the expectation that they will remain at a distance from political debate. More generally, under our system of government the judge is very largely a passive actor. A judge does not reach out and find a case to decide or a legal issue to resolve; rather, the "case or controversy" is brought to the judge and argued by partisan advocates, with the judge expected to play the role of disinterested observer and decision-maker.

Finally, perhaps the most important reason that federal judges generally did not more actively engage the proponents of the federal Sentencing Guidelines was the widely shared belief that their concerns or opposition would be ascribed to guild interest. The judges would appear self-serving. If judges' concerns were attributed merely to disgruntlement at the prospect of limitations on judicial authority, the concerns themselves would be discredited.

The federal judiciary's reluctance to step forward earlier was regrettable, for there is no group better able—by virtue of training, experience, and disinterestedness—to forge a structure for criminal sentencing that is both workable and fair. We hope that the organized federal judiciary will emerge from its reclusiveness on this issue, to vindicate not only its own institutional interests but also the interests of the broader society in a just system of sentencing. In particular, we recommend:

The Sentencing Commission should be replaced with a sentencing committee whose members (who need not all be judges) are chosen by the Judicial Conference of the United States, the governing body of the federal courts. The task of this committee would be to develop sentencing procedures and advisory guidelines—true guide-

lines—that seek to use judicial knowledge and experience, rather than to suppress or replace judgment by judges. Congress would have final authority to approve the committee's proposed guidelines.

This modest recommendation recalls one made nearly two decades ago by Kenneth Culp Davis in his thoughtful analysis of discretion in the criminal justice system.[142] It might be claimed (in an echo of the "self-serving" argument noted above) that a committee of the judiciary itself would be reluctant to place any restrictions on judges—that is, on themselves. In fact, we suppose the opposite would be true, because judges on any such committee would be guiding primarily *other* judges. Moreover, in the wake of the federal Sentencing Guidelines and Congress's continuing interest in criminal sentencing, it is inconceivable that such a committee would simply propose a return to the era of discretionary sentencing. In any event, Congress would retain ultimate authority to approve or disapprove the committee's guidelines.[143]

WE HESITATE TO SUGGEST in detail the work of this committee. The Judicial Conference itself is the best place to consider how we might start anew. We only sketch one possible scenario here. Among the committee's primary responsibilities might be to assume certain functions now assigned by statute to the Sentencing Commission: to serve "as a clearinghouse and information center for the collection, preparation, and dissemination of information on Federal sentencing practices," to assist federal courts and agencies in developing sound sentencing practices, to collect and sponsor empirical research drawing upon both public and private sources of expertise, "to publish data concerning the sentencing process," to conduct seminars and training programs, to make recommendations to Congress concerning matters "necessary and advisable to carry out an effective, humane and rational sentencing policy," and "to collect systematically and disseminate information concerning sentences actually imposed."[144]

The last of these bears further refinement. The proposed Judicial Conference sentencing committee should ensure that before each sentencing proceeding, the district judge receives from the court's probation office information regarding past sentences imposed on defendants convicted of similar crimes.[145] Data could be provided for the period of the Sentencing Guidelines and for the pre-Guidelines period. The judge would learn the proportion of other such defendants who received terms of probation only, the proportion who received terms of confinement, the mean term of imprisonment, and some sense of the range. In order to take account of various mitigating and aggravating circumstances, the committee might further subcategorize the data—for instance, noting the different averages and ranges for defendants with different criminal histories, and for defendants with various roles in the crime. As we noted in the previous chapter, there is good evidence that federal judges on the whole agree more on the *ordinal ranking* of hypothetical case scenarios than they do on the *cardinal magnitudes* of appropriate sentences.[146] That is, judges may agree that the defendant in a particular case should be sentenced relatively leniently and the defendant in another case relatively harshly, but tend to disagree on whether a particular term of years is "lenient" or "harsh" for either case. Information on average sentences for a variety of "heartland" case scenarios[147] would provide quantitative guideposts to judges.

If Congress concludes that more concrete guidance is necessary to ensure systematic and principled articulation of sentencing criteria—that is, if we are not willing to wait for the development of these criteria by the courts in a federal common law of sentencing—this committee of the Judicial Conference could take on the task of writing sentencing guidelines that authentically offered guidance. The overriding purpose of these sentencing guidelines would not be to reduce "disparity" in sentencing, but to ensure that every defendant is sentenced in a manner that is fair—that is, *reasoned* and *reasonable.* Over time, the sentencing committee might be able, on the basis of the developing common law of sentencing,[148] to propose advisory or even presumptive sentences for certain crimes and situations, perhaps those constituting "heartland" crimes. The presumptive sentences might well be based on past average sentences for "heartland" scenarios; the judge would be required to explain how the case at hand matches or is different from the "heartland" crime.

Any such committee should avoid, however, the elaborate fact-finding requirements of the present Sentencing Guidelines, which become an end in themselves and too often prevent the court from considering the individual circumstances of the case at hand. And as we have argued, either party should have the right to appellate review of the sentence, on an abuse-of-discretion standard.

Replacement of the Guidelines as we know them in favor of judicial discretion tempered by advisory principles and appellate review would take us neither back to the old system nor into uncharted waters. Indeed, a simplified sentencing system of the sort we suggest here would build upon two of the major accomplishments of the Sentencing Reform Act of 1984—the requirement of an explanation of the sentence by the trial judge and the right of appeal by both sides. It would also move us toward a solution favored by several state and foreign governments. New Zealand, Finland, Sweden, and Germany all base their sentencing regimes on judicial discretion checked by nonbinding guidelines, appellate review, or both. Several states have adopted only nonbinding guidelines or guidelines in "narrative" format (rather than a grid like the Sentencing Table, see appendix A), and no other jurisdiction has produced sentencing guidelines that come close to matching the United States Sentencing Guidelines in complexity and rigidity.[149] In 1989, the legislature of Maine, consciously rejecting a system of administrative sentencing guidelines, charged the judiciary itself "with the task of creating a law of sentencing as a product of the appellate process."[150]

IN A WORLD IN WHICH discretion cannot be avoided—because justice must be administered by human beings—we must learn once again to trust the exercise of judgment in the courtroom, especially where it is subject to review by appellate courts. Fed by a fear of the exercise of discretion—by a fear of judging—and by a technocratic faith in experts and central planning, the federal sentencing reforms of the 1980s sought to relocate authority from individual sentencing judges to a distant administrative tribunal of experts not influenced by the particulars of each case at hand.

Eventually, we must come to grips with the consequences of this system—a system built on what Vaclav Havel has called "the proud belief that man, as the pinnacle of everything that exists, [is] capable of objectively describing, explaining and controlling everything . . . and of possessing the one and only truth about the world."[151] In sentencing, as in other human affairs, no mechanical solution can satisfy the demands of justice. As Havel has explained:

> We cannot devise . . . a system that will eliminate all the disastrous consequences of previous systems. . . . We have to abandon the arrogant belief that the world is merely a puzzle to be solved, a machine with instructions for use waiting to be discovered, a body of information to be fed into a computer in the hope that, sooner or later, it will spit out a universal solution.[152]

APPENDIX A

Sentencing Table of the United States Sentencing Guidelines

Offense Level	Criminal History Category (Criminal History Points) I (0 or 1)	II (2 or 3)	III (4, 5, 6)	IV (7, 8, 9)	V (10, 11, 12)	VI (13 or more)
1	0–6	0–6	0–6	0–6	0–6	0–6
2	0–6	0–6	0–6	0–6	0–6	1–7
3	0–6	0–6	0–6	0–6	2–8	3–9
4	0–6	0–6	0–6	2–8	4–10	6–12
5	0–6	0–6	1–7	4–10	6–12	9–15
6	0–6	1–7	2–8	6–12	9–15	12–18
7	0–6	2–8	4–10	8–14	12–18	15–21
8	0–6	4–10	6–12	10–16	15–21	18–24
9	4–10	6–12	8–14	12–18	18–24	21–27
10	6–12	8–14	10–16	15–21	21–27	24–30
11	8–14	10–16	12–18	18–24	24–30	27–33
12	10–16	12–18	15–21	21–27	27–33	30–37
13	12–18	15–21	18–24	24–30	30–37	33–41
14	15–21	18–24	21–27	27–33	33–41	37–46
15	18–24	21–27	24–30	30–37	37–46	41–51
16	21–27	24–30	27–33	33–41	41–51	46–57
17	24–30	27–33	30–37	37–46	46–57	51–63
18	27–33	30–37	33–41	41–51	51–63	57–71
19	30–37	33–41	37–46	46–57	57–71	63–78
20	33–41	37–46	41–51	51–63	63–78	70–87
21	37–46	41–51	46–57	57–71	70–87	77–96
22	41–51	46–57	51–63	63–78	77–96	84–105
23	46–57	51–63	57–71	70–87	84–105	92–115
24	51–63	57–71	63–78	77–96	92–115	100–125
25	57–71	63–78	70–87	84–105	100–125	110–137
26	63–78	70–87	78–97	92–115	110–137	120–150
27	70–87	78–97	87–108	100–125	120–150	130–162
28	78–97	87–108	97–121	110–137	130–162	140–175
29	87–108	97–121	108–135	121–151	140–175	151–188
30	97–121	108–135	121–151	135–168	151–188	168–210
31	108–135	121–151	135–168	151–188	168–210	188–235
32	121–151	135–168	151–188	168–210	188–235	210–262
33	135–168	151–188	168–210	188–235	210–262	235–293
34	151–188	168–210	188–235	210–262	235–293	262–327
35	168–210	188–235	210–262	235–293	262–327	292–365

Offense Level	Criminal History Category (Criminal History Points) I (0 or 1)	II (2 or 3)	III (4, 5, 6)	IV (7, 8, 9)	V (10, 11, 12)	VI (13 or more)
36	188–235	210–262	235–293	262–327	292–365	324–405
37	210–262	235–293	262–327	292–365	324–405	360–life
38	235–293	262–327	292–365	324–405	360–life	360–life
39	262–327	292–365	324–405	360–life	360–life	360–life
40	292–365	324–405	360–life	360–life	360–life	360–life
41	324–405	360–life	360–life	360–life	360–life	360–life
42	360–life	360–life	360–life	360–life	360–life	360–life
43	life	life	life	life	life	life

APPENDIX B

"Relevant Conduct" Guideline (as amended through 1997)

§1B1.3. *Relevant Conduct (Factors That Determine the Guideline Range)*

(a) *Chapters Two (Offense Conduct) and Three (Adjustments)*. Unless otherwise specified, (i) the base offense level where the guideline specifies more than one base offense level, (ii) specific offense characteristics and (iii) cross references in Chapter Two, and (iv) adjustments in Chapter Three, shall be determined on the basis of the following:

(1)(A) all acts and omissions committed, aided, abetted, counseled, commanded, induced, procured, or willfully caused by the defendant; and

(B) in the case of a jointly undertaken criminal activity (a criminal plan, scheme, endeavor, or enterprise undertaken by the defendant in concert with others, whether or not charged as a conspiracy), all reasonably foreseeable acts and omissions of others in furtherance of the jointly undertaken criminal activity,

that occurred during the commission of the offense of conviction, in preparation for that offense, or in the course of attempting to avoid detection or responsibility for that offense;

(2) solely with respect to offenses of a character for which §3D1.2(d) would require grouping of multiple counts, all acts and omissions described in subdivisions (1)(A) and (1)(B) above that were part of the same course of conduct or common scheme or plan as the offense of conviction;

(3) all harm that resulted from the acts and omissions specified in subsections (a)(1) and (a)(2) above, and all harm that was the object of such acts and omissions; and

(4) any other information specified in the applicable guideline.

(b) *Chapters Four (Criminal History and Criminal Livelihood) and Five (Determining the Sentence)*. Factors in Chapters Four and Five that establish the guideline range shall be determined on the basis of the conduct and information specified in the respective guidelines.

Commentary

Application Notes:

1. The principles and limits of sentencing accountability under this guideline are not always the same as the principles and limits of criminal liability. Under subsections (a)(1) and (a)(2), the focus is on the specific acts and omissions for which the defendant is to be held accountable in determining the applicable

guideline range, rather than on whether the defendant is criminally liable for an offense as a principal, accomplice, or conspirator.

2. A "jointly undertaken criminal activity" is a criminal plan, scheme, endeavor, or enterprise undertaken by the defendant in concert with others, whether or not charged as a conspiracy.

In the case of a jointly undertaken criminal activity, subsection (a)(1)(B) provides that a defendant is accountable for the conduct (acts and omissions) of others that was both:

(i) in furtherance of the jointly undertaken criminal activity; and

(ii) reasonably foreseeable in connection with that criminal activity.

Because a count may be worded broadly and include the conduct of many participants over a period of time, the scope of the criminal activity jointly undertaken by the defendant (the "jointly undertaken criminal activity") is not necessarily the same as the scope of the entire conspiracy, and hence relevant conduct is not necessarily the same for every participant. In order to determine the defendant's accountability for the conduct of others under subsection (a)(1)(B), the court must first determine the scope of the criminal activity the particular defendant agreed to jointly undertake (i.e., the scope of the specific conduct and objectives embraced by the defendant's agreement). The conduct of others that was both in furtherance of, and reasonably foreseeable in connection with, the criminal activity jointly undertaken by the defendant is relevant conduct under this provision. The conduct of others that was not in furtherance of the criminal activity jointly undertaken by the defendant, or was not reasonably foreseeable in connection with that criminal activity, is not relevant conduct under this provision.

In determining the scope of the criminal activity that the particular defendant agreed to jointly undertake (i.e., the scope of the specific conduct and objectives embraced by the defendant's agreement), the court may consider any explicit agreement or implicit agreement fairly inferred from the conduct of the defendant and others.

Note that the criminal activity that the defendant agreed to jointly undertake, and the reasonably foreseeable conduct of others in furtherance of that criminal activity, are not necessarily identical. For example, two defendants agree to commit a robbery and, during the course of that robbery, the first defendant assaults and injures a victim. The second defendant is accountable for the assault and injury to the victim (even if the second defendant had not agreed to the assault and had cautioned the first defendant to be careful not to hurt anyone) because the assaultive conduct was in furtherance of the jointly undertaken criminal activity (the robbery) and was reasonably foreseeable in connection with that criminal activity (given the nature of the offense).

With respect to offenses involving contraband (including controlled substances), the defendant is accountable for all quantities of contraband with which he was directly involved and, in the case of a jointly undertaken criminal activity, all reasonably foreseeable quantities of contraband that were within the scope of the criminal activity that he jointly undertook.

The requirement of reasonable foreseeability applies only in respect to the conduct (i.e., acts and omissions) of others under subsection (a)(1)(B). It does not apply to conduct that the defendant personally undertakes, aids, abets, counsels, commands, induces, procures, or willfully causes; such conduct is addressed under subsection (a)(1)(A).

A defendant's relevant conduct does not include the conduct of members of a conspiracy prior to the defendant joining the conspiracy, even if the defendant knows of that conduct (e.g., in the case of a defendant who joins an ongoing drug distribution conspiracy knowing that it had been selling two kilograms of cocaine per week, the cocaine sold prior to the defendant joining the conspiracy is not included as relevant conduct in determining the defendant's offense level). The Commission does not foreclose the possibility that there may be some unusual set of circumstances in which the exclusion of such conduct may not adequately reflect the defendant's culpability; in such a case, an upward departure may be warranted.

Illustrations of Conduct for Which the Defendant Is Accountable

(a) Acts and omissions aided or abetted by the defendant

(1) Defendant A is one of ten persons hired by Defendant B to off-load a ship containing marihuana. The off-loading of the ship is interrupted by law enforcement officers and one ton of marihuana is seized (the amount on the ship as well as the amount off-loaded). Defendant A and the other off-loaders are arrested and convicted of importation of marihuana. Regardless of the number of bales he personally unloaded, Defendant A is accountable for the entire one-ton quantity of marihuana. Defendant A aided and abetted the off-loading of the entire shipment of marihuana by directly participating in the off-loading of that shipment (i.e., the specific objective of the criminal activity he joined was the off-loading of the entire shipment). Therefore, he is accountable for the entire shipment under subsection (a)(1)(A) without regard to the issue of reasonable foreseeability. This is conceptually similar to the case of a defendant who transports a suitcase knowing that it contains a controlled substance and, therefore, is accountable for the controlled substance in the suitcase regardless of his knowledge or lack of knowledge of the actual type or amount of that controlled substance.

In certain cases, a defendant may be accountable for particular conduct under more than one subsection of this guideline. As noted in the preceding paragraph, Defendant A is accountable for the entire one-ton shipment of marihuana under subsection (a)(1)(A). Defendant A also is accountable for the entire one-ton shipment of marihuana on the basis of subsection (a)(1)(B) (applying to a jointly undertaken criminal activity). Defendant A engaged in a jointly undertaken criminal activity (the scope of which was the importation of the shipment of marihuana). A finding that the one-ton quantity of marihuana was reasonably foreseeable is warranted from the nature of the undertaking itself (the importation of marihuana by ship typically involves very large quantities of marihuana). The specific circumstances of the case (the defendant was one of ten persons off-loading the marihuana in bales) also support this finding. In an actual case, of course, if a defendant's accountability for particular conduct is established under one provision of this guideline, it is not necessary to review alternative provisions under which such accountability might be established.

(b) Acts and omissions aided or abetted by the defendant: requirement that the conduct of others be in furtherance of the jointly undertaken criminal activity and reasonably foreseeable

(1) Defendant C is the getaway driver in an armed bank robbery in which $15,000 is taken and a teller is assaulted and injured. Defendant C is accountable for the money taken under subsection (a)(1)(A) because he aided and abetted the act of taking the money (the taking of money was the specific objective of the offense he joined). Defendant C is accountable for the injury to the teller under subsection (a)(1)(B) because the assault on the teller was in furtherance of the jointly undertaken criminal activity (the robbery) and was reasonably foreseeable in connection with that criminal activity (given the nature of the offense).

As noted earlier, a defendant may be accountable for particular conduct under more than one subsection. In this example, Defendant C also is accountable for the money taken on the basis of subsection (a)(1)(B) because the taking of money was in furtherance of the jointly undertaken criminal activity (the robbery) and was reasonably foreseeable (as noted, the taking of money was the specific objective of the jointly undertaken criminal activity).

(c) Requirement that the conduct of others be in furtherance of the jointly undertaken criminal activity and reasonably foreseeable; scope of the criminal activity

(1) Defendant D pays Defendant E a small amount to forge an endorsement on an $800 stolen government check. Unknown to Defendant E, Defendant D then uses that check as a down payment in a scheme to fraudulently obtain $15,000 worth of merchandise. Defendant E is convicted for forging the $800 check and is accountable for the forgery of this check under subsection (a)(1)(A). Defendant E is not accountable for the $15,000 because the fraudulent scheme to obtain $15,000 was not in furtherance of the criminal activity he jointly undertook with Defendant D (i.e., the forgery of the $800 check).

(2) Defendants F and G, working together, design and execute a scheme to sell fraudulent stocks by telephone. Defendant F fraudulently obtains $20,000. Defendant G fraudulently obtains $35,000. Each is convicted of mail fraud. Defendants F and G each are accountable for the entire amount ($55,000). Each defendant is accountable for the amount he personally obtained under subsection (a)(1)(A). Each defendant is accountable for the amount obtained by his accomplice under subsection (a)(1)(B) because the conduct of each was in furtherance of the jointly undertaken criminal activity and was reasonably foreseeable in connection with that criminal activity.

(3) Defendants H and I engaged in an ongoing marihuana importation conspiracy in which Defendant J was hired only to help off-load a single shipment. Defendants H, I, and J are included in a single count charging conspiracy to import marihuana. Defendant J is accountable for the entire single shipment of marihuana he helped import under subsection (a)(1)(A) and any acts and omissions in furtherance of the importation of that shipment that were reasonably foreseeable (see the discussion in example (a)(1) above). He is not accountable for prior or subsequent shipments of marihuana imported by Defendants H or I because those acts were not in further-

ance of his jointly undertaken criminal activity (the importation of the single shipment of marihuana).

(4) Defendant K is a wholesale distributor of child pornography. Defendant L is a retail-level dealer who purchases child pornography from Defendant K and resells it, but otherwise operates independently of Defendant K. Similarly, Defendant M is a retail-level dealer who purchases child pornography from Defendant K and resells it, but otherwise operates independently of Defendant K. Defendants L and M are aware of each other's criminal activity but operate independently. Defendant N is Defendant K's assistant who recruits customers for Defendant K and frequently supervises the deliveries to Defendant K's customers. Each defendant is convicted of a count charging conspiracy to distribute child pornography. Defendant K is accountable under subsection (a)(1)(A) for the entire quantity of child pornography sold to Defendants L and M. Defendant N also is accountable for the entire quantity sold to those defendants under subsection (a)(1)(B) because the entire quantity was within the scope of his jointly undertaken criminal activity and reasonably foreseeable. Defendant L is accountable under subsection (a)(1)(A) only for the quantity of child pornography that he purchased from Defendant K because the scope of his jointly undertaken criminal activity is limited to that amount. For the same reason, Defendant M is accountable under subsection (a)(1)(A) only for the quantity of child pornography that he purchased from Defendant K.

(5) Defendant O knows about her boyfriend's ongoing drug-trafficking activity, but agrees to participate on only one occasion by making a delivery for him at his request when he was ill. Defendant O is accountable under subsection (a)(1)(A) for the drug quantity involved on that one occasion. Defendant O is not accountable for the other drug sales made by her boyfriend because those sales were not in furtherance of her jointly undertaken criminal activity (i.e., the one delivery).

(6) Defendant P is a street-level drug dealer who knows of other street-level drug dealers in the same geographic area who sell the same type of drug as he sells. Defendant P and the other dealers share a common source of supply, but otherwise operate independently. Defendant P is not accountable for the quantities of drugs sold by the other street-level drug dealers because he is not engaged in a jointly undertaken criminal activity with them. In contrast, Defendant Q, another street-level drug dealer, pools his resources and profits with four other street-level drug dealers. Defendant Q is engaged in a jointly undertaken criminal activity and, therefore, he is accountable under subsection (a)(1)(B) for the quantities of drugs sold by the four other dealers during the course of his joint undertaking with them because those sales were in furtherance of the jointly undertaken criminal activity and reasonably foreseeable in connection with that criminal activity.

(7) Defendant R recruits Defendant S to distribute 500 grams of cocaine. Defendant S knows that Defendant R is the prime figure in a conspiracy involved in importing much larger quantities of cocaine. As long as Defendant S's agreement and conduct is limited to the distribution of the 500 grams, Defendant S is accountable only for that 500 gram amount (under subsection (a)(1)(A)), rather than the much larger quantity imported by Defendant R.

(8) Defendants T, U, V, and W are hired by a supplier to backpack a quantity of marihuana across the border from Mexico into the United States. Defendants T, U, V, and W receive their individual shipments from the supplier at the same time and coordinate their importation efforts by walking across the border together for mutual assistance and protection. Each defendant is accountable for the aggregate quantity of marihuana transported by the four defendants. The four defendants engaged in a jointly undertaken criminal activity, the object of which was the importation of the four backpacks containing marihuana (subsection (a)(1)(B)), and aided and abetted each other's actions (subsection (a)(1)(A)) in carrying out the jointly undertaken criminal activity. In contrast, if Defendants T, U, V, and W were hired individually, transported their individual shipments at different times, and otherwise operated independently, each defendant would be accountable only for the quantity of marihuana he personally transported (subsection (a)(1)(A)). As this example illustrates, in cases involving contraband (including controlled substances), the scope of the jointly undertaken criminal activity (and thus the accountability of the defendant for the contraband that was the object of that jointly undertaken activity) may depend upon whether, in the particular circumstances, the nature of the offense is more appropriately viewed as one jointly undertaken criminal activity or as a number of separate criminal activities.

3. "Offenses of a character for which §3D1.2(d) would require grouping of multiple counts," as used in subsection (a)(2), applies to offenses for which grouping of counts would be required under §3D1.2(d) had the defendant been convicted of multiple counts. Application of this provision does not require the defendant, in fact, to have been convicted of multiple counts. For example, where the defendant engaged in three drug sales of 10, 15, and 20 grams of cocaine, as part of the same course of conduct or common scheme or plan, subsection (a)(2) provides that the total quantity of cocaine involved (45 grams) is to be used to determine the offense level even if the defendant is convicted of a single count charging only one of the sales. If the defendant is convicted of multiple counts for the above noted sales, the grouping rules of Chapter Three, Part D (Multiple Counts) provide that the counts are grouped together. Although Chapter Three, Part D (Multiple Counts) applies to multiple counts of conviction, it does not limit the scope of subsection (a)(2). Subsection (a)(2) merely incorporates by reference the types of offenses set forth in §3D1.2(d); thus, as discussed above, multiple counts of conviction are not required for subsection (a)(2) to apply.

As noted above, subsection (a)(2) applies to offenses of a character for which §3D1.2(d) would require grouping of multiple counts, had the defendant been convicted of multiple counts. For example, the defendant sells 30 grams of cocaine (a violation of 21 U.S.C. §841) on one occasion and, as part of the same course of conduct or common scheme or plan, attempts to sell an additional 15 grams of cocaine (a violation of 21 U.S.C. 846) on another occasion. The defendant is convicted of one count charging the completed sale of 30 grams of cocaine. The two offenses (sale of cocaine and attempted sale of cocaine), although covered by different statutory provisions, are of a character for which §3D1.2(d) would require the grouping of counts, had the defendant been convicted of both counts. Therefore, subsection (a)(2) applies and the total amount of cocaine (45 grams) involved is used to determine the offense level.

4. "Harm" includes bodily injury, monetary loss, property damage and any resulting harm.

5. If the offense guideline includes creating a risk or danger of harm as a specific offense characteristic, whether that risk or danger was created is to be considered in determining the offense level. See, e.g., §2K1.4 (Arson; Property Damage by Use of Explosives); §2Q1.2 (Mishandling of Hazardous or Toxic Substances or Pesticides). If, however, the guideline refers only to harm sustained (e.g., §2A2.2 (Aggravated Assault); §2B3.1 (Robbery)) or to actual, attempted or intended harm (e.g., §2F1.1 (Fraud and Deceit); §2X1.1 (Attempt, Solicitation, or Conspiracy)), the risk created enters into the determination of the offense level only insofar as it is incorporated into the base offense level. Unless clearly indicated by the guidelines, harm that is merely risked is not to be treated as the equivalent of harm that occurred. When not adequately taken into account by the applicable offense guideline, creation of a risk may provide a ground for imposing a sentence above the applicable guideline range. See generally §1B1.4 (Information to be Used in Imposing Sentence); §5K2.0 (Grounds for Departure). The extent to which harm that was attempted or intended enters into the determination of the offense level should be determined in accordance with §2X1.1 (Attempt, Solicitation, or Conspiracy) and the applicable offense guideline.

6. A particular guideline (in the base offense level or in a specific offense characteristic) may expressly direct that a particular factor be applied only if the defendant was convicted of a particular statute. For example, in §2S1.1, subsection (a)(1) applies if the defendant "is convicted under 18 U.S.C. §1956(a)(1)(A), (a)(2)(A), or (a)(3)(A)." Unless such an express direction is included, conviction under the statute is not required. Thus, use of a statutory reference to describe a particular set of circumstances does not require a conviction under the referenced statute. An example of this usage is found in §2A3.4(a)(2) ("if the offense was committed by the means set forth in 18 U.S.C. §2242").

An express direction to apply a particular factor only if the defendant was convicted of a particular statute includes the determination of the offense level where the defendant was convicted of conspiracy, attempt, solicitation, aiding or abetting, accessory after the fact, or misprision of felony in respect to that particular statute. For example, §2S1.1(a)(1) (which is applicable only if the defendant is convicted under 18 U.S.C. §1956(a)(1)(A), (a)(2)(A), or (a)(3)(A)) would be applied in determining the offense level under §2X3.1 (Accessory After the Fact) where the defendant was convicted of accessory after the fact to a violation of 18 U.S.C. §1956(a)(1)(A), (a)(2)(A), or (a)(3)(A).

7. In the case of a partially completed offense (e.g., an offense involving an attempted theft of $800,000 and a completed theft of $30,000), the offense level is to be determined in accordance with §2X1.1 (Attempt, Solicitation, or Conspiracy) whether the conviction is for the substantive offense, the inchoate offense (attempt, solicitation, or conspiracy), or both. See Application Note 4 in the Commentary to §2X1.1. Note, however, that Application Note 4 is not applicable where the offense level is determined under §2X1.1(c)(1).

8. For the purposes of subsection (a)(2), offense conduct associated with a sentence that was imposed prior to the acts or omissions constituting the instant federal offense (the offense of conviction) is not considered as part of the same course of conduct or common scheme or plan as the offense of conviction.

Examples: (1) The defendant was convicted for the sale of cocaine and sentenced to state prison. Immediately upon release from prison, he again sold cocaine to the same person, using the same accomplices and *modus operandi.* The instant federal offense (the offense of conviction) charges this latter sale. In this example, the offense conduct relevant to the state prison sentence is considered as prior criminal history, not as part of the same course of conduct or common scheme or plan as the offense of conviction. The prior state prison sentence is counted under Chapter Four (Criminal History and Criminal Livelihood). (2) The defendant engaged in two cocaine sales constituting part of the same course of conduct or common scheme or plan. Subsequently, he is arrested by state authorities for the first sale and by federal authorities for the second sale. He is convicted in state court for the first sale and sentenced to imprisonment; he is then convicted in federal court for the second sale. In this case, the cocaine sales are not separated by an intervening sentence. Therefore, under subsection (a)(2), the cocaine sale associated with the state conviction is considered as relevant conduct to the instant federal offense. The state prison sentence for that sale is not counted as a prior sentence; see §4A1.2(a)(1).

Note, however, in certain cases, offense conduct associated with a previously imposed sentence may be expressly charged in the offense of conviction. Unless otherwise provided, such conduct will be considered relevant conduct under subsection (a)(1), not (a)(2).

9. "Common scheme or plan" and "same course of conduct" are two closely related concepts.

(A) Common scheme or plan. For two or more offenses to constitute part of a common scheme or plan, they must be substantially connected to each other by at least one common factor, such as common victims, common accomplices, common purpose, or similar *modus operandi.* For example, the conduct of five defendants who together defrauded a group of investors by computer manipulations that unlawfully transferred funds over an eighteen-month period would qualify as a common scheme or plan on the basis of any of the above listed factors; i.e., the commonality of victims (the same investors were defrauded on an ongoing basis), commonality of offenders (the conduct constituted an ongoing conspiracy), commonality of purpose (to defraud the group of investors), or similarity of *modus operandi* (the same or similar computer manipulations were used to execute the scheme).

(B) Same course of conduct. Offenses that do not qualify as part of a common scheme or plan may nonetheless qualify as part of the same course of conduct if they are sufficiently connected or related to each other as to warrant the conclusion that they are part of a single episode, spree, or ongoing series of offenses. Factors that are appropriate to the determination of whether offenses are sufficiently connected or related to each other to be considered as part of the same course of conduct include the degree of similarity of the offenses, the regularity (repetitions) of the offenses, and the time interval between the offenses. When one of the above factors is absent, a stronger presence of at least one of the other factors is required. For example, where the conduct alleged to be relevant is relatively remote to the offense of conviction, a stronger showing of similarity or regularity is necessary to compensate for the absence of temporal proximity. The nature of the offenses may also be a relevant consideration (e.g., a defendant's failure to file tax returns in three consecutive years appropriately would be considered as part of the same course of conduct because such returns are only required at yearly intervals).

10. In the case of solicitation, misprision, or accessory after the fact, the conduct for which the defendant is accountable includes all conduct relevant to determining the offense level for the underlying offense that was known, or reasonably should have been known, by the defendant.

Background: This section prescribes rules for determining the applicable guideline sentencing range, whereas §1B1.4 (Information to be Used in Imposing Sentence) governs the range of information that the court may consider in adjudging sentence once the guideline sentencing range has been determined. Conduct that is not formally charged or is not an element of the offense of conviction may enter into the determination of the applicable guideline sentencing range. The range of information that may be considered at sentencing is broader than the range of information upon which the applicable sentencing range is determined.

Subsection (a) establishes a rule of construction by specifying, in the absence of more explicit instructions in the context of a specific guideline, the range of conduct that is relevant to determining the applicable offense level (except for the determination of the applicable offense guideline, which is governed by §1B1.2(a)). No such rule of construction is necessary with respect to Chapters Four and Five because the guidelines in those Chapters are explicit as to the specific factors to be considered.

Subsection (a)(2) provides for consideration of a broader range of conduct with respect to one class of offenses, primarily certain property, tax, fraud and drug offenses for which the guidelines depend substantially on quantity, than with respect to other offenses such as assault, robbery and burglary. The distinction is made on the basis of §3D1.2(d), which provides for grouping together (i.e., treating as a single count) all counts charging offenses of a type covered by this subsection. However, the applicability of subsection (a)(2) does not depend upon whether multiple counts are alleged. Thus, in an embezzlement case, for example, embezzled funds that may not be specified in any count of conviction are nonetheless included in determining the offense level if they were part of the same course of conduct or part of the same scheme or plan as the count of conviction. Similarly, in a drug distribution case, quantities and types of drugs not specified in the count of conviction are to be included in determining the offense level if they were part of the same course of conduct or part of a common scheme or plan as the count of conviction. On the other hand, in a robbery case in which the defendant robbed two banks, the amount of money taken in one robbery would *not* be taken into account in determining the guideline range for the other robbery, even if both robberies were part of a single course of conduct or the same scheme or plan. (This is true whether the defendant is convicted of one or both robberies.)

Subsections (a)(1) and (a)(2) adopt different rules because offenses of the character dealt with in subsection (a)(2) (i.e., to which §3D1.2(d) applies) often involve a pattern of misconduct that cannot readily be broken into discrete, identifiable units that are meaningful for purposes of sentencing. For example, a pattern of embezzlement may consist of several acts of taking that cannot separately be identified, even though the overall conduct is clear. In addition, the distinctions that the law makes as to what constitutes separate counts or offenses often turn on technical elements that are not especially meaningful for purposes of sentencing. Thus, in a mail fraud case, the scheme is an element of the offense and each mailing may be the basis for a separate count; in an embezzlement case, each taking may provide a basis for a separate count. Another consideration is that in a pattern of small thefts, for example, it is important to take into account the full range of related conduct. Relying on the entire range of conduct, regardless of the number of counts that are alleged or on which a conviction is obtained, appears to be the most reasonable approach to writing workable guidelines for these offenses. Conversely, when §3D1.2(d) does not apply, so that convictions on multiple counts are considered separately in determining the guideline sentencing range, the guidelines prohibit aggregation of quantities from other counts in order to prevent "double counting" of the conduct and harm from each count of conviction. Continuing offenses present similar practical problems. The reference to §3D1.2(d), which provides for grouping of multiple counts arising out of a continuing offense when the offense guideline takes the continuing nature into account, also prevents double counting.

Subsection (a)(4) requires consideration of any other information specified in the applicable guideline. For example, §2A1.4 (Involuntary Manslaughter) specifies consideration of the defendant's state of mind; §2K1.4 (Arson; Property Damage By Use of Explosives) specifies consideration of the risk of harm created.

Historical Note: Effective November 1, 1987. Amended effective January 15, 1988 (see Appendix C, amendment 3); November 1, 1989 (see Appendix C, amendments 76–78 and 303); November 1, 1990 (see Appendix C, amendment 309); November 1, 1991 (see Appendix C, amendment 389); November 1, 1992 (see Appendix C, amendment 439); November 1, 1994 (see Appendix C, amendment 503).

APPENDIX C

The Complexity of Criminal History

The following excerpt is from a United States Sentencing Commission staff memorandum prepared and circulated by the Sentencing Commission in 1995. The memorandum details the steps that must be taken to calculate the number of Criminal History points to be assigned to a prior sentence of three years imprisonment imposed on the defendant twenty years ago:

> First, it appears that §4A1.1(a) requires assignment of three points to the prior sentence because the sentence imposed exceeded one year and one month. However, Application Note 1 in the commentary to §4A1.1 contains some limitations on the application of this guideline, including the applicable time period in which convictions can be counted. According to this application note, this conviction would not be counted, unless the sentence was imposed within 15 years of the commencement of the instant offense or the term of imprisonment on the sentence extended into the 15 year time period. This requires a determination of the date of release from imprisonment to determine whether or not the sentence is counted. However, before a final determination can be made, Application Note 1 to §4A1.1 references eight additional places in §4A1.2 for further definitions and instructions that impact application: §4A1.2 for the definition of "prior sentence"; §4A1.2(b) for the definition of "sentence of imprisonment"; §4A1.2(e) for the applicable time periods; §4A1.1 2(d) [*sic*] if the offense was committed prior to the defendant's eighteenth birthday; §4A1.2(h),(j) and the Commentary to §4A1.2 for offenses involving expunged, foreign, or invalid convictions; and finally §4A1.2(k) for prior sentences that involve revocations of probation and parole. Note that these are only the sections referenced in Application Note 1 at §4A1.1. There are many other sections that could be applicable.

APPENDIX D

How Sentencing Works

CALCULATING A FEDERAL SENTENCE

Federal sentences used to be decided simply by judge's decree. Today they are based on calculations tied to the facts of an individual crime and the defendant's criminal history, and detailed in reports by probation officers. Much of that information is provided by prosecutors and federal agents—for example, the amount of money lost or the defendant's level of involvement. Such factors are totaled to determine the "offense level." Aspects of the defendant's criminal record have point values too and are figured into a "criminal history level." Except in extraordinary circumstances, the judge can sentence only in the range where the two levels meet on the sentencing grid. The path below shows how the point values for certain crimes, characteristics and criminal records might combine to determine a sentence.

CRIMINAL HISTORY

Whether points are applied for prior sentences depends on their length, how long ago they were served and whether the defendant was a juvenile. The points shown here are applicable for recent, adult convictions.

Previously convicted of hitchhiking, loitering or speeding	If crime was committed less than two years after release from prison	Each prior sentence less than 60 days	Each prior sentence from 60 days to 13 months
+0	+2	+1 Up to +4	+2

OFFENSE LEVEL

DRUG CRIME

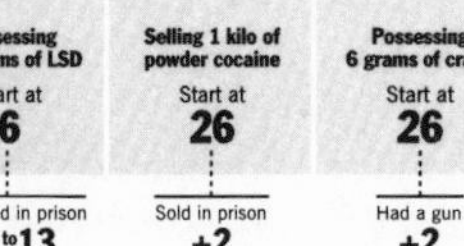

Possessing 20 grams of LSD	Selling 1 kilo of powder cocaine	Possessing 6 grams of crack	Selling drugs to a child
Start at 6	Start at 26	Start at 26	Start at 26
Possessed in prison Jump to 13	Sold in prison +2	Had a gun +2	

WHITE-COLLAR CRIME

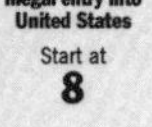

Illegal entry into United States	Fraud worth $25,000	Embezzling $150,000	Extorting more than $1.5 million
Start at 8	Start at 10	Start at 13	Start at 23
	Hid funds in foreign account Jump to 12		Threatened injury +2

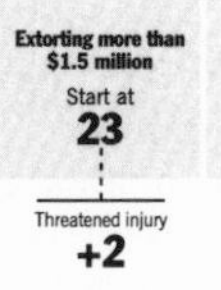

Level might be subject to changes

OFFENSE LEVEL

Did defendant lead five or more participants?	Did defendant manage five or more?	Did defendant lead or manage fewer than five?	Was de... mi... parti...
+4	+3	+2	–

VIOLENT CRIME

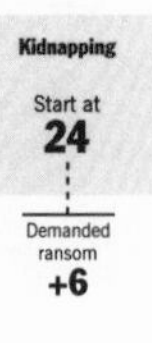

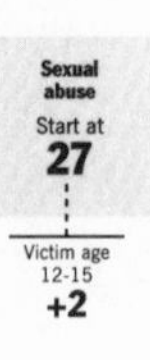

Aggravated assault	Kidnapping	Sexual abuse	First-degree murder
Start at 15	Start at 24	Start at 27	Start at 43
Seriously injured victim +4; Discharged a gun +5	Demanded ransom +6	Victim age 12-15 +2	

SOURCES: U.S. Sentencing Commission Guidelines Manual; court records

GRAPHIC BY LINDA PERLSTEIN AND LAURA STANTON—THE WASHINGTON POST

Each prior sentence nore than 13 months **+3** | If crime committed while defendant on parole or probation **+2** | Two prior violent crime or drug convictions mark you "career offender" Start at **13** (Category VI)

Total the points to determine category

A minor participant? **−2** | Was the crime a hate crime? **+3** | Did defendant abuse a position of trust? **+2** | Did defendant use a special skill? **+2** | Did defendant obstruct justice? **+2** | Did defendant accept responsibility? **−2 or −3** Depending on offense level

Total the points to determine offense level

FEDERAL SENTENCING GRID

Ranges specified in the grid are shown as months in prison.

OFFENSE LEVEL	CRIMINAL HISTORY CATEGORY I (0-1 point)	II (2-3 points)	III (4-6 points)	IV (7-9 points)	V (10-12 points)	VI (13 or more)
1	0-6 mos.	0-6	0-6	0-6	0-6	0-6
2	0-6	0-6	0-6	0-6	0-6	1-7
3	0-6	0-6	0-6	0-6	2-8	3-9
4	0-6	0-6	0-6	2-8	4-10	6-12
5	0-6	0-6	1-7	4-10	6-12	9-15
6	0-6	1-7	2-8	6-12	9-15	12-18
7	0-6	2-8	4-10	8-14	12-18	15-21
8	0-6	4-10	6-12	10-16	15-21	18-24
9	4-10	6-12	8-14	12-18	18-24	21-27
10	6-12	8-14	10-16	15-21	21-27	24-30
11	8-14	10-16	12-18	18-24	24-30	27-33
12	10-16	12-18	15-21	21-27	27-33	30-37
13	12-18	15-21	18-24	24-30	30-37	33-41
14	15-21	18-24	21-27	27-33	33-41	37-46
15	18-24	21-27	24-30	30-37	37-46	41-51
16	21-27	24-30	27-33	33-41	41-51	46-57
17	24-30	27-33	30-37	37-46	46-57	51-63
18	27-33	30-37	33-41	41-51	51-63	57-71
19	30-37	33-41	37-46	46-57	57-71	63-78
20	33-41	37-46	41-51	51-63	63-78	70-87
21	37-46	41-51	46-57	57-71	70-87	77-96
22	41-51	46-57	51-63	63-78	77-96	84-105
23	46-57	51-63	57-71	70-87	84-105	92-115
24	51-63	57-71	63-78	77-96	92-115	100-125
25	57-71	63-78	70-87	84-105	100-125	110-137
26	63-78	70-87	78-97	92-115	110-137	120-150
27	70-87	78-97	87-108	100-125	120-150	130-162
28	78-97	87-108	97-121	110-137	130-162	140-175
29	87-108	97-121	108-135	121-151	140-175	151-188
30	97-121	108-135	121-151	135-168	151-188	168-210
31	108-135	121-151	135-168	151-188	168-210	188-235
32	121-151	135-168	151-188	168-210	188-235	210-262
33	135-168	151-188	168-210	188-235	210-262	235-293
34	151-188	168-210	188-235	210-262	235-293	262-327
35	168-210	188-235	210-262	235-293	262-327	292-365
36	188-235	210-262	235-293	262-327	292-365	324-405
37	210-262	235-293	262-327	292-365	324-405	360-life
38	235-293	262-327	292-365	324-405	360-life	360-life
39	262-327	292-365	324-405	360-life	360-life	360-life
40	292-365	324-405	360-life	360-life	360-life	360-life
41	324-405	360-life	360-life	360-life	360-life	360-life
42	360-life	360-life	360-life	360-life	360-life	360-life
43	life	life	life	life	life	life

A REAL-LIFE EXAMPLE

The case of Martin Miller *of Bethesda illustrates how the grid works. Last September, U.S. District Judge Paul Friedman sentenced Miller for defrauding his business partners. An offense level of 14 and criminal history category of I put Miller in the range of 15 to 21 months. In the end, Friedman gave him 15 months in prison.*

How Miller's offense level was determined:

Fraud	**6**
Loss between $173,017 and $200,000	+7
More than minimal planning	+2
Abused position of trust	+2
	17
Accepted responsibility	−3
	Level: 14

How Miller's criminal history level was determined:

No criminal record	**Points: 0**
	Category I

NOTES

Introduction

1. See Stith and Cabranes 1997; Stith and Koh 1993; Cabranes 1992a; Cabranes 1992b, 27.

2. Cohen 1933, 261.

3. S. Rep. No. 225, 98th Cong., 1st Sess. 52, 56 (1984).

4. In this respect and others, the federal Sentencing Guidelines build upon the efforts of the United States Parole Commission, begun in the mid-1970s, to formalize the parole process. See pages 36–37.

5. The IRS Code has been accumulating since 1913; the Sentencing Guidelines Manual only since 1987.

6. A recent survey by the Federal Judicial Center showed that 86 percent of federal judges believe "somewhat" or "strongly" that the Guidelines give too much power to federal prosecutors. Federal Judicial Center 1997, 6. In chapter 4, we argue that prosecutorial power has been increased *relative* to judicial power.

7. Koon v. United States, 116 S. Ct. 2035 (1996).

8. The *Koon* case is discussed at pages 100–103.

9. Prisoners may still earn "good time" credits in prison, however, which can amount to as much as 15 percent of the sentence. Once released from prison, federal offenders are supervised for a period of time imposed by the judge as part of the sentence; the Guidelines require that nearly all felony offenders be sentenced to at least two years of supervised release following incarceration. U.S.S.G. §§5D1.1, 1.2.

10. We discuss the various sources of sentencing disparity in chapter 4.

11. Weich 1996, 97.

12. Judges have published numerous articles, essays, and letters that express deep criticism of the Guidelines regime. See Bauer 1987, C19 (criticizing Guidelines and arguing that the "judging of fellow human beings is too important to reduce its application to a computer"); Becker 1990 (criticizing Guidelines' amendment procedure for breeding "uncertainty, confusion, and extra work"); Bright 1993; Broderick 1991 (criticizing U.S. Sentencing Commission for failing to incorporate judicial feedback in Guidelines); Broderick and Wolf 1991 (criticizing Guidelines for excessively restricting judges' capacity to fashion fair sentence); Coughenour 1995, 142 (noting that "charging and sentencing disparity was a traditional feature of the criminal justice system, that has not necessarily been curtailed by the guidelines"); Eisele 1991, 16, 20 (criticizing Guidelines as "a dark, sinister, and cynical crime management program" reminiscent of "those systems prevalent in Central and Eastern European countries 150 years ago"); Gerber 1993, 232 (arguing that Guidelines-driven sentencing "betrays the constitutional ideal of individual due process"); Heaney 1992, 774 (criticizing Guidelines for increasing disparity); Heaney 1991, 226, 230 (criticizing Guidelines for failing to meet stated goals and for violating constitutional norms of due process); Karlton 1991 (reporting "deep disaffection" with Guidelines motivated by "a profound sense that the goals and price of the system are out of whack"); Lay

1992, 1761 (criticizing Guidelines for exacting "abhorrent social and economic costs" and providing "nothing more than a . . . negative contribution to a serious societal problem"); Miner 1992, 692 (criticizing excessive severity of guidelines sentences generally and inflexibility of statutory minimum sentences in drug cases in particular); Oakes 1995, 391 (arguing that Judge Learned Hand would have "vehemently" opposed Guidelines because he "was far too much a craftsman to countenance so rigid an intrusion on the discretion of a judge"); Oberdorfer 1987; Schwarzer 1992, 41 (noting that "it is undisputed that sentencing guidelines have made sentencing more time-consuming and burdensome for district court judges—not to mention appellate judges who must hear appeals from sentencing decisions"); Schwarzer 1991 (criticizing Guidelines for exacting "a high price in terms of the integrity of the criminal justice process, in terms of human life and the moral capital of the system" while yielding "arbitrary results"); Schwarzer 1990 (criticizing Guidelines for promoting "gross disparities in sentencing"); Sweet 1987 (testimony before subcommittee of House Judiciary Committee, urging that Guidelines not be put into effect); Trott 1994 (criticizing Guidelines system as "hopelessly out of control"); Van Graafeiland 1986, 1293 (agreeing with "[t]he consensus of most knowledgeable critics . . . that the Commission's sentencing by numbers approach is too depersonalized, too complicated, too punitive, and too burdensome of application"); Wald 1992, 82–83 (criticizing Guidelines for "profoundly distanc[ing] the judge from the violent consequences of the sentence" and arguing that judges "need to retain the humanizing sense of accountability" in sentencing); Weinstein 1994, 27–29 (criticizing Guidelines for forcing judges to choose between law and morality); Weinstein 1992, 366 (criticizing Guidelines for promoting "bureaucratic mentality" that denies each defendant's identity as "unique human being"); Weis 1992 (canvassing various flaws in Guidelines and arguing that they have failed to comport with their stated goals).

Other judges who have been generally supportive of the Guidelines nonetheless recognize significant difficulties with the regime, see Selya and Massaro 1994, 844 (concluding that criticism of guidelines due to their "ultra-uniformity" is fair if exaggerated); Tacha 1995, 654 (expressing respect for "the many federal judges who have opposed the Federal Sentencing Guidelines . . . based in large measure upon a legitimate concern that the best sentencing decisions are those made by the sentencing judge who knows the details of the case, the crime, and the defendant").

Judges have also criticized the Guidelines in their judicial opinions. A full catalogue of such opinions would impossibly expand the length of this note; indeed, in the years between the passage of the Sentencing Reform Act and the Supreme Court's decision upholding its constitutionality, United States v. Mistretta, 488 U.S. 361 (1989), over two hundred district judges held the SRA unconstitutional. See U.S.S.C. Annual Report 1989, 11. A review of judicial opinions critical of the Guidelines appears in Cooper 1995 (concluding that "[a]nyone who reads a large number of judicial opinions is likely to come away with a sense that few judges have great fondness for the present system. Critical words—for Congress, the Sentencing Commission, and other courts—far outnumber words of praise"). See also New York Times 1990, 22 (reporting resignation of federal District Judge J. Lawrence Irving, who stated that Guidelines' inherent injustice prevented him from enforcing them "in good conscience"); Margolick 1992, 1 (noting that Guidelines have "evoked a chorus of criticism from normally reticent judges of all ideological stripes"); Torry 1993, F7 (quoting federal District Judge Stanley Sporkin as asserting that Guidelines require sentences "out of touch with reality"); Treaster 1993, 1 (reporting announcements by Senior District Judges Jack B. Weinstein and Whitman Knapp, as semi-retired judges able to select their cases, that they would no longer preside over drug cases as a protest against particular harshness and inflexibility of Guidelines in that area).

13. Federal Judicial Center 1997. See also Federal Judicial Center 1994 (over two-thirds of federal trial judges and nearly two-thirds of federal appellate judges "strongly" or "moderately" oppose retention of mandatory sentencing guidelines).

14. DeBenedictis 1993 (45 percent of federal judges say that Sentencing Guidelines should "be scrapped," 45 percent disagree, and 10 percent don't know).

15. Earlier surveys of federal judges reported even less satisfaction with the Guidelines than do the more recent surveys mentioned at text. See Federal Courts Study Committee 1990, 137 (consulting 82 percent of sitting federal judges and recommending that Guidelines be rendered nonbinding); Burns 1993, 529 n.12 (reporting that when ninety federal judges assembled at conference were asked by professor whether they favored Guidelines, only one, a member of the U.S. Sentencing Commission, answered affirmatively); Dunworth and Weisselberg 1992, 104 n.12 (noting that in August 1991, the Ninth Circuit Judicial Conference "overwhelmingly passed a resolution that asks the Judicial Conference of the United States to recommend that Congress repeal all mandatory minimum sentences and make the sentencing guidelines permissive and nonbinding") (citation omitted); McCall 1993, 473 n.21 (noting that in May 1991, the Eleventh Circuit Judicial Council resolved that the Guidelines and mandatory minimum sentencing "'foster disparate sentencing'" and "'impede . . . the elimination of unwarranted sentencing disparity'") (citation omitted).

Chapter One

1. Proponents of mandatory sentencing guidelines have been reluctant to acknowledge the long history of judicial sentencing discretion in this country. See, e.g., Nagel 1990, 892–93 (stating that "up through 1870, legislators retained most of the discretionary power over criminal sentencing"; that "the period of incarceration was generally prescribed with specificity by the legislature"; and that Congress initially provided a "fixed statutory penalty structure," which only later was "abandoned in favor of increased judicial discretion"). Professor Nagel was an original member of the Sentencing Commission.

2. See Reese 1990, 328–29 (only in Arkansas, Kentucky, Mississippi, Missouri, Oklahoma, Tennessee, Texas, and Virginia does the jury play any role in sentencing in noncapital cases). For examples of jury recommendations of mercy, see United States v. Randall, 27 F. Cas. 696 (D.C.C.D. Or. 1886).

3. See Dorszynski v. United States, 418 U.S. 424, 432–43 (1974). Appellate review of criminal convictions in federal court included authority to review sentences for only a brief interlude of time. See Act of Mar. 3, 1879, ch. 176, 20 Stat. 354 (providing that the appellate court "shall proceed to pronounce final sentence"). This provision was interpreted to permit appellate courts to consider not only whether the sentence imposed was lawful—within statutory limitations—but also whether it was excessive, and, if so, to modify it. See, e.g., United States v. Wynn, 11 F. 57 (C.C.E.D. Mo. 1882). This power of sentencing review was limited to appeals by the defendant, since the government may not appeal an acquittal. In 1891, when Congress created the Circuit Courts of Appeals, it provided that these courts would have appellate jurisdiction "in all cases . . . arising under the criminal laws." Although the better view is that the 1891 enactment did intend to permit the new circuit courts to review criminal sentences,

cf. Hanley v. United States, 123 F. 849 (2d Cir. 1903), ultimately the view prevailed that Congress in the 1891 Act had repealed appellate review over sentences. See Freeman v. United States, 243 F. 353 (9th Cir. 1917). See generally Kutak and Gottschalk 1974, 464–71; Richey 1978. Had the 1891 statute clearly permitted appellate review (as England permitted, for instance), we might never have been confronted with the federal Sentencing Guidelines.

4. See An Act to Regulate the Collection of the Duties, ch. 5, §35, 1 Stat. 29, 46–47 (1789). Two months later, Congress enacted the Judiciary Act of 1789, ch. 20, 1 Stat. 73 (1789), which established the lower federal courts (the Constitution itself having provided in Article III for the Supreme Court).

5. See Crimes Act of 1790, ch. 9, 1 Stat. 112.

6. Id. §7, 1 Stat. at 113, 116.

7. An Act to Punish Frauds Committed on the Bank of the United States, ch. 611, §1, 1 Stat. 573. (1798); see also An Act for the Punishment of Certain Crimes against the United States, 1 Stat. 596 (1798) (providing for imprisonment from six months to five years for conspiracy to commit sedition).

8. See Henderson 1985, 8–9, 37. The Crimes Act of 1790 also authorized state courts to entertain some federal prosecutions, as did subsequent statutes until 1815. Dwight Henderson reports that there has been no study of the frequency or the nature of such prosecutions. Id. at 37–38.

9. See, e.g., An Act More Effectually to Provide for the Punishment of Certain Crimes against the United States, ch. 65, §1, 4 Stat. 115 (1825) (providing death penalty for arson in arsenals and navy yards). It was apparently not until 1872 that Congress provided for a sentence of life imprisonment. Act of June 8, 1872, §285, 17 Stat. 320 (mandatory life term of hard labor for second conviction of postal robbery or injuring postal employee during robbery or using dangerous weapon during postal robbery).

10. See generally Howe 1939; Stith 1995.

11. See, e.g., United States v. Bevans, 16 U.S. (3 Wheat.) 336 (1818) (Marshall, C.J.) (reversing conviction for murder on ship docked in Boston Harbor because that harbor was not "on the high seas or in any river, harbor, basin, or bay, out of the jurisdiction of any particular state" under the Crimes Act of 1790).

12. See Henderson 1985, 47, 146–47. The pardon power is granted in U.S. Constitution art. II, §2, cl. 1.

13. See Hay 1975; Hindus 1980; Beattie 1986. Of 111 capital sentences imposed in the federal courts prior to 1829, only 42 were carried out. (Sixty-four defendants were pardoned; the remaining five defendants died, escaped, or are unaccounted for.) See House Judiciary Committee, H.R. Rep. No. 108, 54th Cong., 2d Sess. (Jan. 22, 1896), appendix at 4–5 (table 1, reprinted from H.R. Exec. Doc. No. 146, 20th Cong., 2d Sess. (Feb. 26, 1829)). Reports from later years are consistent. For instance, during the single year 1890, 120 homicides were presented to federal grand juries, resulting in 77 indictments for murder, 16 convictions of murder (plus 6 convictions of manslaughter), and 48 jury acquittals. Ten murderers were actually executed. Id. at 5 (table 2). In 1897, Congress eliminated the death penalty for all but three of the eighteen nonmilitary crimes for which it had nominally been provided. Capital Punishment Act of 1897, ch. 20, 29 Stat. 487 (1897) (retaining capital punishment only for treason, murder, and rape).

14. See Joint Committee on New York Drug Law Evaluation 1978 (evaluation of "Rockefeller Drug Laws"); U.S.S.C. 1991b.

15. See, e.g., An Act to Establish the Post Office and Post Roads, ch. 7, 1 Stat. 232 (minimum fine of $100 for "fraudulent demand of postage") (1792); Act of Mar. 3, 1825, ch. 64, §§16, 21, 22, 23, 28, 4 Stat. 102, 106–10 (providing for

mandatory minimum terms of imprisonment, usually of one year, for a variety of crimes related to U.S. mails); Act of June 8, 1872, §§281, 285, 287, 288, 290, 291, 297, 298, 17 Stat. 283–330 (defining numerous new crimes relating to U.S. mails and providing for mandatory minimum penalties, usually of six months or one year).

16. See, e.g., An Act in Addition to the Act Entitled An Act for the Punishment of Certain Crimes against the United States, ch. 74, §1, 1 Stat. 596, 596 (1798) (six months to five years for conspiracy to commit sedition); An Act to Prohibit the Importation of Slaves, ch. 22, §7, 2 Stat. 426, 428 (1807) (two to four years for importation of slaves in ship); Act of Mar. 3, 1825, ch. 64, §22, 4 Stat. 102, 108–9 (five to ten years for robbery of mails, two to ten years for attempted robbery; one to three years for larceny); An Act to Prevent Correspondence with Rebels, ch. 60, §1, 12 Stat. 696, 696 (1863) (six months to five years for correspondence with rebels); An Act to Define and Punish Certain Crimes, ch. 193, §1, 14 Stat. 557, 557 (1867) (one to ten years for robbery of U.S. property); An Act Imposing Taxes on Distilled Spirits and Tobacco, ch. 186, §95, 15 Stat. 125, 164 (1868) (six months to three years for sale of untaxed cigars); Act of June 8, 1782, ch. 335, §281, 17 Stat. 283, 318–19 (one to five years for larceny from U.S. mails).

17. Ch. 64, §23, 4 Stat. 102, 109 (1825). Similarly, the criminal provision of the Ku Klux Klan Act of 1871 provided for a fine from $500 to $5000 and imprisonment from six months to six years ("with or without hard labor, as the court may determine"); also, the defendant could be both fined and imprisoned "as the court shall determine," ch. 22, §2, 17 Stat. 13, 14 (1871).

18. See United States v. Gilbert, 25 F. Cas. 1318 (C.C.N.D. Ohio 1873) (No. 15,205); United States v. Blaisdell, 24 F. Cas. 1162 (S.D.N.Y. 1869) (No. 14,608).

19. Ch. 335, §146, 17 Stat. 283, 302.

20. See 18 U.S.C. §1703 (1994).

21. Montesquieu 1748.

22. Beccaria 1764, at 1986.

23. Thomas Jefferson wrote to Edmund Pendleton in 1776: "Punishments I know are necessary, and I would provide them, strict and inflexible, but proportioned to the crime. Death might be inflicted for murther [*sic*] and perhaps for treason. . . . Rape, buggery &c. punish by castration. All other crimes by working on high roads, rivers, gallies &c. a certain time to be proportioned to the offence." Jefferson 1776, 503, 505.

24. See Bentham 1830. Bentham explained, id. at 396, "General prevention is effected by the denunciation of punishment, and by its application, which, according to the common expression, *serves for an example*. . . . General prevention ought to be the chief end of punishment, as it is its real justification." Like Beccaria before him, Bentham went on to argue, id. at 402, that there must be a "proportion between crimes and punishments [because in] matters of importance, every one calculates." Crime, he said "will be more successfully combated, the more carefully the law turns the balance of profit against it."

25. See Beccaria 1764, 23 ("[T]he purpose of punishments is not to torment and afflict a sentient being or to undo a crime which has already been committed. . . . The purpose of punishment, then, is nothing other than to dissuade the criminal from doing fresh harm to his compatriots and to keep other people from doing the same.").

26. See Montesquieu 1748, 89–91. See also Locke 1698 ("retribute" to the criminal "so far as calm reason and conscience dictates, what is proportionate to his Transgression, which is so much as may serve for R*eparation* and R*estraint*").

27. Beccaria 1764, 46.

28. Id. at 12, 39–53.

29. See Tappan 1958 (noting that even in France, within twenty years "the excessive rigidity of the system had been recognized, and it was modified in the Code of 1810 and by subsequent laws of 1824 and 1832, which permitted a measure of judicial discrimination in sentencing in accordance with mitigating or aggravating circumstances").

30. See Hall 1951.

31. See United States v. Coolidge, 25 F. Cas. 619, 620 (C.C.D. Mass. 1813) (Story, J., sitting as Circuit Justice), *rev'd,* 14 U.S. (1 Wheat.) 415 (1816).

32. See United States v. Hudson and Goodwin, 11 U.S. (7 Cranch) 32 (1812); United States v. Coolidge, 14 U.S. (1 Wheat.) 415 (1816). See generally Rowe 1992.

33. Beccaria had been adamantly opposed to any leeway permitted judges to interpret the law. See Beccaria 1764, 10–11 ("[T]he authority to interpret penal law can scarcely rest with criminal judges for the good reason that they are not lawmakers. . . . In every criminal case, the judge should come to a perfect syllogism: the major premise should be the general law; the minor premise, the act which does or does not conform to the law; and the conclusion, acquittal or condemnation. If the judge were constrained to form even two syllogisms, or if he were to choose to do so, then the door to uncertainty would be opened.")

34. See Crimes Act of 1825, ch. 65, §2, 4 Stat. 115, 115. Virtually every section of this comprehensive criminal enactment (except those providing for the death penalty) provided for a maximum fine and a maximum term of imprisonment. Appended to each specification of the maximum sentence was the direction "according to the aggravation of the offense." Interestingly, the postal crimes statute enacted shortly afterwards did not contain this direction, see *supra* text at note 17. See also Contempt Act of 1831, ch. 103, §2, 4 Stat. 447, 488, which provided for "a fine not exceeding five hundred dollars, or by imprisonment, not exceeding three months, or both, according to the nature and aggravation of the offence."

35. This wording appears in the Robbery Act of 1867, ch. 193, 14 Stat. 557; the Ku Klux Klan Act of 1871, ch. 22, §2, 17 Stat. 13, 14; and the Post Office Act of 1872, ch. 335, §§146, 147, 17 Stat. 283, 302, as well as in statutes enacted prior to 1825. See, e.g., An Act to Prohibit American Vessels from Proceeding to, or Trading With, the Enemies of the United States, §1, 1 Stat. 778 (providing for forfeiture of unbonded ship and fine up to $100 and imprisonment up to twelve months, "according to the discretion of the court").

36. Postema 1986. In Bentham's words: "For minimizing evil, the main caution is, in no case, on no occasion, to lay down inflexible rules. . . . The pretence in this case is, the avoiding to place arbitrary power in the hands of the judge. But the good thus sought is illusory." Id. at 409 (quoting Bentham). As Professor Postema has shown, Bentham's mature theory of adjudication is actually quite nuanced in its treatment of the issue of judicial discretion, providing for almost complete judicial discretion in adjudication; importantly, however, Bentham would not grant *law-making* power to judges and thus would have no system of judicial precedent. Id. at 403–35.

37. Ferri 1921, 3–4, 180–81. The Ferri proposal provided, for instance, "If there occurs only once circumstance of greater dangerousness, the judge shall apply the sanction in a measure not less than half between the minimum and the maximum set for the offense. . . . If there occurs only one circumstance of less dangerousness the judge shall apply the sanction in a measure less than half between the minimum and the maximum." Id. at 163–64, 354–55.

38. Glueck 1958, 468. For a modern version of this sort of judging, see page 85 below, text at note 23.

39. See Exodus 21. The Biblical *lex talionis,* Exodus 21:24, is translated popularly as "an eye for an eye." In context, this was a call for lenient punishment—instead of more than an eye for an eye. Thomas Jefferson adopted a similar proportionality principle; see Jefferson 1779, 498 ("[W]hosoever . . . shall maim another, or shall disfigure him . . . shall be maimed or disfigured in like sort.").

40. 15 F. Cas. 1183, 1185 (C.C.D. Vt. 1798).

41. Bacon v. United States, 97 F. 35, 44 (8th Cir.), *cert. denied,* 175 U.S. 726 (1899).

42. See, e.g., United States v. Nye, 27 F. Cas. 210, 211 (C.C.D. Mass. 1855) (No. 15,906) (court held that in prosecution for an "endeavor to make a revolt" at sea, the disrepair of the vessel was irrelevant to guilt; however, this fact and the fact that the defendants "came on board sober, and fit for duty," as well as the absence of violence itself during the offense, were taken into account in imposing sentence of thirty days, where the maximum sentence provided by statute was three years imprisonment and a fine of $1000).

43. United States v. Randall, 27 F. Cas. 696 (D.C.D. Or. 1869) (No. 16,118) (sentencing defendant to twelve years' imprisonment; statute provided minimum term of ten years and maximum term of twenty-one years.)

44. The American colonies briefly experimented with prisons in the late seventeenth century, but it was not until after the Revolution that states had significant prison capacity and began relying on imprisonment as a punishment for a wide variety of offenses. See Barnes and Teeters 1959, 328–37 ("The Genesis and Development of the Penitentiary"); Lewis 1922, 16–24; Fogel 1975, 3–18.

45. Lewis 1922, 22, paraphrasing Benjamin Rush, *An Inquiry into the Effects of Punishments upon Criminals and upon Society.*

46. Id.

47. See An Act for the Punishment of Certain Crimes, ch. 42, 5 Laws of New Hampshire 596, 596–98 (1791) (Rumford 1916).

48. Kant 1797, 100. Kant specifically addressed Beccaria's proposals at 100–102, 104–6.

49. "Only the Law of retribution (*jus talionis*) can determine exactly the kind and degree of punishment; it must be well understood, however, that this determination [should be made] in the chambers of a court of justice (and not in your private judgment)." Id. at 101.

50. Id. at 100.

51. See Stephen 1883; Hart 1968, 11–12; Packer 1968, 64–69.

52. It has been suggested that when penitentiaries were first established in the United States in the late eighteenth century, the sole purpose of the penitentiary was to provide an alternative to capital punishment. See Rothman 1990, 61–62. Rothman's introduction states, however, that as instituted both in Europe and the United States, penitentiaries sought "to transform the inmate's character so that he would leave the institution a different person." Id. at xxv.

53. Rothman describes the two schools of prison reformation in the early nineteenth century: the Auburn, New York "congregate" plan whereby prisoners were to "labor together in a workshop during the day for the course of their fixed sentences in the penitentiary . . . forbidden to converse with fellow inmates or even exchange glances," and the rival Pennsylvania system which "isolated each prisoner for the entire period of his confinement . . . to leave the institution as ignorant of the identity of other convicts as on the day they entered." Id. at 82.

54. Twentieth Century Fund Task Force on Criminal Sentencing 1976.

55. Rothman 1990, 250.

56. In the 1860s, "[o]fficials sometimes talked as if reform was still a primary goal, but the declarations sounded pro forma." Rothman 1990, 243. "Nevertheless, the penitentiaries remained central to criminal punishment. They continued to thrive long after their original rationale and practices were abandoned." Id. at 245.

57. Rothman 1990, 249–51.

58. See Morse 1939, *quoting* S. J. May of the Prison Association of New York 1847.

59. The particulars of how this fear led to enactment of the federal Sentencing Guidelines is chronicled in chapter 2. The question whether this fear is justified is examined in chapter 4.

60. Morse 1939, *quoting* S. J. May of the Prison Association of New York 1847.

61. Rothman 1990, 251.

62. See Ryerson 1977.

63. The 1870 meeting in Cincinnati, Ohio of the American Prison Association has been recognized as the key event in the rise of what became the medical model of rehabilitation in American penology. The Declaration of Principles adopted at that meeting asserted that "the supreme aim of prison discipline is the reformation of criminals, not the infliction of vindictive suffering." See Lindsey 1925, 18–21, *quoting Declaration of Principles,* National Congress on Penitentiary and Reformatory Discipline (1870).

64. See An Act to Provide for Deductions from the Terms of Sentence of United States Prisoners, ch. 145, 18 Stat. 479, 479–80 (1875); An Act to Shorten the Terms of Imprisonment in the Jail, ch. 33, 26 Stat. 20 (1890).

65. The New York statute is quoted in Lindsey 1925, 22–23.

66. Id.

67. See generally Campbell 1991; Lovejoy 1994, 24.

68. An Act to Parole United States Prisoners, ch. 387, 36 Stat. 819 (1910) (creating boards of parole at each United States Penitentiary). By this time Congress had also established three federal penitentiaries, to which federal prisoners, previously confined in state facilities, were transferred. Specifically, on March 31, 1891, Congress provided for the erection of federal prisons, An Act For the Erection of United States Prisons, ch. 529, 26 Stat. 839.

69. Crimes Act of 1909, ch. 321, 35 Stat. 1088.

70. Id. As of 1909, twelve crimes still carried some form of minimum penalty. Three of these carried a potential death penalty: treason, first degree murder, and rape. For the latter two, the jury could reduce the sentence to life imprisonment, and for treason the mandatory minimum penalty was only five years. Various forms of mutiny, murder, robbery by piracy, and engaging in the trade of slaves carried mandatory life sentences. Second degree murder and plundering a ship in distress carried penalties of ten years to life. The remaining 270 crimes carried no minimum penalty of imprisonment, and all but thirteen had maximum terms of ten years or less.

71. "Good time" was introduced in the federal system in 1875. See Act of Mar. 3, 1875, ch. 145, 18 Stat. 479, 480. The rate was increased to ten days per month in 1910 and remained at that rate until the Sentencing Reform Act of 1984. See 18 U.S.C. §4161 (1982) (repealed 1984).

72. An Act to Parole United States Prisoners, ch. 387, §1, 36 Stat. 819, 819 (1910), subsequently codified at 18 U.S.C. §§4202–8 (repealed 1984).

73. See Augustus 1852.

74. See generally Cromwell et al. 1985; Evjen 1975, 3 ("at least 60 [federal]

districts in 39 states were suspending sentence" before the Supreme Court denied such authority).

75. See Ex parte United States, 242 U.S. 27 (1916), which includes accounts of the history of sentence "suspension" in the federal courts and state courts. In the case itself, the defendant had pleaded guilty to embezzlement from a national bank and had already made restitution; the federal district court sentenced him to the minimum prison term (five years) specified by Congress. But the Court then ordered that "execution of the sentence be, and it is hereby suspended during the good behavior of the defendant." Although holding that the district court had no such power absent authorization from Congress, the Supreme Court stayed issuance of its judgment "so as to afford ample time for executive clemency or such other action as may be required to meet [this] situation."

76. Probation Act of 1925, ch. 521, §1, 43 Stat. 1259, 1259.

77. See 18 U.S.C. §3651 (repealed 1984).

78. Cromwell et al. 1985, 12.

79. The boards of parole that Congress had created in 1910 at each federal prison were consolidated into a single Board of Parole in 1948. Act of June 25, 1948, ch. 645, §4201, 62 Stat. 683, 854. In 1976, parole was significantly restructured, and the name of the federal authority was changed to the United States Parole Commission. See Parole Commission and Reorganization Act, Pub. L. No. 94-233, §2, 90 Stat. 219 (1976) (codified at 18 U.S.C. §4202) (repealed 1984).

80. Some of these laws were targeted to rehabilitation for particular classes of offenders. See Federal Youth Corrections Act, 18 U.S.C. §§5005–26 (repealed 1984); Narcotics Addiction Act, 18 U.S.C. §§4251–55 (repealed 1984); Juvenile Delinquency Act, 18 U.S.C. §§5031–42 (repealed 1984). Parole law was also amended to permit judges to provide that a defendant would immediately be eligible for parole or to provide parole eligibility at some point prior to service of one-third of sentence, see 18 U.S.C. §4205(b) (repealed 1984), but few judges used these provisions. Additionally, some offenders were effectively denied eligibility for probation or parole. See 18 U.S.C. §3575 (repealed 1984) ("dangerous special offenders"); 21 U.S.C. §849 ("dangerous special drug offenders").

81. As of the late 1960s, every state also still had essentially indeterminate sentencing. During the 1970s, as criticism of the indeterminate model mounted (see pages 29–37), several states, including California and New Jersey, led the way in adopting legislatively determinate sentencing. See generally Shane-DuBow et al. 1985.

82. 18 U.S.C. §3651 (1994). See generally Low 1970, 1246–58; *Reform of the Federal Criminal Laws: Hearings on S. 1437 and S. 1722 before the Subcommittee on Criminal Laws and Procedures of the Committee on the Judiciary, 91st Cong.–96th Cong.* (1971–1979). The criminal provisions of federal law are primarily set forth in Title 18 of the U.S. Code; many of these have not been altered in essential respects since the nineteenth century.

83. 18 U.S.C. §4205(a) (repealed 1984) (if sentence greater than one year, prisoner eligible for parole after one-third of sentence is served or after ten years, whichever is less).

84. Between 1970 and 1972, the sentencing judge permitted immediate parole eligibility—subject to the parole board's discretion—in 28.6 percent of cases. See United States Board of Parole 1970–72, 14–15.

85. In providing enhanced penalties for use of a firearm during a federal felony, for instance, Congress provided for a minimum penalty of one year for a first offense (in addition to the sentence for the underlying felony). For a second

conviction, however, Congress expressly provided that "such person shall be sentenced to imprisonment for twenty years. . . . Notwithstanding any other provision of law, the court shall not place on probation or suspend the sentence of any person convicted of this subsection." 18 U.S.C. §924(c)(1). This provision was amended in 1984 to provide *mandatory* minimum sentences in all cases, and was subsequently amended to provide for higher mandatory penalties.

86. See Weinstein 1989 (listing range of nonprison sentences, including fines, day prison, "halfway" houses, home detention with or without electronic monitoring, community service, treatment programs, employment programs, and supervised probation).

87. See Bureau of Justice Statistics, 1994 Sourcebook of Criminal Justice Statistics, table 5.27 (giving historical data from 1950–1987).

88. See U.S.S.C. 1987b, 68 (reporting percentage of defendants receiving "split sentence" under pre-Guidelines practice ranged from 1 percent of those convicted of robbery, to 36 percent of income tax offenders). Split sentences were authorized by 18 U.S.C. §3651 and were available except where the offense of conviction was punishable by death or life imprisonment. If the defendant violated the terms of probation, he could be resentenced "for any part of the remaining balance of the originally prescribed term of imprisonment." 18 U.S.C. §3653. The Sentencing Reform Act of 1984 repealed the authority for imposition of split sentences.

89. See Glueck 1928, 455 (emphasis omitted).

90. Id. at 475.

91. See 18 U.S.C. §4202 (establishing Parole Commission, which replaced federal Parole Board, "as an independent agency in the Department of Justice," consisting of nine members appointed by the President with Senate confirmation, serving six-year terms.)

92. "Before 1976, California was the state most thoroughly committed to the idea that criminal sentences should be indeterminate. The judge merely sentenced the offender to 'the term prescribed by law,' which often was one year to life in prison. The actual period of confinement (and the subsequent period of parole supervision) was set by the Adult Authority, an administrative agency which exercised practically unsupervised discretion. . . . All this changed with the passage of the Determinate Sentencing Act of 1976." Johnson 1995, 121–22.

93. Hart 1968, 8–13, 25–27.

94. See generally Singer and Gardner 1989, 255–325 (explaining derivation and significance of the mens rea requirement in American law).

95. See, e.g., Ratzlaf v. United States, 510 U.S. 135, 140–41 (1994); Morissette v. United States, 342 U.S. 246 (1952) (Jackson, J.).

96. See, e.g., Ariz. Rev. Stat. Ann. §13-1904 (1996) (defining armed robbery as robbery when armed with, using, or threatening to use "a deadly weapon or a simulated deadly weapon").

97. 18 U.S.C. §1341 (1994).

98. See Rakoff 1980, 771 ("To federal prosecutors of white collar crime, the mail fraud statute is . . . our true love . . . with its simplicity, adaptability, and comfortable familiarity.").

99. See, e.g., McNally v. United States, 483 U.S. 350 (1987) (reversing mail fraud conviction on ground that indictment covered conduct not within the federal prohibition); United States v. Margiotta, 688 F.2d 108 (2d Cir. 1982) (upholding conviction under mail fraud statute over dissent of Judge Ralph K. Winter that "limitless expansion of the mail fraud statute subjects virtually every active participant in the political process to potential criminal investigation and prosecution," id. at 143).

100. See Model Penal Code §2.02 Comment at 229–44.

101. See Model Penal Code §1.02(2) (referring to provisions on punishment as provisions on "sentencing and treatment"); id. art. 6 ("Authorized Disposition of Offenders"); id. §7.01(1) (prohibiting imposition of term of imprisonment unless, inter alia, "defendant is in need of correctional treatment").

102. Model Penal Code §7.01 Comment at 227.

103. Id. §2.02 (General Requirements of Culpability) (defining terms "purposely," "knowingly," "recklessly," and "negligently").

104. Id. §6.06(2).

105. Id. §7.01(1).

106. Id. §221.2(1).

107. Id. §§223.1 et seq.

108. Id. §7.01(2).

109. Id.

110. Lynch 1994, 112.

111. See, e.g., In re Winship, 397 U.S. 358 (1970) (due process implies presumption of innocence and requirement of proof beyond a reasonable doubt); Miranda v. Arizona, 384 U.S. 436 (1966) (police must inform suspect of rights before interrogation); Gideon v. Wainwright, 372 U.S. 335 (1963) (constitutional right to counsel requires appointment of counsel for indigent defendants); Mapp v. Ohio, 367 U.S. 643 (1961) (excluding evidence obtained in violation of Fourth Amendment).

112. 337 U.S. 241, 245–47 (1949).

113. See, e.g., Federal Rules of Evidence 1101(d)(3) (providing that rules, other than with respect to evidentiary privileges, do not apply to sentencing); McMillan v. Pennsylvania, 477 U.S. 79 (1986) (preponderance of evidence standard for disputed facts at sentencing hearing); United States v. Grayson, 438 U.S. 41 (1978) (permitting sentencing court to take into account apparent perjury by defendant who took stand at trial; no mention of standard of proof required); Roberts v. United States, 445 U.S. 552 (1980) (permitting sentencing court to take into account defendant's refusal to cooperate not based upon privilege against compelled self-incrimination); United States v. Butler, 680 F.2d 1055 (5th Cir. 1982) (exclusionary rule for Fourth Amendment violations not applicable to sentencing).

114. 337 U.S. at 248–49.

115. 438 U.S. 41 (1978).

116. McMillan v. Pennsylvania, 477 U.S. 79 (1986).

117. Wisconsin v. Mitchell, 508 U.S. 476 (1993).

118. Id. at 485.

119. See Greenholtz v. Inmates of Nebraska Penal and Correctional Complex, 442 U.S. 1 (1979) (noting, in case concerning procedural due process, the subjectivity and complexity of the parole decision). However, to the extent that a state makes parole decisions *nondiscretionary,* revocation of parole must be accompanied by certain minimum requirements of due process—including notice, opportunity to be heard and to confront witnesses, counsel in certain cases, and "neutral and detached" parole officials. See Gagnon v. Scarpelli, 411 U.S. 778 (1973); Morrissey v. Brewer, 408 U.S. 471 (1972).

120. See Fed. R. Crim. P. 32(c).

121. See, e.g., United States v. Fatico, 458 F. Supp. 388 (E.D.N.Y. 1978), *aff'd,* 603 F.2d 1053 (2d Cir. 1979), *cert. denied,* 444 U.S. 1073 (1980).

122. See Weber 1904, 2:886.

123. See Savelsberg 1992.

124. See Hayner 1958, 482–83. Professor Alan M. Dershowitz has concluded

that incapacitation of apparently dangerous criminals "has always been practiced, to some degree, by every society in history regardless of the jurisprudential rhetoric it has employed"; the methods have included capital punishment, banishment, and imprisonment. See Dershowitz 1974b, 1, 57.

125. See Rubin 1956, 344–47; Van Vechten 1937, 638. But see Tappan 1958, 535–36 (a thorough review of sentence lengths in the few jurisdictions with definite sentencing reveals that time served before release is similar to that in jurisdictions with indefinite sentencing).

126. See Mitford 1973; New York State Special Commission on Attica 1972, 93–102 ("operation of the parole system was a primary source of tension and bitterness within the walls"); Emmrich 1978, C1. There had been earlier complaints that apparent disparity in treatment leads to prison unrest. See Ashe 1941, 26.

127. In 1928, Dr. Karl Menninger, on behalf of a committee of the American Psychiatric Association, urged the "permanent legal detention of the incurably inadequate, incompetent, and anti-social offenders irrespective of the particular offense committed." Menninger 1928, 376; see also Menninger 1945, 448–49 ("The scientific attitude as shown in psychiatry must sooner or later totally displace existing legal methods.").

128. See Wertham 1955, 338; Hall 1956. Dr. Menninger apparently revised his views, as did Professor Glueck to a lesser extent. See Hall and Menninger 1953, 701–2; Glueck 1958; see generally Morris 1974, 1–34.

129. American Friends Service Committee 1971.

130. See Orland 1973, 55–56, *quoting* J. Edgar Hoover, "The Dire Consequences of the Premature Release of Dangerous Criminals through Probation and Parole," *F.B.I. Law Enforcement Bulletin* 27, no. 11 (1958): 1.

131. See Messinger and Johnson 1978; Casper 1984, 236 (explaining that "[c]onservatives and law enforcement interests" desired determinate sentencing because "parole boards seemed often to release prisoners who continued to pose a danger to society" and judges seemed "reluctant to send 'marginal defendants' to prison").

132. See Everson 1919; Gaudet et al. 1933; Gaudet 1949, 449–61; Hogarth 1971.

133. See, e.g., Sellin 1935 and the earlier studies discussed and criticized in Sutton 1978.

134. See Partridge and Eldridge 1974, 9.

135. Model Penal Code §§6.01–6.13, 7.01 (Proposed Official Draft 1962).

136. National Council on Crime and Delinquency 1963; see also ABA Standards Relating to Sentencing Alternatives and Procedures (Approved Draft 1968) (similar).

137. Model Penal Code §7.01(1); see also §7.0, Comment at 224.

138. One crude way to gauge leniency in criminal sentencing is to measure incarceration rates in the nation. In 1933, the first year in which reliable statistics are available, the incarceration rate in the United States was approximately 110 per 100,000 population, and rose to nearly 140 per 100,000 population in 1939. After a reduction in the incarceration rate during the Second World War, the rate remained between approximately 110 and 120 per 100,000 until the 1960s. In that decade, however, the rate of incarceration fell to less than 100 per 100,000 population by 1968. The rate remained relatively constant until the mid-1970s, and since that time has assumed a steady, continual growth upward until it is now, in 1996, over 350 per 100,000 population. Donohue and Siegelman 1996, 10–11 (unpublished manuscript, citing Bureau of Justice statistics; manuscript on file with authors).

139. O'Donnell et al. 1977, 70.

140. The Brown Commission's Final Report was not issued until 1971. National Commission on Reform of Federal Criminal Laws 1971.

141. President's Commission on Law Enforcement and Administration of Justice 1967, 351–52, 358.

142. Davis 1969.

143. Id. at 43.

144. Id. at 18–20.

145. Id. at 139–40 (emphasis added).

146. See Coffee 1978, 977 (referring to *Struggle for Justice* and *Law without Order* as "bombshells" contributing to collapse of rehabilitative ideal).

147. American Friends Service Committee 1971.

148. Mitford 1973.

149. Twentieth Century Fund Task Force on Criminal Sentencing 1976.

150. See, e.g., Dershowitz 1970; 1974a.

151. Von Hirsch 1976. Von Hirsch's book was the *Report of the Committee for the Study of Incarceration,* whose membership included Alan M. Dershowitz. The American Friends Service Committee report, Frankel's book (see below), and Von Hirsch's book were all published by Hill and Wang, New York.

152. Van den Haag 1975.

153. See Becker 1968; Posner 1973, 364–67.

154. See Wilson 1975.

155. See Martinson 1974, 25 (emphasis omitted). Martinson's article was based on a thorough review of the empirical literature on the effectiveness of rehabilitation, see Lipton et al. 1975. Subsequently, Martinson essentially recanted his earlier conclusion. See Martinson 1979, 252; Vitiello 1991.

156. See Allen 1981, 29–30. Allen had long been skeptical of the rehabilitative model of sentencing. See Allen 1964.

157. In this period, a significant scholarly call for continuation of discretionary sentencing and parole was that of Morris 1977; Morris's book also called for reduced reliance on imprisonment.

158. Frankel 1973.

159. 128 Cong. Rec. 26503 (1982)

160. Frankel 1973, 5.

161. Id. at 122, 123.

162. Id. at 15.

163. Id. at 22–23.

164. Id. at 103.

165. Id. at 119–20.

166. Id. at 113–14.

167. See Alschuler 1978. See also pages 106–12.

168. See O'Donnell et al. 1977.

169. See Newman 1977; Newman 1987; Kennedy 1979b, 356 n.10 ("In recent years, Judge Frankel has secured the support of an articulate ally," citing Judge Newman).

170. See page 51.

171. See Freed 1992, 1681 n.7 (discussing Yale's, and Freed's, involvement with sentencing reform from 1974 through to present time as editor of the bimonthly Federal Sentencing Reporter, which we cite frequently throughout this book).

172. See 38 Fed. Reg. 26,652 (Sept. 24, 1973); 38 Fed. Reg. 31942 (Nov. 19, 1973).

173. Genego et al. 1975, 822–23.

174. See also pages 71–72.

175. Parole Commission and Reorganization Act, Pub. L. No. 94-233, 90 Stat. 219 (1976) (codified in various sections of Title 5 and Title 18 of the United States Code) (repealed 1984).

176. 18 U.S.C. §4203(a)(1) required continuation of parole guidelines. The notification requirement was at 18 U.S.C. §4208(a). Both sections were repealed in 1984.

177. See Gottfredson 1979; United States General Accounting Office 1982.

Chapter Two

1. Goldstein 1977, D14. Also present at the dinner were Professor James Vorenberg of the Harvard Law School and Professor Norval Morris of the University of Chicago Law School. Id.

2. Judge Frankel's book, the Second Circuit sentencing study, and the Yale study are discussed at pages 35–37.

3. See Kennedy 1976a, 209; Kennedy 1976b, 4; Kennedy 1979a, 453, 455; Kennedy 1979b, 353; Kennedy 1980, 424–26.

4. See S. 1437, 95th Cong. (1977); S. 1722, 96th Cong. (1979); S. 1630 and Title 4 of S. 2572, 97th Cong. (1981); Title 2 of S. 1762, 98th Cong. (1983).

5. See Stith and Koh 1993.

6. See, e.g., *Text of Reagan Press Conference,* July 24, 1984, *in* 42 Congressional Quarterly 1841 (1984); see also Cohodas 1984, 2752.

7. The most controversial provisions of "S.1," as it was called after its initial Senate bill number, related to extortion provisions opposed by organized labor, an "official secrets" provision criminalizing the disclosure of classified documents, and abolition of the insanity defense. See Kennedy 1976b, 8.

8. See Cohen 1990, A10.

9. See Eaton 1988, 3 & nn.10–12; Lewis 1977, A33. Senator Thurmond worked closely with Senator Kennedy on several significant legislative programs over the course of three decades. See Atkinson 1990, E12; Eaton 1988, 16.

10. Wilkins 1977, A10.

11. 130 Cong. Rec. 838 (1984) (Sen. Thurmond).

12. S. 1437, 95th Cong., 2d Sess. (1978); S. 1722, 96th Cong., 1st Sess. (1980); S. 1630, 97th Cong., 1st Sess. (1981); S. 2572, 97th Cong., 2d Sess. (1982); S. 1762, 98th Cong., 1st Sess. (1983).

13. This provision became 28 U.S.C. §991(b)(1)(B).

14. These provisions became 28 U.S.C. §994(k) (rehabilitation and treatment not appropriate purposes in imposing sentence of imprisonment); 18 U.S.C. §2302(a) (abolishing parole); 18 U.S.C. §3583 (providing for term of supervised release after imprisonment).

15. See S. 1437, 95th Cong., 2d Sess. §124. This provision became part of 28 U.S.C. §991(a).

16. Every bill provided that the upper bound of each sentencing range could not exceed the lower bound by more than 25 percent. This provision became 28 U.S.C. §994(b)(2).

17. This language is in the Senate Report accompanying the final legislation. S. Rep. No. 225, 98th Cong., 2d Sess. 79 (1984). Virtually identical wording is in S. Rep. No. 605, 95th Cong., 1st Sess. 1167 (1977) (accompanying S. 1437).

18. S. 1437, 95th Cong., 2d Sess. §§101, 124 (1978). As amended, this provision became 28 U.S.C. §994(d) (1988).

19. As amended, this provision became 18 U.S.C. §3742 (1988).

20. See 5 U.S.C. §706 (Administrative Procedure Act provision for judicial

review of regulations). The Sentencing Reform Act does require that the Sentencing Commission comply with the notice and comment provisions of the Administrative Procedure Act, 5 U.S.C. §533. See 28 U.S.C. §994(x). However, the Senate Report makes clear that the Guidelines are not subject to appellate review under 5 U.S.C. §§701 et seq. See S. Rep. No. 225, 98th Cong., 2d Sess. 181 (1984). The Report offers that "[t]here is ample provision for review of the guidelines by the Congress and the public; no additional review of the guidelines as a whole is either necessary or desirable."

21. Kennedy 1979b, 374.

22. S. 1437, 95th Cong., 1st Sess. §101(a) (1977). This provision as modified is 18 U.S.C. §3553(a).

23. S. 1437, 95th Cong., 1st Sess. §101(b) (1977). This provision as modified is 18 U.S.C. §3553(c).

24. See S. 204, 95th Cong., 1st Sess. (1977). The cosponsor of this competing bill was liberal New York Republican Senator Jacob K. Javits.

25. 124 Cong. Rec. 209 (1978) (unprinted amendment no. 1100 adopted Jan. 23, 1978) (emphasis added).

26. See 18 U.S.C. §3553(b).

27. Compare 18 U.S.C. §3742(a), with S. 1437, 95th Cong., 1st Sess. §101 (1977) (as originally introduced by Senator Kennedy).

28. S. 1437, 95th Cong., 1st Sess. §241 (as introduced by Senators Kennedy and McClellan on May 2, 1977). The Judicial Conference of the United States is discussed at pages 153–59.

29. See 124 Cong. Rec. 381 (1978) (unprinted amendment no. 1097).

30. See S. 1722, 96th Cong., 1st Sess. (1980). The bill that the Senate passed in 1978 had instructed both the sentencing judge and the Sentencing Commission to "consider" the possible relevance of a wide variety of personal characteristics. See S. 1437, 95th Cong., 2d Sess. §§101, 124 (1978). The bill reported by Senator Kennedy's Judiciary Committee in 1980, however, amended that provision to make clear that the Commission had the power to decide that some or all of the listed personal characteristics were *never* relevant to sentencing. This section became 28 U.S.C. §994(c). As if to underscore its skepticism regarding the relevance of personal characteristics, the Judiciary Committee in 1980 also added two more provisions in the same vein. One required that the guidelines be "entirely neutral as to the race, sex, national origin, creed, and socioeconomic status of offenders." This section became 28 U.S.C. §994(d). The second noted "the general inappropriateness" of considering education, vocational skills, employment record, community ties, and family responsibilities in imposing a sentence of imprisonment. This section became 28 U.S.C. §994(e). Elsewhere, Senator Kennedy strongly suggested that education, employment record, and family responsibilities should have "little or no bearing on a decision to imprison an offender." Kennedy 1979b, 373.

31. S. 1437, 95th Cong., 2d Sess. (1978).

32. See Drinan et al. 1981, 514.

33. H.R. 6915, 96th Cong., 2d Sess. (1980).

34. H.R. Rep. No. 1396, 96th Cong., 2d Sess. 489 (1980).

35. Rodino 1984, 231.

36. See Griset 1991, 40–46 (discussing move toward determinate sentences); Frase 1995 (discussing history of state sentencing commissions). Most of these early state guideline systems were nonbinding. However, in 1980, Minnesota adopted presumptive sentencing guidelines tied to correctional resources. See Parent 1988.

37. See Comprehensive Drug Penalty Act of 1982, H.R. 7140, 97th Cong., 2d Sess. (1982); Violent Crime and Drug Enforcement Improvements Act of 1982, S. 2572, 97th Cong., 2d Sess. (1982).

38. Laws passed in the 98th Congress mandating minimum prison terms included the Controlled Substance Act, Pub. L. No. 98-473, §503(a), amending 21 U.S.C. §845(a) (1982); id. §212(a)(2), amending 18 U.S.C. §3561(b)(1) (1982); id. §1006(a), codified as amended at 18 U.S.C. §929 (1988). Mandatory sentencing laws passed in the following Congress included the Firearm Owners Protection Act, Pub. L. No. 99-308, §104(a)(2)(A)–(E), amending 18 U.S.C. §924(c) (1982); the Anti-Drug Abuse Act of 1986, Pub. L. No. 99-570, §1402(a), amending 18 U.S.C. §924(e)(1) (1982). Laws passed in the 100th Congress imposing mandatory minimum sentences included the Omnibus Anti-Drug Abuse Act of 1988, Pub. L. No. 100-690, §6470(a), amending 18 U.S.C. §981(a)(1). The pattern continued thereafter and widened to include laws dealing with financial crimes and sex offenses. See U.S.S.C. 1991b, 8–10.

39. See S. 2572, 97th Cong., 2d Sess. (1982); S. 1762, 98th Cong., 2d Sess. (1984).

40. The 1978 vote had been 75 to 15; see 124 Cong. Rec. 1463 (1978). The 1982 vote was 95 to 1; see 128 Cong. Rec. 26,581 (1982). The vote in 1984 was 91 to 1. See 130 Cong. Rec. 1587 (1984); see also Taylor 1984a, A1.

41. Other titles of the 1984 Act provided for preventive detention for certain persons awaiting trial, seizure of the assets and profits of drug dealers, and limitations on the insanity defense. See S. 1762, 98th Cong., 1st Sess., titles 3, 4 (1983).

42. One new subsection would operate almost as a mandatory minimum sentence provision, requiring "a term of imprisonment at or near the maximum term authorized" for repeat violent offenders and drug offenders. See Sentencing Reform Act, 28 U.S.C. §994(h). Another provision set forth a presumption in favor of imprisonment for crimes of violence. See id. §994(j). Another required "a substantial term of imprisonment" for drug offenders. See id. §994(i).

43. This amendment was part of a group of floor amendments considered en bloc. See 128 Cong. Rec. 26,515–16 (1982). It became 28 U.S.C. §994(*l*).

44. See S. 1762, 98th Cong., 2d Sess. §207 (1984).

45. See id.; S. 668, 98th Cong., 2d Sess. (1984). These provisions, as subsequently slightly modified, became 28 U.S.C. §991(a).

46. See 130 Cong. Rec. 973 (1984).

47. Id. at 976.

48. Congressional Digest 1984, 182.

49. 130 Cong. Rec. 975 (1984).

50. 130 Cong. Rec. 973 (1984).

51. S. 1437, 95th Cong., 1st Sess. §241 (1977).

52. 28 U.S.C. §991(a).

53. The concern was justified. The Supreme Court decision upholding the constitutionality of the Sentencing Commission insisted that the agency was entirely "independent" of the executive branch. See Mistretta v. United States, 488 U.S. 361, 368, 385–97 (1989). It may also be noted that because of its placement in the judicial branch, the Sentencing Commission is not bound by the requirements of the Administrative Procedure Act. See 5 U.S.C. §701(b)(1)(B) (Act not applicable to "the courts").

54. This provision became 18 U.S.C. §3742(e).

55. Werner 1984.

56. 130 Cong. Rec. 2616 (1984) (typographical error deleted).

57. Id.

58. See 128 Cong. Rec. 32,936 (1982).

59. Congressional Quarterly 1984, 1841; see also Cohodas 1984, 2752.

60. See S. Rep. No. 225, 98th Cong., 2d Sess. 65 (1984).

61. See H.R. Rep. No. 1017, 98th Cong., 2d Sess. 34–35, 93–94 (1984).

62. See H.R. 6012, 98th Cong., 2d Sess. (1984).

63. See H.R. Rep. No. 1017, 98th Cong., 2d Sess. 35–37, 105–6 & 145–46.

64. Id. at 243–50 (dissenting statement of Rep. Conyers); see also Conyers 1985, 68.

65. See H.R. Rep. No. 1017, 98th Cong., 2d Sess. 251, 253 (dissenting statement).

66. See Judicial Conference of the United States 1984, 69 (meeting of Judicial Conference informed that Senate anticrime bill was dead and House compromise measure probably would reach floor vote).

67. H.R.J. Res. 648, 98th Cong., 2d Sess. (1984).

68. See Tiefer 1989, 459 (motion to recommit, though seldom used, permits opponents of bill under consideration to achieve effect of an amendment from the floor, even when such amendments are prohibited).

69. See 130 Cong. Rec. 26,834–38 (1984).

70. Tate 1984, 2357.

71. 130 Cong. Rec. 26,835–36 (1984).

72. Tate 1984, 2355 (quoting Rep. Trent Lott, R-Miss).

73. See 130 Cong. Rec. at 26,837–38 (1984); see also Tolchin 1984, A1.

74. See 130 Cong. Rec. 29,870 (1984) ("Thurmond Agreement" of Oct. 4, 1984).

75. Senator Mathias had unsuccessfully sought to add this language, based on language in the sentencing reform bill under consideration in the House of Representatives, earlier in 1984. See 130 Cong. Rec. 836 (1984) (Amendment No. 2648). At that time, the amendment was defeated under strenuous opposition from both the Reagan administration and the Senate sponsors of sentencing reform. See 130 Cong. Rec. 840–411, 986 (1984); Brenner, 1984. See also H.R. Rep. No. 1017, 98th Cong., 2d Sess. 93–94 (1984).

76. 130 Cong. Rec. 29,870 (1984) (Oct. 4, 1984). Although the amendment was formally part of a package of last-minute amendments proposed by Senator Thurmond on behalf of himself, Senator Kennedy, and other Senate sponsors of sentencing reform, the provision on imposing the least severe sentence has been attributed to Senator Mathias. See Conyers 1985, 69.

77. See Taylor 1984b, A1; see also Cohodas 1984, 2752.

78. See Frankel 1973, 53–60 (noting that a sentencing commission could be politically insulated, and result in fewer severe sentences), 118–23 (advocating formation of a sentencing commission and elucidating its possible advantages, such as reducing arbitrariness, increasing "truth in sentencing," harnessing expertise, and formalizing deliberation); Orland 1978, 46–51.

79. A highly readable and informative summary comparing state and federal sentencing commissions and guidelines is Tonry 1996, 27–39. See also page 177.

80. See generally Almanac of the Federal Judiciary 1996; Judicial Staff Directory 1993.

81. See, e.g., Breyer 1979; Breyer 1982; Breyer et al. 1980; Breyer 1983; Breyer and Stewart 1985.

82. Indeed, Breyer was the only judicial nominee of President Carter to be confirmed by the Senate during the Carter-Reagan interregnum.

83. During his time on the staff of the Senate Judiciary Committee, Breyer had played a leading role in the deregulation of airline fares. Coyle and Lavelle 1994.

84. Breyer 1993, 61.

85. As enacted in 1984, the Sentencing Reform Act required that all three federal judges be "active" judges, rather than on "senior" status. The statute was quietly amended in April 1985 to remove this requirement. Pub. L. No. 99-22, §1(1), amending 28 U.S.C. §991(a). Later, the statutory deadline for promulgation of the guidelines was extended from April 1986 to April 1987. Pub. L. No. 99-217, amending 28 U.S.C. §994(q) and 18 U.S.C. §3551.

86. In addition to numerous articles, Professor Nagel had published two books. See Nagel and Freeman 1975; Bernstein 1976.

87. Robinson and Grall 1983.

88. Block 1989, 19.

89. Coyle and Strasser 1989, 5. Corrothers was the first African-American and the first woman to become a prison warden in Arkansas. McHenry 1994, 37.

90. See page 40; chapter 4, note 1.

91. See 18 U.S.C. §3553(a)(2); 28 U.S.C. §991(b).

92. 28 U.S.C. §991(b)(1)(C).

93. 488 U.S. 361 (1989).

94. 488 U.S. at 407, 412.

95. 28 U.S.C. §§991(b)(1)(A), 994(f).

96. 488 U.S. at 427 (Scalia, J., dissenting).

97. The Sentencing Reform Act required that the Guidelines

1. sentence repeat felony offenders "to a substantial term of imprisonment," 28 U.S.C. §994(i);
2. sentence repeat violent and drug offenders "at or near the maximum term [statutorily] authorized," 28 U.S.C. §994(h);
3. be "entirely neutral as to the race, sex, national origin, creed, and socioeconomic status of offenders," 28 U.S.C. §994(d);
4. reflect the "general inappropriateness" of considering education, employment record, or family and community ties in determining sentences of imprisonment, 28 U.S.C. §994(e);
5. impose an additional incremental penalty for each separate offense in a case where the defendant is convicted of multiple offenses, 28 U.S.C. §994(l);
6. set the maximum of each sentencing range no more than 25 percent above the minimum of that range, 28 U.S.C. §994(b)(2); and
7. "reflect the fact that, in many cases, current sentences do not accurately reflect the seriousness of the offense," 28 U.S.C. §994(m).

98. See, e.g., 28 U.S.C. §994(h), (i), (m).

99. 28 U.S.C. §994(g).

100. 18 U.S.C. §991(b)(1)(B).

101. 28 U.S.C. §994(e).

102. 18 U.S.C. §994(b)(2); see *supra* note 16.

103. See, e.g., Parent 1988, 34–39, 51–63; Hauptly and Knapp 1992; Orland and Reitz 1993.

104. See generally Marc Miller 1992, 437–50.

105. Robinson 1987a, 18,121–23; Robinson 1987b, 6–27, 53–58.

106. U.S.S.C. 1986.

107. See, e.g., Cohn 1986; Strasser 1986; Anderson 1986; Bureau of National Affairs 1986; Kurtz 1987a.

108. Strasser 1986.

109. Kurtz 1987a.

110. U.S.S.C. 1987b.

111. Parker and Block 1990, 292; see also Block 1989, 19.

112. In one article, Block explained that the formula for determining the optimal penalty is

$$F^* = (L + C')/P_f$$

where F* is the optimal penalty, L is the total social harm resulting from the crime, C′ is the incremental cost of detecting a violation, and P_f is the probability that a violation will be detected. Block 1991, 397.

113. See U.S.S.G. §1A3 (1987). This discussion has been amended slightly in later versions of the Guidelines Manual. See also U.S.S.C. 1987c, 16 ("little practical difference in result" between the two approaches).

114. Breyer 1988, 15–18.

115. See 28 U.S.C. §994(*l*) (requiring incremental penalties for each *conviction* only).

116. See pages 68–70.

117. This approach, in both the Robinson draft and in the final Guidelines, may be usefully compared to the more flexible approach the Commission took in an interim draft issued in late January 1987. That "revised draft," as it was called, assigned a range of severity levels and adjustment magnitudes and remitted the choice of a precise value to the discretion of the sentencing judge. See U.S.S.C. 1987a.

118. See Robinson 1987a, at 18,123–30.

119. U.S.S.C. 1987c, 15–16; see also U.S.S.G. §1A3 (summary of philosophical dispute and Commission's resolution thereof).

120. See 28 U.S.C. §994(p) (providing that Guidelines become effective six months after final promulgation, unless legislatively disapproved).

121. See generally Wright 1991a; Buffone 1991.

122. 28 U.S.C. §994(x).

123. See *supra* note 20.

124. See 61 Fed. Reg. 52,825 (Oct. 8, 1996); 61 Fed. Reg. 39,493 (July 29, 1996). See also Buffone 1996 ("While it is laudable that the Commission has now proposed rules . . . the proposals are little more than a recitation of the existing inadequate procedures.").

125. Wright 1994, 58, 64. See also Wright 1991a, 7–23 (discussing administrative insulation of Sentencing Commission).

126. 5 U.S.C. §706(2)(A); see *supra* note 20.

127. See United States v. Lopez, 938 F.2d 1293, 1297 (D.C. Cir. 1991) (holding that Administrative Procedure Act's judicial review provisions do not apply to rule making by Sentencing Commission).

128. See *Sentencing Commission Guidelines: Hearing before the Committee on the Judiciary, U.S. Senate,* 100th Cong., 1st Sess. (1987).

129. See *Sentencing Guidelines: Hearings before the Subcommittee on Criminal Justice of the Committee on the Judiciary, U.S. House of Representatives,* 100th Cong., 1st Sess. (1987).

130. U.S.S.C. 1987a.

131. See Kurtz 1987a. See also *supra* note 117.

132. Bureau of National Affairs 1987.

133. Kurtz 1987b.

134. Santos 1987.

135. Feinberg 1987. See also Wermeil 1987 (while Guidelines reduce judicial discretion, they "nevertheless would give judges considerable flexibility by allowing them to depart . . . whenever they believe it is necessary").

136. Noble 1987.

137. Wermeil 1987 ("Breyer's draft"). But see also Moran 1987 (final Guidelines are a "last-minute 'merging' of a heavily reworked January version . . . with a wholly new draft, dubbed 'Draft X,' drawn up by two staffers in early March"); Kurtz 1987b ("Draft X" was "engineered by" Commissioners Breyer, Block, and Nagel).

138. Moran 1987.

139. Coyle and Strasser 1987.

140. See *Sentencing Guidelines: Hearings Before the Subcommittee on Criminal Justice of the Committee on the Judiciary, U.S. House of Representatives,* 100th Cong., 1st Sess. (1987).

141. 28 U.S.C. §994(p).

142. See Stinson v. United States, 508 U.S. 36, 41–47 (1993) (Commentary that explains or interprets a Guideline is authoritative); Williams v. United States, 503 U.S. 193, 201 (1992) (Policy Statements are authoritative). The Commission has said that Commentary is the "legal equivalent of a policy statement," U.S.S.G. §1B1.7.

Some federal appellate courts have held, however, that when the Commission does not issue formal Guidelines concerning a particular issue, but only Commentary or Policy Statements, these are *not* binding on the federal courts. See, e.g., United States v. Cohen, 99 F.3d 69, 70–71 (2d Cir. 1996) (per curiam); United States v. McCormick, 58 F.3d. 874, 878 (2d Cir. 1995); United States v. Hofierka, 83 F.3d 357, 360–61 (11th Cir.) (per curiam), *modified on other grounds on denial of reh'g,* 92 F.3d 1108 (11th Cir. 1996); United States v. Escamilla, 70 F.3d 835 (5th Cir. 1995) (per curiam), *cert. denied,* 116 S. Ct. 1368 (1996); United States v. West, 59 F.3d 32, 33–36 (6th Cir.), *cert. denied,* 116 S. Ct. 486 (1995). With respect to most issues, Commentary and Policy Statements do relate to particular Guidelines, and therefore they are ordinarily binding.

143. U.S.S.C. 1987c, 16–18.

144. Breyer 1988, 17; see also Parker and Block 1990, 315–18.

145. See *supra* notes 143, 144. Two Commissioners carefully avoided making this claim in their retrospective law review articles. See Nagel 1990, 930–32 (Commission was "anchored," but not bound by past practice, apparently for all crime categories); Wilkins 1988, 184 (past practices simply provided a "realistic guide for informed decision-making"). Additionally, Commissioner Robinson in his dissent from the Guidelines issued in 1987 argued, inter alia, that the Commission had not completely relied on past practice. Robinson 1987a, 18,122–23.

146. See, e.g., Frank O. Bowman, III 1996a, 733–34 (arguing that Commission increased penalties for narcotics and "white collar" cases, but not for all others, the latter including robbery and immigration); Cohen and Scheffman 1989, 336–37 ("With a few exceptions, the Sentencing Commission based the 1987 Guidelines on the statistical estimates of past practice."); Parker 1993, 403 & n.17 ("The initial sentencing guidelines for individuals followed the general punishment levels and, with some exceptions, the distribution of punishment under past practice."); Sunstein 1995, 1744 (discussing Commission's decision to use "past averages," citing the 1988 article by Judge Breyer).

147. See Hauptly and Knapp 1992, 679–85.

148. 28 U.S.C. §994(m). The legislative history of this provision is discussed at pages 43–44.

149. See Parker and Block 1990, 315–18, quoting S. Rep. No. 225, at 59 (1984).

150. Robinson 1987a.

151. 28 U.S.C. §994(m).

152. 28 U.S.C. §994(h), (i).

153. U.S.S.C. 1987c, 18–19.

154. See *supra* note 41.

155. U.S.S.C. 1987c, 18; Schulhofer 1992, 854; Tonry 1992b, 358. For example, under present law, selling between five and fifty grams of crack cocaine requires a prison sentence of at least five years. 21 U.S.C. §841. The Sentencing Guidelines go beyond that requirement, prescribing a range of up to ten years for a first offender whose offense involves fifty grams of crack cocaine. U.S.S.G. §2D1.1(c) (Drug Quantity Table—Offense Level 30). Moreover, the Guidelines apply statutory minimum sentences to the quantity *attributable* to the defendant under the "relevant conduct" principle, which we discuss below, even though the statutory minimum applies only to amounts for which the defendant was formally convicted.

156. U.S.S.C. 1987c, 18.

157. 28 U.S.C. §994(m). See also S. Rep. No. 225 at 177 (1984) .

158. U.S.S.C. 1987c, 19 (emphasis supplied).

159. See, e.g., U.S.S.C. 1997b, 6 (drug offenses constitute 40 percent of all convictions, firearms and robbery cases constitute another 10 percent of convictions, and varieties of white collar crime another 13 percent).

160. U.S.S.C. 1987c, 18 n.59.

161. The presentence report, prepared by a federal probation officer, is discussed at pages 79–80, 85–89.

162. U.S.S.C. 1987c, 22–39.

163. See U.S.S.G. §2B3.1(b)(1)–(5); §3B1.1; §4A1.1.

164. See id. §5H1.2–1.12.

165. See 28 U.S.C. §994(d); *supra* note 30.

166. Nagel 1990, 924.

167. See Bureau of Justice Statistics Sourcebook 1994, table 5.27. See also U.S.S.C. Annual Report 1989, table B-7 (providing rates of imprisonment from 1984–1989).

168. U.S.S.C. 1997b, 20 (12 percent of all defendants sentenced to probation; another 7.2 percent sentenced to combination of confinement for short period, followed by probation).

169. The Sourcebook of Criminal Justice Statistics, published by the Bureau of Justice Statistics within the Department of Justice, has long been an exceptionally useful compendium of federal prison and sentencing statistics. While data are broken down by race, however, they were not broken down by sex until recent years. The Sentencing Commission does publish information each year showing the percentage of offenders of each sex for each major crime category. See, e.g., U.S.S.C. Annual Report 1995, 47 (women were 14.9 percent of all sentenced defendants in 1995).

170. See Coughenour 1995, 142 (since mid-1980s, number of men in federal correctional institutions has grown by less than 200 percent, while number of women has grown by nearly 400 percent). Compare U.S.S.C. 1997b, table 5 (women were 15.4 percent of all sentenced defendants in 1996), with Newton, Glazer, and Blackwell 1995, 148 (in 1985, women were 17.8 percent of all sentenced defendants).

171. However, neither table 1 nor the Sentencing Commission's own data includes the terms of confinement served by offenders in community confinement, intermittent confinement in prison or jail, or home detention (all pursuant to U.S.S.G. §5C1.1). The Sentencing Commission counts these sentences as "zero months'" terms of imprisonment. See, e.g., U.S.S.C. 1997b, table 13 at 22 & n.1. Of the more than forty thousand individuals sentenced in 1996, more than three thousand were sentenced to these forms of confinement (along with terms

of probation). See id. table 12 at 21. By treating such sentences the same as probation-only sentences, both our table 1 and the Sentencing Commission's own tables understate the overall severity of sentencing under the Guidelines.

172. See *supra* note 14.

173. The Sentencing Reform Act eliminated parole, but provided that defendants through "good time" credits could reduce their terms of imprisonment by up to fifty-four days per year. 18 U.S.C. §3624(b).

174. Bureau of Justice Statistics Sourcebooks for 1979, 1980, 1981, 1983, 1984, 1985, 1986, and 1987 indicate that federal offenders released in these years served on average about 47 percent of their nominal prison sentences. This percentage had remained stable since at least 1950.

175. See U.S.S.C. 1997b, 22–23 (average sentence for drug offenders sentenced to prison is nearly seven years, whereas average prison sentence overall is slightly over four years); *supra* note 155 (explaining how Guidelines are more severe than statutory minimums). See also page 125, text at note 112 (discussing significance of Commission's treatment of statutory minimums).

176. The "safety valve" was enacted as a provision of the Violent Crime Control and Law Enforcement Act of 1994, Pub. L. No. 103-322, §80001(a), 18 U.S.C. §3553(f). The "safety valve" applies only to defendants who have a Criminal History score of zero or one, who did not possess a weapon, who did not engage in violence, who were not leaders or supervisors, and who cooperate with prosecutorial authorities by "truthfully provid[ing] information and evidence the defendant has" concerning all of their relevant conduct. The Sentencing Commission provided a reduction of only two points in calculation of Base Offense Level for defendants who meet the "safety valve" requirements. U.S.S.G. §2D1.1(b)(4).

177. See Yost 1989b. See also 18 U.S.C. §924(c) (providing for mandatory five-year sentence in certain robbery cases).

178. The 1987 Supplementary Report estimated that the Guidelines would have the effect of increasing prison population by only between 2 percent and 7 percent in the aggregate. See U.S.S.C. 1987b, 53–66; Block and Rhodes 1989, 52, 54, 64–65.

179. 28 U.S.C. §994(m); see pages 43–44.

180. See Alschuler 1989, 56, 86.

181. See *supra* note 42.

182. Moran 1987.

183. Corporate Crime Reporter 1991, 4–5 (quoting David Lombardero, former Chief Counsel of the Sentencing Commission, identified as "a principal author of the federal sentencing guidelines").

184. Corporate Crime Reporter 1991, 4 (quoting John R. Lott, Jr., former Chief Economist at Sentencing Commission, in reference to organizational guidelines issued by Commission in 1989).

185. Yost 1989a.

186. Yost 1989b.

187. See United States General Accounting Office 1990, 3, 12–15; Marcus 1990, A25; Tonry 1996, 84–95.

188. See, e.g., Alschuler 1989; Lay 1992, 1755–56; Robinson 1987a, 18,122.

189. See, e.g., Yellen 1993.

190. See Wilkins and Steer 1990, 501 ("The Senate version, while it did not expressly specify, seemed to lean toward a real offense system.") (citations omitted).

191. 28 U.S.C. §§994(b)(1)(B), 994(c).

192. Lear 1993, 1192–94; Nagel 1990, 925–27, 925 n.228; Breyer 1988, 8–11; Tonry and Coffee 1987, 152–54.

193. See S. Rep. No. 225 at 63, 167–83 (1984); Schulhofer 1980, 748–60; Schulhofer 1979, 2, 47–52; Tonry and Coffee 1987 (discussing "real-offense" sentencing); Alschuler 1983, 1044–48 (discussing sentencing reform and the abolition of plea-bargaining).

194. See U.S.S.G. §1A.4(a). In its preliminary draft Guidelines, issued in September 1986, the Commission adopted a policy that it described as "modified real offense" sentencing. U.S.S.C. 1986, 10–18. The revised draft Guidelines issued in January 1987 employed a system under which the offense charged in the indictment would be a more significant determinant of sentence. U.S.S.C. 1987a. See also U.S.S.G. §1A.4(a) (1987) (describing drafting history).

195. See pages 32–33, 39.

196. U.S.S.G. §2B1.1.

197. U.S.S.G. §2A3.1.

198. This is the most common Guidelines arithmetic for taking account of "specific offense characteristics." Alternatively, the Guidelines may specify two or more different "Base Offense Levels," depending on the presence or absence of a specified aggravating factor. For instance, burglary of a residence is assigned a Base Offense Level of 17; burglary of any other structure is assigned a Base Offense Level of 12. See U.S.S.G. §2B2.1(a).

199. For example, if a gun is "brandished, displayed, or possessed" during a robbery, the Base Offense Level is increased by five points. See U.S.S.G. §2B3.1(G)(2) (add seven points if firearm "discharged," six points if firearm otherwise "used," five points if firearm "brandished, displayed or possessed"). If, on the other hand, any other "dangerous weapon" is "brandished, displayed, or possessed" in the course of a robbery, the Base Offense Level will be increased by only three points. See U.S.S.G. §2B3.1(G)(2)(E). For drug trafficking, in contrast, "possession" of any dangerous weapon (including a firearm) increases the Base Offense Level by two points. See U.S.S.G. §2D1.1(b)(1).

200. See U.S.S.G. §2A2.2(g)(3).

201. Compare U.S.S.C. 1987b, 27–39, with U.S.S.C. 1987 Guidelines Manual.

202. See pages 53–56.

203. See Lynch 1994, 113.

204. See U.S.S.G. §2B1.1(b)(1) (loss table for larceny, embezzlement, theft, and receiving stolen property).

205. U.S.S.G. §2L1.1.

206. In a conversation with one of the authors, a federal prosecutor in the Southern District of California reported that her office and other U.S. Attorneys in border districts had sought to convince the Commission to specify an offense characteristic relating to the conditions of smuggling, to no avail because of the subjective nature of such an inquiry. Yet judges were reluctant to "depart" from the Guidelines because dangerous conditions may be sufficiently common in alien-smuggling cases as to not qualify as "atypical" (see discussion at pages 99–103).

Finally, in 1996 Congress directed the Commission to provide for enhanced penalties for risk of death or serious bodily injury. See Illegal Immigration Reform and Immigrant Responsibility Act of 1996, Pub. L. No. 104-20008, §203. In 1997 the Commission amended U.S.S.G. §2L1.1 accordingly.

207. See U.S.S.G. §1B1.3 (Commentary). We discuss the preponderance standard and issues of due process at pages 148–49.

208. Wilkins and Steer 1990, 495–96. Technically, the "relevant conduct" rules are "Policy Statements" rather than "Guidelines."

209. Id. at 499 n.27.

210. See pages 96–97.

211. See U.S.S.G. §3A1.1(b) (increase Offense Level by two points if defen-

dant knew or should have known that victim was unusually vulnerable due to age, mental condition, or physical condition).

212. See U.S.S.G. §3B1.1 (increase Offense Level by four points if defendant was leader or organizer of criminal activity involving five or more participants, three points if he was manager or supervisor of same, and two points if defendant otherwise played major role).

213. See U.S.S.G. §3C1.1 (increase Offense Level by two points for obstructing or impeding administration of justice). Adjustments may amount to "double counting" when used in connection with offenses that almost always involve the underlying adjustment factors. So long as the adjustment factor is not actually listed as a specific offense characteristic or as an element of the offense, the adjustment is applicable in conjunction with that offense. Thus, for example, the "restraint of victim" adjustment does not apply to kidnapping because the Guidelines here recognize that restraint of a victim is a statutory element of the offense of kidnapping. See U.S.S.G. §3A1.3 (Commentary, Application Note 2).

214. See U.S.S.G. §3E1.1. As originally promulgated, the Guidelines permitted only a two-point adjustment.

215. See 28 C.F.R. §2.20(e); page 39; U.S.S.C. 1987c, 42–43 (noting influence of Parole Commission's approach to criminal history).

216. Additionally, and curiously, some aspects of a defendant's criminal history may affect not only his Criminal History Category but also his *Offense Level.* For instance, if the defendant's crime was "part of a pattern of criminal conduct engaged in as a livelihood," his Offense Level will be at least 11—regardless of the level that might otherwise be calculated under the separate Offense Level instructions. See U.S.S.G. §4B1.3.

217. 28 U.S.C. §991(b)(1)(B). It may be noted that the statutory directive does not say anything about the *weight* to be accorded criminal history. See also Nagel 1990, 924 (Commission decided to have defendant's criminal history "dramatically affect" sentence).

218. U.S.S.C. 1987c, 42.

219. For defendants in the highest Criminal History Category, previous convictions account, on average, for half of total sentence severity. See appendix A: For any given offense level, the sentencing range for Category VI is approximately twice the range for Category I. The impact of criminal record is not uniform across offense levels, however, with the effect of criminal history highest at Offense Level 9—where criminal history approximately triples the sentencing range. See Roberts 1994, 22–24. The author of this article calculates what he calls the "recidivist premium" implicit in the Sentencing Guidelines. The premium is highest at Offense Level 9, and is lowest at Offense Levels 29 and higher.

220. For instance, prior sentences imposed in "unrelated" cases are counted as separate convictions, whereas prior sentences in "related" cases are counted as a single conviction. See U.S.S.G. §4A1.2(a)(2). But "related" convictions may occur years apart, and "unrelated" convictions may occur in the same proceeding. See, e.g., United States v. Metcalf, 898 F.2d 43, 46 (5th Cir. 1990). The distinction between "related" and "unrelated" cases is similar to, *but not the same as,* the concept of "relevant conduct." Compare U.S.S.G. §4A1.2 with U.S.S.G. §1B1.3 and U.S.S.G. §3D1.2.

221. See Hoffman and Beck 1996, 192–94.

222. Unlike sentencing guidelines in other jurisdictions, the federal Guidelines do not permit any mitigation if the defendant has been law-abiding for sustained periods of time. See Roberts 1994, 26 (discussing systems in Canada and Washington that do mitigate for crime-free periods).

223. This standard for departure is stated both in the Sentencing Reform

Act, 18 U.S.C. §3553(b), and in the Guidelines, U.S.S.G. §5K2.0 (Policy Statement). The original language in the Sentencing Reform Act was slightly different, see page 41, text at note 25, but was amended before the Guidelines took effect. See Sentencing Act of 1987, Pub. L. No. 100-182, 101 Stat. 1266 (amending 18 U.S.C. §3553(b)). The Senate sponsors of the amendment asserted that the addition of the terms "of a kind or to a degree" did not expand or otherwise alter the standard for departure. See 133 Cong. Rec. S16,644, 16,646–48 (1987) (joint statement of Senators Biden, Thurmond, Kennedy, and Hatch). In the same 1987 amendment to the Sentencing Reform Act, another sentence was added requiring that the determination of "adequacy" be based *solely* on "the sentencing guidelines, policy statements, and official commentary of the Sentencing Commission." See 18 U.S.C. §3553(b).

224. See 18 U.S.C. §3742(f)(2); Koon v. United States, 116 S. Ct. 2035, 2046–47, 2052–53 (1996); Williams v. United States, 503 U.S. 193, 194 (1992); United States v. Stephenson, 921 F.2d 438, 441 (2d Cir. 1990).

225. Because the Guidelines never *require* a judge to depart, a decision not to depart from the Guidelines range is not reviewable on appeal. 18 U.S.C. §3742(a)(1), (2); §3742(b)(1), (2). See United States v. Chabot, 70 F.3d 259, 60–61 (2d Cir. 1995); United States v. Brown, 98 F.3d 650, 654 (2d Cir. 1996) (per curiam).

226. See generally Stith 1990.

227. See page 72, text at note 223. See also 133 Cong. Rec. 31,947–49 (1987) (statement of Representative Conyers); Freed 1992, 1734 ("Congress no doubt delegated the evaluation of 'adequacy' to the sentencing court"). We briefly consider this interpretation of the Sentencing Reform Act at pages 167–68.

228. See U.S.S.G. §1A.4(b). The original version of this Policy Statement contained an even broader assertion of authority: "In principle, the Commission, by specifying that it has adequately considered a particular factor, could prevent a court from using it as grounds for departure." U.S.S.C., Guidelines Manual 1987, §1A.4(b). In 1990, the Commission excised the language quoted but asserted that it was not altering its substantive position. Amendment 307, reprinted in U.S.S.C., Guidelines Manual 1995, appendix C.

229. See, e.g., U.S.S.G. §2G1.1 (Commentary, Application Note 1) (encouraging 8-level downward departure from Base Offense Level of 14 where "transportation for purpose of prostitution" was not committed for profit and did not involve force).

230. See U.S.S.G. §5K2.0 (Policy Statement).

231. See U.S.S.G. §5K2.1–2.9, 2.14, 2.17–2.18 (listing twelve grounds for upward departure) (Policy Statement).

232. U.S.S.G. §5K2.0 (Policy Statement).

233. See U.S.S.G. §4A1.3 (Policy Statement), §4A1.3 (Commentary).

234. See, e.g., United States v. Fonner, 920 F.2d. 1330, 1332–33 (7th Cir. 1990) (upholding upward departure based on acquitted conduct, but remanding for new calculation of extent of departure).

235. See U.S.S.C. 1997b, 40 (35 percent of all upward departures were based on inadequacy of criminal history score in reflecting seriousness of past crimes, and another 12.6 percent were based on inadequacy of score in reflecting likelihood of future crimes). In comparison, less than 5 percent of all *downward* departures were on the ground that the criminal history score *over-represented* the seriousness of the defendant's prior criminal conduct. See id. at 40–41 (out of a total of 12,046 downward departures, only 550 were due to over-representation in criminal history score; this represents approximately 12 percent of non-substantial assistance downward departures).

236. See U.S.S.G. §§5K2.10–2.13, 2.16. See also page 99.

237. See United States v. Tsosie, 14 F.3d 1438, 1441–42 (10th Cir. 1994); United States v. Andruska, 964 F.2d 640, 644–46 (7th Cir. 1992); United States v. Garlich, 951 F.2d 161, 164 (8th Cir. 1991); United States v. Ritchey, 949 F.2d 61, 63 (2d Cir. 1991); United States v. Glick, 946 F.2d 335, 338 (4th Cir. 1991); United States v. Takai, 941 F.2d 738, 743–44 (9th Cir. 1991); United States v. Russell, 870 F.2d 18, 20 (1st Cir. 1989). At least one circuit has interpreted the aberrant act principle quite broadly. See United States v. Takai, 941 F.2d at 743–44 (not-for-profit involvement in multiple efforts over multi-week period to obtain green cards for relatives and friends).

238. U.S.S.G. §1A.4(d). In 1995, the aberrant act principle was invoked in 10 percent of cases in which judges departed downward, not including substantial assistance departures. See U.S.S.C. Annual Report 1995, 87. In 1996, it was invoked in 6 percent of non-substantial assistance downward departures. U.S.S.C. 1997b, 41.

239. As one commentator has noted, the Introduction to the Guidelines Manual (said to have been drafted largely by Commissioner Breyer) generally strikes a more flexible and conciliatory tone than the actual rules that follow. Freed 1992, 1703, 1718 (referring to Introduction of Guidelines Manual as "well-reasoned" and "flexible"). It seems unlikely that the reference in the Introduction to aberrant behavior was intended to set forth a new and independent ground for departure; the reference is not even contained in the portion of the Introduction entitled "Departures," but, rather, in the portion entitled "Probation and Split Sentences."

240. 28 U.S.C. §994(d).

241. See U.S.S.G. §5H1.10 (sentencing court may never consider race, sex, national origin, creed, religion, and socioeconomic status) (Policy Statement).

242. U.S.S.G. §5H1.4 (Policy Statement). Drug or alcohol dependence thus may be a basis for upward departure.

243. 28 U.S.C. §994(e).

244. See U.S.S.G. §5H1.1 (age), 1.2 (education and vocational skills), 1.3 (mental and emotional condition), 1.5 (employment record), 1.6 (family ties and responsibilities, and community ties) (Policy Statement).

245. See *supra* note 170; Newton, Glazer, and Blackwell 1995, 151–52 (noting that women tend to have more parental responsibility, listed by the Guidelines as "ordinarily" not relevant, and are more likely to be first offenders, who are generally imprisoned under the Guidelines).

246. See United States v. McCaleb, 908 F.2d 176, 179 (7th Cir. 1990) (departure on grounds of defendant's military service permitted in some circumstances); United States v. Lara, 905 F.2d 599, 605 (2d Cir. 1990) (justifying departure on grounds of defendant's extreme vulnerability in prison due to physique); United States v. Neil, 903 F.2d 564, 566 (8th Cir. 1990) (departure on grounds of defendant's military service permitted in some circumstances); United States v. Big Crow, 898 F.2d 1326, 1330–32 (8th Cir. 1990) (downward departure permitted on grounds of defendant's exemplary employment record and efforts to overcome deprivations of Indian reservation).

247. See U.S.S.G. §5H1.4 (Policy Statement).

248. See U.S.S.G. §5H1.11 (Policy Statement).

249. See U.S.S.G. §5H1.12 (Policy Statement) (emphasis added).

250. See U.S.S.G. §5K2.0 (Policy Statement) (as amended, Nov. 1, 1994). In addition, the case at hand must differ from "heartland" cases in "a way that is important to the statutory purposes of sentencing."

251. S. Rep. No. 225, 98th Cong., 2d Sess. 169 (1984).

252. See U.S.S.G. §1A.4(b).
253. See *supra* note 239 (discussing Introduction to Guidelines Manual).
254. See Breyer 1988, 14 n.79, 45 (appendix).
255. See United States v. Rivera, 994 F.2d 942, 947–52 (1st Cir. 1993).
256. 116 S. Ct. 2035 (1996).
257. See pages 100–103.
258. The 1986 amendment requires the Commission to ensure that the Guidelines "reflect the general appropriateness of imposing a lower sentence . . . to take into account a defendant's substantial assistance in the investigation or prosecution" of others. 28 U.S.C. §994(n).
259. U.S.S.G. §5K1.1 (Policy Statement).
260. See U.S.S.C. 1997b, 39. In 1995, two-thirds of all departures were for substantial assistance to authorities. See U.S.S.C. Annual Report 1995, 89.
261. See U.S.S.C. 1997b, 41. Another 7 percent of all downward departures are listed by the Commission as being "pursuant to plea agreement." Id. at 40.
262. See U.S.S.G. §5K1.1 (stating that court may depart "[u]pon motion of the government") (Policy Statement).
263. 18 U.S.C. §3553(e). While Congress requires prosecutorial approval before a judge may sentence below *statutory* minimum requirements, however, it has not imposed a similar requirement on departures below the *Guidelines* range. The latter is a policy choice made by the Sentencing Commission itself. See 18 U.S.C. §3553(b).
264. See U.S.S.C. 1997b, 39 (showing growth in percentage from 3.5 percent in 1989 to 19.5 percent in 1994, 19.7 percent in 1995, and 19.2 percent in 1996).
265. See Joost 1997.
266. Id. at 211. The Brown Commission is briefly noted at pages 32–33, 39.
267. See 28 U.S.C. §994(p), discussed at pages 56–57.

Chapter Three

1. See 8 Oxford English Dictionary 326 (2d ed. 1989) (describing *Justicia* as "often represented in art as a goddess holding balanced scales or a sword, sometimes also with veiled eyes, betokening impartiality"); Curtis and Resnik 1987.
2. See also Curtis and Resnik 1987, 1728 (quoting Professor Robert Cover: "The temptation to raise the blindfold may be . . . the temptation to see—to overcome the elusiveness of indirection.").
3. Aristotle (Barnes ed. 1984), 1796.
4. See pages 19–20 & chapter 1, note 83.
5. Prior to 1974, presentence reports were prepared only upon request of the sentencing judge. In 1974, Rule 32(c) of the Federal Rules of Criminal Procedure was amended to require a report in nearly every case, unless the defendant waived its preparation; another amendment required disclosure of the report to the defendant upon request.
6. Administrative Office of the United States Courts, Division of Probation 1978. Prior instructions from the Probation Division in Washington had stressed even more strongly the "social work" role. See generally Bunzel 1995, 946–48. The father of one of the authors, Judge Cabranes, served in the 1940s as Chief United States Probation Officer for the District of Puerto Rico.
7. Fed. R. Crim. P. 11(e)(1)(B) governs both pleas where the prosecutor agrees to "recommend" a sentence, and pleas where the prosecutor agrees not to oppose the defendant's requests.
8. Although many state systems permit prosecutors and defendants to agree on a particular sentence as part of a plea-bargain, such sentence-bargains were

highly unusual in the federal system. The Federal Rules of Criminal Procedure do permit the parties in a criminal case to agree to a specific sentence, which is "binding" *if* the judge agrees to accept the plea agreement. Fed. R. Crim. P. 11(e)(1)(C). There is general consensus that in federal court, very few cases have proceeded under this rule. See United States v. Pimentel, 932 F.2d 1029, 1033–34 (2d Cir. 1991) (plea-bargains seldom premised on a particular sentence, at least prior to Guidelines).

9. See chapter 1, note 3.

10. See Fed. R. Crim. P. 11(c), (d).

11. Fed. R. Crim. P. 11(f). It has been argued that judges have been too passive in this respect. See Goldstein 1981, 39–47.

12. See United States v. Davern, 970 F.2d 1490, 1516 (6th Cir. 1992) (N. Jones, J., dissenting) (describing sentencing as "an intensely human process"), *cert. denied,* 507 U.S. 923 (1993); United States v. Naugle, 879 F. Supp. 262, 265 (E.D.N.Y. 1995) (Weinstein, J.) (stressing "the necessity for human interaction when sentence is imposed. It is then that the judicial system relates most powerfully to the defendant as a person.").

13. See Dworkin 1977, 44–48 (distinguishing between principles and rules in law).

14. Kronman 1993, 41.

15. See U.S.S.C. 1997b, 1 (there were 42,436 sentencings under the Guidelines in fiscal year 1996). Fewer than 10 percent of these defendants were convicted after a trial; the remainder entered pleas of guilty, usually pursuant to plea agreements with federal prosecutors. Id. at 16. See also Administrative Office of the United States Courts 1996, table D-4 (reporting 52,270 defendants, including corporations and other entities, convicted and sentenced in 1996; 91.6 percent convicted by plea of guilty).

16. The rules governing departure are discussed at pages 73–77, 98–103.

17. Gilbert 1991, 109 (quoting an unnamed but "well-known and highly respected jurist"; author is Chief U.S. Probation Officer, District of Oregon).

18. Van Graafeiland 1986, 1293–94.

19. Cardozo 1921, 18–19 ("[T]he judge must look to the common law for the rule that fits the case."); Holmes 1881, 36 ("And as the law is administered by able and experienced men, who know too much to sacrifice good sense to a syllogism, it will be found that, when ancient rules maintain themselves in the way that has been and will be shown in this book, new reasons more fitted to the time have been found for them. . . .").

20. See Weinstein 1992, 363–64 (1992) (noting that judges in Eastern District of New York spend less time than they had prior to the Guidelines discussing substantive issues of punishment).

21. See pages 51–66.

22. Kafka (Glatzer ed. 1971), 3.

23. Flaherty and Biskupic 1996, A1 (first of five articles in series entitled "Justice by the Numbers").

24. Frank O. Bowman, III 1996a, 732.

25. Fed. R. Crim. P. 32(c)(2)(B).

26. Administrative Office of the United States Courts, Division of Probation 1987, 4–5.

27. Id. (emphasis added); see also Goodwin 1996.

28. Piotrowski 1991, 97 (author is Supervising Probation Officer for the District of Massachusetts); see also Sarner 1996, 329 (author, an assistant federal public defender, argues against "proactive" fact investigations by probation officers, who "are not trained law enforcement agents").

29. See Piotrowski 1991, 96.

30. Bunzel 1995, 965–66; see also Francesca D. Bowman 1991 (author is Deputy Chief Probation Officer for the District of Massachusetts); Cook 1991 (author is Chief Judge of the U.S. District Court for the Eastern District of Michigan).

31. Departure authority for "atypical" cases is further discussed at pages 100–103.

32. As recognized in the Federal Rules of Criminal Procedure, information in the presentence report about the defendant's personal history may be of importance to correctional officials. See Fed. R. Crim. P. 32(b)(4)(A) (requiring presentence report to include "information about . . . any circumstances that, because they affect the defendant's behavior, may be helpful in imposing sentence *or in correctional treatment*") (emphasis added).

33. Francesca D. Bowman 1996, 305.

34. Piotrowski 1991, 97; Bunzel 1995, 960, 963.

35. Lynch 1997.

36. The Commission has two sets of Worksheets: one set for calculating sentences for individuals, and a second set for calculating sentences for corporations and other organizations. The Commission also has a telephone "hotline" for judges, probation officers, prosecutors, and defense attorneys. It is open between 8:30 A.M. and 5:30 P.M. See U.S.S.C. 1997a, 1, 34. The Commission has also made a "variety of exercises, visual aids, and other training materials designed by the Commission's training staff . . . available to the public." Id. at 1–2. There are many other compendiums of Guidelines jurisprudence. See *infra* note 83.

37. Federal Courts Study Committee 1990, 138. One of the authors, José A. Cabranes, was a member of the Federal Courts Study Committee.

38. Varnon 1991, 64 (author is Chief U.S. Probation Officer for the Eastern District of California).

39. Jaffe 1989, 12; see also Varnon 1991, 64 (noting among prosecutors "the perception that officers are now making findings of fact and law which we [probation officers] are not trained or competent to make").

40. See Denzlinger and Miller 1991, 50–51 (describing how the probation officer is seen as a "third adversary" in the courtroom); Heaney 1991, 200 (recounting public defender's description of probation officers as more adversarial than prosecutors in Guidelines regime); Piotrowski 1991, 98 (noting that when defendants are interviewed by probation officers, their attorneys frequently direct them not to answer questions).

41. Piotrowski 1991, 97; see also Sarner 1996, 329 (alleging that "probation officers' version [of offense] too often attributes greater culpability to the defendant").

42. See Edmunds 1996, 319 (noting tension between probation officers and prosecutors).

43. See Chambers 1990, 13–14; Gleeson 1996, 315; see also Frank O. Bowman, III 1996b, 325–26 (discussing common prosecutorial practice of not advising probation officer of facts concerning offenses not readily provable beyond a reasonable doubt).

44. 18 U.S.C. §3602(a) (1994).

45. See Cook 1991, 113; Heaney 1991, 168–69; Nagel and Schulhofer 1992, 538.

46. Weinstein 1992, 364. See also United States v. O'Meara, 895 F.2d 1216, 1223 (8th Cir.) (Bright, J., dissenting in part), *cert. denied,* 498 U.S. 943 (1990).

47. The origin of this characterization is obscure, but it has been widely adopted by many commentators, including defense attorneys, see Clarke 1989, and probation officers themselves, see Gilbert 1991, 110.

48. See Jensen 1991, 95 (responding to judges and others who complain

about probation officers in the Guidelines era, asserting that probation officers are simply doing their job and that "[i]t is of no use to kill the messenger" when what is really at issue is the "message"—that is, the Sentencing Guidelines).

49. 28 U.S.C. §991(a) (1994). For the legislative history of this provision, see page 45.

50. Cook 1991, 113.

51. Bureau of National Affairs 1995, 1518 (quoting Wayne R. Anderson, United States District Judge for the Northern District of Illinois); see also Gleeson 1996, 315 (arguing that judges should welcome bargains that agree to a compromise Guidelines range because this "conserves judicial resources at both the district and appellate levels").

52. Weinstein 1992, 365 (quoting unnamed judge in the Eastern District of New York).

53. See Francesca D. Bowman 1996, 306 (chief probation officers report in survey that in most cases sentencing judge defers to plea agreement).

54. See Goodwin 1996, 71.

55. See United States v. Aguilar, 884 F. Supp. 88, 90–91 (E.D.N.Y. 1995) (Weinstein, J.). Cf. Gleeson 1996, 317 (a district judge, formerly a federal prosecutor, urging that Guidelines should be amended to clarify legitimacy of "sentence bargains").

56. See *supra* note 8.

57. The District Courts and the Courts of Appeals are the courts of general jurisdiction in the federal system, and the judges thereof are generally recognized as "generalists." Federal Courts Study Committee 1990, 121. These courts hear all serious federal criminal cases and all federal civil cases except those filed in specialized courts.

58. See Administrative Office of the United States Courts 1995, 53 (recording 10,162 criminal appeals filed in fiscal year 1995, 8731 involving defendants sentenced under the Guidelines; four-fifths of those cases involved claims under the Guidelines). See also U.S.S.C. 1997b, 71 & A-9 (recording total of only 6480 cases, including multi-defendant cases, involving appeals by defendants sentenced under the Guidelines; 62.3 percent of these involved claims about the Guidelines).

59. U.S.S.G. §3B1.2 (1995).

60. Cf. United States v. Rivera, 96 F.3d 41 (2d Cir. 1996) (recounting sentencing judge's rejection of finding in presentence report that defendant was due two-level reduction for acceptance of responsibility, despite prosecutor's and defense attorney's agreement that reduction was due; probation officer orally undermined presentence report finding).

61. A WESTLAW search on Sept. 15, 1996, found 869 cases reported on this distinction alone.

62. See, e.g., United States v. Costales, 5 F.3d 480, 484–88 (11th Cir. 1993); United States v. Caballero, 936 F.2d 1292, 1299 (D.C. Cir. 1991).

63. Compare United States v. Speenburgh, 990 F.2d 72, 74–76 (2d Cir. 1993) (no, but departure by analogy may be made), with *Costales,* 5 F.3d at 486 (no, and departure also not available).

64. Compare United States v. Valdez-Gonzalez, 957 F.2d 643, 648–50 (9th Cir. 1992) (permitting adjustment to be applied on basis of role in offense of conviction only), with United States v. Webster, 996 F.2d 209, 210–11 (9th Cir. 1993) (overruling *Valdez-Gonzalez* because new amendment to Sentencing Guidelines provides that adjustment for role in offense is based on relevant conduct).

65. See United States v. Lopez-Gil, 965 F.2d 1124, 1131 (1st Cir. 1992); United States v. Rossy, 953 F.2d 321, 326 (7th Cir. 1992).

66. See United States v. Mustread, 42 F.3d 1097, 1103–5 (7th Cir. 1994); United States v. LaValley, 999 F.2d 663, 666 (2d Cir. 1993).

67. See United States v. Lopez, 937 F.2d 716, 728 (2d Cir. 1991) (holding that defendant's role should be compared to that of the "average participant" in such a crime); United States v. Thomas, 932 F.2d 1085, 1092 (5th Cir. 1991) (holding that it is not enough that defendant participated "less" than other defendants).

68. See Federal Judicial Center 1997, 13, 19; see also U.S.S.G. §1B1.11 (1995) (stating, inter alia, that "[i]f the defendant is convicted of two offenses, the first committed before, and the second after, a revised edition of the Guidelines Manual became effective, the revised edition of the Guidelines Manual is to be applied to both offenses."); United States v. Patasnik, 89 F.2d 63, 70 (2d Cir. 1996) (applying new "Commentary" violates Constitution's *ex post facto* clause if amendment does more than "clarify" already-existing rules).

69. See Federal Judicial Center 1997, 72–78, 81–82 (summarizing in brief, abbreviated form, the holdings of numerous recent cases).

70. Id. at 31–35.

71. Id. at 35–37.

72. Id. at 39–42.

73. Id. at 61–64.

74. Id. at 72–73, 75–77 (role), 88–90 (special skill), 96–97 (concealment).

75. Id. at 63–64.

76. See United States v. Clements, 73 F.2d 1330, 1340 (5th Cir. 1996).

77. See Federal Judicial Center 1997, 65–67.

78. Id. at 84–86.

79. Id. at 107–8.

80. See, e.g., United States v. Mullens, 65 F.3d 1560, 1564 (11th Cir. 1995).

81. See Federal Judicial Center 1997, 135.

82. Id. at 130. Compare U.S.S.G. §4B1.1 (Commentary, note 1) with 18 U.S.C. §924(e) (1994) (meaning not the same).

83. See, e.g., Federal Judicial Center 1997; the "Guideline Grapevine" printed semi-annually by the Library of the United States Court of Appeals for the Second Circuit; the Vera Institute's quarterly journal, Federal Sentencing Reporter. Leading treatises on the federal Sentencing Guidelines include Haines et al. 1994; Hutchinson and Yellen 1989. The Commission itself publishes annually (1) the Guidelines Manual, incorporating all amendments to the Guidelines, (2) an Annual Report which summarizes important case law developments, as well as providing data on sentencings, (3) a pamphlet entitled "Selected Guidelines Application Decisions," (4) another entitled "Amendment Highlights," (5) a looseleaf entitled "Most Frequently Asked Questions about the Sentencing Guidelines," and (6) an on-line newsletter called "Guidelines: News from the U.S. Sentencing Commission" (http://www.ussc.gov/news.htm).

84. U.S.S.G. §5K2.0 (1995) (Commentary to Policy Statement); U.S.S.G. §§5H1.1–1.6, 1.9–1.12 (1995) (listing factors and circumstances that are irrelevant in most or all cases). See also United States v. Ives, 984 F.2d 649, 650–51 (5th Cir. 1993) (disparity among codefendants not relevant); United States v. Arjoon, 964 F.2d 167, 170–71 (2d Cir. 1992) (disparity among unrelated cases is not relevant); United States v. Frazier, 979 F.2d 1227, 1231 (7th Cir. 1992) (remanding where sentencing court had sentenced to probation on ground that there was "nothing to be gained" by imprisonment); United States v. Bruder, 945 F.2d 167, 173 (7th Cir. 1991) (en banc) (Guidelines' reduction for "acceptance of responsibility" already takes into account defendant's rehabilitative efforts post-arrest); United States v. Carpenter, 914 F.2d 1131, 1135–46 (9th Cir. 1990) (disparity among codefendants not relevant).

85. See pages 56–57.

86. Compare 18 U.S.C. §§1501–16 (1994) with U.S.S.G. §3C1.1 (1995) (making "non-exhaustive" enumeration of nine types of conduct constituting obstruction within meaning of Guidelines; the last of these is "conduct prohibited by 18 U.S.C. §§1501–16").

87. See page 70. As Judge Wilkins explained in his 1990 law review article heralding the "relevant conduct" principle, there are really three different dimensions to the principle, and each of these reaches criminal behavior beyond the offense of conviction. The first dimension is temporal, reaching the defendant's conduct not just during the offense of conviction, but also during preparation for that offense and any attempt to avoid detection after the offense is committed. U.S.S.G. §1B1.3(a)(1). A second aspect of relevant conduct reaches all criminal conduct committed by the defendant's partners-in-crime, as long as that conduct was "reasonably foreseeable" to the defendant. U.S.S.G. §1B1.3(a)(1)(A), (B). The third, and potentially broadest, dimension reaches *other crimes* (committed by the defendant or his accomplices) that are part of the same "conduct or scheme" as the offense of conviction. U.S.S.G. §1B1.3(a)(2). See Wilkins and Steer 1990, 504–17.

88. See, e.g., Fed. R. Evid. 404(b) ("Evidence of other crimes . . . may . . . be admissible [to prove] motive, opportunity, intent, *plan* . . . ."). Conduct that constitutes a "common scheme or plan" with the offense of conviction is *one* type of "relevant conduct." See U.S.S.G. §1B1.3(a)(2) (1995). The term "common scheme or plan" (and the related, but differently defined, term "same course of conduct") are defined in the Commentary, Application Note 9 of the Relevant Conduct rules.

89. See, e.g., 18 U.S.C. §2 (1994) (extending criminal liability not only to the primary actor, but also to one who "aids, abets, counsels, commands, induces, or procures," or "wilfully causes" the crime). The Guidelines include as *one* type of relevant conduct, "all acts and omissions committed, aided, abetted, counseled, commanded, induced, procured, or willfully caused by the defendant" that occurred "during the commission of the offense of conviction, in preparation for that offense, or in the course of attempting to avoid detection or responsibility for that offense." U.S.S.G. §1B1.3(a)(1)(A) (1995).

90. See, e.g., 18 U.S.C. §371 (1994). The Guidelines include as *one* type of relevant conduct, "all reasonably foreseeable acts and omissions of others in furtherance of" criminal activity "jointly undertaken" with the defendant. Jointly undertaken criminal activity is further defined as "a criminal plan, scheme, endeavor, or enterprise undertaken by the defendant in concert with others, whether or not charged as a conspiracy." U.S.S.G. §1B1.3(a)(1)(B) (1995).

91. See Federal Judicial Center 1997, 1–8, 19–20. A Sentencing Commission staff discussion paper on the relevant conduct rules reported in 1995 that the Commission's "training staff has found that the relevant conduct guideline has been among the most troublesome for application and that the guideline's application has been very inconsistent across districts and circuits." U.S.S.C. 1995, 5.

92. The amendments became effective January 15, 1988, November 1, 1989, November 1, 1990, November 1, 1991, and November 1, 1994.

93. 18 U.S.C. §401 (1994).

94. United States v. Ortiz, 84 F.3d 977, 980 (7th Cir. 1996) (decided on May 24).

95. United States v. Versaglio, 85 F.3d 934, 943 (2d Cir. 1996) (decided on June 3).

96. United States v. Cefalu, 85 F.3d 964, 969–70 (2d Cir. 1996) (decided on June 4).

97. Ultimately, the district judge was affirmed in both cases. After the opinions in *Versaglio* and *Cefalu* were issued, the defendant sought rehearing in the former case, while the government sought rehearing in the latter case. Three months later, the *Versaglio* panel withdrew its judgment and opinion, and issued a new decision consistent with *Cefalu*. See United States v. Versaglio, 96 F.3d 637 (2d Cir. 1996) (on rehearing).

98. The Commission proceeded on the assumption that the Sentencing Reform Act prohibited any exercise of judicial discretion beyond the choice of the final sentence within the Guidelines' 25 percent range. See Goodwin 1995, 109; pages 55–56.

99. See Wilkins and Steer 1993, 74–75. There may be much merit in *not* attempting to resolve circuit conflicts as soon as they arrive. The merits of "percolation" rather than immediate resolution of inter-circuit conflicts were noted in Federal Courts Study Committee 1990, 124. Such an approach permits different circuits to try out different resolutions of an ambiguous or difficult area of law and permit several circuits to consider such an issue before it is definitively resolved.

100. U.S.S.C. 1994 (listing amendments).

101. Alito 1992, 168.

102. See Berman 1994, 145.

103. See Braxton v. United States, 500 U.S. 344, 347–49 (1991); Wright 1991b, 58.

104. See page 73, text at notes 228–30.

105. U.S.S.G. §§5K2.1–2.8, 2.15.

106. Id. §§5K2.9–2.13.

107. Id. §4A1.3.

108. See id. §3C1.2 (Commentary, notes 2, 6).

109. Several guidelines in chapter 2 of the Guidelines Manual, which instructs the sentencing court how to calculate the defendant's Base Offense Level, also explicitly or implicitly invite departures on particular grounds. See, e.g., id. §2A6.1 (Commentary, note 1) (noting that the "Threatening Communication" guideline deals with wide range of conduct and that "[f]actors not incorporated" expressly may be a basis for departure).

110. See U.S.S.G. §§3A1.2(b), 3C1.2, 5K2.10–2.13.

111. See, e.g., United States v. Merritt, 988 F.2d 1298, 1305–11 (2d Cir. 1993) (permitting upward departure for defendant's "profound corruption and dishonesty" and "fraudulent manipulation . . . designed to preserve" monetary gains of crime); United States v. Fan, 36 F.3d 240, 246–47 (2d Cir. 1994) (affirming upward departure for "obstruction of justice" by perjury); United States v. Cantu, 12 F.3d 1506 (9th Cir. 1993) (considering Post Traumatic Stress Disorder as mental disorder which can support downward departure); United States v. Johnson, 956 F.2d 894 (9th Cir. 1992) (Noonan, J.) (considering partial duress as a mitigating factor warranting departure); United States v. Lieberman, 971 F.2d 989, 995–96 (3d Cir. 1992) (affirming downward departure for post-conviction conduct evincing acceptance of responsibility); United States v. Johnson, 952 F.2d 565, 583–84 (1st Cir. 1991) (permitting upward departure for "cool, deliberative, calculated" planning regarding terrorist weapons and threat to national security), *cert. denied,* 506 U.S. 816 (1992).

112. We use the term "guided departure" to refer to all instances where the Commission identifies a ground that may be an appropriate basis for departure, upward or downward. The Commission itself uses this term more narrowly—to refer to those few instances in which the Guidelines both identify a ground for possible departure *and* recommend the amount of a departure through precise

quantitative specification or by cross-referencing another guideline. See U.S.S.G. §1A.4(b) (1995) (discussing "guided departures").

113. See, e.g., United States v. Hendrickson, 22 F.3d 170, 175 (7th Cir.), *cert. denied,* 513 U.S. 878 (1994); United States v. Jones, 18 F.3d 1145, 1149 (4th Cir. 1994); United States v. Cherry, 10 F.3d 1003, 1010–12 (3d Cir. 1993); United States v. Kelly, 1 F.3d 1137, 1139–41 (10th Cir. 1993), *cert. denied,* 513 U.S. 939 (1994); United States v. Castro-Cervantes, 927 F.2d 1079, 1081–82 (9th Cir. 1990); United States v. Kikumura, 918 F.2d 1084, 1116 (3d Cir. 1990); United States v. McDowell, 902 F.2d 451, 453–54 (6th Cir. 1990).

114. See pages 74–76.

115. See Ellingstad 1992 (First, Third, Sixth, and Seventh Circuits have generally rejected downward departures, while the Second and Eighth Circuits have generally upheld them).

116. United States v. Farah, 991 F.2d 1065 (2d Cir. 1993).

117. United States v. Poff, 926 F.2d 588 (7th Cir. 1991) (en banc); United States v. Russell, 917 F.2d 512 (11th Cir. 1990).

118. United States v. Jackson, 30 F.3d 199 (1st Cir. 1994); United States v. Goff, 20 F.3d 918 (8th Cir. 1994); United States v. Rimell, 21 F.3d 1281 (8th Cir. 1994); United States v. Hawley, 984 F.2d 252 (8th Cir. 1993); United States v. Guajardo, 950 F.2d 203 (5th Cir. 1991), *cert. denied,* 503 U.S. 1009 (1992); United States v. White, 945 F.2d 100 (5th Cir. 1991).

119. United States v. Guajardo, 950 F.2d 203 (5th Cir. 1991), *cert. denied,* 503 U.S. 1009 (1992).

120. United States v. Vela, 927 F.2d 197 (5th Cir. 1991); United States v. Prestemon, 929 F.2d 1275 (8th Cir. 1991).

121. United States v. Fairman, 947 F.2d 1479 (11th Cir. 1991), *cert. denied,* 503 U.S. 947 (1992).

122. United States v. Chestna, 962 F.2d 103 (1st Cir.), *cert. denied,* 506 U.S. 920 (1992); United States v. Cacho, 951 F.2d 308 (11th Cir. 1992); United States v. Berlier, 948 F.2d 1093 (9th Cir. 1991).

123. United States v. Porter, 948 F.2d 1283 (4th Cir. 1991).

124. United States v. O'Brien, 950 F.2d 969 (5th Cir. 1991), *cert. denied,* 506 U.S. 819 (1992).

125. United States v. Desormeaux, 952 F.2d 182 (8th Cir. 1991); United States v. Sklar, 920 F.2d 107 (1st Cir. 1990); United States v. Pharr, 916 F.2d 129 (3d Cir. 1990).

126. United States v. Chubbuck, 32 F.3d 1458 (10th Cir. 1994).

127. United States v. Harotunian, 920 F.2d 1040, 1047 (1st Cir. 1990); United States v. Williams, 891 F.2d 962, 965 (1st Cir. 1989).

128. United States v. Peters, 978 F.2d 166, 170 (5th Cir. 1992) (holding that defendant's receipt of two Purple Hearts and a Distinguished Flying Cross was not a basis for departure from the Guidelines).

129. See U.S.S.C. Annual Report 1995, 21–24 (listing eight cases during the year approving downward departures, thirteen cases disapproving downward departures, nineteen cases approving upward departures, and three cases disapproving upward departures); U.S.S.C. Annual Report 1994, 15–20 (listing nine cases approving downward departures, thirty-five cases disapproving downward departures; sixteen cases during the year approving upward departures, seven cases disapproving upward departures); U.S.S.C. Annual Report 1993, 25–29 (listing eight cases approving downward departures, fourteen cases disapproving downward departures; thirty-two cases during the year approving upward departures, seventeen cases disapproving upward departures). The Commission's Annual Report for 1996 does not provide comparable tables.

130. See, e.g., United States v. Reyes, 8 F.3d 1379, 1385 (9th Cir. 1993).

131. 21 U.S.C. §841(b).

132. See, e.g., United States v. Canales, 91 F.3d 363, 370 (2d Cir. 1996); United States v. Maxwell, 25 F.3d 1389 (8th Cir. 1994). In 1996, Congress rejected the Commission's proposal, by a vote of 4 to 3, that the penalties for powdered cocaine and crack cocaine be equalized. Pub. L. No. 104-38 (Oct. 30, 1995).

133. See, e.g., United States v. Betts, 16 F.3d 748 (7th Cir. 1994); United States v. Piche, 981 F.2d 706 (4th Cir. 1992), *cert. denied,* 508 U.S. 916 (1993).

134. See, e.g., United States v. Barbontin, 907 F.2d 1494 (5th Cir. 1990).

135. See, e.g., United States v. Smith, 27 F.3d 649, 668 (D.C. Cir. 1994); United States v. Nnanna, 7 F.3d 420 (5th Cir. 1993); United States v. Crook, 9 F.3d 1422 (9th Cir. 1993), *cert. denied,* 511 U.S. 1086 (1994).

136. See, e.g., United States v. Pozzy, 902 F.2d 133, 137 (1st Cir. 1990).

137. 116 S. Ct. 2035 (1996).

138. See chapter 2, section B(4).

139. U.S.S.G. §5K2.0 (Policy Statement).

140. 116 S. Ct. at 2047.

141. 18 U.S.C. §3742(e).

142. 116 S. Ct. at 2046.

143. See, e.g., Bureau of National Affairs 1996a.

144. 116 S. Ct. at 2046.

145. Frank O. Bowman, III 1996b.

146. Cases that read *Koon* as increasing discretion to depart include United States v. Sablan, 114 F.3d 913 (9th Cir. 1997) (6–5 en banc panel); United States v. Galante, 111 F.3d 1029 (2d Cir. 1997), *reh'g in banc denied,* 128 F.3d 788 (1997); United States v. Joost, 92 F.3d 7 (1st Cir. 1996) (upholding upward departure on basis specifically identified by Commission as warranting upward departure; but also citing deference language of *Koon*).

147. See, e.g., United States v. Rybicki, 96 F.3d 754, 758 (4th Cir. 1996) ("While we review this ultimate departure decision for abuse of discretion, . . . if the court's departure is based on a misinterpretation of the Guidelines, our view of that underlying ruling is de novo."); United States v. Lewis, 90 F.3d 302, 304, 306 (8th Cir. 1996) (citing *Koon* for the proposition that departure relied on error of law and thus was "by definition" an abuse of discretion); United States v. McNeil, 90 F.3d 298 (8th Cir. 1996) (declining to give deference to district court's decision that criminal history calculation was not adequate); United States v. Taylor, 88 F.3d 938 (11th Cir. 1996) (affirming upward departure on grounds specifically identified by Guidelines as possibly warranting upward departure; quoting *Koon* at length without suggesting it had changed effective standard of review); United States v. Weinberger, 91 F.3d 642, 644 (4th Cir. 1996); United States v. Weise, 89 F.3d 502 (8th Cir. 1996) (ordering remand over partial dissent which argued that *Koon* requires more deference to district court than recognized by majority).

After a thorough review of *Koon* and other Supreme Court cases involving departures under the Guidelines, Professor Cynthia Lee has concluded that the standards for appellate review of district court departures remain confused. Lee 1997. See also U.S.S.C. Annual Report 1996, 19–21 (post-*Koon* discussion citing more cases affirming upward than downward departures, and more cases reversing downward than upward departures).

148. 18 U.S.C. §3553(b) (permitting judge to depart on own motion only if "there exists an aggravating or mitigating circumstance of a kind, or to a degree, not adequately taken into consideration by the Sentencing Commission"); for the legislative history of this key provision, see page 41, text at notes 24–26.

149. 18 U.S.C. §3553(b). See chapter 2, note 223.

150. See 116 S. Ct. at 2052–53 (stating that because Commission already took factor into account, sentencing court "abused its discretion" by considering that factor).

151. United States v. Barber, 93 F.3d. 1200, 1203 (4th Cir. 1996).

152. 116 S. Ct. at 2052 (stating that a factor present to an extent considered by the Commission does "not take the case out of the heartland"). *Koon* explicitly reaffirmed the rule that reviewing courts should consider *de novo* (that is, without deference) the "legal conclusions" that a district court makes in asserting departure authority, noting that "[a] district court by definition abuses its discretion when it makes an error of law." Id. at 2047.

153. See pages 74–75.

154. Among the prominent factors thus considered by the Commission are the presence or absence of a criminal record, the defendant's role in the offense, the quantity of harm, and whether the defendant has accepted responsibility for the crime. See also U.S.S.G. §§1.1 (age ordinarily not relevant); 1.2 (educational and vocational skills ordinarily not relevant); 1.5 (employment record ordinarily not relevant); 1.6 (family or community responsibilities ordinarily not relevant); 1.11 (military, civic, charitable, or public service ordinarily not relevant).

155. See United States v. Weinberger, 91 F.3d 642, 644 (4th Cir. 1996) ("Given the comprehensive sentencing structure embodied in the guidelines, '[o]nly rarely will we conclude that a factor was not adequately taken into consideration by the Commission.'") (quoting pre-*Koon* Fourth Circuit cases); see also Stith and Koh 1993, 246–47.

156. 116 S. Ct. at 2052 (stating that factor relied on by sentencing court "is to be expected . . . so we conclude these consequences were adequately considered by the Commission").

157. United States v. Pullen, 89 F.3d 368, 371 (7th Cir. 1996).

158. Frank O. Bowman, III 1996b, 19.

159. Weinstein 1992, 365–66.

160. Frank O. Bowman, III 1996a, 732.

Chapter Four

1. See generally chapter 2. See also Nagel and Schulhofer 1992, 501; Schulhofer and Nagel 1989, 237 (characterizing disparity reduction as the Act's "overriding goal"); Wilkins, Newton and Steer 1993.

2. Letter from Hon. Stephen S. Trott, Associate Attorney General, on behalf of the U.S. Department of Justice to Hon. William W. Wilkins, Jr., Chairman of the U.S. Sentencing Commission (Apr. 7, 1987) (urging sentencing guidelines that permit only narrow judicial discretion). To complete the record, it should be noted that the author of this statement, now Judge Stephen S. Trott of the U.S. Court of Appeals for the Ninth Circuit, has more recently (November 9, 1994) written to the Hon. Richard Conaboy, the present Chairman of the Sentencing Commission, explaining that experience under the Guidelines had caused him to conclude that "the cure is worse than the disease." Both letters are reprinted in 8 Federal Sentencing Reporter 196–99 (1995).

3. See, e.g., Stith and Koh 1993, 261–62.

4. S. Rep. No. 225, 98th Cong., 2d Sess. 38–39, 41–66, 49, 52, 65, 75, 161 (1984).

5. 18 U.S.C. §3553(a); 28 U.S.C. §§991(b)(1)(B), 994(f).

6. See, e.g., the remarks of Senators Biden and Thurmond, in Wilkins, Newton and Steer 1993, 366–67; Stith and Koh 1993, 278.

7. 28 U.S.C. §991(b)(a)(B) ("The purposes of the United States Sentencing

Commission are to provide certainty and fairness in meeting the purposes of sentencing, avoiding unwarranted disparities among defendants with similar records who have been found guilty of similar criminal conduct while maintaining sufficient flexibility to permit individualized sentences when warranted. . . .").

8. S. Rep. No. 225, 98th Cong., 2d Sess. 161 (1984).

9. Compare Frank O. Bowman, III 1996a, 714–24 (asserting that no study has demonstrated that disparity has *increased* under the Guidelines). Inasmuch as the purpose of the Guidelines was to reduce disparity, it would seem that the burden of proof on this issue is on those who support the Guidelines.

10. Frankel 1973; see pages 35–36.

11. The most comprehensive review of empirical literature on sentencing during this period is Hagan and Bumiller 1983. They note that only seven of the studies involve the federal courts.

12. S. Rep. No. 225, 98th Cong., 2d Sess. 65 (1984) ("The shameful disparity in criminal sentences is a major flaw in the existing criminal justice system. . . ."). See also pages 31, 38.

13. Weisburd 1992.

14. McDonald and Carlson 1993, 25.

15. McDonald is now Senior Social Scientist at Abt Associates, Inc. of Cambridge, Massachusetts.

16. McDonald 1982.

17. See generally Stith and Koh 1993.

18. See Cook 1979, 227–71; Alschuler 1978; Flaxman 1979; Krattenmaker 1978, 1323–26; see also Diamond 1981, 402–3 (noting complexity in sources of inter-judge variations in sentencing).

19. In addition to these four studies, the Senate Report also briefly mentioned four others. Three of these did not concern the federal courts: Wilkins et al. 1976; Austin and Williams 1977; Baab and Furgeson 1967, 45:471. The fourth study cited in the Senate Report was Diamond and Zeisel 1975, but this review of experimental sentencing councils actually showed less variation in judges' independent sentencing decisions than did the four studies that featured more prominently in the Senate Report. Id. at 115, 120 (judges in Sentencing Council study agreed 70 percent of the time whether defendant should receive probation or imprisonment, whereas the study of sentencing judges in Second Circuit Study, relied on by the Senate, showed agreement only 20 percent of the time).

20. See S. Rep. No. 225, 98th Cong., 2d Sess. 41–45 (1984).

21. Seymour 1973, reprinted in 119 Cong. Rec. 6060 (1973).

22. Seymour 1973, 67, quoted in Senate Rep. No. 225, 98th Cong., 2d Sess. 41 n.21 (1984).

23. Administrative Office of the United States Courts 1972, app. table X-4, reprinted in S. Rep. No. 225, 98th Cong., 2d Sess. 45 (1984).

24. Heaney 1991. See also pages 116–18.

25. U.S.S.C. Annual Report 1995, appendix B, entries for Central District of California, District of Columbia, and Eastern District of Pennsylvania.

26. Wilkins 1992, 799.

27. Heaney 1992, 237 ("If such methods of comparison were valid to show pre-guidelines disparity, they are equally valid to show the existence of disparity under the guidelines.").

28. See Partridge and Eldridge 1974, 9.

29. Frankel 1973; see also Frankel 1972. See generally pages 35–36.

30. Twentieth Century Fund Task Force on Criminal Sentencing 1976, 103.

31. Partridge and Eldridge 1974.

32. Id. at 10.

33. Id. at 41–54.

34. Confidential conversation with one of the authors in 1987.

35. Heumann 1993 (summarizing research presentation by Wheeler et al. 1986).

36. The Senate Report cites two publications that analyzed the results of this Department of Justice Study. See Bartolomeo et al. 1981, and INSLAW et al. 1981.

37. Bartolomeo 1981, 10–18; appendix 2, 78–80; INSLAW 1981, III-27 n.3.

38. INSLAW 1981, III-11.

39. INSLAW 1981, III-16, cited in S. Rep. No. 225, 98th Cong., 2d Sess. 44 (1984).

40. Bartolomeo et al. 1981, 21–31; INSLAW 1981, III-17. The remaining variation was ascribed to "interaction effects" among case attributes and the judge effect.

41. Payne 1997, 2 (conclusion regarding non-Guidelines sentences imposed in Southern District of New York, Eastern District of New York, and Eastern District of Pennsylvania between 1980 and 1991).

42. Partridge and Eldridge 1974, 14–16 (discussing "paper defendant" problem).

43. See McDonald and Carlson 1993, 24–26 (reviewing both simulation studies and studies examining actual federal sentencing decisions prior to the introduction of the sentencing guidelines; noting as to each that race was not found to be a statistically significant factor).

44. McDonald and Carlson 1993, 27.

45. Cognitive psychologists Amos Tversky and Daniel Kahneman have noted that people "assess the frequency of a class . . . by the ease with which instances or occurrences can be brought to mind. . . . In addition to familiarity, other factors, such as salience, affect the retrievability of instances." Tversky and Kahneman 1982, 11; see also id. at 9–10 (discussing failure of observers to perceive likelihood of regression toward the mean, and thus likelihood that an extreme observation will be followed by a less extreme observation).

46. See Partridge and Eldridge 1974, appendix C ("Ranks of Sentences of Individual Judges in Thirteen Cases"); Bartolomeo et al. 1981, technical appendix 4.

47. Wheeler et al. 1988, 12 & n.35 (re-analyzing data in Partridge and Eldridge 1974).

48. Wheeler et al. 1988, 167 (Wheeler here is referring to his own empirical analysis, not his reanalysis of Partridge and Eldridge 1974).

49. Bartolomeo et al. 1981, 58.

50. Bartolomeo et al. 1981, 65 (emphasis in original).

51. See Clancy et al. 1981, 553–54; see also Diamond 1981.

52. 28 U.S.C. §994(a)(2).

53. U.S.S.C. 1991a, executive summary at 85.

54. See Wilkins 1992, 820; Nagel and Schulhofer 1992; Wilkins and Steer 1993, 64.

55. U.S.S.C. 1991a, 288, 292, 296, 299.

56. United States General Accounting Office 1992; Weisburd 1992, 151–52; Tonry 1992a, 147 n.1. A second part of the Commission's 1991 self-evaluation sought to determine whether sentences under the Guidelines were related to several factors that the Guidelines consider irrelevant to sentence, including race, age, sex, marital status, employment status, and education. The analysis

was limited to 25 percent of the cases sentenced in the second half of 1990 for four specific offense/offender combinations. The Commission cautioned that its findings were preliminary, that many of its sample sizes were extremely small, and thus that, for many of the variables considered, no statistically significant conclusions could be reached. On the basis of its analysis, the Commission concluded that there were no statistically significant correlations between severity of sentence and the factors it deemed impermissible. The reanalysis by the GAO, using somewhat more sophisticated statistical techniques, found small but statistically significant correlations for all such variables except education. United States General Accounting Office 1992, 12, 62–110.

57. McDonald and Carlson 1993, 31–32. They say: "[A] comparison of maximum court-imposed sentences in pre-guideline cases (which were designed to include a parole term after release from prison) with "real time" sentences under the guidelines is misleading. The [shift to "real time" sentences] under the guidelines . . . alone would have accounted for a narrower dispersion of sentences. . . ."

58. Rhodes 1992, 153.

59. See, e.g., Weisburd 1992, 151–52; Tonry 1992a, 147.

60. This is noted in Tonry 1992a, 147; McDonald and Carlson 1993, 31–32; Rhodes 1992, 153.

61. U.S.S.C. 1991a, 281.

62. We note this variation at page 117, table 2.

63. See page 80.

64. In the middle of 1990, when the Commission assumed responsibility for collecting federal sentencing data from the Administrative Office of the U.S. Courts (the support bureaucracy for the federal courts), the Commission began gathering information related to Sentencing Guidelines categories but *stopped* collecting some types of information that the Administrative Office had routinely compiled. For example, the Commission does not collect information about offender characteristics, such as socioeconomic status and family and community ties, that the Guidelines deem irrelevant (or nearly so) to sentencing decisions. Such "limitations and inconsistencies in data available" led the GAO to urge the Commission to give up trying to make before-and-after comparisons of this type, and to conclude that "it is impossible to determine how effective the sentencing Guidelines have been in reducing overall sentencing disparity." United States General Accounting Office 1992, 10, 23; see also McDonald and Carlson 1993, 5–6.

65. Alschuler 1991, 917.

66. United States General Accounting Office 1992, 13 ("The Commission maintained that as long as the sentences imposed are within the guidelines range, . . . unwarranted disparity cannot exist.").

67. See also Schulhofer 1992, 845 (disparity reduced in the 65–80 percent of plea-bargained cases that do not attempt evasion of the Guidelines).

68. U.S.S.G. §5H1.1 (age not relevant for imposing sentence outside of Guidelines range, except for certain circumstances involving aged and infirm defendants).

69. U.S.S.C. 1991a; see also Wilkins 1992, 801.

70. Heaney 1991. Plea bargaining and hidden disparity are further discussed at pages 130–42.

71. Another study that sought to compare pre- and post-Guidelines sentencing variation in a few federal districts concluded that "the guidelines are significantly reducing the sentence variations on an overall scale for most offenses." Karle and Sager 1991, 407. Unfortunately, the study "had several important

flaws," including inaccurate differentiation between Guidelines and non-Guidelines cases in the transition years after 1987. McDonald and Carlson 1993, 28–29.

72. The General Accounting Office, in its re-analysis of the Commission's 1991 self-evaluation, likewise confirmed significant disparities among circuits both in levels of departures and in the position of sentences within Guidelines ranges. United States General Accounting Office 1992, 68–85.

73. U.S.S.C. Annual Report 1991, table 56, at 140–42.

74. U.S.S.C. 1997b, 39–41 (19.5 percent in 1994, 19.7 percent in 1995, 19.2 percent in 1996).

75. The standard deviation is a measure of the variation around the mean. Assuming that the variation in use is normally distributed, as appears to be the case, two-thirds of all districts will be within one standard deviation of the mean, one-sixth will be more than one standard deviation below the mean, and one-sixth will be more than one standard deviation above the mean. In 1995, for instance, one-sixth of districts granted substantial assistance motions in less than 9.6 percent of cases, while one-sixth granted such motions in more than 29.6 percent of cases.

76. See pages 106–12; see also Rhodes 1991, 1009–10.

77. U.S.S.C. Annual Report 1995, table 31.

78. See U.S.S.C. 1997b, 41–43; Annual Report 1992, table 50; Annual Report 1993, table 66; Annual Report 1994, table 33.

79. See U.S.S.C. Annual Report 1994 at 83 (rate of 8.5 percent); Annual Report 1993 at 161 (rate of 6.6 percent); Annual Report 1992 at 127 (rate of 8.8 percent). The substantial assistance departure rate for the District of Connecticut rose to approximately 15 percent in 1995 and fell back to 10.8 percent in 1996. See U.S.S.C. Annual Report 1995 at 89; U.S.S.C. 1997b, 41.

80. See pages 91–97. See also Lawrence and Hofer 1992, discussed at pages 129–30.

81. Waldfogel 1991; see also Waldfogel 1994.

82. In some districts, there may be opportunities for judge-shopping as a result of local rules or practices governing arraignments and the taking of guilty pleas. In some districts, for example, the rules may provide that a criminal case will be assigned to the judge who presides over the defendant's initial arraignment, if the defendant pleads guilty at that arraignment. If the schedule of assignments to the "arraignment part" is known to counsel, there will be bargaining not only for a plea of guilty but also for arraignment before a particular judge. This was true, for example, in the Southern District of New York until 1987, when the local practices were changed to provide assurances of random distribution of all criminal proceedings. See Lubasch 1987, B1 (reporting that although cases in the Southern District of New York are randomly assigned to judges when the defendant at arraignment enters plea of "not guilty," any "guilty" plea is taken by the presiding arraignment judge, whose identity and dates of service are known to prosecutors and defense attorneys in advance); Connelly and Douglas 1987 (reporting that judges in the Southern District had voted unanimously to have all cases, including guilty pleas, assigned randomly).

83. See pages 111–12, text at note 46.

84. Researchers have complained, at times bitterly, about this limitation. See Cohn 1994, 139–40; Freed and Miller 1993, 3–5; Walker 1995.

85. Waldfogel 1991, 153.

86. Payne 1997, 338, 357–58.

87. Moreover, while we used the same pre-Guidelines time period as had Waldfogel (1984–1988), our post-Guidelines period (1988–1992) was longer. In

addition, unlike Waldfogel, we did not include in our post-Guidelines data set any sentences for pre-1987 crimes, because the Guidelines only apply to crimes committed after November 1, 1987. Our data was more limited than Waldfogel's in one important respect, however: it covered only a limited subset of federal crimes. Specifically, our data covered only four routine, and not particularly controversial, categories of federal crime: tax evasion, fraud, larceny, and embezzlement.

88. For instance, whereas Waldfogel found that the mean disparity in the District of Connecticut had increased from 4.2 months to 9.9 months under the Guidelines, we found that for our subset of crimes it had decreased from 3.3 months to 2.6 months.

89. The other members of the research group are James Anderson, Yale Law School Class of 1995, and Jeffrey Kling of the Massachusetts Institute of Technology.

90. See U.S.S.G. §2D1.1. See generally pages 68–70.

91. Alschuler 1991.

92. Schulhofer 1992.

93. Alschuler 1991, 950–51; Schulhofer 1992, 861.

94. U.S.S.C. 1991b, ii.

95. Id.

96. Id.

97. See pages 130–42 for a discussion of plea-bargaining and prosecutorial discretion under the Guidelines.

98. See Lowenthal 1993; Harvard Law Review, "Determinate Sentencing and Judicial Participation in Democratic Punishment," 108:947, 949 (1995) (student review).

99. We use the term to refer to the reaction beginning in the late 1960s against indeterminacy in sentencing, see pages 30–37.

100. See also Griset 1991; Casper 1984, 236–37; Stith and Koh 1993, 227–28.

101. See, e.g., 21 U.S.C. §841(b)(1)(A)(i)–(viii) (prescribing mandatory minimum for specified weights of drugs).

102. See generally pages 66–77.

103. The median of the sentencing ranges for Offense Level 20 is approximately eight times that of the ranges for Offense Level 8. See appendix A (Sentencing Table).

104. McDonald and Carlson 1993. In addition to reviewing previous empirical analyses of sentencing disparity in the federal courts, the study examined federal sentencing data from 1986 through 1990, including all sentencings from January 20, 1989 to June 30, 1990 that were subject to the Sentencing Reform Act of 1984. Id. at 37–38.

105. McDonald and Carlson 1993, 1, 24–26, 44–49.

106. Id. at 1, 45, 181.

107. Id. at 1.

108. Id.

109. Id. at 1–2, 178–89. In 1997, Attorney General Janet Reno and White House drug policy director Barry R. McCaffrey urged that the differential between powdered cocaine and crack cocaine be significantly reduced. Wren 1997.

110. 21 U.S.C. §841(b)(1)(A).

111. McDonald and Carlson 1993, 192. The report does not provide similar statistics for a reduction in white/Hispanic disparity, though it does report that without the crack cocaine/powdered cocaine distinction the average sentences for drug trafficking by Hispanics would have been reduced. Id. at 192–94.

112. Id. at 191–93. The Commission not only links its Base Offense Levels to

statutory minimums, but also imposes these Base Offense Levels even in cases where the statutory minimum would not apply. The statutory minimum applies only to the quantity of drugs in the offense of conviction, whereas the Guidelines attribute additional quantities to a defendant through application of its "relevant conduct" principle. See page 70.

113. A similar analysis may be undertaken with respect to the question of whether the Guidelines have increased or decreased sentencing disparity on the basis of sex. Professor Ilene Nagel, one of the original members of the Sentencing Commission, has demonstrated that in the pre-Guidelines era, women were sentenced more leniently than men, see Nagel and Hagan 1983, 134. In deciding that the Guidelines should be "neutral" as to sex, that judges may not take sex into account in sentencing, and that family responsibilities are not usually relevant in determining the sentencing range, the Congress and the Sentencing Commission made a series of *choices* that have resulted in the incarceration of many more female offenders. See pages 74–75, text at notes 240–45.

114. See chapter 2, note 225.

115. The Guidelines seek to limit the amount of a Criminal History departure by requiring that the judge consider and reject each intermediate departure amount before deciding on a final Criminal History Category. U.S.S.G. §4A1.3 (Commentary); United States v. Mendez-Colon, 15 F.3d 188 (1st Cir. 1994). Some appellate courts have appeared to impose a similar "bunny hop" requirement on departures along the Offense Level axis. See, e.g., United States v. Lira-Barraza, 941 F.2d 745, 747–51 (9th Cir. 1991) (en banc); United States v. Hogan, 54 F.3d 336, 342 (7th Cir. 1995). The Supreme Court decision in Koon v. United States, by failing to address the issue, may be read as indicating that appellate courts should not review the magnitude of departure. See 116 S. Ct. 2035 (1996); United States v. Sablan, 114 F.3d 913 (9th Cir. 1997) (en banc).

116. Cf. United States v. Rivera, 994 F.2d 942, 949 (1st Cir. 1993) (Breyer, J.) (advising that with respect to sentencing factors unmentioned in the Guidelines, judges should consider "structure and theory" of the Guidelines in deciding whether departure is permissible).

117. See page 90.

118. See Heaney 1991.

119. Nagel and Schulhofer 1992, 546.

120. Id.; Heaney 1991.

121. Administrative Office of the United States, Division of Probation 1984, 3–4.

122. See pages 86–89; Forde 1996, 397 (noting that Guidelines have "radically altered the weight and importance of evidence that is considered at sentencings").

123. See the various essays by probation officers published in the Federal Sentencing Reporter in 1991 cited in chapter 3. See also Garoppolo 1996 (author is Deputy Chief U.S. Probation Officer for the Eastern District of New York).

124. Francesca D. Bowman 1996.

125. See page 87.

126. See Judicial Conference of the United States, Committee on Probation 1987.

127. Lawrence and Hofer 1992.

128. Id. For another defendant, a majority of officers assigned a Base Offense Level of 20, but the median was between Levels 22 and 23, and three officers assigned an Offense Level of 32. For the final defendant, the majority response

was an Offense Level of 24, but the median Level was 26, and two officers assigned an Offense Level of 32. Id.

129. Hofer 1992, 335. See generally appendix B.

130. See, e.g., Federal Courts Study Committee 1990, 138; Heaney 1991, 168–75, 190–203; Freed and Miller 1991, 175–76; Weintraub 1991, 148; Yellen 1992, 569–72; Weis 1992, 825; United States General Accounting Office 1992, 14–16.

131. See, e.g., Schulhofer and Nagel 1989, 285–87; Nagel and Schulhofer 1992, 557.

132. United States General Accounting Office 1992.

133. As to the last of these, see pages 76–77.

134. U.S. Department of Justice, Bureau of Justice Statistics, 1987 Sourcebook of Criminal Justice Statistics, table 5.22; 1988 Sourcebook, table 5.28; U.S.S.C. Annual Report 1994, table 19, at 51; U.S.S.C. Annual Report 1995, table 17, at 56.

135. U.S.S.G. §6B1.2(a).

136. See Gleeson 1996; Goodwin 1996.

137. See Fed. R. Crim. P. 11(e).

138. Id. 11(e)(1)(C) (parties may "agree that specific sentence is appropriate disposition of the case"); id. 11(e)(2) ("the court may accept or reject the agreement, or may defer its decision . . . until there has been an opportunity to read the presentence report").

139. See Gleeson 1996, 316 (pleas under Rule 11(e)(1)(C) "occur only occasionally"). Cf. United States v. Pimentel, 932 F.2d 1029, 1033 (2d Cir. 1991) (obliquely referring to practice prior to Guidelines, and urging more "sentencing bargaining" given the Guidelines).

140. See Wilkins and Steer 1990, 499 n.27, quoted at page 70.

141. See chapter 2, note 193.

142. See generally Garoppolo 1996.

143. U.S.S.G. §6B1.2(a) (emphasis added).

144. U.S.S.G. §6B1.4(a) (emphasis added).

145. U.S.S.G. §6B1.2(b)(2), (c)(2).

146. See also Wilkins and Steer 1990, 500 (to avoid plea-bargaining manipulation, "the presentence report and recommended guideline application of the probation officer play an important role").

147. U.S.S.G. §6B1.1(c).

148. U.S.S.G. §6A1.1 (and Commentary) (emphasis added).

149. U.S.S.G. §6B1.4(d) (emphasis added).

150. See Fed. R. Crim. P. 11(e)(2)–(4) and *supra* note 138. See generally Abraham S. Goldstein 1981, 39 et seq.

151. See Wilkins and Steer 1990, 500–501.

152. U.S.S.G. §6B1.2(a) ("actual offense behavior").

153. See pages 68–70.

154. Lynch 1997.

155. U.S.S.G. §6B1.2.

156. See pages 72–77, 98–103.

157. See Wilkins and Steer 1990, 501; see also Wilkins 1990, 13 ("justifiable reasons" means reasons that satisfy "statutory criteria for a valid departure").

158. See Breyer 1988, 30–31; see also Breyer 1990, 13 ("justifiable reasons" include caseload pressure in the district).

159. U.S.S.G. §1(A)(4)(c).

160. See Schulhofer and Nagel 1989, 242–43.

161. Wilkins 1992, 802 (safeguards against prosecutorial "abuse" and "manipulat[ion]"). See also Wilkins 1988, 189–90 (failing to include this statement in listing of Guidelines provisions that endeavor "to ensure that truth in sentencing will not be sacrificed under any circumstances").

162. See Breyer 1988, 31.

163. Schulhofer and Nagel 1989, 243.

164. Before the implementation of the Sentencing Guidelines, the Department of Justice did not attempt to regulate or monitor either the charging or plea-bargaining process with much specificity. The United States Attorney within each of the nation's ninety-six judicial districts had significant authority in employing his prosecutorial resources, bringing charges, accepting pleas, and deciding whether to recommend sentence. See Vorenberg 1981, 1543–44.

In 1980, the Department did issue a set of guidelines entitled *Principles of Federal Prosecution.* Largely the work of Philip B. Heymann, who was on leave from his professorship at Harvard Law School and serving as chief of the Criminal Division, these guidelines laid down general principles and were not "intended . . . [to] require a given prosecutorial decision in any particular case." Id. (A)(2) (Comment). Although the *Principles* did attempt to limit the parameters of prosecutorial discretion, most particularly by defining the permissible bases for plea-bargaining, they were written at a high level of generality, deliberately employed subjective concepts, and contained very few categorical prescriptions. Nor was their implementation monitored or enforced. (One of the present authors was a special assistant to Heymann when the *Principles* were drafted.)

165. See Thornburgh 1989. The memorandum, entitled *Plea Policy for Federal Prosecutors: Plea Bargaining under the Sentencing Reform Act,* is reprinted in Federal Sentencing Reporter 1994, 6:347–49. The Thornburgh Memorandum was actually preceded by a memorandum issued under the signature of William Weld, who was the chief of the Criminal Division. The Weld directive, generally referred to as "The Redbook" on plea-bargaining, was issued on November 1, 1987, the day the Sentencing Guidelines went into effect. The Redbook contained no claim that it would be monitored and enforced by the Department of Justice.

166. Thornburgh 1989.

167. Id.

168. Id.

169. Nagel and Schulhofer 1992, 542.

170. See id. at 563 n.79 ("Despite our efforts, some AUSAs may have incorrectly inferred that we were checking *on them.* If so, their responses may have been defensive, or they may have obscured some of the evasion that had actually occurred."). See also Yellen 1992, 569.

171. Nagel and Schulhofer 1992, 516 ("If the negotiation occurs before indictment, . . . circumvention is almost impossible for us to detect.").

172. Yellen 1992, 569–70.

173. See Reno 1993. The Reno Memorandum is reprinted at Federal Sentencing Reporter 1994, 6:352. Its title was, simply, *Principles of Federal Prosecution,* the same title that the Department had used in 1980 when it published general and nonbinding prosecutorial guidelines, see *supra* note 164. Like those *Principles,* which were still in effect (if little noticed), the Reno Memorandum advised prosecutors to charge "the most serious offense that is consistent with the nature of the defendant's conduct, that is likely to result in a sustainable conviction." Philip B. Heymann, the principal drafter of the 1980 *Principles,* was Deputy Attorney General when the Reno Memorandum was issued.

174. See, e.g., Liebman and Snyder 1994, 1 (prosecutors are "liberated" from constraints of Thornburgh Memorandum); Daniels 1994, 304.

175. See Reno 1994. The letter to Senator Hatch is dated March 8, 1994. It responded to the Senator's public concern that the Reno Memorandum had essentially left federal prosecutors free to bargain around the Guidelines. Both Senator Hatch's letter to the Attorney General and her letter to him are reprinted at Federal Sentencing Reporter 1994, 6:353.

176. See, e.g., Gleeson 1996.

177. Garoppolo 1996, 405. See also Bunin 1996, 477 (taking issue with Garoppolo on grounds that (1) fact bargaining does not occur in all districts, and (2) probation officers may not have the "true facts").

178. Francesca D. Bowman 1996. The survey was sent to ninety-four districts; responses were received from eighty-five of these. Id. at 304.

179. Id. Question 2 (sentence-stipulated pleas are entered more than half of the time in 7 percent of districts).

180. Id. Question 1 (13 percent of respondents report such plea agreements in 95–100 percent of all pleas; 21 percent in 80–90 percent of pleas; 16 percent in 25–75 percent of pleas; 16 percent in 10–20 percent of pleas; 34 percent of respondents report such stipulations in 5 percent or fewer of pleas).

181. See United States v. Pimentel, 932 F.2d 1029, 1033 (2d Cir. 1991).

182. Francesca D. Bowman 1996, Question 6. Slightly over half of all respondents reported that stipulations were accurate and complete in a majority of cases. Id.

183. Id. Question 4 (prosecutor provides information more than 80 percent of time in nearly 90 percent of districts reporting).

184. Id. Question 5 (45 percent reporting that all information was provided in 95 percent or more of cases; 31 percent reporting that all information was provided in 80–90 percent of cases; 21 percent reporting all information was provided in 25–75 percent of cases; 3 percent reporting that all information provided in less than 20 percent of cases).

185. Garoppolo 1996, 406.

186. See pages 116–17.

187. Heaney 1991, 184; see also page 117.

188. Nagel and Schulhofer 1992, 556.

189. Id. at 539.

190. Id. at 524.

191. See Bureau of National Affairs 1996 (quoting defense attorney Alan Chaset of Alexandria, Virginia, noting that the Department of Justice had failed to address the wide variance in policies on what will be claimed as "relevant conduct" at sentencing); see also pages 129–30 (probation officers differ in applying "relevant conduct" rules).

192. United States v. Miller, 910 F.2d 1321, 1332 (6th Cir. 1990) (Merritt, C. J., dissenting), *cert. denied,* 498 U.S. 1094 (1991).

193. See Brief of Appellee at 17–18, United States v. Fulton, No. 96-1029 (2d Cir. 1996).

194. Nagel and Schulhofer 1992, 533, 535–36.

195. See 933 F. Supp. vii–xxviii (1996) (table listing both active and senior district judges).

196. See Gleeson 1996. It should be noted, however, that until the Supreme Court recognized the existence and legitimacy of plea bargaining in Brady v. United States, 397 U.S. 742 (1970), it was seldom acknowledged in open court—as is true of much Guidelines bargaining today. See Beale 1994, 311.

197. See, e.g., Wayte v. United States, 470 U.S. 598, 607 (1985).

198. See, e.g., United States v. Armstrong, 116 S. Ct. 1480 (1996).

199. These are among the factors that prosecutors are advised to consider in *Principles of Federal Prosecution* (B)(3) (1980), the guidelines written under the direction of Assistant Attorney General Philip B. Heymann. Those guidelines are discussed in *supra* note 164.

200. The Department of Justice recognizes that considerations such as race, religion and national origin are illegitimate. See *Principles of Federal Prosecution* (B)(6) (1980); see also, e.g., United States v. Al Jibori, 90 F.3d 22 (2d Cir. 1996).

201. See, e.g., United States v. Giles, 768 F. Supp. 101 (S.D.N.Y.), *aff'd,* 953 F.2d 636 (2d Cir. 1991), *cert. denied,* 503 U.S. 949 (1992); United States v. Streeter, 907 F.2d 781 (8th Cir. 1990); United States v. Dickey, 924 F.2d 836 (9th Cir.), *cert. denied,* 502 U.S. 943 (1991). Cf. Heaney 1991 ("reverse sting" operations, where defendant purchases drugs supplied by government agent, create opportunities for wide disparity in sentencing of like offenders).

202. See United States v. Staufer, 38 F.3d 1103, 1106–98 (9th Cir. 1994) ("sentencing entrapment"); United States v. Brewster, 1 F.3d 51, 55 (1st Cir. 1993) (concern about sentencing "manipulation" that would "overbear the will" of defendant); United States v. McClelland, 72 F.3d 717, 724–26 (9th Cir. 1995) (downward departure for "imperfect entrapment"), *cert. denied,* 116 S. Ct. 1448 (1996). See also United States v. Egemony, 62 F.3d 425, 427 (1st Cir. 1995) ("improper" enlargement of offense by agents); United States v. Gomez, 103 F.3d 249, 256 (2d Cir. 1997) (noting, but not deciding at this time, issue of sentencing factor "manipulation" by law enforcement agents); United States v. Jones, 102 F.3d 804, 809 (6th Cir. 1996) (similar).

The Commission in 1993 amended the Guidelines to permit a judge to depart downward where agents artificially lower the price of drugs, "thereby leading to the defendant's purchase of a significantly greater quantity . . . than his available resources would have allowed." U.S.S.G. §2D1.1 (Commentary, note 17). Mitchell 1996 has urged, more generally, that "imperfect entrapment" be recognized as a ground for downward departure, analogous to the Guidelines' treatment of an imperfect defense of coercion or duress in U.S.S.G. §5K2.12.

Chapter Five

1. See tables listing dates of judicial service, at 129 F.3d vii–xv (1997) and 979 F. Supp. vii–xxvii (1997) (figures as of December 1997).

2. Altogether, Congress has passed more than twenty statutes since 1987 that direct the Commission to alter its Guidelines to take account of some specified aggravating factor. See listing in the Guidelines Manual, appendix A.

3. Treasury, Postal Service and General Government Appropriations Act of 1992, §632, 18 U.S.C. §944 note.

4. Most of the policy directives in the Sentencing Reform Act are codified at 28 U.S.C. §994(d)–(n). The accumulation of these directives occurred over the seven years in which Congress considered the Sentencing Reform Act. See pages 38–48.

5. U.S.S.C. 1991b, 118–24 (statutory instructions to the Commission "offer advantages" over mandatory minimum sentences).

6. For discussion of the terms of appointment and constitutional status of the Sentencing Commission, see pages 44–45, 48.

7. See generally pages 121–26.

8. See pages 132–40.

9. See pages 102–3.

10. Melendez v. United States, 116 S. Ct. 2057, 2061 (1996).

11. We have used the term "guided departure" to refer to all those factors that the Sentencing Guidelines identify as *possibly warranting* departure, while the Commission has used the term more narrowly to encompass only those situations in which the Commission both identifies a departure factor and specifies the weight to be accorded that factor. See page 99 & chapter 3, note 112.

12. See page 73 & chapter 2, note 229.

13. See pages 55–56, 91–93.

14. See pages 67–72.

15. 18 U.S.C. §3742(e) (with respect to sentences outside Guidelines range, court of appeals must determine not only whether sentence violates Guidelines, but also whether it is "unreasonable").

16. See pages 148–63.

17. Because the Sentencing Reform Act requires that the Commission establish a sentencing range "for each category of offense *involving each category of defendant,*" 28 U.S.C. §994(b) (emphasis added), it would not be possible to have pure "offense of conviction" Guidelines ranges.

18. See page 77 (Guidelines as an adjunct criminal code); pages 22–24 (Guidelines as complex form of mandatory sentencing); Lynch 1994, 113 (Guidelines as criminal code).

19. See pages 70, 96–97; Tonry 1996, 94.

20. U.S.S.G. §3C1.1.

21. U.S.S.G. §3C1.1 (Commentary, note 3(e)).

22. See United States v. Watts, 117 S. Ct. 633 (1997); Witte v. United States, 515 U.S. 389 (1995).

23. One of the country's most knowledgeable students of sentencing policy, Professor Michael Tonry, states that the single feature of the federal Sentencing Guidelines that judges in other countries (and state judges in our country) find "most astonishing" is the "relevant conduct" principle. See Tonry 1996, 94.

24. See U.S.S.G. §6A1.3 (Commentary) ("disputes regarding application of the guidelines to the facts of a case" are appropriately resolved under a "preponderance of the evidence standard").

25. See pages 19–21, 81–82.

26. 337 U.S. 241 (1949).

27. Id. at 247–50.

28. 18 U.S.C. §3661: "No limitation shall be placed on the information concerning the background, character, and conduct of a person convicted of an offense which a court of the United States may receive and consider for the purpose of imposing an appropriate sentence." As originally codified in 1970, this provision was 18 U.S.C. §3577; it was renumbered but not eliminated by the Sentencing Reform Act of 1984.

29. See generally Young 1994, 308–17.

30. See McMillan v. Pennsylvania, 477 U.S. 79, 91 (1986) (sentencing judges have traditionally weighed evidence about various facts "without any prescribed burden of proof at all"). One of the first cases to impose an evidentiary burden of proof at sentencing was United States v. Fatico, 603 F.2d 1053 (2d Cir. 1979), *cert. denied,* 444 U.S. 1073 (1980) (imposing standard of proof where parties dispute presence of factors that judge explicitly takes into account at sentencing).

31. McMillan v. Pennsylvania, 477 U.S. 79 (1986).

32. See Witte v. United States, 515 U.S. 389, 402–5 (1995). Two federal circuits had sought to apply a double jeopardy bar in cases where the Department of Justice prosecuted defendants for crimes that had already led to sentence

enhancement under the "relevant conduct" principle of the Guidelines. See United States v. McCormick, 992 F.2d 437, 439–41 (2d Cir. 1993); United States v. Koonce, 945 F.2d 1145, 1149–54 (10th Cir. 1991).

33. In its initial Guidelines of 1987, the Sentencing Commission did not address the issue of standard of proof in Guidelines adjudications. The federal appellate courts, however, determined that the "preponderance" standard should apply. The leading cases on the subject were written by then-Judge Stephen G. Breyer of the First Circuit, United States v. Wright, 873 F.2d 437, 441–42 (1st Cir. 1989), and Judge William W. Wilkins, Jr. of the Fourth Circuit, United States v. Urrego-Linares, 879 F.2d 1234, 1237–38 (4th Cir. 1989). Other circuits soon followed suit, and the Sentencing Commission adopted the "preponderance" rule in 1991, U.S.S.G. §6A1.3. Of course, Judge Breyer was a member of the Sentencing Commission, and Judge Wilkins was the Chairman of the Commission.

34. United States v. Watts, 117 S. Ct. 633 (1997) (per curiam).

35. United States v. Clark, 792 F. Supp. 637, 644 (E.D. Ark. 1992) (Eisele, J.).

36. See 28 U.S.C. §994(k) (1994), discussed at page 40.

37. United States v. Wise, 976 F.2d 393, 408 (8th Cir. 1992) (en banc) (Richard S. Arnold, C. J., dissenting) (arguing that procedures for determining "role in offense," a mandatory sentencing factor under the Guidelines, violate the Constitution's Confrontation and Due Process Clauses).

38. See id.; United States v. Silverman, 976 F.2d 1502, 1525–27 (6th Cir. 1992) (en banc) (Merritt, C. J., dissenting) (relevant conduct rule violates Article III separation of powers principle, right against compelled self incrimination, and rights to notice, grand jury indictment, and confrontation of adverse witnesses); United States v. Galloway, 976 F.2d 414, 436–45 (8th Cir. 1992) (en banc) (Bright, J., dissenting) (relevant conduct principle violates rights to grand jury indictment, notice, speedy and public jury trial, and confrontation of adverse witnesses); United States v. Jewel, 947 F.2d 224, 240 (7th Cir. 1991) (Easterbrook, J., concurring) (use of illegally obtained evidence at sentencing under Guidelines violates Fourth Amendment); United States v. Payne, 940 F.2d 286, 295 (8th Cir. 1991) (Heaney, J., dissenting) (relevant conduct principle violates defendant's right to have criminal conduct proven beyond a reasonable doubt); United States v. Clark, 792 F. Supp. 637 (E.D. Ark. 1992) (Eisele, J.).

39. See United States v. Kikumura, 918 F.2d 1084, 1101–3 (3d Cir. 1990) (adopting clear and convincing evidence standard when upward adjustments would dramatically increase sentence). See also United States v. Gigante, 94 F.3d 53, 55–57 (2d Cir. 1996) (upholding preponderance of the evidence standard, but holding that the judge must depart downward if a series of upward adjustments based on facts proven by that standard lead to a significantly increased sentence that is unsupported by the weight of the evidence); United States v. Washington, 11 F.3d 1510, 1516 (10th Cir. 1993) (noting "strong arguments" in favor of higher standard of proof where relevant conduct dramatically increases sentence, and noting that in *McMillan* itself, the Supreme Court seemed to warn against a statutory scheme in which the enhancement is far greater than the underlying punishment, whereby the enhancement would be "a tail which wags the dog of the substantive offense," 477 U.S. at 88).

40. One circuit and some individual district and circuit judges have concluded that the Fourth Amendment exclusionary rule which prohibits admission into evidence at trial of illegally seized evidence should be applied at a sentencing hearing under the Guidelines, despite the judges' recognition that the rule was properly not applied in such hearings in the discretionary pre-

Guidelines era. See United States v. Nichols, 979 F.2d 402, 410–11 (6th Cir. 1992), *aff'd on other grounds,* 511 U.S. 738 (1994); United States v. Jewel, 947 F.2d 224, 240 (7th Cir. 1991) (Easterbrook, J., concurring); United States v. Gilmer, 811 F. Supp. 578, 586 (D. Colo. 1993). See also United States v. Rullo, 748 F. Supp. 36, 45 n.6 (D. Mass. 1990) (judge applied the exclusionary rule at a sentencing hearing on the basis that a police officer had lied about having beaten the defendant to obtain the evidence in question); United States v. Cabrera, 756 F. Supp. 134, 135–36 (S.D.N.Y. 1991), *rev'd sub nom.* United States v. Tejada, 956 F.2d 1256 (2d Cir. 1992).

The Court of Appeals for the Second Circuit recently held that "in order to balance [the] broad executive discretion" reflected in the prosecutor's power to veto a departure on the basis of "substantial assistance" to authorities, the defendant has a right to have his counsel present at any debriefing interview that law enforcement authorities conduct with a defendant who has decided to cooperate. United States v. Ming He, 94 F.3d 782, 787–93 (2d Cir. 1996).

41. See United States v. Watts, 117 U.S. 633 (1997), discussed *supra.* Cases holding that the exclusionary rule does not apply to Guidelines sentencing hearings include United States v. Kim, 25 F.3d 1426, 1432–36 (9th Cir. 1994); United States v. Montoya-Ortiz, 7 F.3d 1171, 1181–82 (5th Cir. 1993); United States v. Jenkins, 4 F.3d 1338, 1344–45 (6th Cir. 1993); United States v. Lynch, 934 F.2d 1226, 1234–37 (11th Cir. 1991); United States v. McCrory, 930 F.2d 63, 67–69 (D.C. Cir. 1991); United States v. Torres, 926 F.2d 321, 322–25 (3d Cir. 1991). See also United States v. Tejada, 956 F.2d 1256, 1260–63 (2d Cir. 1992) (illegally seized evidence admissible at sentencing unless seized in order to enhance sentence). See generally Forde 1996, 379.

42. 28 U.S.C. §994(a)(2).

43. See page 155.

44. U.S.S.G. §6A1.3.

45. In the Sentencing Reform Act itself, Congress amended Rule 32(c) of the Federal Rules of Criminal Procedure to make it highly likely that a presentence report will be prepared in every case, even when the defendant is willing to waive its preparation. In its prior form, Rule 32(c) permitted a defendant to waive preparation of a presentence report.

46. U.S.S.G. §6A1.3.

47. U.S.S.G. §6A1.3 and Commentary.

48. U.S.S.G. §6B1.2 (Commentary).

49. Id.

50. U.S.S.G. §6A1.3(a).

51. See pages 130–42.

52. See pages 85–91.

53. See pages 132–36.

54. See 28 U.S.C. §994(a)(2).

55. See, e.g., United States v. Cohen, 99 F.3d 69 (2d Cir. 1996) (per curiam); chapter 2, note 142.

56. See also Hutchison and Yellen 1989, 406 ("Nothing in [the Sentencing Reform Act] authorizes the Commission to prescribe evidentiary rules.").

57. 28 U.S.C. §§2071–72 (1994). Pursuant to the Rules Enabling Act, the Chief Justice of the United States appoints advisory committees in each area of court procedure; there is an Advisory Committee on the Criminal Rules, one on the Civil Rules, one on the Rules of Evidence, and so on. Each Advisory Committee is directed "to carry on a continuous study of the operation and effect of the general rules of practice and procedures in its particular field, taking into consideration suggestions and recommendations received from any source, new

statutes and court decisions affecting the rules, and legal commentary." Administrative Office of the U.S. Courts 1993 (quoting 28 U.S.C. §331).

58. See 28 U.S.C. §994(p) (1994).

59. In April 1995, a bare majority of the Commission proposed that Congress equalize the quantities of powdered cocaine and crack cocaine that trigger various statutory mandatory sentences, and proposed to alter its Guidelines accordingly. Congress rejected the proposed amendments, declined to adjust statutory penalties, and directed the Sentencing Commission to conduct further review of the issue. Pub. L. No. 104–38 (Oct. 30, 1995).

60. 28 U.S.C. §994(p) (1994). The Commission has not always subjected amendments of "Commentary" to public notice and comment, but has submitted all such proposed changes to Congress.

61. One of the authors, Kate Stith, is presently serving as a member of the Advisory Committee on the Federal Rules of Criminal Procedure, having been appointed in 1995.

62. See 28 U.S.C. §2074 (1994). Proposals for amendments to the rules governing procedures in the federal courts typically begin in the appropriate Advisory Committee, see *supra* note 57. The members of these committees represent a variety of perspectives; the Advisory Committee on the Criminal Rules, for instance, is presently composed of two federal appellate judges, one state supreme court justice, four federal district judges, a federal magistrate-judge, a representative from the Department of Justice, two private attorneys, one federal public defender, and a professor of law. The Advisory Committee's proposals are submitted, along with official Advisory Committee Notes that explain in significant depth the reasons for the proposal, to the Standing Committee on Rules of Practice and Procedure. If that Committee approves the proposal, it is published for public notice and comment (including public hearings where warranted). At the conclusion of the public comment period, the reporter of the Standing Committee prepares a summary of the comments and testimony received. The matter is returned to the Advisory Committee for further modification, and then to the Standing Committee. If the Standing Committee again approves the proposal, it is forwarded to the Judicial Conference itself. If the Conference, composed of federal trial and appellate judges representing each of the twelve federal circuits, approves the proposal, it is forwarded to the Supreme Court. Only if the Supreme Court approves the proposal is it finally laid before Congress, becoming effective unless Congress within seven months disapproves it. Congress virtually always holds hearings on proposed changes to the Federal Rules.

63. Federal Courts Study Committee 1990, 139. One of the authors, José A. Cabranes, served as a member of the Federal Courts Study Committee.

64. The Judicial Conference was equally cautious, and generally acquiescent, as Congress considered and debated the Sentencing Reform Act, even though that legislation would radically alter the judge's role in sentencing. See pages 173–74; Stith and Koh 1993.

65. Fed. R. Crim. P. 7(c)(1).

66. Id. 10.

67. Id. 11(a).

68. Id. 7(f).

69. See id. 12–31.

70. Id. 11(c)(1).

71. Id. 11(c)(3).

72. Id. 11(d).

73. Id. 11(f).

74. Id. 11(c)(4).
75. Id. 11(c)(1).
76. Id.
77. See pages 82–85.
78. See Fed. R. Crim. P. 32, 18 U.S.C.A. (1998 cumulative annual pocket part).
79. See Young 1994 (recommending higher burden of proof for all sentence enhancement factors); Yellen 1993, 459 (recommending that "other offenses" be proved by clear and convincing evidence); Becker and Orenstein 1992, 891 (1992) (arguing for heightened standard of proof, depending on significance of "relevant conduct" to the sentence to be imposed); Adair 1992 (arguing for higher standard of proof for sentencing facts); Clarke 1992 (recommending "beyond a reasonable doubt" standard for proving offenses not part of offense of conviction and clear and convincing standard for facts that are part of offense of conviction); Herman 1992, 345–48 (arguing for application of balancing test to determine standard of proof on a case-by-case basis); Husseini 1990 (advocating standard of "clear and convincing evidence"). United States v. Kikumura, 918 F.2d 1084 (3d Cir. 1990), held that the burden of proof should be "clear and convincing evidence" to justify an extraordinary upward departure (from a Guidelines range of less than three years to a sentence of thirty years).
80. See Becker 1993, 21–30 (arguing for limitations on the use of hearsay evidence in sentencing proceedings); Becker and Orenstein 1992, 885–91 (arguing for application of "selected" Rules of Evidence in sentencing proceedings); Berger 1992 (arguing for increased limitations on use of hearsay evidence at sentencing); Herman 1992, 348–49; Yellen 1993, 459 (recommending application of rules of evidence to sentencing proceedings); Harvard Law Review, "An Argument for Confrontation under the Federal Sentencing Guidelines," 105: 1880 (1992) (student note).
81. United States v. Miller, 910 F.2d 1321, 1332 (6th Cir. 1990) (Merritt, C. J., dissenting), *cert. denied,* 498 U.S. 1094 (1991).
82. See discussion at pages 139–40.
83. Weinstein 1992, 363.
84. See pages 157–58.
85. Fed. R. Crim. P. 11 Advisory Committee's Note, reprinted in 18 U.S.C.A. (1998 cumulative annual pocket part).
86. Id.
87. U.S.S.G. §6B1.2 (Commentary), discussed at page 153.
88. As this book was being written, this proposal was submitted at a meeting of the Advisory Committee on the Federal Rules of Criminal Procedure; it was not adopted, by a 7–5 vote of the members present.
89. See pages 82–87.
90. See Fed. R. Crim. P. 7.
91. See, e.g., United States v. Rose, 20 F.3d 367, 372–73 (9th Cir. 1994) ("[A]lthough Rose and Peterson were convicted on money laundering counts involving only around $275,000, designation of uncharged money laundering counts as relevant conduct permits the 'value of funds' for sentencing purposes . . . to exceed $2 million for each of them.").
92. See pages 67–72.
93. See Fed. R. Crim. P. 11(e)(4); United States v. Hyde, 117 S. Ct. 1630 (1997). See also page 138, text at notes 179–80 (such pleas not common in federal court).
94. See Fed. R. Crim. P. 11(e)(2) (judge may defer until sentencing stage

decision to accept a plea agreement that specifies sentence or drops charges); U.S.S.G. §6B1.1 (judges should defer acceptance of such plea agreements until sentencing stage).

95. See pages 150–52.

96. The statute is quoted in full at *supra* note 28.

97. United States v. Watts, 117 S. Ct. 633 (1997) (per curiam, with only Justice Stevens dissenting on the merits). While the Guidelines do not explicitly address the status of acquitted conduct, the Supreme Court and nearly every lower court had reasonably interpreted this silence as implying that acquitted conduct be considered to the same extent as any other conduct deemed relevant by the Guidelines and proven at a sentencing hearing. As the Supreme Court noted, there is no logical inconsistency between conduct not being proved "beyond a reasonable doubt" at a criminal trial, and the same conduct being proved to a "preponderance of the evidence" at a sentencing hearing.

98. 117 S. Ct. at 635.

99. Id. at 638 (Scalia, J.).

100. Id. (Breyer, J.).

101. See 62 Fed. Reg. 151 (Jan. 1, 1997). The Commission had also put the issue on its agenda in 1992. See 57 Fed. Reg. 62,832 (1992).

102. Bureau of National Affairs 1997 (quoting Commissioner Michael Goldsmith).

103. See, e.g., 28 U.S.C. §994(c), (d). See generally pages 38–48.

104. U.S.S.G. §1B1.4.

105. Tonry 1996, 98–99.

106. Id. at 91. See also Lee 1994. While we can hypothesize cases where a departure for substantial assistance is warranted despite the government's conclusion to the contrary, such cases are surely few and far between. We recognize that the present rule is symbolically powerful as an assertion of mistrust in judges: The most significant instance of judicial discretion permitted by the Guidelines is itself conditioned on the approval of the prosecutor.

107. Tonry 1996, 91–93. As Tonry notes, this would not necessarily result in lower sentences on average, but it would restore a sentencing option to a class of cases where sometimes that option makes sense.

108. See page 130 & chapter 4, note 134.

109. See discussion at pages 132–36.

110. United States v. Aguilar, 884 F. Supp. 88, 90 (E.D.N.Y. 1995). The government was unable to appeal this decision because it was formally a "binding" plea under Fed. R. Crim. P. 11(e)(1)(C), and hence not appealable. See 18 U.S.C. §3742 (c). See also pages 90–91.

111. See pages 136–40.

112. See pages 38–48.

113. 18 U.S.C. §3553(a).

114. 28 U.S.C. §994(a)(2)(E) (among matters on which Commission may issue "general policy statements" is "authority granted under rule 11(e)(2) of the Federal Rules of Criminal Procedure to accept or reject a plea agreement").

115. See pages 85–91.

116. Maria Rodrigues McBride, 1996.

117. U.S.S.G. §1A.4(b) (Commentary).

118. U.S.S.G. §1A.2 (Commentary)

119. The "heartland" concept is discussed at pages 75–76, 100–103.

120. See U.S.S.C. Annual Report 1995, 12–13 (Commission intends to "improve federal sentencing by working closely with the judiciary and others to simplify and refine the Guidelines," to conduct a "systematic look at the effectiveness of the guidelines" in reducing disparity, and to assess "magnitude of effect" of relevant conduct on sentence severity).

121. See Bureau of National Affairs 1996b (Commission's priorities for 1997 include "simplification" of relevant conduct guideline, but Commissioner Michael Goldsmith reports at ABA convention that "current commission is satisfied, as a whole, with the first commission's treatment of relevant conduct"). See also Goldsmith 1996 (Commissioner Michael Goldsmith concluding that Guidelines succeed in customizing sentences, and that they are not unduly complex or mechanistic); Bureau of National Affairs 1995 (Judge Deanell R. Tacha, present Sentencing Commissioner, noting that Commission is focusing on "simplification," which might mean, for instance, "a little more discretion within categories").

122. Bureau of National Affairs 1997 (quoting Commissioner Michael Goldsmith).

123. Koon v. United States, 116 S. Ct. 2035, 2046 (1996); see also Williams v. United States, 503 U.S. 193, 205 (1992) (Sentencing Reform Act "did not alter a court of appeals' traditional deference to a district court's exercise of its sentencing discretion"). *Koon* is discussed at pages 100–103.

124. 18 U.S.C. §3742(e) (1994) ("Upon review of the record, the court of appeals shall determine whether the sentence . . . is outside of the applicable guideline range, and is unreasonable. . . .").

125. See pages 94–103; see also United States v. Davern, 970 F.2d 1490 (6th Cir. 1992) (rejecting interpretation similar to that set forth in text).

126. 18 U.S.C. §3553(b). For the legislative history of this provision, see page 41.

127. See generally pages 82–85.

128. Weinstein 1992, 366.

129. See generally pages 11–37.

130. R. Callis, Upon the Statute of Sewers 113 (1622) (quoted in Pattenden 1982, 4).

131. Weinstein et al. 1989b, §401[01], at 401–8.

132. In a survey of two volumes of the Federal Reporter consisting of published federal appellate court opinions in the early 1980s, Judge Joseph Sneed of the Ninth Circuit Court of Appeals determined that one-quarter of all appeals involve matters committed to the discretion of the trial court; the appellate courts approved the exercise of discretion over two-thirds of the time. See generally Sneed 1982 (unpublished presentation before judges of the Second Circuit, Yale Law School, 1982).

133. See Dorszynski v. United States, 418 U.S. 424, 432 (1974) (sentences reviewable only for lawfulness under pertinent statutes); chapter 1, note 5.

134. See, e.g., Tonry 1996, 89–99; Freed 1992.

135. See pages 38–40; Stith and Koh 1993.

136. 123 Cong. Rec. 13,063 (1977).

137. See generally pages 38–40, 106–12.

138. See generally Stith and Koh 1993.

139. See pages 112–42.

140. See Stith and Koh 1993, 251–57, 263–77, 287–89.

141. See pages 34–37.

142. See pages 33–34.

143. Congress retains ultimate authority to approve or disapprove the Federal Rules of Procedure and the Federal Rules of Evidence, see *supra* notes 57, 62, both those that repose discretion in judges and those that do not.

144. See 28 U.S.C. §995(a)(12)–(21).

145. Statutory or other categories might be used. The Sentencing Commission's nineteen generic categories of crime might be an especially useful way to organize sentencing data. See U.S.S.G. §2B.

146. See Wheeler et al. 1988, cited in chapter 4, notes 47, 48.

147. This is the approach proposed by Alschuler 1991.

148. As to the failure of the Sentencing Commission to welcome judges in contributing to the growth and elaboration of federal sentencing law, see pages 97–99.

149. See Jareborg 1995 (voluntary guidelines in Sweden); Henham 1993, 271–72, 275–76 (voluntary guidelines in Finland and Germany); East 1990, 11 (appellate review without guidelines in New Zealand). See Tonry 1996, 27 for a discussion of state sentencing guidelines systems. The presumptive sentencing guidelines in Minnesota, Washington, and Pennsylvania differ from the federal guidelines in these respects, among others. For other insightful discussions of state guidelines systems, see Frase 1995, Orland and Reitz 1993, Tonry 1993, Hauptly and Knapp 1992.

150. Wathen 1991, 612. Me. Rev. Stat. Ann. tit. 15, §§2151–57. The legislation was based on a model set forth by the Chief Justice of Maine, Daniel E. Wathen, the previous year, see Wathen 1988.

151. Havel 1992.

152. Id.

BIBLIOGRAPHY

Adair, David N., Jr. 1992. "House Built on a Weak Foundation: Sentencing Guidelines and the Preponderance Standard of Proof." *Federal Sentencing Reporter* 4:292.

Administrative Office of the United States Courts. 1972. *Federal Offenders in United States District Courts.* Washington, D.C.: Administrative Office of the United States Courts.

———. 1993. *The Federal Rules of Practice and Procedure: A Summary for Bench and Bar.* Washington, D.C.: Administrative Office of the United States Courts.

———. 1995. *Judicial Business of the United States Courts: 1995 Report of the Director.* Washington, D.C.: Administrative Office of the United States Courts.

———. Division of Probation. 1978. *The Presentence Investigation Report.* Washington, D.C.: Administrative Office of the United States Courts.

———. 1984. *The Presentence Investigation Report.* Washington, D.C.: Administrative Office of the United States Courts.

———. 1987. *Presentence Investigation Reports under the Sentencing Reform Act of 1984.* Washington, D.C.: Administrative Office of the United States Courts.

Alexander, Susan, ed. 1996. *Almanac of the Federal Judiciary.* 2 vols. Chicago: Law-Letters, 1984–96.

Alito, Samuel A. 1992. "Reviewing the Sentencing Commission's 1991 Annual Report." *Federal Sentencing Reporter* 5:166.

Allen, Francis A. 1964. *The Borderland of Criminal Justice.* Chicago: University of Chicago Press.

———. 1981. *The Decline of the Rehabilitative Ideal.* New Haven: Yale University Press.

Alschuler, Albert W. 1978. "Sentencing Reform and Prosecutorial Power: A Critique of Recent Proposals for 'Fixed' and 'Presumptive Sentencing.'" *University of Pennsylvania Law Review* 126:550.

———. 1983. "Implementing the Criminal Defendant's Right to Trial: Alternatives to the Plea Bargaining System." *University of Chicago Law Review* 50:931.

———. 1989. "The Selling of the Sentencing Guidelines: Some Correspondence with the U.S. Sentencing Commission." In *The U.S. Sentencing Guidelines,* edited by Dean J. Champion. New York: Praeger Publishing.

———. 1991. "The Failure of Sentencing Guidelines: A Plea for Less Aggregation." *University of Chicago Law Review* 58:901.

American Bar Association. 1968. *Standards Relating to Sentencing Alternatives and Procedures.* Chicago: American Bar Association.

American Friends Service Committee. 1971. *Struggle for Justice.* New York: Hill and Wang.

"An Argument for Confrontation under the Federal Sentencing Guidelines." 1992. *Harvard Law Review* 105:1880.

Anderson, David C. 1986. "The Editorial Notebook: Tinkering with Justice." *New York Times,* 4 December, 34.

Aristotle. *Nicomachean Ethics.* In *The Complete Works of Aristotle,* edited by Jonathan Barnes. Princeton: Princeton University Press, 1984.

"As Corporate Sentencing Guidelines Take Hold, Former U.S. Sentencing Commission Staffers Open Fire." 1991. *Corporate Crime Reporter* 4 (42): 5.

Ashe, Stanley P. 1941. "A Warden's Views on Inequality in Sentences." *Federal Probation* (January–March): 26.

Atkinson, Rick. 1990. "The Survivor: Ted Kennedy Weathers Fall from Grace in the '80s to Become a Force in the Senate." *Los Angeles Times,* 29 April, E12.

Augustus, John. 1852. *John Augustus: First Probation Officer.* Boston: Wright and Hasty. Reprinted, with an introduction by Sheldon Glueck. New York: National Probation Association, 1939.

Austin, William, and Thomas A. Williams, III. 1977. "A Survey of Judges' Responses to Simulated Legal Cases." *Journal Criminal Law, Criminology, and Police Science* 68:306.

Baab, George William, and William Royal Furgeson, Jr. 1967. "Texas Sentencing Practices: A Statistical Study." *Texas Law Review* 45:471.

Barnes, Harry E., and Negley K. Teeters. 1959. *New Horizons in Criminology.* New Jersey: Prentice Hall.

Bartolomeo, John, et al. 1981. *Sentence Decision Making: The Logic of Sentence Decisions and the Extent and Sources of Sentence Disparity.* Washington, D.C.: U.S. Department of Justice.

Bauer, William J. 1987. "Federal Sentencing Guidelines Need More Study." *Chicago Tribune,* 4 September, C19.

Beale, Sara Sun. 1994. "The New Reno Bluesheet: A Little More Candor Regarding Prosecutorial Discretion." *Federal Sentencing Reporter* 6:310.

Beattie, John M. 1986. *Crime and the Courts in England, 1660–1800.* Princeton: Princeton University Press.

Beccaria, Cesare. 1764. *On Crimes and Punishments.* Translated by David Young. Indianapolis: Hackett, 1986.

Becker, Edward R. 1990. Judge Becker on Behalf of the Judicial Conference Committee on Criminal Law and Probation Administration to the Sentencing Commission, statement, March. Reprinted in *Federal Sentencing Reporter* 2:238.

———. 1993. "Insuring Reliable Fact Finding in Guidelines Sentencing." *Capital University Law Review* 22:1.

Becker, Edward R., and Aviva Orenstein. 1992. "The Federal Rules of Evidence after Sixteen Years." *George Washington Law Review* 60:857.

Becker, Gary S. 1968. "Crime and Punishment: An Economic Approach." *Journal of Political Economy* 76:169.

Bentham, Jeremy. 1830. "Principles of Penal Law." *The Works of Jeremy Bentham.* Vol. 1. Edinburgh: William Tait, 1843.

Berger, Margaret A. 1992. "Rethinking the Applicability of Evidentiary Rules at Sentencing." *Federal Sentencing Reporter* 5:96.

Berman, Douglas A. 1994. "The Sentencing Commission as Guidelines Supreme Court: Responding to Circuit Conflicts." *Federal Sentencing Reporter* 7:142.

Bernstein, Ilene Nagel, ed. 1976. *Validity Issues in Evaluation Research.* Beverly Hills: Sage Publications.

Block, Michael K. 1989. "Crime and Punishment in the Boardroom: Balance Costs and Benefits in Setting Business Fines." *Legal Times,* 13 February, 19.

———. 1991. "Optimal Penalties, Criminal Law and the Control of Corporate Behavior." *Boston University Law Review* 71:395.

Block, Michael K., and William M. Rhodes. 1989. "Forecasting the Impact of the Federal Sentencing Guidelines." *Behavioral Sciences and the Law* 7:51.

Bowman, Francesca D. 1991. "The Greening of Probation Officers in Their New Role." *Federal Sentencing Reporter* 4:99.

———. 1996. "Probation Officers Advisory Group Survey." *Federal Sentencing Reporter* 8:303.

Bowman, Frank O., III. 1996a. "The Quality of Mercy Must Be Restrained, and Other Lessons in Learning to Love the Federal Sentencing Guidelines." *Wisconsin Law Review* 1996:679.

———. 1996b. "Places in the Heartland: Departure Jurisprudence after *Koon.*" *Federal Sentencing Reporter* 9:19.

Brenner, Eliot. 1984. "Washington News." *United Press International,* 30 January.

Breyer, Stephen G. 1979. "Analyzing Regulatory Failure: Mismatches, Less Restrictive Alternatives, and Reform." *Harvard Law Review* 92:547.

———. 1982. *Regulation and Its Reform.* Cambridge: Harvard University Press.

———. 1983. "Two Models of Regulatory Reform." *South Carolina Law Review* 34:629.

———. 1988. "The Federal Sentencing Guidelines and the Key Compromises upon Which They Rest." *Hofstra Law Review* 17:1.

———. 1990. *Testimony before the Federal Courts Study Committee,* 31 January, Washington, D.C.

———. 1993. *Breaking the Vicious Circle.* Cambridge: Harvard University Press.

Breyer, Stephen G., et al. 1980. "A Fresh Look at Federal Regulatory Strategies." *Administrative Law Review* 32:165.

Breyer, Stephen G., and Richard Stewart. 1985. *Administrative Law and Regulatory Policy,* 2d ed. Boston: Little, Brown and Company.

Bright, Myron H. 1993. "These Sentences Defy Reason, But as I Have Already Noted—Such Is Our System." *Overcrowded Times* 4 (3): 20.

Broderick, Vincent L. 1991. Judge Broderick to Judge Avern Cohn, 13 June. Reprinted in *Federal Sentencing Reporter* 4:48.

Broderick, Vincent L., and Mark L. Wolf. 1991. Judges Broderick and Wolf to the U.S. Sentencing Commission, statement, 5 March. Reprinted in *Federal Sentencing Reporter* 3:276.

Buffone, Samuel J. 1991. "Control of Arbitrary Sentencing Guidelines: Is Administrative Law the Answer?" *Federal Sentencing Reporter* 4:137.

———. 1996. "The Federal Sentencing Commission's Proposed Rules of Practice and Procedure." *Federal Sentencing Reporter* 9:67.

Bunin, Alexander. 1996. "Whose Facts? Counterpoint to Probation Offficer's View on Fact Bargaining." *BNA Criminal Practice Manual* 10:447.

Bunzel, Sharon. 1995. "The Probation Officer and the Federal Sentencing Guidelines: Strange Philosophical Bedfellows." *Yale Law Journal* 104:933.

Bureau of Justice Statistics. 1979–1994. *Sourcebook of Criminal Justice Statistics.* Washington, D.C: Bureau of Justice Statistics, U.S. Department of Justice.

Bureau of National Affairs. 1986. "Sentencing Commission's First Effort Receives Outpouring of Criticism." *Daily Report for Executives* 16 December, C1.

———. 1987. "Sentencing Commission Holds Hearing on New Draft Guidelines." *Antitrust and Trade Regulation Report,* 52:628.

———. 1995. "Sentencing Commission Member Discusses Commission's Wish to 'Simplify Guidelines.'" *Criminal Law Reporter* 57:1516.

———. 1996a. "Koon Decision: Mere Lip Service to Sentencing Discretion?" *Criminal Practice Manual* 10:285.

———. 1996b. "Sentencing Commissioners Discuss Effort to Simplify Guidelines." *Criminal Law Reporter* 59:1517.

———. 1997. "Sentencing Commission Unlikely to Submit Amendments on Broad Issues This Year." *Criminal Law Reporter* 60:1523.

Burns, Megan E. 1993. "The Presentence Interview and the Right to Counsel: A Critical Stage under the Federal Sentencing Structure." *William and Mary Law Review* 34:527.

Cabranes, José A. 1992a. "Sentencing Guidelines: A Dismal Failure." *New York Law Journal,* 11 February, 2.

———. 1992b. "A Failed Utopian Experiment." *National Law Journal* 27 July, 17.

Campbell, Arthur W. 1991. *The Law of Sentencing.* Deerfield, Ill.: Clark, Boardman, Callaghan.

Cardozo, Benjamin N. 1921. *The Nature of the Judicial Process.* New Haven, Conn.: Yale University Press.

Casper, Jonathan D. 1984. "Determinate Sentencing and Prison Crowding in Illinois." *University of Illinois Law Review* 1984:231.

Chambers, Marcia. 1990. "Probation Officers Sit in Judgment." *National Law Journal,* 16 April, 13.

Clancy, Kevin, et al. 1981. "Sentence Decisionmaking: The Logic of Sentence Decisions and the Extent and Sources of Sentence Disparity." *Journal of Criminal Law and Criminology* 72:524.

Clarke, Judy. 1989. "Ruminations on *Restrepo.*" *Federal Sentencing Reporter* 2:135.

———. 1992. "The Need for a Higher Burden of Proof for Fact Finding under the Guidelines." *Federal Sentencing Reporter* 4:300.

Coffee, John C., Jr. 1978. "The Repressed Issues of Sentencing: Accountability, Predictability and Equality in the Era of the Sentencing Commission." *Georgetown Law Journal* 66:975.

Cohen, Gerald S. 1990. "How Kennedy Became 'King of the Hill.'" *San Francisco Chronicle,* 27 March, A10.

Cohen, Mark A., and David T. Scheffman. 1989. "The Antitrust Sentencing Guideline: Is the Punishment Worth the Cost?" *American Criminal Law Review* 27:331.

Cohen, Morris Raphael. 1933. *Law and the Social Order.* New York: Harcourt, Brace.

Cohn, Alan. 1986. "U.S. Judges Ask Changes in Plan for Sentencing." *New York Law Journal,* 4 December, 1.

Cohn, Avern. 1994. "The Sentencing Commission's 1993 Annual Report." *Federal Sentencing Reporter* 7:137.

Cohodas, Nadine. 1984. "Enactment of Crime Package Culmination of 11-Year Effort." *Congressional Quarterly* 42:2752.

Connelly, Mary, and Carlyle C. Douglas. 1987. "'Judge Shopping' Made Harder." *New York Times,* 3 May, sec. 4, p. 6.

"Controversy over Federal Criminal Sentencing Policy: Pro and Con." 1984. *Congressional Digest* (June–July): 182.

Conyers, John Jr., 1985. "Unresolved Issues in the Federal Sentencing Reform Act." *Federal Bar News and Journal* 32:68.

Cook, Beverly B. 1979. "Sentencing Problems and Internal Court Reform." In *The Study of Criminal Courts: Political Perspectives,* edited by Peter F. Nardulli. Cambridge, Mass.: Ballinger.

Cook, Julian Abele, Jr. 1991. "The Changing Role of the Probation Officer in the Federal Court." *Federal Sentencing Reporter* 4:112.

Cooper, Jeffrey O. 1995. "Judicial Opinions and Sentencing Guidelines." *Federal Sentencing Reporter* 8:46.

Coughenour, John C. 1995. "Separate and Unequal: Women in the Federal Criminal Justice System." *Federal Sentencing Reporter* 8:142.

Coyle, Marcia, and Fred Strasser. 1987. "Final Sentence." *National Law Journal,* 19 October, 9.

———. 1989. "Internal Fights Rend Sentencing Commission." *National Law Journal,* 4 September, 5.

Coyle, Marcia, and Marianne Lavelle. 1994. "Risk Regulation Stance May Prove a 'Breyer Patch.'" *National Law Journal,* 30 May, A12.

"Criticizing Sentencing Rules, U.S. Judge Resigns." 1990. *New York Times.* 1990. 30 September, 22.

Cromwell, Paul F., Jr., et al. 1985. *Probation and Parole in the Criminal Justice System.* St. Paul: West Publishing.

Curtis, Dennis E., and Judith Resnik. 1987. "Images of Justice." *Yale Law Journal* 96:1727.

Daniels, Deborah J. 1994. "Sentencing Guidelines and Prosecutorial Discretion: The Justice Department's 'Clarification' of the Thornburgh Memo." *Federal Sentencing Reporter* 6:302.

Davis, Kenneth C. 1969. *Discretionary Justice.* Baton Rouge: Louisiana State University Press.

DeBenedictis, Don J. 1993. "The Verdict Is In." *American Bar Association Journal* 79:78.

Denzlinger, Jerry D., and David E. Miller. 1991. "The Federal Probation Officer: Life before and after Guideline Sentencing." *Federal Probation* (December): 49.

Dershowitz, Alan M. 1970. "The Law of Dangerousness: Some Fictions about Predictions." *Journal of Legal Education* 23:24.

———. 1974a. "Indeterminate Confinement: Letting the Therapy Fit the Harm." *University of Pennsylvania Law Review* 123:297.

———. 1974b. "The Origins of Preventive Confinement in Anglo-American Law—Part I: The English Experience." *University of Cincinnati Law Review* 43:1.

"Determinate Sentencing and Judicial Participation in Democratic Punishment." 1995. *Harvard Law Review.* 108:947.

Diamond, Shari S. 1981. "Exploring Sources of Sentence Disparity." In *The Trial Process,* edited by Bruce D. Sales. New York: Plenum Press.

Diamond, Shari S., and Hans Zeisel. 1975. "Sentencing Councils: A Study of Sentence Disparity and Its Reduction." *University of Chicago Law Review* 43:109.

Donohue, John, and Peter Siegelman. 1996. "Is the United States at the Optimal Rate of Crime?" Unpublished manuscript.

Drinan, Robert F., et al. 1981. "The Federal Criminal Code: The Houses Are Divided." *American Criminal Law Review* 18:509.

Dunworth, Terence, and Charles D. Weisselberg. 1992. "Felony Cases and the Federal Courts: The Guidelines Experience." *Southern California Law Review* 66:99.

Dworkin, Ronald. 1977. "Is Law a System of Rules?" In *The Philosophy of Law.* New York: Oxford University Press.

East, Paul. 1990. "Modern Sentencing Developments." *New Zealand Law Journal* (January): 11.

Eaton, William J. 1988. "Kennedy Emerging as Superpower in the Senate." *Los Angeles Times,* 26 July, 16.

Edmunds, Robert H., Jr. 1996. "Analyzing the Tension Between Prosecutors and Probation Officers over 'Fact Bargaining.'" *Federal Sentencing Reporter* 8:318.

Eisele, G. Thomas. 1991. "The Sentencing Guidelines System? No. Sentencing Guidelines? Yes." *Federal Probation* (December): 16.

Ellingstad, Susan E. 1992. "Note, The Sentencing Guidelines: Downward Departures Based on a Defendant's Extraordinary Family Ties and Responsibilities." *Minnesota Law Review* 76:957.

Emmrich, Stuart. 1978. "Pen Inmates Air Gripes." *Atlanta Constitution,* 5 December, C1.

Everson, George. 1919. "The Human Element in Justice." *Journal of the American Institute of Criminal Law and Criminology* 10:90.

Evjen, Victor H. 1975. "The Federal Probation System: The Struggle to Achieve It and Its First 25 Years." *Federal Probation* (June): 3.

Federal Courts Study Committee. 1990. *Report.* Washington, D.C.: Administrative Office of the U.S. Courts.

Federal Judicial Center. 1994. *Planning for the Future: Results of a 1992 Federal Judicial Center Survey of United States Judges.* Washington, D.C.: Federal Judicial Center.

———. 1995. *Guideline Sentencing: An Outline of Appellate Case Law on Selected Issues.* Washington, D.C.: Federal Judicial Center.

———. 1997. *The United States Sentencing Guidelines, Results of the Federal Judicial Center's 1996 Survey.* Washington, D.C.: Federal Judicial Center.

Ferri, Enrico. 1921. "Relazione sul Progetto Preliminare di Codice Penale Italiano," as quoted in Glueck, Sheldon, "Principles of a Rational Penal Code." *Harvard Law Review* 41:453, 1928.

Flaherty, Mary Pat, and Joan Biskupic. 1996. "Despite Overhaul, Federal Sentencing Still Misfires." *Washington Post,* 6 October, A1.

Flaxman, Kenneth N. 1979. "The Hidden Dangers of Sentencing Guidelines." *Hofstra Law Review* 7:259.

Fogel, David. 1975. ". . . *We Are the Living Proof* . . ." Cincinnati: W. H. Anderson.

Forde, Michael K. 1996. "The Exclusionary Rule at Sentencing: New Life under the Federal Sentencing Guidelines?" *American Criminal Law Review* 33:379.

Forer, Lois G. 1994. *A Rage to Punish: The Unintended Consequences of Mandatory Sentencing.* New York: W. W. Norton and Company.

Frankel, Marvin E. 1972. "Lawlessness in Sentencing." *University of Cincinnati Law Review* 41:1.

———. 1973. *Criminal Sentences: Law without Order.* New York: Hill and Wang.

Frase, Richard. 1995. "State Sentencing Guidelines: Still Going Strong." *Judicature* 78:173.

Freed, Daniel J. 1992. "Federal Sentencing in the Wake of the Guidelines: Unacceptable Limits on the Discretion of Sentencers." *Yale Law Journal* 101:1681.

Freed, Daniel J., and Marc Miller. 1991. "Plea Bargained Sentences, Disparity, and 'Guideline Justice.'" *Federal Sentencing Reporter* 3:175.

———. 1993. "Editors' Observations." *Federal Sentencing Reporter* 6:59.

Garoppolo, Tony. 1996. "Fact Bargaining: What the Sentencing Commission Hath Wrought." *BNA Criminal Practice Manual* 10:405.

Gaudet, Frederick J. 1949. "The Sentencing Behavior of the Judge." In *Encyclopedia of Criminology,* edited by Vernon C. Branham and Samuel B. Kutash. New York: Philosophical Library.

Gaudet, Frederick J., George S. Harris, and Charles W. St. John. 1933. "Individual Differences in the Sentencing Tendencies of Judges." *Journal of Criminal Law and Criminology* 23:811.

Genego, William J., Peter D. Goldberg, and Vicki C. Jackson. 1975. "Project: Parole Release Decisionmaking and the Sentencing Process." *Yale Law Journal* 84:810.

Gerber, Rudolph J. 1993. "A System in Collapse: Appearance vs. Reality in Criminal Justice." *St. Louis University Public Law Review* 12:225.

Gilbert, Frank S. 1991. "The Probation Officer's Perception of the Allocation of Discretion." *Federal Sentencing Reporter* 4:109.

Gleeson, John. 1996. "Sentencing Bargaining under the Guidelines." *Federal Sentencing Reporter* 8:314.

Glueck, Sheldon. 1928. "Principles of a Rational Penal Code." *Harvard Law Review* 41:453.

———. 1958. "Predictive Devices and the Individualization of Justice." *Law and Contemporary Problems* 23:461.

Goldsmith, Michael. 1996. "Sentencing Reform That Works." *Washington Post,* 14 November, A21.

Goldstein, Abraham S. 1981. *The Passive Judiciary: Prosecutorial Discretion and the Guilty Plea.* Baton Rouge: Louisiana State University Press.

Goldstein, Tom. 1977. "Judicial Discretion Faces Curb in Senate Bill on Sentencing Methods." *New York Times,* 16 June, D14.

Goodwin, Catharine M. 1995. "Background of the AO Memorandum Opinion on the 25% Rule." *Federal Sentencing Reporter* 8:109.

———. 1996. "The Independent Role of the Probation Officer at Sentencing and in Applying *Koon v. United States.*" *Federal Probation* (September): 71.

Gottfredson, Michael R. 1979. "Parole Guidelines and the Reduction of Sentencing Disparity: A Preliminary Study." *Journal of Research on Crime and Delinquency* 16:218.

Griset, Pamala L. 1991. *Determinate Sentencing: The Promise and the Reality of Retributive Justice.* Albany, N.Y.: State University of New York Press.

Hagan, John, and Kristin Bumiller. 1983. "Making Sense of Sentencing: A Review and Critique of Sentencing Research." In *Research on Sentencing: The Search for Reform II,* edited by Alfred Blumstein et al. Vol. 2. Washington, D.C.: National Academy Press.

Haines, Roger W., Jr., Kevin Cole, and Jennifer C. Woll. 1994 (with semi-annual supplement). *Federal Sentencing and Forfeiture Guide.* Cosa Mesa, Cal.

Hall, Ford W. 1951. "The Common Law: An Account of Its Reception in the United States." *Vanderbilt Law Review* 4:791.

Hall, Jerome. 1956. "Psychiatry and Criminal Responsibility." *Yale Law Journal* 65:761.

Hall, Jerome, and Karl Menninger. 1953. "Book Review." *Iowa Law Review* 38:687.

Hart, H. L. A. 1958. "Positivism and the Separation of Law and Morals." *Harvard Law Review* 71:593.

———. 1968. *Punishment and Responsibility.* New York: Oxford University Press.

Hatch, Orrin. 1994. Senator Hatch to the Attorney General, 13 January. Reprinted in *Federal Sentencing Reporter* 6:353.

Hauptly, Denis J., and Kay A. Knapp. 1992. "State and Federal Sentencing Guidelines: Apples and Oranges." *University of California at Davis Law Review* 25:679.

Havel, Vaclav. 1992. "The End of the Modern Era." *New York Times,* 1 March, 4–15.

Hay, Douglas. 1975. "Property, Authority, and the Criminal Law." In *Albion's Fatal Tree: Crime and Society in Eighteenth Century England,* edited by Douglas Hay et al. New York: Pantheon.

Hayner, Norman S. 1958. "Sentencing by an Administrative Board." *Law and Contemporary Problems* 23:477.

Heaney, Gerald W. 1991. "The Reality of Sentencing Guidelines: No End to Disparity." *American Criminal Law Review* 28:161.

———. 1992. "Revisiting Disparity: Debating Guidelines Sentencing." *American Criminal Law Review* 29:771.

Henderson, Dwight F. 1985. *Congress, Courts, and Criminals: The Development of Federal Criminal Law, 1801–1929.* Westport, Conn.: Greenwood Press.

Henham, Ralph. 1993. "The European Context of Sentencing Violent Offenders." *International Journal of the Sociology of the Law* 21:265.

Herman, Susan N. 1992. "The Tail That Wagged the Dog: Bifurcated Fact-Finding under the Federal Sentencing Guidelines and the Limits of Due Process." *Southern California Law Review* 66:289.

Heumann, Milton. 1993. "Empirical Questions and Data Sources: Guideline and Sentencing Research in the Federal System." *Federal Sentencing Reporter* 6:15.

Hindus, Michael S. 1980. *Prison and Plantation: Crime, Justice and Authority in Massachusetts and South Carolina, 1767–1878.* Chapel Hill: University of North Carolina Press.

Hofer, Paul J. 1992. "Implications of the Relevant Conduct Study for the Revised Guideline." *Federal Sentencing Reporter* 4:334.

Hoffman, Peter B., and James L. Beck. 1996. "The Origin of the Federal Criminal History Score." *Federal Sentencing Reporter* 9:192.

Hogarth, John. 1971. *Sentencing as a Human Process.* Toronto: University of Toronto Press.

Holmes, Oliver Wendell Jr. 1881. *The Common Law.* Boston: Little, Brown and Company.

Howard, Philip K. 1994. *The Death of Common Sense.* New York: Random House.

Howe, Mark D. 1939. "Juries as Judges of Criminal Law." *Harvard Law Review* 52:582.

Husseini, Richard. 1990. "The Federal Sentencing Guidelines: Adopting Clear and Convincing Evidence as the Burden of Proof." *University of Chicago Law Review* 57:1387.

Hutchinson, Thomas W., and David Yellen. 1989. *Federal Sentencing Law and Practice.* St. Paul: West Publishing Company.

INSLAW, Inc. et al. 1981. *Federal Sentencing: Toward a More Explicit Policy of Criminal Sanctions.*

Jaffe, Harry Joe. 1989. "The Presentence Report, Probation Officer Accountability, and Recruitment Practices: Some Influences of Guideline Sentencing." *Federal Probation* (September): 12.

Jareborg, Nils. 1995. "The Swedish Sentencing Reform." In *The Politics of Sentencing Reform,* edited by Chris Clarkson and Rod Morgan. Oxford: Clarendon Press.

Jefferson, Thomas. 1776. "Letter to E. Pendleton." In *Papers of Thomas Jefferson,* edited by Julian P. Boyd. Vol. 1. Princeton: Princeton University Press, 1950.

———. 1779. "A Bill for Proportioning Crimes and Punishments in Cases Heretofore Capita." In *Papers of Thomas Jefferson,* edited by Julian P. Boyd. Vol. 2. Princeton: Princeton University Press, 1950.

Jensen, Magdeline E. 1991. "Has the Role of the U.S. Probation Officer Really Changed?" *Federal Sentencing Reporter* 4:94.

Johnson, Phillip E. 1995. *Criminal Law,* 5th ed. St. Paul: West Publishing.

Joint Committee on New York Drug Law Evaluation. 1978. *The Nation's Toughest Drug Law: Evaluating the New York Experience.* Washington, D.C.: U.S. Government Printing Office.

Joost, Robert H. 1997. "Federal Criminal Code Reform: Is It Possible?" *Buffalo Criminal Law Review* 1:195.

Judicial Conference of the United States. 1984. Report of Proceedings, 19–20 September.

———. Committee on Probation. 1987. *Model Local Rule for Guideline Sentencing.*

Judicial Staff Directory. 1993. Edited by Ann L. Brownson. Mount Vernon, Va.: Staff Directories, Ltd.

Kafka, Franz. 1883–1924. "Before the Law." In *The Complete Stories and Parables of Kafka,* edited by Nahum N. Glatzer. Translated by Willa and Edwin Muir. New York: Schocken Books, 1971.

Kant, Immanuel. 1797. *The Metaphysical Elements of Justice.* Translated by John Ladd. New York: Bobbs-Merrill, 1965.

Kaplan, Sheila. 1991. "Shock of the New." *Legal Times,* 7 October, 5.

Karle, Theresa Walker, and Thomas Sager. 1991. "Are the Federal Sentencing Guidelines Meeting Congressional Goals? An Empirical and Case Law Analysis." *Emory Law Journal* 40:393.

Karlton, Lawrence K. 1991. Letter to editors, 20 November, *Federal Sentencing Reporter* 4:186.

Kennedy, Edward M. 1976a. "Criminal Sentencing: A Game of Chance." *Judicature* 60:208.

———. 1976b. "Reforming the Federal Criminal Code: A Congressional Response." *North Carolina Central Law Review* 8:1.

———. 1979a. "Federal Criminal Code: An Overview." *George Washington Law Review* 47:451.

———. 1979b. "Toward a New System of Criminal Sentencing: Law with Order." *American Criminal Law Review* 16:353.

———. 1980. "Commentary—The Federal Criminal Code Reform Act and New Sentencing Alternatives." *West Virginia Law Review* 82:423.

Krattenmaker, Thomas G. 1978. "Book Review." *Georgetown Law Review* 66:1317.

Kronman, Anthony T. 1993. *The Lost Lawyer: Failing Ideas of the Legal Profession.* Cambridge: Harvard University Press, Belknap Press.

Kurtz, Howard. 1987a. "Judges to Retain Latitude in Sentencing; Proposed Guidelines Won't Try to Restrict Federal Judiciary's Discretion Sharply." *Washington Post,* 26 January, A4.

———. 1987b. "Judges to Retain Sentencing Discretion." *Washington Post,* 14 April, A9.

Kutak, Robert J., and Michael Gottschalk. 1974. "In Search of a Rational Sentence: A Return to the Concept of Appellate Review." *Nebraska Law Review* 53:463.

Lawrence, Pamela B., and Paul J. Hofer. 1992. "An Empirical Study of the Application of the Relevant Conduct Guideline §1B1.3." *Federal Sentencing Reporter* 4:330.

Lay, Donald P. 1992. "Rethinking the Guidelines: A Call for Cooperation." *Yale Law Journal* 101:1755.

Lear, Elizabeth T. 1993. "Is Conviction Irrelevant?" *UCLA Law Review* 40:1179.

Lee, Cynthia K. Y. 1994. "Prosecutorial Discretion, Substantial Assistance, and the Federal Sentencing Guidelines." *UCLA Law Review* 42:105.

———. 1997. "A New 'Sliding Scale of Deference' Approach to Abuse of Discretion: Appellate Review of District Court Departures under the Federal Sentencing Guidelines." *American Criminal Law Review* 35:1.

Lewis, Anthony. 1977. "Politics of the Possible." *New York Times,* 14 November, A33.

Lewis, Orlando F. 1922. *The Development of American Prisons and Prison Customs, 1776–1845.* Albany, N.Y.: Prison Association of New York.

Liebman, Jonathan, and Orin S. Snyder. 1994. "Joint Guilty Pleas: 'Group Justice' in Federal Plea Bargaining." *New York Law Journal,* 8 September, 1.

Lindsey, Edward. 1925. "Historical Sketch of the Indeterminate Sentence and Parole System." *Journal of Criminal Law and Criminology* 16:9.

Lipton, Douglas, et al. 1975. *The Effectiveness of Correctional Treatment.* New York: Praeger Publishing.

Locke, John. 1698. *Two Treatises of Government.* Edited by Peter Laslett. Cambridge: Cambridge University Press, 1988.

Lovejoy, James K. 1994. "Abolition of Court Member Sentencing in the Military." *Military Law Review* 142:1.

Low, Peter W. 1970. *Working Papers of the National Commission on Reform of Federal Criminal Laws.* Washington, D.C.: U.S. Government Printing Office.

Lowenthal, Gary T. 1993. "Mandatory Sentencing Laws: Undermining the Effectiveness of Determinate Sentencing Reform." *California Law Review* 81:61.

Lubasch, Arnold H. 1987. "Judge-Shopping in Federal Court: Lawyers' Quest for Leniency." *New York Times,* 4 March, B1.

Lynch, Gerard E. 1994. "The Sentencing Guidelines as a Not-So-Model Penal Code." *Federal Sentencing Reporter* 7:112.

———. 1997. Reader Report prepared for University of Chicago Press and sent to authors by Professor Lynch.

Marcus, Ruth. 1990. "'Disarray' at Sentencing Commission: GAO Study Questions Panel's Ability to Assess New Guidelines." *Washington Post,* 8 March, A25.

Margolick, David. 1992. "Full Spectrum of Judicial Critics Assail Prison Sentencing Guides." *New York Times,* 12 April, A1.

Martinson, Robert. 1974. "What Works?—Questions and Answers about Prison Reform." *The Public Interest* (spring): 22.

———. 1979. "New Findings, New Views: A Note of Caution Regarding Sentencing Reform." *Hofstra Law Review* 7:243.

McBride, Maria Rodrigues. 1996. Letter from Chief Probation Officer, District of Connecticut, to José A. Cabranes, 12 December.

McCall, Jack H. Jr., 1993. "The Emperor's New Clothes: Due Process Considerations under the Federal Sentencing Guidelines." *Tennessee Law Review* 60:467.

McDonald, Douglas. 1982. *On Blaming Judges: Criminal Sentencing Decisions in New York Courts: Are Guidelines Needed to Restrain Judges?* New York: Citizens' Inquiry on Parole and Criminal Justice.

McDonald, Douglas, and Kenneth E. Carlson. 1993. *U.S. Department of Justice, Sentencing in the Federal Courts: Does Race Matter? The Transition to Sentencing Guidelines, 1986–1990.* Washington, D.C.: Bureau of Justice Statistics, 1993.

McHenry, Susan. 1994. *Working Woman,* 19 July, 37.

Menninger, Karl A. 1928. "Medicolegal Proposals of the American Psychiatric Association." *Journal of Criminal Law and Criminology* 19:367.

———. 1945. *The Human Mind,* 3d ed. New York: A. A. Knopf.

Messinger, Sheldon L., and Phillip E. Johnson. 1978. *California's Determinate Sentencing Statute: History and Issues in Determinate Sentencing: Reform or Regression?* Washington, D.C.: U.S. Department of Justice.

Miller, Marc. 1992. "Purposes at Sentencing." *Southern California Law Review* 66:413.

Miner, Roger J. 1992. "Crime and Punishment in the Federal Courts." *Syracuse Law Review* 43:681.

Mitchell, Suzanne. 1996. "Clarifying the United States Sentencing Guidelines' Focus on Government Conduct in Reverse Sting Sentencing." *George Washington Law Review* 64:746.

Mitford, Jessica. 1973. *Kind and Usual Punishment; the Prison Business,* 1st ed. New York: A. A. Knopf.

Montesquieu, Charles de Secondat, baron de. 1748. *The Spirit of the Laws.* Translated by Thomas Nugent. New York: Hafner, 1949.

Moran, Terence. 1987. "'Final' Sentencing Rules Are Far from Final." *Legal Times,* 20 April, 4.

Morris, Norval. 1974. *The Future of Imprisonment.* Chicago: University of Chicago Press.

———. 1977. "Toward Principled Sentencing." *Maryland Law Review* 37:267.

Morse, Wayne L. et al., eds. 1939. *Attorney General's Survey of Release Procedures.* Vol. 4. Washington, D.C.: U.S. Government Printing Office.

Nagel, Ilene H. 1990. "Structuring Sentencing Discretion: The New Federal Sentencing Guidelines." *Journal of Criminal Law and Criminology* 80:883.

Nagel, Ilene H., and H. E. Freeman. 1975. *Academic and Entrepreneurial Research: The Consequences of Diversity in Federal Evaluation Studies.* New York: Russell Sage Foundation.

Nagel, Ilene H., and John Hagan. 1983. "Gender and Crime: Offense Patterns and Criminal Court Sanctions." In *Crime and Justice: An Annual Review of Research,* edited by Michael Tonry and Norval Morris, 4:91.

Nagel, Ilene H., and Stephen J. Schulhofer. 1992. "A Tale of Three Cities: An

Empirical Study of Charging and Bargaining Practices under the Federal Sentencing Guidelines." *Southern California Law Review* 66:501.

National Commission on Reform of Federal Criminal Laws. 1971. "Final Report." Reprinted in *Reform of the Federal Criminal Laws: Hearings before the Subcomittee on Criminal Laws and Procedures of the Senate Committee on the Judiciary,* 92d Cong., 1st Sess. 29–514.

National Council on Crime and Delinquency. Advisory Council of Judges. 1963. *Model Sentencing Act.* New York: National Council on Crime and Delinquency.

New York State Special Commission on Attica. 1972. *Attica.* New York: Praeger Publishers.

Newman, Jon O. 1977. "A Better Way to Sentence Criminals." *American Bar Association Journal* 63:1563.

———. 1987. "Federal Sentencing Guidelines: A Risk Work Taking." *The Brookings Review* (summer): 29.

Newton, Phyllis J., Jill Gazer, and Kevin Blackwell. 1995. "Gender, Individuality and the Federal Sentencing Guidelines." *Federal Sentencing Reporter* 8:148.

Noble, Kenneth B. 1987. "Q&A: Stephen G. Breyer; With Uniform Sentencing—Same Crime, Same Time." *New York Times,* 19 April, D5.

Oakes, James L. 1995. "Personal Reflections on Learned Hand and the Second Circuit." *Stanford Law Review* 47:387.

Oberdorfer, Louis. 1987. "Remarks at the Forty-Eighth Judicial Conference of the District of Columbia Circuit." *Federal Rules Decisions* 119:610.

O'Donnell, Pierce, et al. 1977. *Toward a Just and Effective Sentencing System: Agenda for Legislative Reform.* New York: Praeger Publishers.

Orland, Leonard. 1973. *Justice, Punishment, Treatment: The Correctional Process.* New York: Free Press.

———. 1978. "From Vengeance to Vengeance: Sentencing Reform and the Demise of Rehabilitation." *Hofstra Law Review* 7:29.

Orland, Leonard, and Kevin R. Reitz. 1993. "Epilogue: A Gathering of State Sentencing Commissions." *Colorado Law Review* 64:837.

Packer, Herbert L. 1968. *The Limits of the Criminal Sanction.* Stanford, Calif.: Stanford University Press.

Parent, Dale G. 1988. *Structuring Criminal Sentences: The Evolution of Minnesota's Sentencing Guidelines.* Edited by Daniel J. Freed. Stoneham, Mass.: Butterworth.

Parker, Jeffrey S. 1993. "Rules Without . . . : Some Critical Reflections on the Federal Corporate Sentencing Guidelines." *Washington University Law Quarterly* 71:397.

Parker, Jeffrey S., and Michael K. Block. 1990. "The Sentencing Commission, P. M. Sunshine or Sunset?" *American Criminal Law Review* 27:289.

Partridge, Anthony, and William B. Eldridge. 1974. *The Second Circuit Sentencing Study: A Report to the Judges and Justices of the Second Circuit.* Washington, D.C.: Federal Judicial Center.

Pattenden, Rosemary. 1982. *The Judge, Discretion and the Criminal Trial.* Oxford: Clarendon Press.

Payne, A. Abigail. 1997. "Does Inter-Judge Disparity Really Matter? An Analysis of the Effects of Sentencing Reforms in Three Federal District Courts." *International Review of Law and Economics* 17:337.

Piotrowski, Michael. 1991. "The Enhanced Role of the Probation Officer in the Sentencing Process." *Federal Sentencing Reporter* 4:96.

Posner, Richard A. 1973. *An Economic Analysis of Law,* 1st ed. Boston: Little, Brown.

Postema, Gerald J. 1986. *Bentham and the Common Law Tradition.* Oxford: Clarendon.

President's Commission on Law Enforcement and Administration of Justice.

1967. *The Challenge of Crime in a Free Society.* Washington, D.C.: U.S. Government Printing Office.

Rakoff, Jed S. 1980. "The Federal Mail Fraud Statute (Part I)." *Duquesne Law Review* 18:771.

Reagan, Ronald. "Text of Reagan Press Conference." 1984. *Congressional Quarterly* 42:1841.

Reese, Craig. 1990. "Jury Sentencing in Texas: Time for a Change?" *South Texas Law Journal* 31:331.

Reno, Janet. 1993. Attorney General to Federal Prosecutors, memorandum. "Principles of Federal Prosecution." Reprinted in *Federal Sentencing Reporter* 6 (1994): 352.

———. 1994. Letter from Attorney General to Senator Orrin Hatch, 8 March. Reprinted in *Federal Sentencing Reporter* 6:353.

Rhodes, William. 1991. "Federal Criminal Sentencing: Some Measurement Issues with Application to Pre-Guideline Sentencing Disparity." *Journal of Criminal Law and Criminology* 81:1002.

———. 1992. "Sentence Disparity, Use of Incarceration, and Plea Bargaining: The Post-Guideline View from the Commission." *Federal Sentencing Reporter* 5:152.

Richey, Charles R. 1978. "Appellate Review of Sentencing: Recommendation for a Hybrid Approach." *Hofstra Law Review* 7:71.

Roberts, Julian V. 1994. "The Role of Criminal Record in the Federal Sentencing Guidelines." *Criminal Justice Ethics* 13:21.

Robinson, Paul H. 1987a. "Dissenting View of Commissioner Paul H. Robinson on the Promulgation of the Sentencing Guidelines by the United States Sentencing Commission." *Federal Register* 52:18,121.

———. 1987b. "A Sentencing System for the 21st Century?" *Texas Law Review* 66:1.

Robinson, Paul H., and Jane A. Grall. 1983. "Element Analysis in Defining Criminal Liability: The Model Penal Code and Beyond." *Stanford Law Review* 35:681.

Rodino, Peter W. Jr. 1984. "Federal Criminal Sentencing Reform." *Journal on Legislation* 11:218.

Rothman, David J. 1990. *The Discovery of the Asylum: Social Order and Disorder in the New Republic,* 2d ed. Boston: Little, Brown and Company.

Rowe, Gary D. 1992. "The Sounds of Silence: *United States v. Hudson and Goodwin,* the Jeffersonian Ascendancy, and the Abolition of Federal Common Law Crimes." *Yale Law Journal* 101:919.

Rubin, Sol. 1956. "Long Prison Terms and the Form of Sentence." *National Probation and Parole Association Journal* 2:344.

Ryerson, Ellen. 1977. *The Best-Laid Plans: America's Juvenile Court Experiment.* New York: Hill and Wang.

Santos, Lori. 1987. "Sentencing Deadline Ends Two Years of Controversy." *United Press International,* 12 April.

Sarner, Felicia. 1996. "'Fact Bargaining' under the Sentencing Guidelines: The Role of the Probation Department." *Federal Sentencing Reporter* 8:328.

Savelsberg, Joachim J. 1992. "Law That Does Not Fit Society: Sentencing Guidelines as a Neoclassical Reaction to the Dilemmas of Substantivized Law." *American Journal of Sociology* 97:1346.

Schulhofer, Stephen J. 1979. *Prosecutorial Discretion and Federal Sentencing Reform.* Washington, D.C.: Federal Judicial Center.

———. 1980. "Due Process of Sentencing." *University of Pennsylvania Law Review* 128:733.

———. 1992. "Assessing the Federal Sentencing Process: The Problem Is Uniformity Not Disparity." *American Criminal Law Review* 29:833.

Schulhofer, Stephen J., and Ilene H. Nagel. 1989. "Negotiated Pleas under the Federal Sentencing Guidelines: The First Fifteen Months." *American Criminal Law Review* 27:231.

Schwarzer, William W. 1990. "Statement Concerning Mandatory Minimum Sentences," 29 January. Reprinted in *Federal Sentencing Reporter* 2:186.

———. 1991. "Judicial Discretion in Sentencing." *Federal Sentencing Reporter* 3:339.

———. 1992. "Sentencing Guidelines and Mandatory Minimums: Mixing Apples and Oranges." *Southern California Law Review* 66:405.

Sellin, Thorston. 1935. "Race Prejudice in the Administration of Justice." *American Journal of Sociology* 41:212.

Selya, Bruce M., and John C. Massaro. 1994. "The Illustrative Role of Substantial Assistance Departures in Combatting Ultra-Uniformity." *Boston College Law Review* 35:799.

Seymour, Whitney N., Jr. 1973. "1972 Sentencing Study for the Southern District of New York." *New York State Bar Journal* 45:163.

Shane-DuBow, Sandra, et al. 1985. *Sentencing Reform in the United States: History, Content, and Effect.* Washington, D.C.: National Institute of Justice.

Singer, Richard G., and Martin R. Gardner. 1989. "The Importance of Mens Rea." In *Crimes and Punishment: Cases, Materials, and Readings in Criminal Law.* New York: Matthew Bender.

Sneed, Joseph. 1982. *Trial Court Discretion: Exercise by Trial Courts and Review by Appellate Courts.* Paper presented before judges of the Second Circuit, Yale Law School, New Haven, Conn.

Stephen, James F. 1883. *A History of the Common Law of England.* London: Macmillan.

Stith, Kate. 1990. "The Risk of Legal Error in Criminal Cases: Some Consequences of the Asymmetry in the Right to Appeal." *University of Chicago Law Review* 57:1.

———. 1995. "The Criminal Jury in Our Time." *Virginia Journal of Social Policy & the Law 3:133.*

Stith, Kate, and José A. Cabranes. 1997. "Judging under the Federal Sentencing Guidelines." *Northwestern University Law Review* 91:1247.

Stith, Kate, and Steve Y. Koh. 1993. "The Politics of Sentencing Reform: The Legislative History of the Federal Sentencing Guidelines." *Wake Forest Law Review* 28:223.

Strasser, Fred. 1986. "Is Sentencing Panel on the Rocks? Last Summer's Hopes Dashed." *National Law Journal,* 8 December, 3.

Sunstein, Cass R. 1995. "Commentary—Incompletely Theorized Agreements." *Harvard Law Review* 108:1733.

Sutton, Paul L. 1978. *Federal Criminal Sentencing: Perspectives of Analysis and a Design for Research.* Washington, D.C.: U.S. Dept. of Justice.

Sweet, Robert W. 1987. Statement and Testimony before Subcommittee on Criminal Justice of the Committee on the Judiciary, U.S. House of Representatives. 100th Cong., 1st Sess. 233.

Tacha, Deanell Reece. 1995. "Independence of the Judiciary for the Third Century." *Mercer Law Review* 46:645.

Tappan, Paul W. 1958. "Sentencing under the Model Penal Code." *Law and Contemporary Problems* 23:528.

Tate, Dale. 1984. "Congress Loads Up Emergency Funding Bill." *Congressional Quarterly* 42:2355.

Taylor, Stuart, Jr. 1984a. "Senate Approves an Anticrime Bill." *New York Times,* 3 February, A1.

———. 1984b. "New Crime Act a Vast Change, Officials Assert." *New York Times,* 15 October, A1.

Thornburgh, Richard. 1989. Attorney General to Federal Prosecutors, memorandum. "Plea Policy for Federal Prosecutors: Plea Bargaining under the Sentencing Reform Act." Reprinted in *Federal Sentencing Reporter* 6 (1994): 347.

Tiefer, Charles. 1989. *Congressional Practice and Procedure.* Westport, Conn.: Greenwood Press.

Tolchin, Martin. 1984. "House Votes Anticrime Measure and Senate Eases Abortion Rules." *New York Times,* 26 September, A1.

Tonry, Michael. 1992a. "GAO Report Confirms Failure of U.S. Guidelines." *Federal Sentencing Reporter* 5:144.

———. 1992b. "Salvaging the Sentencing Guidelines in Seven Easy Steps." *Federal Sentencing Reporter* 4:355.

———. 1993. "The Success of Judge Frankel's Sentencing Commission." *University of Colorado Law Review* 64:713.

———. 1996. *Sentencing Matters.* New York: Oxford University Press.

Tonry, Michael, and John C. Coffee, Jr. 1987. "Enforcing Sentencing Guidelines: Plea Bargaining and Review Mechanisms." In *The Sentencing Commission and Its Guidelines,* edited by Andrew von Hirsch, Kay A. Knapp, and Michael Tonry. Boston: Northeastern University Press.

Torry, Saundra. 1993. "Some Federal Judges Just Say No to Drug Cases." *Washington Post,* 17 May, F7.

Treaster, Joseph B. 1993. "Two Judges Decline Drug Cases, Protesting Sentencing Rules." *New York Times,* 17 April, 1.

Trott, Stephen S. 1987. Letter from U.S. Department of Justice to Chairman of the United States Sentencing Commission, 7 April. Reprinted in *Federal Sentencing Reporter* 8 (1995): 196.

———. 1994. Letter from Trott to United States Sentencing Commission, 9 November. Reprinted in *Federal Sentencing Reporter* 8 (1995): 199.

Tversky, Amos, and Daniel Kahneman. 1974. "Judgment under Uncertainty: Heuristics and Biases." *Science* 185:1124.

Twentieth Century Fund Task Force on Criminal Sentencing. 1976. *Fair and Certain Punishment.* New York: McGraw-Hill.

United States Board of Parole. 1970–72. *Biennial Report.* Washington, D.C.

United States Department of Justice 1980. *Principles of Federal Prosecution.*

United States Department of Justice 1989. "Plea Policy for Federal Prosecutors: Plea Bargaining under the Sentencing Reform Act."

United States Department of Justice 1993. "Principles of Federal Prosecution."

United States General Accounting Office. 1982. *Federal Parole Practices: Better Management and Legislative Changes Are Needed.* Washington, D.C.: U.S. Government Printing Office.

———. 1990. *U.S. Sentencing Commission: Changes Needed to Improve Effectiveness.* Washington, D.C.: U.S. General Accounting Office.

———. 1992. *Sentencing Guidelines: Central Questions Remain Unanswered.* Washington, D.C.: U.S. General Accounting Office.

United States Sentencing Commission. *Guidelines Manual.* Washington, D.C.: U.S. Sentencing Commission (as amended through 1997; cited as U.S.S.G.).

———. 1986. "Sentencing Guidelines—Preliminary Draft." Reprinted in *Federal Register* 51 (1987): 13,123.

———. 1987a. "Sentencing Guidelines—Revised Draft, January 1987." Reprinted in *Federal Register* 52:3921.

———. 1987b. "Preliminary Observations of the Commission on Commissioner Robinson's Dissent." Reprinted in *Federal Register* 52:18,133.

———. 1987c. *Supplementary Report on the Initial Sentencing Guidelines and Policy Statements.* Washington, D.C.: U.S. Sentencing Commission.

———. 1989–1996. *Annual Report.* Washington, D.C.: U.S. Sentencing Commission.

———. 1991a. *The Federal Sentencing Guidelines: A Report on the Operation of the Guidelines System and Short-Term Impacts on Disparity in Sentencing, Use of Incarceration, and Prosecutorial Discretion and Plea Bargaining.* Washington, D.C.: U.S. Sentencing Commission.

———. 1991b. *Special Report to the Congress: Mandatory Minimum Penalties in the Federal Criminal Justice System.* Washington, D.C.: U.S. Sentencing Commission.

———. 1994. *Circuit Conflicts Addressed by Commission Amendment.* Washington, D.C.: Office of General Counsel.

———. 1995. *Discussion Paper: Relevant Conduct and Real Offense Sentencing.* Washington, D.C.: U.S. Sentencing Commission.

———. 1997a. *A Guide to Publications and Resources.* Washington, D.C.: U.S. Sentencing Commission.

———. 1997b. *1996 Sourcebook of Federal Sentencing Statistics.* Washington, D.C.: U.S. Sentencing Commission.

van den Haag, Ernest. 1975. *Punishing Criminals.* New York: Basic Books.

Van Graafeiland, Ellsworth A. 1986. "Some Thought on the Sentencing Reform Act of 1984." *Villanova Law Review* 31:1291.

Van Vechten, Courtland C. 1937. "The Parole Violation Rate." *Journal of Criminal Law and Criminology* 27:638.

Varnon, Charlie E. 1991. "The Role of the Probation Officer in the Guidelines System." *Federal Sentencing Reporter* 4:63.

Vitiello, Michael. 1991. "Reconsidering Rehabilitation." *Tulane Law Review* 65:1011.

Von Hirsch, Andrew. 1976. *Doing Justice: The Choice of Punishments.* New York: Hill and Wang.

Vorenberg, James. 1981. "Decent Restraint of Prosecutorial Discretion." *Harvard Law Review* 94:1521.

Wald, Patricia M. 1992. "Violence under the Law: A Judge's Perspective." In *Law's Violence,* edited by Austin Sarat and Thomas R. Kearns. Ann Arbor: University of Michigan Press.

Waldfogel, Joel. 1991. "Aggregate Inter-Judge Disparity in Federal Sentencing: Evidence from Three Districts." *Federal Sentencing Reporter* 4:151.

———. 1994. "Does Inter-Judge Disparity Justify Empirically Based Sentencing Guidelines?" Unpublished manuscript.

Walker, John M. 1995. *Is the Commission Fulfilling Its Mandate? A Review of the Sentencing Commission's 1994 Annual Report. Federal Sentencing Reporter* 8:106.

Wathen, Daniel E. 1988. "Disparity and the Need for Sentencing Guidelines in Maine: A Proposal for Enhanced Appellate Review." *Maine Law Review* 40:1.

———. 1991. "Judges on Judging: Making Law the Old Fashioned Way—One Case at a Time." *Ohio State Law Journal* 52:611.

Weber, Max. 1904. *Economy and Society.* Edited by Guenther Roth and Glaus Wittich. Translated by Ephraim Fischoff et al. Berkeley: University of California Press, 1978.

Weich, Ronald. 1996. "The Battle against Mandatory Minimums: A Report from the Front Lines." *Federal Sentencing Reporter* 9:94.

Weinstein, Jack B. 1989. "Prisons Need Not Be Mandatory." *Judges' Journal* 28:16.

———. 1992. "A Trial Judge's Second Impression of the Federal Sentencing Guidelines." *Southern California Law Review* 66:357.

———. 1994. "Limits on Judges' Learning, Speaking, and Acting." *Dayton Law Review* 20:1.

Weinstein, Jack B., et al. 1989. "Weinstein's Evidence." Vol. 1. New York: Matthew Bender.

Weintraub, Benson B. 1991. "Hidden Disparity under the Sentencing Guidelines." *Federal Sentencing Reporter* 4:148.

Weis, Joseph F., Jr. 1992. "The Federal Sentencing Guidelines—It's Time for a Reappraisal." *American Criminal Law Review* 29:823.

Weisburd, David. 1992. "Sentencing Disparity and the Guidelines: Taking a Closer Look." *Federal Sentencing Reporter* 5:149.

Werner, Leslie Maitland. 1984. "Of Crime and the Bermuda Triangle." *New York Times,* 14 June, B3.

Wermeil, Stephen J. 1987. "Sentencing Panel Scraps Recent Draft, Rushes to Finish Guidelines for Judges." *Wall Street Journal,* 9 April, A18.

Wertham, Fredric. 1955. "Psychoauthoritarianism and the Law." *University of Chicago Law Review* 22:336.

Wheeler, Stanton, et al. 1988. *Sitting in Judgment: The Sentencing Of White-Collar Criminals.* New Haven: Yale University Press.

Wilkins, Leslie T., et al. 1976. *Sentencing Guidelines: Structuring Judicial Discretion.* Washington, D.C.: U.S. Government Printing Office.

Wilkins, Roger. 1977. "Reform of the U.S. Criminal Code: Parole Provisions Bother Liberals." *New York Times,* 12 November, A10.

Wilkins, William W., Jr. 1987. Chairman of U.S. Sentencing Commission to Associate Attorney General, May. Reprinted in *Federal Sentencing Reporter* 8 (1995): 199.

———. 1988. "Plea Negotiations, Acceptance of Responsibility, Role of the Offender, and Departures: Policy Decisions in the Promulgation of Federal Sentencing Guidelines." *Wake Forest Law Journal* 23:181.

———. 1990. Testimony before the Federal Courts Study Committee, 31 January, Washington, D.C.

———. 1992. "Response to Judge Heaney." *American Criminal Law Review* 29:795.

Wilkins, William W., Jr., and John R. Steer. 1990. "Relevant Conduct: The Cornerstone of the Federal Sentencing Guidelines." *South Carolina Law Review* 41:495.

———. 1993. "The Role of Sentencing Guideline Amendments in Reducing Unwarranted Sentencing Disparity." *Washington and Lee Law Review* 50: 63.

Wilkins, William W., Jr., Phyllis J. Newton, and John R. Steer. 1993. "Competing Sentencing Policies in a 'War on Drugs' Era." *Wake Forest Law Review.* 28:305.

Wilson, James Q. 1975. *Thinking about Crime.* New York: Basic Books.

Wren, Christopher S. 1997. "Reno and Top Drug Official Urge Smaller Gap in Cocaine Sentences." *New York Times,* 22 July, A1.

Wright, Ronald F. 1991a. "Sentencers, Bureaucrats, and the Administrative Law Perspective on the Federal Sentencing Commission." *California Law Review* 79:1.

———. 1991b. "Sentencing Law in the Supreme Court's 1990–91 Term." *Federal Sentencing Reporter* 4:58.

———. 1994. "Amendments in the Route to Sentencing Reform." *Criminal Justice Ethics* (winter/spring): 58.

Yellen, David N. 1992. "Two Cheers for *A Tale of Three Cities.*" *Southern California Law Review* 66:567.

———. 1993. "Illusion, Illogic and Injustice: Real-Offense Sentencing and the Federal Sentencing Guidelines." *Minnesota Law Review* 78:403.

Yost, Paula. 1989a. "The Long Term Debate; Charges of Politics Dog Sentencing Panel." *Washington Post,* 4 July, A21.

———. 1989b. "Sentencing Panel Member Resigns over Research; Block Charges Lack of Commitment by Commissioners to Base Decisions on Data." *The Washington Post,* 23 August, A25.

Young, Deborah. 1994. "Fact-Finding at Federal Sentencing: Why the Guidelines Should Meet the Rules." *Cornell Law Review* 79:229.

Index